RAY STRACHEY (1887–1940) was born into a distinguished American Quaker family. Daughter of Mary Pearsall Smith (Mrs Bernard Berenson), she was the niece of the essayist Logan Pearsall Smith and of Alys Russell, first wife to Bertrand Russell.

Educated at Newnham College Oxford, where she read mathematics, and at Bryn Mawr College in the USA, she also studied electrical engineering. Deeply committed to the Suffrage Movement, a close friend and colleague of the Suffragist leader Millicent Fawcett, she took part in the fight for the vote during the critical years. She was one of the first women to stand for Parliament after the vote was won and became political adviser to Lady Astor, the first woman MP. Editor of the Suffragist newspaper *The Common Cause*, she was deeply committed to the advancement of women, serving on many committees and organizations, and founding the Women's Employment Federation. A prolific writer and broadcaster, she wrote numerous articles, pamphlets and books, including a notable biography of Millicent Fawcett.

In 1911 Ray Strachey married Oliver Strachey, brother of Lytton. She had two children, one of whom writes the preface to this edition of her most famous work. *The Cause* tells the history of the emancipation of women in Great Britain. Since 1928, when it was first published, this vigorous and far-sighted book has become accepted as a standard work of suffrage history.

THE CAUSE

A SHORT HISTORY OF THE WOMEN'S MOVEMENT IN GREAT BRITAIN

BY

RAY STRACHEY

NEW PREFACE BY BARBARA STRACHEY

"The eighteenth century proclaimed the rights of man, the nineteenth shall proclaim the rights of woman."
VICTOR HUGO.

Virago

London

Published by VIRAGO PRESS Limited 1978
20-23 Mandela Street, Camden Town, London NW1 0HQ

Reprinted 1978, 1988, 1989

First published 1928 by G. Bell & Sons Limited

British Library Cataloguing in Publication Data
A CIP Catalogue record for this book is
available from the British Library.

Printed in Great Britain
by The Guernsey Press Ltd, C.I.

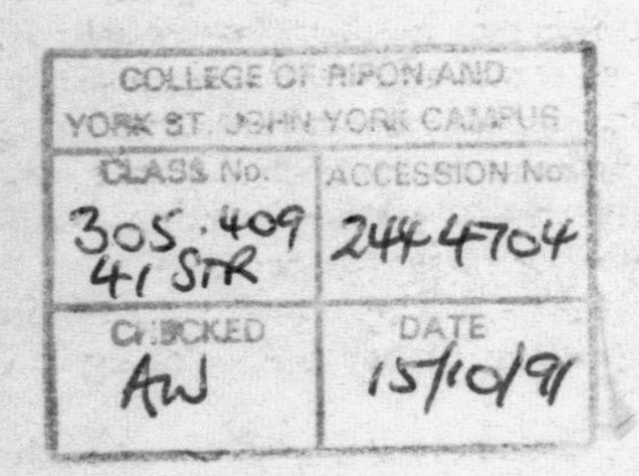

The photographs of Josephine Butler, Millicent Fawcett and Elizabeth Garrett Anderson on the cover are reproduced by kind permission of Radio Times Hulton Picture Library and that of Florence Nightingale by kind permission of the Mary Evans Picture Library

NEW PREFACE

In 1905, when she was still seventeen, Ray Costelloe paid a long visit to her mother, Mary, and her stepfather, Bernard Berenson, in Florence. Mary had run away from her first husband, Frank Costelloe, some years before to join Berenson, leaving her two daughters Ray and Karin to be fought for, and finally (since Costelloe died when the children were still very young) to be brought up by her own mother, Hannah Whitall Smith.

Hannah, who had been born a Quaker in Philadelphia, was a remarkable woman. She had written many religious books, one of which, *The Christian's Secret of a Happy Life*, became a classic, and is still in print today. She was wise and witty, radical in politics and a true feminist from her earliest days, and she had a lasting influence on her granddaughter.

Mary, however, believed that it would be good for Ray to acquire some experience of the world before going to Cambridge, so she deliberately threw her into the company of a young American cousin who was in Florence at the time. The result was to inspire Ray with utter disgust for the arrogance of the contemporary young man and his belief that females should only be educated so that they could appreciate and admire male excellence. She was driven to purge herself of the experience by transmuting it into a novel, and as the book was not without merit for a first effort, Mary financed its publication – a generous action, for it was complimentary neither to her nor to the young man.

This episode was an important one for Ray, for it marked the start of both the main preoccupations of her life: writing and feminism.

She went on to Newnham, where she read mathematics, but in the years between 1905 and 1909 the suffrage movement had reached so exciting a stage that she spent much more time on suffrage marches, Parliamentary campaigns and caravan speaking tours than she did on mathematics, with the result that she came 280th out of 286 candidates in her Tripos.

After much heart searching she had decided that in spite of the glamour and heroism of the suffragettes, it was the law-abiding suffragists who would have the greater effect in the long run, and she began what was to be a lifelong cooperation and friendship with Mrs Fawcett, their leader. She still hankered, however, after the life of a writer, and was torn between the attractions of literature and politics.

There was yet a third career she nearly chose. After Cambridge, she took a course in electrical engineering, which she found even more fascinating than mathematics, and was much tempted to go on and qualify, and become the first woman to practise. However, in 1911 she married Oliver Strachey, brother of Lytton, himself a convinced feminist. He was out of a job at the time, having just returned from India, so for a period they tried writing together and then Ray went back to suffrage work, leaving Oliver to do the housekeeping – at which he was unfortunately so incompetent that she very soon had to take it over again herself.

She stood for Parliament in 1919, the first election after women got the vote, but she stood as an Independent and failed to get in, and failed again in 1922. Neither defeat, however, in the least diminished her energy and optimism. She was editor of the suffragist paper *The Common Cause*, and founder of the Women's Employment Federation; she wrote novels, biographies, almost daily articles, broadcast on a multitude of subjects, sat on innumerable committees and spoke at innumerable meetings. When Lady Astor entered the House of Commons, Ray was "drafted" to be her political adviser, to brief her and write speeches for her, and endeavoured to provide that ebullient pioneer with strategy, ballast and moderation. This, too, led to a lifelong cooperation and friendship.

She put her considerable organizational abilities into her family affairs as well, for in spite of her horrifyingly full working life, her children never doubted for a moment that they came first in all her plans.

Ray was excellent company – utterly scornful of appearances, being liable, for instance, to go out to grand political parties with her dress on inside out; she loved swimming and bricklaying and learning new "skills" such as playing the piano or painting in oils, which she did very badly indeed, but with rapture. She died at 53 in 1940 – much too young – but she had already achieved a great deal for the "cause" she embraced. Not the least of her achievements was her history of the Movement, *The Cause*, in which she was able at last to combine her two main ambitions by writing a book which will, I think, remain a classic – honest, scholarly, immensely readable and, even to so stern a critic as a teenage daughter, truly inspiring.

1978 BARBARA STRACHEY

PREFACE

THE records of the Women's Movement are easily accessible, and most of the events are still within living memories. The facts upon which this book is based are thus not greatly in dispute, nor particularly hard to amass. My difficulty in writing it has lain in the opposite direction—in the excess of evidence and material, and the overlapping of the events themselves. The sudden development of the personal, legal, political, and social liberties of half the population of Great Britain within the space of eighty years has inevitably crowded tendencies, causes, results, and consequences one upon the top of another in the most bewildering fashion, and it has been difficult to disentangle them all sufficiently to indicate at once their separate progress and their mutual interaction.

I am conscious indeed that the task of clarification has been very imperfectly achieved, and that much which is both relevant and instructive has been left out. I have, as far as possible, added dates to the page headings, to make the sequence of events plain; but the true history of the Women's Movement is the whole history of the nineteenth century; nothing which occurred in those years could be irrelevant to the great social change which was going on, and nothing was without its share of influence upon it. I have not referred to such events as the Indian Mutiny, the Franco-Prussian War, the Home Rule Agitation, or the Parliament Act, and yet I know that these things undoubtedly had a bearing on the problem and did their part, along with the whole progress of the world, in shaping this special development. But in the writing of history there have to be boundary lines, and I have placed mine as far out as the limits of one volume allow.

I feel bound to confess at the outset that in writing this book I have not been unbiased. I was myself an actor in the later stages of the Suffrage drama, and thus I am both open to and proud of the charge that I cannot take a wholly impartial view. I have conscientiously tried to write history and not propaganda; but my assumptions are undoubtedly feminist, and my eyes perhaps blinded to the virtues of the past.

In the collection and arrangement of material, in the perspective and in the writing of the book I am deeply indebted to my friend Ida O'Malley. We worked together in the study of the period immediately preceding 1837, and found much interesting matter which, however, lies outside the scope of this volume. The pre-pioneer stage of the Movement was in some ways more entertaining than the Movement itself, and of course behind that there lies a fascinating field of research into the history of the status of women from earliest times. I hope that some day Miss O'Malley's discoveries in these directions may be published, and that light may be thrown on that great darkness which has hitherto enveloped the history of the female sex.

A great many other friends have helped me in the preparation of this book. First and foremost I must thank Dame Millicent Fawcett. Her leadership of the Movement needs no thanks from me; it is, I hope, fully made clear in these pages. But I must express my gratitude for the personal kindness, the fund of reminiscences, the jokes and the records with which she has supplied me. The whole extent of the Suffrage side of the Movement, from the first Petition of John Stuart Mill to the final grant of adult enfranchisement, has fallen within her personal experience; and the record bears upon its face the mark of her guiding hand.

I am indebted to so many other people also that it is difficult to make my obligations clear. There are the existing feminist societies, Women's Service (formerly the London

Society for Women's Suffrage), whose librarian has searched out many obscure details for me, whose library has proved a mine of information, and whose records and minute-books have thrown so much light on the inner workings of the agitation; there is the National Union of Societies for Equal Citizenship (formerly the National Union of Societies for Women's Suffrage), whose official records have been placed at my disposal; there is the interesting collection of old feminist books which Mrs Cavendish Bentinck has kindly allowed me to examine; the Blackburn Library at Girton College, for access to which I have to thank Miss Major; and also the London School of Economics, which has allowed me to see a collection of letters and papers of Miss Helen Taylor. I am exceedingly grateful to the late Mrs Pankhurst for discussing the militant phase of the Movement with me; and I have also to thank Miss C. Pine for lending me her unique and fascinating collection of photographs. To Lady Stephen I owe a great debt, not only for the admirable and exact record of the early days of the Education Movement which appears in her book (*Emily Davies and Girton College*), but also for many criticisms and profitable hints. Miss B. A. Clough has helped me greatly in the preparation of the chapters dealing with the Higher Education Movement. To both of these, and also to Mrs Vaughan Nash and to the other members of the family of the late Miss Florence Nightingale I am grateful for permission to publish the fragment "Cassandra" and the hitherto unpublished drawing by Lady Eastlake.

There are many other people who have helped me by the loan of old letters, records, and photographs, and by giving me their personal reminiscences; the late Mr G. W. Johnson, Miss Hope Malleson, Mrs Reid, Miss Crompton, Miss Hart, Mrs Becker, Miss B. L. Hutchins, and the late Miss Edith Palliser among them. The portrait of Josephine Butler, which has never before been published, is the property of Mr George Butler, and the copyright is his. The photographs of militant scenes and of the militant leaders have been lent by Miss C. Pine, that of the Newnham hockey team by Newnham College, of Barbara Bodichon by Girton College, of Lady Astor taking the oath by Viscount Astor, of Miss Emily Davies by Miss M. Llewelyn Davies. The cartoon of Miss Becker has been lent by Miss Crompton, and Lord Grantley has given permission for the portrait of Mrs Norton which is in his possession to be reproduced here. Thanks are due to all these for their great kindness. And, finally, I should like to express my indebtedness to every single one of my comrades of the days of the Women's Suffrage agitation.

RAY STRACHEY.

1924–1928.

CONTENTS

"THE CAUSE"

A SHORT HISTORY OF THE WOMEN'S MOVEMENT IN GREAT BRITAIN

CHAPTER I

THE PRISON-HOUSE OF HOME. 1792–1837

The French Revolution—Mary Wollstonecraft—The early philanthropic movement—The legal, social, and industrial position of women at the beginning of the nineteenth century — Florence Nightingale.

THE organised Women's Movement, which is the subject of this book, is not yet at an end, and may therefore be in some ways unsuitable for treatment as an historical subject. It has, however, reached a stage at which its progress can be tabulated with some exactness; and so many of its aims have been achieved that the various aspects of the movement can be put into their proper perspective in relation to the whole ideal, and the affair surveyed without the heat of controversy or the prejudice of propaganda.

It is possible to select various dates for the true beginning of the Women's Movement, but whatever date we choose it is impossible to isolate it altogether from the events which preceded it. Like every other development of human society it was the result of a multitude of causes, and it might be both profitable and entertaining to search them out. For our purposes, however, most of these fascinating subjects of investigation must be set aside. We must not examine the position of women among savage peoples, nor in ancient civilisations; we must ignore the Middle Ages, and, indeed, we must refuse to be drawn into the history of the status of women at all. Their widespread subjection, with its curious exceptions, has been part of the structure of the world for the whole of recorded, and probably for the greater part of unrecorded, history. It has contributed more to the progress, or rather to the lack of progress, of mankind than has yet been measured; but we must resolutely turn away from this speculation now. Of course there would have been no need for a Women's Movement at all had not this subjection existed; but it was tolerated for a great many centuries, without effective protest, and some other contributing impulse must therefore be found to account for the final emergence of a genuine female revolt in the nineteenth century.

It seems clear that this impulse came from the doctrines and philosophies which inspired the French Revolution, and that it received a further impulse from the economic changes of the Industrial Revolution. The Women's Revolt was, in fact, a by-product of these two upheavals, and although it took more than half a century for anything deliberate to become manifest, the real date for the beginning of the movement is 1792.

In that year Mary Wollstonecraft, inspired by thoughts of "Liberty, Equality, and Fraternity," wrote and published her great book, *A Vindication of the Rights of Woman.* In this book the whole extent of the feminist ideal is set out, and the whole claim for equal human rights is made; and although at the time it was little noticed, it has remained the text of the movement ever since.

After the appearance of this book the subject seemed to die away. English society closed up, as it were, against the theories which had wrought such havoc across the Channel, and there was a desperate effort to keep things exactly as they were, lest the British Constitution or the British Home should be demoralised and destroyed. Things could not be kept as they were, however, and though the ruling classes clung as tightly as they could to the habits, the traditions, and the prejudices of their forefathers, their wicked old eighteenth-century world slipped from them, and the nineteenth century began.

On the surface things were unaltered; but across the apparently immutable state of society there flowed the searchlight of the philanthropic movement, and this illumination left behind it not only movements to improve the social and material conditions of the people, but also a great awakening of conscience. The young women who lived under its influence saw that the world was unsatisfactory in a great many ways: they saw that old people were poor and hungry, that children were wild and ragged, and that rain came in through the cottage roofs: and then they realised that they themselves, being "only women," were powerless to do any substantial good. And from that illumination the Women's Movement sprang.

It may seem strange to maintain that Miss Hannah More and Mrs Trimmer and the other good ladies who started the Sunday School and cottage-visiting fashions were the founders of a movement which would have shocked them so profoundly; but it is clearly true. When Hannah More and her sisters began personally to teach the wild children of the Cheddar Hills they opened up a new field of activity for women. It is true that their educational ambitions were extremely limited. Their main object seemed to be to teach people to be contented with their lot, and, as Hannah More said, "I allow of no writing for the poor!" But all the same, the fact that she was teaching anything at all was a highly revolutionary matter. Without in the least intending to do so, she was marking out a new sphere for the young women of the middle classes, and their revolt against their own narrow and futile lives followed as a matter of course. Once they began to look outside their drawing-rooms, and to see the hard realities which other people had to face, those of them who were intelligent and energetic (and these were more numerous than was generally believed) were bound to revolt against their own ornamental futility. For a little time philanthropy and soup and blankets kept them quiet, but not for long. Many years before there was an organised movement to encourage them, some of these young girls broke away from the traditional courses and made names for themselves in the real world of affairs.

It is not possible for us to tell here the stories of these pioneers, remarkable and fascinating as they are. Jane Austen, Mary Berry, Fanny Burney, Caroline Chisholm, Maria Edgeworth, Elizabeth Fry, Jane Marcet, Harriet Martineau, Mary Somerville—to name only the more famous of them—were all true forerunners of the Women's Movement, and each in her different sphere contributed directly to its approach. But they did their work, and had their effect, before the movement actually began, and so lie outside the scope of this volume. Some of them, indeed, lived on until long after the movement had begun, and naturally they gave it their full support. Most of them had discovered and approved the idea long before any organisation was in existence, and it is interesting to see, in their letters to each other, how a kind of freemasonry of understanding existed among them. They sought each other out, and, as it were, recognised each other, and different though their careers and interests were, they were alike in daring to utter the shocking words, "women's rights," and in supporting with equanimity the terrible epithet, "strong minded."

But there were only a few of these pioneer women, and the world in which they lived was still accepting a very different ideal. By law women were heavily handicapped, and none of the grievous disabilities which had been fastened upon them in the ancient past had yet been removed.

To ordinary women this state of affairs was not grievous. They thought nothing of their legal status, and cared not at all for their "rights." Life, as they knew it, was a mixture of pleasures and pains, and the proportions were not controllable by law. They adjusted themselves to the world in which they found themselves, and if they were fortunate in their family surroundings, as well as being intelligent, or beautiful, or gay, their lives passed pleasantly enough. But their prosperity was built on precarious foundations, and serious dangers lurked beneath it. If their fathers, or their husbands, were ill-disposed, the whole course of their lives might be shattered through no fault of their own. For women were but relative to men, and had no real standing of their own.

Although, as Blackstone [1] put it, "the disabilities a woman lies under are for the most part intended for her protection and benefit, so great a favourite is the female sex in the laws of England," yet the fact was that these laws and customs put her at a severe disadvantage. "By marriage," as Blackstone goes on to say, "the very being or legal existence of a woman is suspended, or at least it is incorporated or consolidated into that of the husband, under whose wing, protection and cover she performs everything, and she is therefore called in our law a feme covert." This, in plainer language, meant that the property, the earnings,[2] the liberty,[3] and even the conscience [4] of a wife all belonged to her husband, as did also the children [5] she might bear. The incorporation and consolidation were complete, "my wife and I are one, and I am he"; and since there was no divorce obtainable for a woman before 1857,[6] there was no way of escape save death.

[1] Sir Wm. Blackstone, *Commentary on the Laws of England*, 1765.

[2] Property and Earnings: See *Women under English Law*, by Arthur Cleveland Rackham, 1896.

[3] Liberty: The right of a man to imprison his wife in his own house was not questioned till 1891 (*Queen* v. *Jackson, Clitheroe* case).

[4] Conscience: Crimes, other than murder or high treason, committed by a woman in the presence of her husband were presumed to have been committed under coercion, and the woman was thus guiltless. This presumption was not abolished until 1925.

[5] Children: Mothers had no guardianship rights at all before 1839, see Chap. II.

[6] Divorce, see Chap. IV. There was a theoretical possibility of Divorce by Act of Parliament, but only in two cases was this ever obtained at the instance of a wife.

"If a woman be of so haughty a stomach," said a learned judge,[1] "that she will choose to starve rather than submit and be reconciled to her husband, she may take her own choice. And if a married woman, who can have no goods of her own to live on, will depart from her husband against his will, let her live on charity, or starve in the name of God."

These were indeed the stark facts of the position of women in the first half of the nineteenth century, and public opinion fully supported them. It was generally agreed to be one of the self-evident laws of nature that men were superior to women — mentally, physically, and morally. Education, therefore, would be wasted upon them; responsibility would overwhelm them, and work would make them ill. They must be sheltered, protected, and indulged—so the theory ran. They were the wives, or the mothers, or the daughters of some man; that was their description and the real justification of their existence. And the virtues and attainments which it was right and proper for them to cultivate were those which would be useful in these capacities. Men differed as to what they wanted from women: some were content with good cooking and wholesome stupidity, others hoped for intelligent companionship and a dash of sympathy: but all were united in feeling that ambition, achievement, and independence were unfeminine attributes, and that obedience, humility, and unselfishness were what was really required.

The women who were brought up on this convention grew accustomed to it, and loved it. They sheltered under the irresponsibility it gave them, and they hugged the "chains" which seemed so protective; and in their turn they brought up their daughters in the good old way, so that all seemed fair and smooth. In the middle and upper classes, women who were exceptionally energetic might carve out for themselves a round of "duties," but the others would

[1] Judge Hide in the case of *Manby* v. *Scot* (reign of Charles II).

sink back into a soft idleness; and men despised them, and women did not mind.

There was, of course, one very uncomfortable consequence of this state of affairs, and that was the existence of superfluous women. A girl could go on being somebody's daughter only so long as her father was alive; and after that, if she had not succeeded in becoming somebody's wife, she was adrift. Without money, or the possibility of earning for herself, she was reduced to being dependent on her male relatives; and the position of being somebody's unmarried sister, or somebody's maiden aunt was far from agreeable. "A single woman with a narrow income," said Jane Austen,[1] "must be a ridiculous old maid, the proper sport of boys and girls; but a single woman of good fortune is always respectable, and may be as sensible and pleasant as anybody else." With the laws of inheritance as they were, the single woman nearly always had narrow means; and her life was passed in trying to be as little in the way as could be managed. Through all the literature of the first half of the nineteenth century the pathetic figure of the old maid is found, a "proper sport" for comedy and satire. The reality, however, must have been bitter indeed, and if society had but looked squarely at it, the hollowness of the "favourite" position of women would have been perceived.

Among the working population conditions were not the same, but the belief in the inferiority of women was equally firmly established. Although women toiled with their hands as hard, and even more incessantly than men, they had less reward for what they did. If they went out to work their rates of pay were pitifully low, and if they did not go out to work there were no rates of pay at all. It was generally believed that if a man was displeased with the way his wife worked for him—or with any other aspect of her conduct—he had a perfect right to beat her with a stick, provided it

[1] *Emma*, by Jane Austen. First published in 1816.

was not thicker than his own thumb. This was all "natural." It was woven into the very fabric of the universe, which it would be ridiculous as well as impious to change. "And if a woman becomes weary, or at last dead, from childbearing," as Luther said, "it matters not; let her only die from bearing, she is there to do it."

Such was the general belief and the general situation of the female inhabitants of the country when a young girl was called to rule over them. Victoria, by the Grace of God, Queen of Great Britain and Ireland, ascended the throne in 1837, and the early Victorian era was ushered in.

In this year the young Queen was eighteen years old, and most of those who were to set on foot the Women's Movement were her contemporaries. Some were a little older—Harriet Martineau, for example, was thirty-five, John Stuart Mill and Elizabeth Barrett were thirty-one, and Mary Carpenter and Caroline Norton were thirty; but others were exactly of her date. Charlotte Brontë was twenty-one, Marian Evans (George Eliot) was eighteen, Louisa Twining, Anne Jemima Clough, and Florence Nightingale were seventeen. There were some younger girls, too, who were destined to be important: Frances Power Cobbe, for example, who was fifteen; Barbara Leigh Smith and Frances Mary Buss who were ten; Josephine Grey who was nine; Emily Davies who was seven, and little Elizabeth Garrett who was just one year old.

The girlhood of Victoria was a special thing, not quite typical of her generation. When she was called downstairs to hear that she was Queen of England she came alone, and this was the first time in her life that she had been allowed to walk down the staircase without someone holding her by the hand. Cramped and guarded as her contemporaries were, it is unlikely that this was true of anyone else; but they all, in their own lives, encountered the peculiar disadvantages of being women, and there is no better way of making the grounds of their coming revolt clear than by describing some of their individual experiences and reactions to them.

The best example is perhaps Florence Nightingale, who brought to her revolt against the restrictions and limitations of young ladyhood the same passionate force which enabled her in later life to carry out her magnificent achievements. She was destined to be one of Victoria's greatest subjects, but until she was more than thirty years old she was shut up tight within the conventions which forbade independent action to a woman.

Florence Nightingale was born in 1820. Her parents were wealthy English people, "well born," as it was called, and well connected, with all the culture and all the conventional pleasures of the world at their disposal. There were two large country houses, formal gardens, foreign travel, the season in town, distinguished friends, the latest literature, and carriages and horses awaiting their daughters when they should be old enough to appreciate such advantages; and Florence, had she been so disposed, could have lived out a happy and a harmless life in this environment. But Florence was not of a pliable and adaptable disposition. From her earliest years she longed to be of some definite use in the world, to take up some heavy absorbing work, and by plunging her life into it, to consecrate her powers to the service of God and mankind. She hated "looking merry and saying something lively mornings, noons, and nights," and above all she chafed and rebelled against the system by which a young lady never had a moment she could call her own. However, this was the system under which she lived, and Florence was obliged to sit patiently while she was read aloud to (" it is like lying on one's back and having liquid poured down one's throat"); she was obliged to devote herself to "company" and to "visits," and to sit in the drawing-room through the long winter evening hours. Learning and culture she might have in plenty, and indeed she did receive a wide and extended education from her father; but there was no comfort in Greek and Latin for a soul like hers. It was action she craved for, not the seductive bypaths of literature, art, or music. "Picking up miscellaneous information for one's self is the most unsatisfactory of all pursuits," she wrote, "I had so much rather live than write; writing is only a substitute for living. . . . I think one's feelings waste themselves in words; they ought all to be distilled into actions which bring results."

This instinctive inner impulse came to Florence as the voice of God. From the time she was a child she felt she had a true vocation, a call, from One on high; and, as the years went by and she grew to young ladyhood, the longing to answer this call grew ever stronger and stronger, until it was the great preoccupation of her thoughts. Casual cottage-visiting and fragmentary scraps of philanthropy, fitted in at odd times, were not enough. It was a real dedication of her life which she envisaged; and it was this that her family and the whole system of society opposed.

Florence was reserved, said little about her intentions, and seemed only very gentle and aloof, even when inwardly she was a whirlwind of rebellion; she thought her thoughts in secret, making a few discreet inquiries, and turning over ways and means in silence. From seventeen to twenty-five she dreamed and prayed; and then at last she attempted to strike out for a useful life, hoping against hope for her family's approval or consent. But it was not to be had.

"I dug after my poor little plan in silence, even from you," she wrote to her most congenial cousin, Hilary Bonham Carter.[1] "It was to go to be a nurse at Salisbury Hospital for these few months to learn the 'prax'; and then to come home and make such wondrous intimacies at West Wellow under shelter of a rhubarb powder and a dressed leg, let alone that no one could ever say to me again, your health will not stand this or that. I saw a poor woman die before

[1] December 1845.

my eyes this summer because there was no one but fools to sit up with her, who poisoned her as much as if they had given her arsenic. And then I had such a fine plan . . . of taking a small house in West Wellow. Well, I do not much like talking about it, but I thought something like a Protestant Sisterhood, without vows, for women of educated feelings, might be established. But there have been difficulties about my very first step, which terrified Mama. I do not mean the physically revolting parts of a hospital, but things about surgeons and nurses which you may guess. . . . Nothing will be done this year at all events, and I do not believe—ever; and no advantage that I see comes of my living on, excepting that one becomes less and less of a young lady every year, which is only a negative one. . . . I shall never do anything . . . and am worse than dust and nothing. I wonder if our Saviour were to walk the earth again, and I were to go to Him and ask, whether He would send me back to live this life again which crushes me into vanity and deceit. Oh, for some strong thing to sweep this loathsome life into the past."

It was not really surprising that Mrs Nightingale was "terrified" by her daughter's unexpected proposal. "It was as if I had wanted to be a kitchen-maid," Florence afterwards admitted—indeed it was worse. For the nurses of those days were drunken, dishonest, and disreputable, and no self-respecting kitchen-maid would associate with them. The depression which settled down upon her in the eight years following the failure of this plan was not lightened by the round of gaiety and of travel with which her mother tried to distract her. Nothing kept her going but the occasional escapes she managed to make from her home atmosphere—the hospitals she slipped away to visit in Rome and Paris, the ragged schools she found her way to (with her manservant at her heels), or the heavy statistical sanitary reports she pored over in her bedroom. An inch here, a foot there, by slow degrees she might acquire the knowledge for which she thirsted. And in time, at least, young ladyhood might be over and she could step out upon the paths of God.

"What in the world and what have I done this last fortnight?[1] I have read the *Daughter at Home* to father, and two chapters of *Mackintosh*; a volume of *Sybil* to Mama. Learnt seven tunes by heart, written various letters. Ridden with Papa. Paid eight visits. Done company. And that is all."

Year after year went by. "O weary days, O evenings that seem never to end! For how many years I have watched that drawing-room clock and thought it would never reach the ten! And for twenty or thirty years more to do thus!"

There seemed to be no way of escape but marriage; and marriage, she thought, must be the same thing in another form. Among the suitors for her hand there was one, indeed, whom she felt she could love. "I have an intellectual nature which requires satisfaction, and that would find it in him. I have a passionate nature which requires satisfaction, and that would find it in him." But this was not enough. "I have a mind, an active nature which requires satisfaction, and that would not find it in his life. . . . I could not satisfy this nature by spending a life with him and arranging domestic things. . . . To be nailed to a continuation and an exaggeration of my present life, without hope of another, would be intolerable to me. Voluntarily to put it out of my power even to be able to seize the chance of forming for myself a true and rich life would seem to me like suicide."

"In my thirty-first year I see nothing but death." "Everything has been tried, foreign travel, kind friends, everything." "My God, what is to become of me?"

By this time it was evident that Florence would never settle down in her mother's world; and she was getting past

[1] Diary, 1846.

a marriageable age, she was more and more restless, more and more determined, and an understanding grew up that some day or other active work might be sanctioned. Inspirited by this hope Florence squeezed out of a foreign journey in 1851 three whole months of training at the Kaiserworth Deaconesses' Institute, and her course was then fixed. Nursing, as she had all along suspected, was the career she was made for; it was the call from God.

The drawing-room clock had to tick round to ten for many months before Florence was free to leave it behind her; but now, with her purpose quite clear and definite, she could wait with better patience.

"I am glad to think that my youth is past [1] and rejoice that it never, never can return—that time of follies and bondage, of unfulfilled hopes and disappointed inexperience, when a man possesses nothing—not even himself." And the waiting time was spent in drawing up a scheme of philosophy, which was to stand her in good stead to the end of her days.

"The last of the old year.[2] I am so glad this year is over. Nevertheless, it has not been wasted, I trust. I have remodelled my whole religious belief, from beginning to end. I have learnt to know God. I have recast my social belief; have them both written, for use when my hour is come."

When! It was close at hand. Hardly a year later she had become head of a small philanthropic nursing home, and in one more after that her great mission had opened. For the Crimean War broke out in the winter of 1853.

All this is well known; but there is an aspect of Florence Nightingale, an essential element in her outlook, which has never yet been fully stated, and that is her real feeling towards the position of her sex. This is a matter which should be intensely illuminating to the student of the Women's

[1] Letter to her father, May 1852.
[2] 1852.

Movement, for Florence Nightingale was a pertinacious and a very individual thinker, and her judgment on the point would throw a truly penetrating light upon the customs and the ideals of her age and generation. But in her published letters and papers it has not been greatly stressed, and it has been generally assumed that it was only among her secondary interests. There is much indeed to give colour to this view, for though she was a feminist of sorts, and signed petitions and believed in Women's Suffrage because "it is the first principle or axiom that every householder or taxpayer should have a voice," she openly declared that she did not "expect much from it."[1] And, further, even while she fought like a tiger for professional status for her nurses, she grew desperately impatient with the inefficiency and lack of mental power she so often met with among women; and did not hesitate to say so. Everyone knows, too, that she shared with Harriet Martineau an active distaste for the feminist writing and propaganda which was multiplying so rapidly during her lifetime. There is indeed a letter of hers to Harriet Martineau[2] in which she says, "I am brutally indifferent to the rights and wrongs of my sex"; and there is the negative evidence of the things she did not do to complete the proof that Florence Nightingale had only an incomplete and easily exhausted sympathy with the organised Women's Movement. In her absorption in her own work she judged the men and women she lived among almost wholly by their usefulness or their uselessness to it; and this outlook of hers is clearly enough shown in the long letter about women and their failings which she wrote in 1861 to Madame Mohl:

"You say 'women are more sympathetic than men.' Now if I were to write a book of my experience, I should begin 'WOMEN HAVE NO SYMPATHY.' Yours is the tradition. Mine is the conviction of experience. I have never found one woman who has altered her life by one iota for me or my opinions . . . Now just

---

[1] 8th October 1861. [2] 13th December 1861.

look at the degree in which women have sympathy—as far as my experience is concerned. And my experience of women is almost as large as Europe. And it is so intimate too. I have lived and slept in the same bed with English Countesses and Prussian Baurinnen. No Roman Catholic Supérieure has ever had charge of women of the different creeds that I have had. No woman has excited ' passions ' among women more than I have. Yet I leave no school behind me. My doctrines have taken no hold among women. Not one of my Crimean following learnt anything from me, or gave herself for one moment after she came home to carry out the lesson of that war or of those hospitals . . . No woman that I know has ever *appris à apprendre*. And I attribute this to want of sympathy. Nothing makes me so impatient as people complaining of their want of memory. How can you remember what you have never heard? . . . It makes me mad, the Women's Rights talk about ' the want of a field ' for them—when I know that I would gladly give £500 a year for a woman secretary . . . They don't know the names of the Cabinet ministers. They don't know the offices at the Horse Guards. They don't know who of the men of the day is dead and who is alive. They don't know which of the Churches have Bishops and which not . . . Women crave for being loved, not for loving. They scream out at you for sympathy all day long, they are incapable of giving any in return for they cannot remember your affairs long enough to do so . . . They cannot state a fact accurately to another, nor can that other attend to it accurately enough for it to become information. Now is not all this the result of want of sympathy? . . . No, no, let each person tell the truth from his own experience."

Even the blindest partisan must recognise that this is the fruit of actual observation, the judgment of a woman who walked alone, upon the woman who did not, and could not walk with her. It expresses, indeed, what Florence Nightingale thought of her fellows, and what she saw upon the surface of contemporary life; and it is a summing-up from which there is no escape. That is what the world was like after the Crimean War, so far as women of the upper classes were concerned; and Florence Nightingale did not much approve of it.

There was more in her mind than this outward valuation, however. Women might be—they were—most trying and imperfect creatures; but that was not all. She had a deep inner thought that they could be otherwise, strong and glorious "saviours," as she called them, if they were but freed from the inanities of their customs and the foolish nonsense of their actual lives. This hope, this inwardly cherished dream, grew up with Florence Nightingale; it stiffened her own fight to win freedom from her own environment, and it lay always burning in her heart, working in ever closer and closer to her most sacred beliefs, and intensifying her devotion to the quite different causes which she made her own.

These may seem exaggerated statements, and would indeed be so were not the evidence very strong. We cannot argue about great people that they "must have" thought this or that, just because their doing so would fit our theories. Human nature is excessively perverse, and Florence Nightingale might perhaps have closed her intelligence to the problems of her own sex, and accumulated her experiences and lived her life without bothering to remember that she was herself a member of a subordinate category. She might have been content, as Queen Victoria and some other able women have been, to consider her own existence a freak of nature, and leave it at that. But Florence Nightingale did not do this. On the contrary, as she brooded over the problems of human life, and as she toiled towards the philosophy of religion in which she finally found satisfaction, she carried this problem always with her. Her thoughts of God and His justice must be made to square with His treatment of her sex; otherwise the whole fabric would be useless and insecure.

Florence Nightingale's thoughts on religion and the woman question were first put together by herself in 1852, and were later amplified into three large volumes entitled, *Suggestions for Thought to Searchers after Religious Truth*, a book which was printed in 1859 but was not published. Taken with her many letters on religious subjects, and read in the light of her own deeds, this book makes clear the philosophy by which Florence Nightingale found a meaning in the universe; and whatever its objective value may be, its importance in understanding the woman herself is clear, for her philosophy was the deepest thing in her nature.

Suggestions for Thought is very long, its arrangement is very confused, and it is a highly wearisome book to read. It is full of repetitions, and of things apparently irrelevant, and there is much in it which is not original. Discussions on belief, on prayer, on free will, occupy many pages, and there is a great deal of space given to the subject of immortality. From the mass of its arguments and illustrations, however, the general outlook emerges clearly enough, namely, a belief that there is a God who acts in and through human beings for their perfecting.

"It is often said that the time is past for individual saviours (male or female). . . . Nevertheless, the world cannot be saved, except through saviours, at present. A saviour means one who saves from errors. . . . There may be, there must be, saviours from actual, from moral evil."

"Male and female saviours"—that was her hope; but in the world as she knew it it was but a faint one. "Why have women passion, intellect, moral activity—these three—" she cried, "and a place in society where no one of the three can be exercised?" This was not according to God's plan, it was monstrous, intolerable, wrong. "I must strive after a better life for women."

That this thought went very deep and lay very close to the centre of her whole philosophy these volumes leave no room for doubt. Again and again, through the whole argument, the subject comes back, often in the most curious juxtapositions. "Is God in the Drawing Room?" she asks, and "Why are Mothers like the Church of England?" and the answers are discouraging indeed.

"We do the best we can to train our women to an idle superficial life; we teach them music and drawing, languages and poor peopling,—' resources ' as they are called, and we hope that if they don't marry they will at least be quiet."

" Women's life is spent in pastime, men's in business. Women's business is supposed to be to find something to pass the ' time.' If young ladies are seen sitting round the table doing worsted work, they are supposed to be appropriately and rightly employed, especially if one is reading aloud. But if men were to be discovered sitting round the table doing worsted work, or even in the evening talking over the fire doing crochet, how women would laugh! . . . But women have never anything to say so important as that they should not be looking at their pattern " . . .

" The maxim of doing things at odd moments is a most dangerous one. . . . Can we fancy Michael Angelo running up and putting a touch to his Sistine ceiling in ' odd moments '? Everything that has ever been done at ' odd moments ' had better never have been done . . . We know what *can* be done at odd times, a little worsted work, acquiring a language, copying something, putting the room to rights, mending a hole in your gloves. . . . What else is there? . . . Nothing, it is evident, which requires a force, a completeness, a beginning and an end. . . ."

" Very few people lead such an impoverishing and confusing and weakening life as the women of the richer classes. What is it? They have made up their minds to live in public, never to have any time to themselves. . . . The brains all become all muddled in company. . . . It is the most confusing life. They have all cultivated general literature. Everybody is reading aloud half a page out of her own book. The mother has a sort of pride in her own daughters being literary ladies, in their having five books lying upon the breakfast-table all at once, and quoting from a heap of authors. . . . You cannot bring forward an opinion without exciting a storm of words. You have made up your mind always to live in this whirlwind. What can be so confusing? . . ."

" A married woman's life consists in superintending what she does not know how to do . . . (She) is to direct the servants, who are to provide conveniences and luxuries not thought of formerly. She has never learnt, and does not know how, but she must take care to provide them. She must superintend the nurse, and the governess of her children, though she knows nothing and has learnt nothing of the nurse's work. And the governess . . . what is she to do? *She* must direct the characters of her pupils. How is she fit for it? . . . Over her, so little prepared, the mother so little prepared is to preside."

" But a mother's situation now requires the impossible. Before she was a mother she had no means of learning how to fulfil its requirements, and if there were means, to learn or to practice all would be impossible. What is she to do? Her best plan would be to have a pursuit of her own; with her family, if any of them like it; without them if they don't or can't do it, like Mrs Fry or Mrs Chisholm. But then what a cry the world makes!"

All this and more to the same effect Florence Nightingale wrote out of the bitterness of her own heart, remembering the exasperations and the disappointments of her own youth. Yet even as she herself had escaped, freed by the desperate strength of her determination, and by the force of her remorseless will, so she believed other women might escape also. "Where do we see the woman with *half* her powers employed?" Not here, in this muddled world, but in the brooding dreams, the fervent hopes, the passionate intention of this saviour of her distracted sex.

Among the chapters composing the *Suggestions for Thought* there is one remarkable fragment, an essay which she has called "Cassandra," which is, as she says, "the voice of one crying in the *crowd* 'Prepare ye the way of the Lord.'" It is a terrible piece of writing, a scornful indictment of society against which there is no possible defence. It is here printed in full [1] and can be left to complete the explanation of the stirring of female discontent. No one who reads it through can wonder any longer that women began to ask more from life than the conventions of the early years of the nineteenth century allowed them.

[1] See Appendix I.

CHAPTER II

THE STIRRING OF DISCONTENT. 1837–1850

The Chartists—Women's political power—Caroline Norton—The Anti-Slavery Convention of 1840—The acceptance of Women's Suffrage among the extreme Radicals.

DISCONTENT and dissatisfaction with the position of women began, as we have seen, in individual hearts. The restrictions, the limitations and the injustices which were a necessary part of their compulsory "protection" fretted and angered those who felt unusual powers, energies, ambitions stirring within them, and one by one, in their own personal lives they carved out an exceptional way for themselves, and proved their own value to the world in which they had been born. But individual triumphs and exceptional cases, even though they multiplied, could not be the final solution of the matter. The average woman, the stupid woman, even the wicked woman had the same right to freedom and to self-development as had the wisest and the best; and, with one exception, all those who escaped their own limitations recognised this fact.

Moreover, during the twenty years between the accession of Queen Victoria and the date when Florence Nightingale worked out her theories of life, a number of public events happened which had a direct bearing on the position of women, and on the "Women's Rights" Movement.

The first, in point of time, was the Chartist Movement, which made its appearance in 1838 and for a brief time flourished exceedingly. There is no need here to discuss its underlying causes, nor to account for its rise and fall; the only point we must notice is that in the first draft of the

Charter of Rights and Liberties itself, Women's Suffrage was specifically mentioned. It was put there by a cabinet-maker called William Lovett, who was at that time the secretary of the Working Men's Association; but it was rapidly struck out again. "Several Members thought its adoption in the Bill might retard the suffrage of men," Lovett reports,[1] and although it appeared again in the third edition, it was again removed for the same cause. The argument was reasonable and true enough; but since it resembles the arguments with which women's causes have had to contend throughout their history, its first appearance is of interest.

Although the Chartists took Women's Suffrage out of their objects they did not reject women's help, and a large number of Women's Political Associations came into existence to further the aims of the Charter. There had been similar associations of women during the Reform Bill agitation, and their members had taken part in the demonstration at Peterloo in 1819, where some of them had been killed. But these women had merely gone along with the men, and had not been thinking for themselves. Their successors were more independently active, however, and in this they received a good deal of encouragement from some of the Chartist leaders. At their ordinary public meetings women were allowed to vote for the resolutions—though this innovation was considered somewhat ludicrous when it was first introduced, and caused mingled shyness and delight to the audiences. Women delegates attended the annual congresses of the Chartist bodies, and there were meetings of women only, sometimes of great size. Now and then, too, these women's associations said a word for themselves, and a discussion of the question of women's rights crept into some of the newspapers of the day.[2] The whole

[1] *Life and Struggles of Wm. Lovett in Pursuit of Bread, Knowledge, and Freedom*, by himself. Reprinted with introduction by R. Tawney, 1920.

[2] *Northern Star*, 8th September and 20th October 1838; *Leeds Times*, 2nd March 1841.

thing, however, was short-lived, and by 1842 most of the enthusiasm and nearly all the organisation had perished.

While the Chartist movement was going its appointed course the feminist idea had begun to show its head in other quarters. The *Westminster Review* had published an article in 1831 by an unknown young woman [1] advocating female suffrage, and in the next year it published another by Mr William Johnston Fox, M.P. for Oldham, to the same effect. On 3rd August of that year Mr Hunt, also a member of the reformed Parliament, actually presented a petition which, as he said, "might be a subject of mirth to some hon. gentlemen, but which was one deserving consideration." It came from a lady of rank and fortune, Mary Smith, of Stanmore in the county of York. The prayer of the petition was that "every unmarried female possessing the necessary pecuniary qualification should be entitled to vote for Members of Parliament." [2] There is no record of the honourable gentlemen's mirth, but it was doubtless hearty and prolonged, and nothing more seems to have been heard of the matter in Parliament for many years.

However, outside Parliament, several developments took place. In 1836 the famous Anti-Corn Law League was formed, and it took a firm hold during the period of bad trade and high prices in 1837. This League, like the Chartist organisations, encouraged women to help its work, and there were social functions, teas, fêtes, soirées, and bazaars for them to arrange in plenty. Of course at that date there was nothing else they could usefully do. Discussions of policy were outside their sphere, public speaking was unheard of for them, and very few even had money of their own to give. Still the limited co-operation of joining the League, and

[1] Afterwards Mrs Mylne. The article was reprinted in 1872, with a preface describing how the subject arose in the author's mind from the study of works by Bentham, and describing also the almost paralysing fright caused by the invitation to publish her ideas. Fear of the task apparently threw the young lady into a decline, and it was only completed under doctor's orders, as the best cure for her complaint.

[2] See *Hansard*, 3rd August 1832.

attending the meetings, and hearing talk about "tariffs, salaries, profits and monopolies" was in itself an education; and a very large proportion of those who later joined the early Women's Suffrage committees had served an apprenticeship in this movement.

There was another kind of interest in public affairs which a few women could take at that date, and that was the personal kind, secured through the relationship, friendship, or love of the men who were conducting the business of government. This brand of political influence, which has been open to women in all periods of the world's history, was sometimes extremely important. Beautiful, clever, or ambitious women have used their personal charms and influence to alter the course of public events time and time again, and this fact was long considered a proof that the female sex had all the rights and powers it could require. The indirect or backstairs method, indeed, was uninformed, capricious and dangerous; it was generally personal in its object as well as in its method, and it was a pernicious element in public life. But it existed; and to a few court beauties and great ladies it provided an exciting and amusing life, and gave a sense of personal importance which they often rapturously enjoyed. Without experience or responsibility, these women played with power, and by so doing wasted their gifts. Sometimes, as in the case of Lady Hester Stanhope, their natural abilities ran off into eccentricity; sometimes, as with Lady Caroline Lamb, they plunged headlong into emotional excitement and fantastic scenes; sometimes they were arrogant, and sometimes spiteful; and the more able they were the more likely was it that they would do harm. Their values were all unreal, and, since they could escape the consequences of their actions, they neither weighed things justly beforehand, nor afterwards profited by experience. And the results of their interventions in public affairs were almost always bad. One such intervention, however, was made in the cause of the Women's

Movement in the first years of Victoria's reign; and although the lady who made it was a professed anti-feminist, and although her methods belonged to the old fashion, the result she achieved was actually the first legislative attempt to improve the position of women.

The heroine of this incident experienced in her own life nearly all the evils of the position of women. Her own personal suffering drove her to action, and her method was the time-honoured one of a woman's importunity. Perhaps in her day and generation she was all the more effective from this fact; and it is appropriate to it that her beauty, her social position, and her charm should have been such important features in her success; for these are the weapons of the weak.

Caroline Norton, who is supposed to have been the original of *Diana of the Crossways*,[1] was one of the three beautiful Miss Sheridans who took London Society by storm in the season of 1826. She was a grand-daughter of the dramatist, and was as witty, as brilliant and as fascinating as Richard Brinsley Sheridan had been himself. She was married at nineteen to the Hon. Richard Norton, and became at once one of the most successful hostesses of fashionable London. Her little house in Storey's Gate was frequented by Lord Melbourne and many of the Whig Ministers, as well as by the literary and fashionable world, and all the great men of the day loudly professed themselves in love with her. Although they had so much social success Caroline and her husband were not happy. They quarrelled a good deal with each other, and lived above their income, and once she ran away from Richard, who had struck and beaten her. The trouble was patched up, and she returned, but after some further painful scenes a final breach occurred. Richard took an opportunity when his wife was visiting her sister

[1] The famous incident of the betrayal of secret information to the *Times* has been fully disproved in connection with Mrs Norton. See George Meredith's preface to the second edition of *Diana of the Crossways*. See also *Life of Caroline Norton*, by Jane G. Perkins.

to carry their three children out of the house, and put them under the charge of a cousin of his own, who refused to let their mother have access to them.

Caroline took refuge with her own family, and then found out the dreadful position in which the law placed her. Not only was she penniless, and unable to keep any money if she earned it, but she had absolutely no rights in her children, and might never see them again until they were of age, if Richard so decreed. She had hardly realised this state of affairs when Richard brought an action against Lord Melbourne for "criminal conversation" with his wife. The case came to trial in June 1836. It was as simple as could be. There were no reputable witnesses, no documents, no evidence at all, and the jury dismissed the case without retiring from the Court, seeing that it was a mere piece of domestic spite and political bluff. But Caroline, outraged and deeply wounded at the attack on herself and at the trouble and distress of her old friend, had still another lesson to learn. For she found that in this trial, which concerned her honour and her good name, she had no standing at all. Being a married woman she could neither sue nor be sued, and could not be represented by counsel in the trial. Legally it was no affair of hers, for legally she could have no affairs, if she was a virtuous and a married woman.

The upshot of the trial did poor Caroline no good. She cleared her good name, indeed, but that had never seriously been in question, and now she secured notoriety of a kind that was exceedingly distressing. And, in regard to the children, it advanced matters not at all. She once succeeded in meeting them by stealth, as they walked in St James's Park; but Richard sent them away to Scotland, and Caroline did not for a long time find out where they were. Her husband refused all her pleadings, refused to give her any allowance, and retained, as was his legal right, the furniture and all the property that was hers. Long and anxious negotiations followed, best described in the words of Sir

John Bagley, the man who had been Mr Norton's chief legal adviser in the trial, but who presently saw his client in his true colours and gave up the connection: "I found Mrs Norton anxious only on one point, and nearly heart-broken about it, namely, the restoration of her children. She treated her pecuniary affairs as a matter of perfect indifference, and left me to arrange them with Mr Norton as I thought fit. I found her husband, on the contrary, anxious only about the pecuniary part of the arrangement, and so obviously making the love of the mother for her offspring a means of barter and bargain that I wrote to him that I could be no party to any arrangement which made money the price of Mrs Norton's fair and honourable access to her children."

Caroline was almost in despair; but not quite. Let the law and the world say what they would, she was determined to see her own children, and, single-handed and penniless as she was, she made up her mind to change her country's laws so that she might do so.

Parliamentary agitation is common enough to-day, and the tactics and procedure of the business are thoroughly well known. In 1836, however, it was a very different thing, and Caroline Norton embarked upon a wholly unexplored field, with the frightful handicap of being a married and yet unprotected woman. She was, however, by no means friendless; and her writings were already well known, so that her passionate pamphlets found their way into the most influential quarters, and were there read and understood.[1] Nor was it surprising that they should have been much noticed. Coming, as they did, straight from her heart, they are moving even after all these years. "A woman's

[1] See *The Natural Claim of a Mother to the Custody of Her Child as Affected by the Common Law Right of the Father, Illustrated by Cases of Peculiar Hardship*, printed for private circulation by Caroline Norton, 1837. Also *Separation of the Mother and Child by the Law of Custody of Infants Considered*, a prose pamphlet printed for private circulation, J. Ridgway, 1837.

suffering is never above half known," she wrote, "for the fact of the publicity of her wrongs is counted to her for disgrace. Well I know how many hundreds, infinitely better than I—more pious, more patient and less rash under injury, have watered their bread with tears. . . ." "I abjure all other writing till I see these laws altered . . . it is the cause of all the women of England. If I could be justified and happy to-morrow, I would still strive and labour in it; and if I were to die to-morrow it would still be a satisfaction to me that I had so striven. Meanwhile, my husband has a legal lien (as he has publicly proved) on the copyright of my works. Let him claim the copyright of THIS. . . ."

The "cases of peculiar hardship" which Caroline adduced were not by any means only her own: there were others even more striking. "There had been an instance where the husband had seized and carried away a suckling infant,[1] as his wife sat in her own mother's house. . . . Another (in which the parties were of high rank) where the husband deserted his wife, claimed the babe born after his desertion (having possession already of his other children) and left her to learn of its death from the newspapers. . . . In all these cases, and in all other cases, the claim of the father was held to be indisputable."

It was to these other cases, indeed, that Caroline's cause owed the support which now became essential to it, namely, that of its Parliamentary champion, Mr Talfourd,[2] a young sergeant at law. He was a man whose knowledge, honesty and motives no one could impeach, and it was he who had decided to introduce an Infants' Custody Bill before ever he met Mrs Norton. He was driven to this, indeed, by some personal experiences of his own, for in the course of his professional career he had twice been counsel for husbands resisting the claims of their wives, and had both times won his

[1] The case of *De Mandeville*.

[2] M.P. for Reading. He was a great friend of Lamb, Dickens, and Wordsworth, and was Lamb's executor. He was responsible for the introduction of the first Bill to secure copyright to authors.

case in accordance with law and in violation of his sense of justice. One of these unfortunate women, Mrs Greenhill, took her case from King's Bench to the Court of Chancery, and Mr Talfourd obtained a sentence of imprisonment against her for keeping her children with her in contempt of Court, even though her husband was at the time living with another woman to whose keeping he proposed to entrust them. Mrs Greenhill, upon this verdict, had fled out of the country with her children, and the lawyer, disgusted with a law which had given him his victory, resolved to devote his energies to its amendment.[1]

Mr Talfourd had been two years in Parliament when he met Mrs Norton in the spring of 1837, and they naturally met often to discuss the policy to be pursued to further the Infants' Custody Bill, and continued in close alliance throughout its progress. But the path of women reformers was a hard one; this collaboration was at once considered suspicious, and the *British and Foreign Review* published a long and insulting attack in which it called Mrs Norton a "she devil" and a "she beast," and coupled her name with Mr Talfourd's in a most impertinent way. Caroline, furious to the last degree, prepared to bring an action for libel, only to realise once more that, as a married woman, she could not sue! "I have learned the law respecting married women piecemeal, by suffering every one of its defects of protection," [2] poor Caroline wrote; it was but too true.

[1] Lord Denman, speaking in the House of Lords on the Infants' Custody Bill in 1839 referred to this case. "In the case of *King* v. *Greenhill*, which was decided in 1836 before myself and the rest of the judges of the Court of the King's Bench, I believe there was not one judge who did not feel ashamed of the state of the law, and that it was such as to render it odious in the eyes of the country." The cases quoted by Mr Talfourd were: *Mrs de Mandeville*, 1804; *Mrs Ball*, 1827; *Mrs McClellan*, 1830; *Mrs Greenhill*, 1835. These few legal cases by no means represented the volume of the abuse. As a rule, when a husband deserted his wife she had not the means to go to law (since he possessed all her property), and if he wished to punish her by keeping the children away from her he was able to do so undisturbed.

[2] *English Law for Women in the Nineteenth Century*, by Caroline Norton, printed for private circulation in 1854.

The Bill, however, survived the scandals, and went its way; and finally reached the House of Lords in December 1848. There, as was so likely to happen, its fate hung in the balance; and it was then that Caroline made her greatest effort. She wrote a pamphlet, "A Plain Letter to the Lord Chancellor," in which she set forth reasonably and yet with tremendous force the case for the Bill, and "as I feared, if they knew it was a woman's writing, it would have less weight," she had it privately printed under the name of Pierce Stevenson.[1] This pamphlet was sent to every Member and to every Peer, and the interest and favourable comment it aroused carried the Bill. In the summer of 1839 the Infants' Custody Act passed into law, a timid and hesitating measure, judged by modern standards, but nevertheless an immense and startling innovation.[2]

Caroline's own affairs improved before the passing of the Act, and in 1839 her husband agreed to let the boys be with her from time to time. But she had worked hard for the victory. "What I suffered respecting those children God knows, and He only," she wrote. "What I endured and yet lived past—of pain, exasperation, helplessness, and despair . . . I shall not even try to explain. I believe men have no more notion of what that anguish is than the blind have of colours. . . . I REALLY wept and suffered in my early youth, for wrong done not BY me but to me. . . . I REALLY suffered the extremity of earthly shame without deserving it (whatever chastisement my other faults may have deserved of Heaven), I REALLY lost my young children —craved for them, struggled for them, was barred from

[1] Detached as this pamphlet is, the discerning eye might have detected the feminine hand. We quote one tell-tale passage, "You cannot get the Peers to sit up till three in the morning listening to the wrongs of separated mothers and the recital of cases . . . they are disturbed at the preposterous importance set by the women on the society of their infant children."

[2] 2 & 3 Vict. c. 54. The Act laid down that a judge in equity might make an order allowing mothers against whom adultery was not proved to have the custody of their children under seven, with right of access to their elder children at stated times.

them—and came too late to see one that had died . . . except in his coffin. I REALLY have gone through much that, if it were invented, would move you; but being of your everyday world, you are willing it should sweep past like a heap of dead leaves on the stream of time and take its place with other things that have gone drifting down."

Poor Caroline! She too, with her bitter memories, her talents, and her charms has been swept away upon the stream of time.[1] But she at least has left a mark behind her, a record written in the very laws of her country, to save others from her own fate. For the breach which she made in the laws relating to mothers and children has widened and deepened, until in the end all the ancient injustices were finally removed by the full equal guardianship of the Infants' Custody Act of 1925.

Mrs Norton's agitation had called the attention of politicians to some of the grievances and disabilities of women, and in 1840 an event occurred which focussed public opinion upon their political standing in a dramatic and interesting fashion.

In that year the World's Anti-Slavery Convention was called by the British and Foreign Anti-Slavery Society, and was held in London. To this convention all the leading Anti-Slavery agitators were summoned, and the American delegation was expected to be particularly distinguished and important. William Lloyd Garrison himself, the head and front of the extreme Abolitionists, was coming, and the whole of the English Radical world was interested in the event.

When the American delegation arrived, however, it was

[1] Caroline's later history may be briefly summarised. Fletcher Norton, her eldest son, entered the diplomatic service in 1847, and his mother travelled abroad with him on many occasions. He died in 1859, being then only 29 years old. Brinsley, her second son, who was also very delicate, married an Italian and settled abroad, and Caroline undertook the education of his children in England. She continued to write stories and poems and to fascinate everyone she met, and she continued to live above her income. Richard Norton died in 1875, and two years later Caroline, then 69 years old, married Sir William Stirling Maxwell, an old and devoted friend. Only three months later she died.

not what had been hoped. Garrison was delayed on the way, and of the seven members who did turn up, four were women! It was a most horrible disappointment. Although women belonged and contributed money to the British Society, none of them had ever yet taken part in its deliberations. The abolition of slavery in British territory in 1833 had been gained without any such indecorous proceeding, so that dismay was now the prevailing note. The leading British representatives said that the claim that women should be part of the Convention was "subversive of the principles and traditions of the country, and contrary to the word of God." It was unthinkable that these females should be admitted. And yet there they were, guests of the Society, fully accredited delegates from the American organisations, and, moreover, eminent and dignified ladies who fully expected to be made welcome! It was a most painful affair.

The whole of the first day's proceedings were devoted to this point, and all through the long hot hours the battle raged. Pending the decision the ladies were put in seats which were fenced off behind a curtain, and of course they were not allowed to speak on their own behalf. Whether they laughed or wept behind the screen no one knew; at any rate they remained quiet, while the men argued and disputed; and in the end they learnt that their credentials had been rejected by an overwhelming majority.

The ladies, as they walked home together down Great Queen Street, took among themselves some solemn resolutions, which bore fruit when they got back to their native land. But for the moment they accepted their defeat, and contented themselves with the fact that all London rang with the doings of the Convention. When the next day's session opened they retired to the gallery, and watched quietly from there. Presently a new sensation was created; William Lloyd Garrison at last arrived. The committee of welcome came forth to meet him. All were agog to see the hero of the hour, and to hear what he had to say, but he, learning what had happened to his companions, was in no mood to be welcomed. Despite all their protests and explanations he declared that he "preferred to join the ladies," and did so. And not a word would he contribute to the debate.

"As the ladies were not allowed to speak in the Convention," an eye-witness tells us, "they kept up a brisk fire morning, noon and night at their hotel on the unfortunate gentlemen who were domiciled at the same house. Mr Birney, with his luggage, promptly withdrew after the first encounter to some more congenial haven of rest, while the Rev. Nathaniel Culver, from Boston, who always fortified himself at breakfast with six eggs well beaten in a large bowl, to the horror of his host and a circle of æsthetic friends, stood his ground to the last."[1] The woman question became the topic of the hour, and almost eclipsed negro slavery itself!

When the Convention was over, and when all that could be said in England had been said, the rejected American delegates went home to put their solemn resolution into practice and to begin a passionate and public demand for their "rights." Before many years were over they had got together a Woman's Rights Convention, the first to be held in any country,[2] and had loudly demanded their full civic, religious, and domestic liberties; and from that beginning the American movement sprang. In England, however, things did not proceed so openly. The new idea spread quietly about, creeping from one person to another and slowly undermining the enemies' defences; and in this process the happenings of that World's Convention of 1840 were an undoubted help.

By 1843, indeed, matters had advanced so far that Mrs Henry Reid was able to publish a definitely propagandist book which had a considerable sale. It was called *A Plea*

[1] *History of Woman Suffrage*, edited by Elizabeth Cady Stanton, Susan B. Anthony, Matilda Jocelyn Gage, and Ida Husted Harper, vol. i, 1881.

[2] The Convention was held at Seneca Falls in 1848.

for Women, and among other things it pointed out that women were entitled to vote for the Directors of the East India Company, and drew the obvious parallels. It was indeed a regular suffrage publication; and three years later the first of the vast tribe of leaflets appeared. This document was drawn up, printed and circulated by Ann Knight, a Quaker lady who lived at Quiet House, Chelmsford, and who was active in all sorts of reforms, including the Anti-Slavery movement. She it was who kept alive the Sheffield Female Political Association which had come into existence during the Chartist agitation. Although most of the others died away, this one lived at any rate until 1851, for in that year it passed a resolution or petition in favour of female suffrage which was presented in the House of Lords by the Earl of Carlisle.[1]

The subject was also mentioned from time to time in the speeches of public men. Richard Cobden, speaking to an audience in Manchester during the Anti-Corn Law agitation, publicly declared that he wished women had the vote, and in 1848 Mr Joseph Hume, supported by Mr Cobden, went so far as to move a resolution in the House of Commons to extend the vote to all householders, including women. Disraeli spoke in its favour,[2] but there was no result, unless indeed the great care with which the word "male" was inserted into the voting clauses of all subsequent Poor Law and Local Government Bills can be attributed to this cause! But at any rate the matter had advanced into the realm of things possible to mention; and the day when it would be considered was at hand.

[1] See *History of Woman Suffrage*, by Elizabeth Cady Stanton and Matilda Jocelyn Gage; English section, vol. iii, by Caroline Ashurst Biggs. See also *Record of Women's Suffrage*, by Helen Blackburn.

[2] "In a country governed by a woman, where you allow women to form part of the estates of the Realm—Peeresses in their own right, for example—where you allow women not only to hold land but to be ladies of the manor and to hold legal courts—where a woman by law may be a church warden and overseer of the poor—I do not see, where she has so much to do with State and Church, on what reasons, if you come to right, she has not the right to vote," Disraeli in the House of Commons, 1848.

CHAPTER III

THE WIDENING CIRCLE. 1837–1850

Conventional young ladyhood and the ideals of the period—Frederick Maurice and the Christian Socialists—The conditions of dress-makers—The problems of factory employment—Women in mines and agriculture—The conditions of governesses—The opening of Queen's College in 1848.

THE first stirrings of the feminist movement began through the awakening of individual women to their own uselessness. As the philanthropic and humanitarian movements advanced, this revelation extended, and by the middle of the century there were quite a noticeable number of people who were familiar with the idea that there was something wrong with the position of women.

The bulk of these people came from among the new Radicals, and particularly from the Unitarian and Quaker families, and from that important and interesting group which made so brilliant a contribution to scientific thought at that epoch. If you were a Buxton, a Gurney, a Fry, a Wedgwood, a Bright, a Fox, a Barclay, or a Darwin it was not such a very great misfortune to be born a woman; though, of course, even in these families you would not share in the main work of your husbands or brothers. Still you would be allowed and expected to be educated and intelligent, and you would be considered an equal in family life, and might, if you chose, take up occupations and interests of your own.

In the journals and lives of the period we get charming glimpses of the intercourse of the young men and women of these families, talking, and talking earnestly, together about the semi-abstract subjects which youth enjoys; the nature of imagination, the refining effect of suffering, the difference between superstition and ceremony, and all the rest. We see them reading German literature together and sitting at the feet of Carlyle, admiring Mazzini and attending scientific congresses and enjoying a companionship and an intellectual interchange which has a distinctly modern flavour.

But neither these nor the brilliant ladies of political society were the models whom public opinion accepted as typical and correct. It was rather the daughter of the small squire or parson who represented the "real lady," and she was still kept close within the hampering limitations of despised womanhood. Little education, few interests, and no activity outside the family circle was the diet for her, with just a faint trickle of ladylike philanthropy to relieve the monotony. It was her only permissible practical activity; and it was much hedged by restrictions, as was everything else in her world. Nevertheless, limited as it was, it did make a tiny crack in the door of life, and that crack admitted the thin end of an entering wedge. But as yet it was not very effective against the misfortune of being a woman. A little gloss of accomplishments, and a false veneer of "polite attentions" was spread over the surface of the monstrosity, but it could not really alter the case. Rich and poor, young and old, women's lives were spent in a round of tedium against which it was all but impossible to prevail.

And it was not only that there was nothing to do. The blight which fell upon each girl at the outset of her life was more insidious and even more irresistible than its compulsory emptiness. For there was a belief strongly held by men and women alike that it would be unnatural, wrong, and, moreover, impossible for any female to do or say or think anything worth serious consideration. Her brain was smaller in cubic content, so that her incapacity for reasoning, generalising, pursuing connected ideas, judging or persevering were natural and inevitable things. She was "inferior" by the act of God, and her lack of intellect was made up for by her vast superiority in "instinct." She might be charming and she should be good, but it was all. For it was her place to minister to man and be content. This convention had flourished for many years, as we have already seen. Florence Nightingale had passionately and successfully revolted against it, and there were, by 1850, a slowly increasing number of young women who longed for release. It was still an all but unchallenged convention, but there was a breath of change in the air which called forth just at this time a definite statement of the whole position. It was as if it were felt necessary to put it into words and to teach in the most deliberate manner the duty of female submissiveness which before had been taken entirely for granted. A host of little books appeared, written for the most part by women, setting forth the whole duty of the sex. *The English Maiden*, *The Feminine Soul*, *Womankind*, *The Afternoon of Unmarried Life*, *Woman —Her Social and Domestic Character*, and a whole series of the *Women, Wives, Mothers and Daughters of England*, which set forth the doctrine to the complete admiration and satisfaction of the day. These books are comic reading now, with their perpetual harping upon self-repression, patience, resignation, and the trivial round of duties which was a woman's highest glory; but they must have seemed deadly enough to the eager young girls for whose repression they were intended. One quotation, out of thousands, will suffice to show the pernicious quality and the subtle poison of these sermons. It is from the chapter headed, "Behaviour to Husbands" in *The Women of England*, by Mrs Ellis, published in 1841. "In the case of a highly-gifted woman, even where there is an equal or superior degree of talent possessed by her husband, nothing can be more injudicious, or more fatal to her happiness, than an exhibition of the least disposition to presume upon such gifts. Let a husband be once subjected to a feeling of jealousy of her importance, which, without the strictest watchfulness, will be liable to arise, and her peace of mind and her free agency are alike destroyed for the rest of her life; or, at any rate, until she can convince him afresh, by a long continuance of the most scrupulous conduct, that the injury committed against him was purely accidental and foreign alike to her feelings and her inclinations. Until this desirable end is accomplished, vain will be all her efforts to render homage to her husband as a superior. He will regard all such attempts as acts of condescension, assumed for no other purpose than that of showing how gracefully she can stoop. In vain may she then endeavour to assist or direct his judgment; he will in such a case most naturally prefer to thwart her, for the purpose of proving his own independence and his power."

The pernicious ideal of marriage which this extract reveals was the outcome of a whole network of fallacies; and it is not surprising that once it had begun to be questioned the number of men and women who revolted against it rapidly increased. The only wonder, indeed, is that it should have been tolerated so long.

While the exhortations of the orthodox were thus goading the young to revolt, a more definite and concrete influence was at work making new "converts" to the cause, namely, the Christian Socialist movement. The ardent little band of people which gathered round Frederick Denison Maurice, the Chaplain of Lincoln's Inn, did not preach feminism it is true, but, nevertheless, their influence told strongly in that direction. For they assumed as a matter of course that women would join in their work, and they admitted them freely to share in their discussions. All they sought was to draw the whole world into the pure, if troubled, region of their own thoughts, and among them, as in the

Kingdom of Heaven, there was "neither male nor female, bond nor free."

The Christian Socialists moved, perhaps, in a somewhat visionary world. Their main preoccupation appeared to be an anxious effort to reconcile the world as they saw it with a Church of their dreams, and most of their subjects of anxiety have long ceased to trouble the religious world. Yet, for all their theological hair-splitting, they were severely practical, and they steadily expressed their ideals in good works which were far more thorough and constructive than the soup-and-blankets charity of the ordinary contemporary parish.

The greater part of the work of Maurice, Kingsley, and their friends falls outside the scope of this book. We have here no direct concern with co-operative production or distribution, or even with the lectures to working men. Neither the measures nor the conceptions inspiring them had anything to do with questions of sex. It was the class structure of society and the class distribution of wealth which they attacked, and essentially they did not care whether it was men or women for whom their experiments were tried. They saw that the improvement of either would be good for society as a whole—and this in itself was a conception of human life more fundamentally in harmony with the women's cause than some of its later and more aggressive developments.

Frederick Maurice, the centre and head of the whole movement, was one of the few men who, in the thirties and forties really believed that women had an existence in this world and the next. Obvious as the thing seems now, it was generally overlooked at that date, and even thoughtful and unselfish men forgot it. That Maurice, from the earliest years, did not, was perhaps partly due to his instinctive fair-mindedness, but also it was partly the consequence of the influences of his childhood. He was the only boy in a family of many children, and his sisters, some of whom were a great deal older than himself, seem all to have been remarkably distinctive persons. The energies and the thought of the whole family centred round problems of religious belief; and Frederick saw these elder sisters taking their own separate ways, and following the promptings of their own individual consciences. Their father grieved over the lines they took, and Frederick, too, disagreed with some of them; but he acknowledged their perfect right, nay, even their absolute duty to follow their own lights. And his attitude to women was thereby determined.

One of the first practical problems which Maurice and his friends tried to attack was the condition of dress-makers and tailors. An opportune strike of the tailors called public attention to their troubles in the first instance, and Thomas Hood in the *Song of the Shirt* (1844) and Charles Kingsley in *Alton Locke* (1850) carried the interest further. Co-operative workrooms were the remedy which the Christian Socialists believed in, and they opened one with high hopes; but, being intelligent people, they realised that the problems of the tailors and those of the tailoresses were almost the same. The seasonal nature of the work, and the unorganised condition of the trade, held good for workers of both sexes; and accordingly they set themselves to look into the women's conditions. A very brief examination showed that it was a good deal worse than that of the men, and the revelations of one of the commissions of inquiry which Lord Shaftesbury had secured showed that the evil was even more widespread. Tailors were sweated, but dressmakers and milliners were still more overdriven.

"In some of what are considered the best regulated establishments during the fashionable season, occupying about four months of the year, the regular hours of work are fifteen. . . ."[1] "In many establishments the hours of work

[1] Report of the Second Commission on the Employment of Women and Children, 1843.

during the season are unlimited . . . very frequently they work all night." A witness from one of those workshops reported that "On the occasion of the general mourning for his majesty William IV. she worked without going to bed from 4 o'clock on Thursday morning till half-past ten on Sunday morning; during this time witness did not sleep at all. In order to keep awake she stood nearly the whole of Friday and Saturday night, only sitting down for half an hour for rest. Two other young persons worked at the same house for the same time." Another witness "has seen young persons in an alarming state of debility and faintness from excessive toil and want of rest." Very often the girls had consumption. They suffered continuously from lassitude, debility, loss of appetite, and pains in the back. "I should think," one witness reports, "that there is not one in twenty who does not suffer from this." "These conditions are worse than in the worst conducted factories. . . . There is no ventilation by day or night, and the work-girls are crowded one upon another in dark rooms." "The dressmakers themselves state their belief that 'no man could sustain the labour which is imposed on these young and delicate women,' and a medical witness declares that 'no men work so long.'"

For all this toil the wages were 4s. 6d. a week, with miserable lodging, and such little food as the poor girls were able to eat. A diet of bread and butter and tea was the usual thing, to which slabs of cold mutton which no one had the courage to touch would sometimes be added.[1] And so they lived while the fashionable season rolled on its way; and for the rest of the year they were short of work.

This report, shocking as were the facts it revealed, did not attract much general attention, but in the following year an "Association for the Aid and Benefit of Milliners and Dressmakers" came into being with the object of making

[1] *Our Homeless Poor*, 1860, by the author of *Helen Lyndsey*. See also Mrs Gaskell's *Ruth*, the novels of Sir Walter Besant, Mary Lamb's essay on "Needlewomen," etc.

the facts of the situation known and awakening sympathy. This association recommended no Sunday work, a twelve-hours' day, with an hour off for dinner and tea, and a minimum wage of nine shillings a week; but modest as these demands were they were accepted by very few employers. The Christian Socialists when they examined this state of affairs understood that it was not merely the hardness of people's hearts which caused these conditions. They saw that the root trouble was the enormous oversupply of workers combined with the seasonal nature of the job. As the commissioners said, a dressmaker's working life was not more than three or four years. "If a constant accession of fresh hands from the country were not provided," a witness told them, "the business could not be carried on." But workers were so many and other openings so few that new victims were always forthcoming. There was nothing else save domestic service for the girls to do; and domestic service was amply supplied. The choice was between dress-making, the streets, or the workhouse; and all too frequently the first led on to the other two in course of time.

The co-operative workrooms, which were opened to alleviate this state of things, broke down completely. Not only did they fail to change the general customs of society, but they did not even pay. After a short and discouraging career they had to be closed, and all effort to help these miserable women seemed to be at an end. The tailors, through their own Trade Union organisation, struggled still with their problems; but the women were too ill, too poorly paid, and too timid to defend themselves, and they appeared to have no hope. It remained for other women, inspired with other ideals, to take the steps which were to improve their lot; for it was the opening of fresh avenues of employment which, in the end, came to the rescue of the dress-makers and milliners and which won for them—far too late, and even now too imperfectly—the protection and improvement they required.

While the Christian Socialists were endeavouring to help the dressmakers, a series of revelations of the actual conditions under which other women workers lived was being made. The problems of factory regulation, which should of course have been considered simultaneously with the growth of factories, were only beginning to attract widespread public attention towards the middle of the century; and by that time the abuses and the scandals had grown to alarming proportions.

The Industrial Revolution began long before the nineteenth century; and all through its course it was accompanied by a decline in the economic importance of women. Their change from partners to parasites was an exceedingly far-reaching social phenomenon, and their collapse from skilled workers to cheap labourers added greatly to the confusions and disasters which accompanied industrial development. As the change proceeded it wrenched away from women great portions of their traditional work, and thus forced them either to follow it into the labour market, or to sit in idleness at home. And both courses led inevitably to demoralisation and discontent. The well-to-do, whose lot was idleness, grew frivolous, artificial, and absurd; the poor, whose lot was wage-earning, were exploited and overdriven; and both rich and poor believed that this was the order of nature and the predestined way of the world.

The miserable condition of working women was not a new phenomenon in the nineteenth century, but it was then that it was first brought to public notice; and the Humanitarian movement which revealed it was not originally concerned with the conditions of women at all, but only with those of children. Lord Shaftesbury, who was the leading spirit of this movement in the thirties and forties, caused a number of commissions of inquiry to be set up, and the revelations which they brought to light shocked even the *laissez-faire* economists of the period. It was all very well to believe that labour would find its own level, and that artificial restrictions hindered trade; but when one learnt that babies of four years old were regularly working for twelve hours a day, one must either alter this state of affairs, or disbelieve it. We cannot here follow the course of the children's agitation, nor describe the abuses which came to light; but it is perhaps not inappropriate to give a thought to the mothers who were forced to drive their children out to work, beating them in the darkness to make them start, and beating them again at night to keep them awake long enough to eat the food so bitterly earned. Heart-rending glimpses of their outlook are to be found in the evidence given before the Government commissions, glimpses of misery and hardness which it is painful to contemplate even after all these years.

It was not only vicarious suffering which the working women had to endure. The conditions of their own work, and the hours and pay they had themselves to accept were enough to shock the public conscience, and as the inquiries went on these facts came to light. Both men and women, it appeared, worked for inordinate hours, and in dangerous and insanitary conditions; and since women were more easily oppressed, and more completely underpaid, their conditions were invariably the worse of the two.

While the revelations of factory conditions were proceeding an agitation began among the factory hands to secure a limitation of the hours of work, but the movement did not venture to proceed in a direct line. It seemed hopeless to ask for a limitation of men's working hours in the face of the solid opposition of the employers and the economic theories current at the time, and so a circuitous route was followed. The tactics were to ask for a limitation of the hours of women and children, in the belief that this would cause a compulsory stoppage of machinery, and so result in the limitation of the hours of men also. The well-known phrase "hiding behind the women's petticoats" had its origin in this attempt; and it was a plan which was moderately successful.

After the publication of numerous exhaustive reports, and after the failure of several small and tentative measures, the Ten Hours Act was passed in 1847, and by this Act the hours of work for women and young persons were limited to ten a day, and the hours of men were, in fact, though not by law, altered to correspond.

It is interesting to note that during the long struggle for this Bill anxiety first began to be expressed by the men workers concerning the numbers of women employed. These numbers were indeed very great. In the cotton mills of Lancashire, for example, there were in 1833 65,000 women (10,721 of whom were married) and only 60,000 men. The cheapness of women's labour, and the fatal ease with which they yielded to longer hours tended to increase the disproportion, and in 1841 some of the short-time committees went so far as to suggest the gradual withdrawal of all females from factory work. Nothing was done on these lines, and even the more moderate suggestion that some comparative ratio of numbers should be fixed fell to the ground, so that the only disabilities which were actually imposed by law on women's labour were such as sprang from the efforts made for their protection. The textile workers adopted the wise plan of organising the men and the women together, and demanding equal piece-work rates for both. This method of meeting the difficulty worked well, but it was only in the cotton and the woollen trades that it was adopted. Elsewhere restrictive methods were gradually imposed by custom, and conventions came into being by which women's progress in industry was severely limited; the present-day restriction of their work, in all but the textile trades, to unskilled and badly paid processes was soon in force, and it brought with it a horde of troubles.

Before the Ten Hours' Day agitation had secured the

passage of the Act of 1847, another matter even more directly concerning the industrial employment of women came suddenly and dramatically before the public. Lord Shaftesbury, early in his fight for the abolition of child labour, had secured the appointment of a Commission on the Employment of Children in Mines and Manufactories, and the first report of this commission appeared in 1842.

The commissioners, wishing to make sure that the report would be read, caused it to be illustrated; effective and terrible as the pictures are, they are not needed to intensify the tale, for the text is enough. There is the evidence of children of six years, or even less, working for more than twelve hours at a stretch underground, in darkness and solitude, tired, cold, and frightened; and of little girls carrying heavy baskets of coal, staggering hour after hour along steep galleries, or on long and dangerous ladders. There, too, are descriptions of girls and women, harnessed like ponies to the trucks, struggling on all fours along the rough, narrow, and insecure passages of the mines, dripping with moisture and stripped to the waist.

"Women always did the lifting or heavy part of the work," said the commissioner, "and neither they nor the children were treated like human beings. . . . Females submit to work in places where no man or even lad could be got to labour in: they work in the bad roads, up to their knees in water, in a posture nearly double: they are below till the last hour of pregnancy; they have swelled haunches and ankles, and are prematurely brought to the grave, or, what is worse, a lingering existence. . . . The state which the females are in after pulling like horses through those holes—their perspiration, exhaustion, and tears very frequently—it is painful in the extreme to witness it; yet, when the work is done, they return to it with a vigour which is surprising, considering how they inwardly hate it."

The women themselves spoke of the matter quite plainly when they gave evidence. "I have a belt round my waist and a chain passing between my legs and go on my hands and feet. The road is very steep and we have to hold by a rope, and when there is no rope by anything we can get hold of. . . . My clothes are wet through almost all day long. . . . I have drawn till I have had the skin off me; the belt and chain is worse when we are in the family way. . . ."

"I had a child born in the pits," said another, "and I brought it up the pit shaft in my skirt." In plain words like these the women told their tale, and the publication of such things naturally made a deep and terrible impression.

Lord Shaftesbury had no difficulty in finding support for his Bill to forbid all women and boys under ten from working underground, and in a few months after the Report had appeared it had passed into law. Everyone wanted to put an end to the scandal, but no one, not even Lord Shaftesbury himself, remembered that when these pit women could no longer crawl through the bowels of the earth to earn their daily bread it might happen that they would starve. The sudden and wholesale closing of their employment did in fact throw numbers [1] of them into a condition of different, but perhaps equally acute, misery, and the few charitable efforts which were afterwards made for their relief were quite insufficient. Public uneasiness was appeased with the closing of this unsuitable employment to women, and the sufferers might fare as best they could. Women's concerns had at best but a brief hold upon the attention of statesmen; were not women in the natural course protected and supported by their husbands? Amid the fictions and sentimentalities of the day the working women were once more forgotten. The curtain of neglect fell over them again, and no more was heard of the female mining population until the pit brow agitation of 1887.

The Report of the Commission on Mines was dreadful

[1] According to the census of 1841 there were 2350 women and girls working underground.

reading, and it was followed by a number of other documents which revealed conditions in other trades hardly less oppressive. In these cases, however, the drastic short cut of forbidding women to work was not attempted, and it was only by the gradual increase of general factory legislation that improvement came; and everywhere, both then and now, the root trouble of the women's relatively worse position, namely, their lower wages, remained untouched. Gradually, as the Trade Union movement strengthened, and as custom hardened and became enshrined in rules and agreements, women's position as the underdogs of industry came to seem a part of the order of the universe. Men's jobs and women's jobs grew clearly marked and sharply differentiated; some of the women's jobs were heavy, some were light, some were skilled and some were simple, but the one common factor of them all was that they were badly paid.

Only one glimmer of cheerfulness comes from a study of the reports on women's labour which appeared in the middle of the century, and its cheerfulness is but comparative. It is the case of the women employed in agriculture, where, as the commissioners observed, the women liked the work, and thought of it as "desirable for health and spirits."

"The general conclusion as to the physical condition of women engaged in agriculture is that it is generally better than that of the same class not so employed. The reason is evident: the means of the family are increased by her earnings, she has more food . . . her health is better. I am speaking now of her own physical condition." [1]

This was something to the good, but the commissioners felt bound to point out that there were drawbacks to the husbands and children. In the case of the children the difficulties were obvious, and the witness who confessed

[1] "Report of the Poor Law Commissioners on the Employment of Women and Children in Agriculture, 1843."

that her heart sank with fear whenever she approached her home lest an accident should have happened must have been typical of many. But even in country districts arrangements must sometimes have been possible, and in any case the children grew up in course of time; the husband problem remained constant, however, and the picture the commissioners drew of his sufferings is pathetic in an unintentional sense.

"To a certain extent also the husband is a sufferer from his wife's absence from home. There is not the same order in the cottage, nor the same attention paid to his comforts as when his wife remains at home all day. On returning from her labour she has to look after the children, and her husband may have to wait for his supper. He may come home tired and wet; he finds his wife has arrived just before him, and she must give her attention to the children; there is no fire, no supper, no comfort, and he goes to the beer shop."

Poor husband! But surely also poor wife? Life at home must have been a dreary thing indeed if this double share of toil was more preferable "for health and spirits" than the woman's task alone!

The sufferings of the industrial and labouring classes had no direct effect upon the Women's Movement. The working women whose lot was so harsh had no thought that they themselves ought to be able to change and control their conditions. They might, indeed, join in some passionate revolt against the wrongs of the poor, or they might dream secretly of riches or of rest; but that they, as women, could ever be relieved of their extra troubles, that they might ever be people on their own account, seems not to have been imagined. Women must be ministers to the comfort of men; that was what they were for, and custom, law and Church all proclaimed it. Their only claim to toleration was this work, this and the bearing of children. And so, in the round of these duties, life went on, and few, if any, realised the forces which were making for change. They did not know that a new social conscience was awakening to their needs, and that their standard of living was going to improve. Sanitation, Education, Factory Inspection, Health Insurance and Old Age Pensions, and all the other improvements of the century were far beyond the range of their ideas; and still farther, still more unimaginable was the movement which was to give them votes. And yet, even as they suffered and toiled, these movements gathered force, and the very same people who were trying to improve their material conditions were furthering the other movement too.

The Christian Socialists, who had not succeeded in helping the tailoresses, had a second object of concern in which they were more effective, and that was the position of governesses. These people, like the seamstresses, suffered from the fact that there were too many of them, and in the thirties and forties they were in a miserable case. Twenty-five pounds a year was the common salary, and on this the governess had to dress "like a lady," to save for illness and old age, and, all too often, to help to support a widowed mother or young sisters and brothers who were dependent on her. The profession was the only one open to a female "of gentle birth"; it was the one resource of impoverished spinsters (of whom there were an alarming number). When, as so often happened, a man made no provision at all for his wife or daughters, and died leaving them penniless, it was the only thought they could entertain. It is true that as a rule they had no training for the profession of teaching, not even the training of a good education; all they could bring to the labour market was their "gentility" and their necessity; and neither of these was a commercial asset. It was no wonder, then, that they were ground down, and that the nervous strain of anxiety and misfortune reduced the level of their competence even further than their total absence of training implied.

In 1841 a Governesses' Benevolent Institution was founded, whose object was to give annuities and to "afford assistance privately and delicately to ladies in temporary distress," and this institution was besieged with hundreds of pitiful cases. For one annuity of twenty pounds, for example, there were 150 applicants over fifty, of whom 83 had not one penny in the world, although they had been brought up in wealth. And this was by no means an exceptional case. The bank failures of the preceding decade had thrown thousands of women into the same position, and there seemed to be no hope for this class save charity.[1]

Frederick Maurice became interested in this subject through the influence of his sister Mary, who had herself become a teacher, and was helping in the heart-breaking work of the institution; and after a visit to her he began talking about the matter to his friends. Benevolence and annuities were all very well, but what he was seeking was something better than a palliative for the evils of society; and after long and earnest discussion the Christian Socialists came to the conclusion that the only real help for this miserable class lay in the improvement of their standards of work. If they could teach better they could command higher salaries; and it was the only way. An effort must therefore be made to improve their education, and for this purpose a committee of professors of King's College, London, came together with the intention of granting certificates of proficiency to governesses, and with the active assistance of Charles Kingsley a series of Lectures to Ladies was begun in 1847.

The decision to give these lectures coincided with an effort which was being independently made by Miss Murray,[2]

[1] It is interesting to note that Jenny Lind, the singer, presented £200 to the Institution in 1849, "because she felt for the sufferers of her sex, having passed through the same trials." *Life of F. D. Maurice*, by his son.

[2] Miss Murray maintained her interest in the Women's Movement, and at the time when Elizabeth Garrett was pursuing her medical studies she often sent for her to come to the palace and tell her how she was

one of the Queen's ladies-in-waiting, to raise money for the improvement of the education of women, and both schemes were united under the Governesses' Benevolent Association. The lectures were such a success, however, that they almost at once developed into a regular institution, and Queen's College for Women came into existence in 1848. The object of this college was to teach "all branches of female knowledge," though it is at least doubtful whether its promoters had a clear and unanimous view of what constituted "female knowledge." Maurice himself, on the occasion of the opening, made a very modest claim. "We are aware," he said, "that our pupils are not likely to advance far in Mathematics, but we believe that if they learn really what they do learn, they will not have got what is dangerous but what is safe." *Punch* and the comic press were not sure of this, however, and squibs about Professors of Bead-Purse Making and Degrees in Crochet Work were considered very telling at the time; but they did not affect the enthusiasm of the students in the least. The women who thronged to the classes really wanted knowledge, whether real or only female, very much indeed, and the professors gave them what they could. Greek was not in the original list of classes, but there were other things to be taught in plenty, and the two hundred students who came in the first year had a considerable choice of lectures. It soon appeared, however, that the chief business of the College would have to be the provision of a grounding in elementary subjects. Those who came, whether they were eager young girls, or elderly women, or governesses of many years' experience, were all alike possessed of a deplorable ignorance of the rudiments of grammar and arithmetic, and before many months had gone by it was apparent that the

getting on. On one such occasion she said to Miss Garrett, "My dear, I think you are doing quite right; and I really believe, if I were a woman myself I would do the same." "If you were a woman yourself?" said Miss Garrett, surprised. "I mean if I were in that station of life," was Miss Murray's explanation!

"female knowledge" which was required was nothing more nor less than the ordinary equipment of a schoolboy. However, the students were not schoolboys, and before long the teachers settled down to a curriculum in which elementary subjects formed the main part, but advanced lectures on English literature, sociology, and even philosophy were also provided. Science, too, was not omitted. Laboratories and practical work were not available, but popular lectures were frequently arranged and were eagerly attended. Indeed, the ordinary courses of scientific lectures which were given at that period were usually crowded with ladies, so much so that in some places they were excluded altogether lest the "real" audience should be shut out. In the same year that Queen's College opened, for example, women were forbidden by the Bishop of London to attend Wheatstone's lectures on electricity at King's College. The reason given was that they had "congregated" too abundantly at Lyell's lectures! But none of the scientists themselves objected to this. Wheatstone, indeed, was so angry at the prohibition that he forthwith resigned his Professorship,[1] and the whole affair made a stir.

The fact was that the crowding in of women to hear lectures and to seek knowledge was a sign of the times. It was so real a demand that a year after Queen's College was opened it was possible for another to be set on foot, and in 1849 Bedford College began. Although the kind of instruction given at Queen's and at Bedford was the same, there was a significant difference between the two institutions. Queen's College, by its constitution, was entirely governed by men, and the only share which women were called upon to take in the management was that of attending the lectures as "Lady Visitors" or chaperones. The other College, however, which was founded by Mrs Reid, adopted the more advanced plan of having a mixed board of management; and though this difference may

[1] *Journal of Caroline Fox.*

seem slight enough now, it was a mighty matter in the middle of the nineteenth century.

To these two institutions many of those who were afterwards to set on foot the organised Women's Movement made their way. In the lives of Barbara Leigh Smith of Octavia Hill, Sophia Jex-Blake, Frances Mary Buss, Dorothea Beale and many more, the companionship, the partial independence and the glimpse of "female knowledge" which these places afforded was exceedingly important. They gave encouragement to their secret and half-realised dreams, and Maurice, Kingsley, and their friends, by sanctioning and encouraging these girls, rendered an immense service to the Women's Movement.

CHAPTER IV

THE DEMAND FORMULATED. 1850–1857

The Radical movement of the fifties and sixties—John Stuart Mill and Mrs Taylor—Barbara Leigh Smith—The first organised Committee for Married Women's Property—Introduction of a Bill—The Marriage and Divorce Act of 1857.

THE Women's Movement before 1850 was scattered and fragmentary, and hardly to be called a movement at all. The ideas and hopes which inspired it existed, indeed, and were growing stronger, but they were manifest chiefly in the lives and aspirations of those few outstanding women who managed to leave some record of themselves upon the world in which they lived. From 1850 onwards, however, it takes on a new aspect, and the individual champions fall more easily into their places in the whole perspective, being supported and surrounded by a growing crowd of followers.

It is difficult to estimate whether it was the Radicals of the fifties and sixties or the philanthropists of the same period who quickened the Women's Movement to life; and it is really unnecessary to weigh them one against the other. The two movements acted and reacted upon each other, as contemporary movements must, and while the one was the head and forefront of the new ideas, the other spread outwards and slowly educated the public mind to accept and even approve of certain activities for women outside the four walls of their homes. We must, however, consider them separately, and, for our purposes, the Radical movement comes first.

This new outlook on society began to be a real force in

English thought many years before it succeeded in altering legislation, and the fact that it came to include the position of women among the things which were in need of change must be directly attributed to the influence of John Stuart Mill.

It is not necessary to retell the story of Mill's early life, nor to describe his extraordinary education. Everyone knows that he began to read Greek when he was three years old, that he studied philosophy, logic, and the calculus before he was twelve, and that his great talents and powers of mind developed, instead of perishing, upon this unusual fare. Mill's mind was always clear, logical, and desperately sincere, and the conviction of "the complete equality in all legal, political, social, and domestic relations which ought to exist between men and women" was, he said,[1] "among the earliest results of the application of my mind to political subjects." In coming to this conviction John Stuart Mill was opposing his father, whose article on Government, contributed to the *Encyclopedia Britannica* in 1823, had asserted that women were quite sufficiently represented by their husbands. The opposite belief was, however, held by Jeremy Bentham, at whose feet the young man Mill sat as a disciple, though indeed in this particular the disciple attached far more importance to the doctrine than did the master, by whom it was considered merely a logical but not particularly important implication of political liberty. Mill, however, brought his force and integrity to the support of these beliefs, and his friendship with Mrs Taylor, which began when he was twenty-four years old, served to intensify and deepen them. "It might be supposed," he wrote,[2] "that my convictions . . . were adopted or learnt from her. This is so far from being the fact that . . . the strength with which I held them was, as I believe, more than anything else, the originating cause of the interest she felt in me."

[1] *Autobiography*, by John Stuart Mill. [2] *Ibid.*

A great deal that is harsh and unkind has been said and implied about the friendship which grew up between these two young people, but the picture which Mill himself draws of their relations is singularly disarming. Their friendship grew slowly, but, after a time they were much together and even travelled abroad; and it became evident to all who knew him that this friendship was the most intense emotion of Mill's life. They must, of course, have loved each other long before it was possible for them to marry, but there was no question of anything beyond the purest friendship between them.

Harriet Taylor, whatever may have been the truth about her intellectual powers, was at any rate as sincere and honest as Mill himself. She spoke openly to her husband of what she felt, and a working arrangement was come to by which she lived for the most part in the country with her daughter Helen, and was visited there by her two sons, but from time to time stayed with her husband in town, and even received Mill there. This situation, in spite of John Taylor's acceptance of it, was too much for most of Mill's friends. One by one they expostulated with him; and one by one, as they did so, they found themselves shut out from his intimacy. He was so strong a defender of Mrs Taylor's good name, and so thoroughly steeped in his friendship, that any unsympathetic reference was intolerable to him, and was violently resented. The consequence of this was that, although hardly any of his friends knew Mrs Taylor at all, and none of them knew her intimately, a violent prejudice grew up against her. It was not scandal of the ordinary sort which was arrayed against her, but rather the jealous animosity of Mill's friends. He quarrelled with his father and his sisters; for the time he broke off all intercourse with Mrs Grote, Mrs Austen, J. A. Roebuck, and Harriet Martineau; and the others maintained their footing only by an anxious and unnatural silence upon the whole subject. In 1849, John Taylor died, and nearly two years later John Mill and Harriet Taylor were married.

Although, of course, it must have been a supreme delight to them both to live together in one household, and have no limits to the close association of their lives, yet their objections to marriage as by law ordained were profound. Mill drew up and signed a statement in which he formally repudiated its legal implications.

"The whole character of the marriage relation," he wrote, "as constituted by law being such as both she and I entirely and conscientiously disapprove, for this among other reasons, that it confers upon one of the parties to the contract, legal power and control over the person, property, and freedom of action of the other party, independent of her own wishes and will; I, having no means of legally divesting myself of these odious powers . . . feel it my duty to put on record a formal protest against the existing law of marriage, in so far as conferring such powers; and a solemn promise never in any case or under any circumstances to use them."

Apart from these considerations the marriage of John Stuart Mill and Harriet Taylor seemed to themselves ideal.

To their friends, however, it was not so welcome. They could no longer ignore the lady, now that she was Mrs Mill, and yet they could not manage to be cordial. The subdued hostility remained and even grew, and when in consequence Mill became less and less available for his friends, the blame settled more and more securely upon his wife. They resented what they called her "ascendancy," they deplored what they called his "hallucination," and they were embarrassed and utterly unconvinced by the things which he wrote in her praise. When the terrible incident of the destruction of the MS. of Carlyle's *French Revolution* occurred in her house, there were some who did not scruple to accuse her of being responsible for it. Housemaids, they said, do not light fires with manuscripts—could not indeed manage to burn up so bulky a parcel inadvertently; they thought that she was jealous, on her husband's behalf, of the success the book would have. It seems, however, incredible that Mrs Mill should have burnt the MS. If she had been the sort of person to whom such an action would be possible, Mill could not have revered her as he did through the whole of his adult life. So clear and honest a man could not have been hopelessly deceived, in so long and intimate an acquaintance, and if it be on his judgment alone, his wife must be acquitted. But although she be cleared from every scandal, and accepted just as Mill wished her to be accepted, as a brilliant and a deep thinker, there must still be something to account for the faint breath of disapproval which still lingers about her name. Perhaps it was the fact that she lived apart from her first husband which put her wrong with the world; perhaps she was always socially on the defensive as well as too exclusively devoted to Mill. Perhaps she cared nothing at all for other people, was unsympathetic or even unkind, impatient of stupidity and of conventions. There may have been a dozen such outward difficulties which hid her from the world, and obscured her image in the records which are to be found in the lives and letters of her day. We cannot now judge what it was that made his friends distrust her. She left nothing of her own by which she can be recreated. One article on the Enfranchisement of Women, published in the *Westminster Review* in 1851, is all that is known to be of her authorship; and that article, admirable and clear as it is, contains nothing personal or self-revealing. Beyond this, and Mill's own descriptions, there is nothing upon which a judgment can be founded. Perhaps, therefore, it is wiser, as well as more charitable, to discard all the unsubstantial criticisms, and to believe Harriet Taylor to have been, as Mill himself described her, a clear-headed and impersonal thinker, honestly absorbed in abstract thought, modifying, widening, and softening their joint outlook, enriching the books which appeared over his name with her grasp of human realities, and filling out his life and her own into a perfect partnership. If Mill is to be believed, they reaped the benefit in their own lives of that complete intellectual and domestic equality which they espoused; and who should know the truth of this statement if not Mill himself?

In any case, whether inspired by or in spite of the influence of Harriet Taylor, John Stuart Mill was a great and an influential man, and in some ways the very centre and mainspring of the new Radical movement. His books, difficult and abstract as they were, had an immense effect in shaping the new political thought, and became the textbooks of the movement.

We are not concerned here with any aspect of Mill's philosophy save the inclusion of women within it; but it was his weight and authority which gave the new dignity and, as it were, solidity to the feminist idea. In his *Political Economy* and in his *Defence of Liberty* this idea was implicit, but in the *Representative Government*, which he published in 1861, three years after his wife's death, he went farther, and clearly and unmistakably advocated Woman Suffrage. Every argument by which he supported representative government applied, he said, with equal force to the inclusion of women; and every principle of justice and of expediency demanded that this fact should be admitted.

In the same year that this book appeared Mill wrote another which he called *The Subjection of Women*. It was eight years more before this book was published, and in those eight years the Woman Suffrage Movement had come into formal existence, and Mill himself brought the subject forward in the House of Commons. It is, however, proper to consider the book now, before describing the later developments, because the outlook to which it gave expression was that which he was always urging upon his followers, and the point of view which it so clearly expresses was the basis of the whole active movement which began before its publication.

The argument of the book is very familiar to-day, and need not even be outlined here. For Mill took the ground that Mary Wollstonecraft had taken before him, and that every defender of the Cause has taken since. The *Subjection of Women*, indeed, is more coloured with logic and less with passion than the *Vindication*, more clearly arranged, more philosophical—and less eloquent. It bears, however, the stamp of full conviction, and of deep and serious thought. Mill had pondered, as no man had pondered before, over the implications and the results of the subjection of a whole sex. He cared not only for the logical completion of his theory of political liberty, but for the personal human consequences which he knew that full enfranchisement must bring. It was not Women's Suffrage only that he demanded, nor only equal laws. It was the removal of the age-long subjection and submission of women from which he hoped so much. His understanding of this wide demand he said he owed to his wife.

"Until I knew her, the opinion was in my mind little more than an abstract principle. . . . But that perception of the vast practical bearing of women's disabilities which found expression in the book *The Subjection of Women* was acquired mainly through her teaching. . . . I am indeed perfectly conscious of how much of her best thoughts on the subject I have failed to reproduce, and how greatly that little treatise falls short of what would have been if she had put on paper her entire mind on this question, or had lived to revise and improve, as she certainly would, my imperfect statement of the case." [1]

Had Mill himself lived to this day he would of course still be working in the same cause, unsatisfied, even though encouraged, by the advance as yet made, and still demanding the economic, the domestic, and the moral equality of men

[1] *Autobiography*, by John Stuart Mill.

and women. "We have had the morality of submission, and that of chivalry; but the time is now come for the morality of justice." So he wrote in 1861, and so he would write to-day. For we have taken as yet but the first steps along the path.

In 1855, six years before Mill's book was written, the first regular feminist committee came into existence, and the person who took the initiative in this matter was a remarkable young woman whose name is now little remembered, but whose share in the first organisation of the Women's Movement was of the utmost importance.

Barbara Leigh Smith, who was a first cousin of Florence Nightingale, was born in 1835, the eldest daughter of Mr Benjamin Smith, Radical Member for Norwich. The family was not only well connected and wealthy, but also extremely enlightened. Mr Smith knew all the reformers and philanthropists of the day, and his daughter moved in legal, political, literary, and artistic circles from her early youth. Left motherless when quite young, Barbara became the hostess of her father's house, and the strong intelligence which she possessed by nature was developed by the circumstances of her life. There seems to have been something particularly vigorous and vivid about Barbara Leigh Smith, who was taken by George Eliot as the model for Romola. Tall, handsome, generous and quite unselfconscious, she swept along, distracted only by the too great abundance of her interests and talents, and the too great outflowing of her sympathies. In her father's circle, brains, honest thinking, and expert knowledge were taken for granted; conventional standards did not count, and worldliness did not exist.

Life was a stirring affair for Barbara. Everything was before her—Art (for her painting was taken seriously by many eminent painters), philanthropy, education, politics—everything lay at her feet. The only trouble was to pick and choose

Barbara's father believed in the good sense of his children. As each came of age, whether sons or daughters, he made over to them an income of £300 a year; and the absolutely unique position which this gave to Barbara added enormously to her joy. Looking about her in the world, she saw hardly another woman so free and fortunate as herself. Her cousins and her girl friends might be well dressed, widely travelled, and continually surrounded with luxuries, but for all that they were personally poor, and their own spending money barely covered the little Christmas presents and the postages of each year. A tiny margin for philanthropy was the utmost any woman could hope to set aside for helping the work of reform, and all real constructive enterprises were hopelessly beyond her sphere. Barbara's married friends were no better off; not only were they as hampered as the others, but they were legally incapable of having any money of their own. One and all, married or single, women were financial nonentities, and Barbara, from her unique position, must have seen it clearly enough. Perhaps it was this, or perhaps it was Harriet Martineau, whom she knew all her life, or perhaps it was one of her father's friends, Lord Brougham or Sergeant Talfourd, who put the idea into her head; at any rate, from wherever it came, Barbara Leigh Smith reached the decision that it was her business to alter and amend the laws of property in England, Scotland, Ireland, and Wales.

She began by mastering the case, and drew up and published a "Brief Summary in plain Language of the most important Laws concerning Women." This summary, which had an immediate and wide sale, was neither long, nor obscure, nor confusing, as many such documents have been, nor was it even side-tracked by argumentation. It was just what it set out to be, a plain statement of facts; and the facts spoke for themselves.

The pamphlet was submitted to Barbara's friend, Mr Davenport Hill, the Recorder of Birmingham, and he placed it before the Law Amendment Society, an organisation he had himself helped to found. This society, which included many distinguished legal luminaries, gave the matter serious attention, and in the following year considered a report, drafted by Sir Erskine Perry, in which it was proposed that property rights and the power to make wills should be extended to married women. A public meeting was then arranged—a thing more rare in those days than it has since become—and when held it proved to be attended by quantities of important people, and by unexpectedly large numbers of ladies. A resolution supporting the proposed reform was of course passed, and a petition was drafted by Miss Leigh Smith and circulated for signature. Other meetings followed, other petitions were set on foot, and within the year, 26,000 men and women had given their approval to the reform. The petitions were then presented in both Houses, and when Lord Brougham took them to the House of Lords they were literally rolled in, and, becoming unrolled as he proceeded up the floor, the one from women alone stretched the whole length of the chamber.

The subject was almost entirely new to public consideration, and, as was natural, the feeling both in support of and in opposition to change was very strong. It would disrupt society, people said; it would destroy the home, and turn women into loathsome, self-assertive creatures no one could live with; it was an intolerable idea. Its supporters went on undismayed, and a Bill was introduced into the House of Commons for the first time in May 1857 by Sir Erskine Perry, and to the delight of Barbara and her friends it passed its Second Reading without much trouble.

Just at this time, however, there was brought forward another Bill, also of great importance to women, and also designed to disrupt society and destroy the home, namely, the Marriage and Divorce Bill.

This important measure was introduced by the Lord Chancellor, Lord Cranworth, and its primary purpose was to abolish the jurisdiction of the ecclesiastical courts, and to make divorce accessible otherwise than through Act of Parliament.

There were now two women's Bills before the country, both dealing with that innermost sanctuary, the home, and to a certain extent they were used to destroy each other. The larger aspirations of feminists were freely used as an argument against both proposals, and the struggle over the Divorce Bill was intense. "Some loose notions have been thrown out of women's intellectual equality with men," ran a horrified pamphlet of the day, "and of their consequently equal right to all the advantages of society . . . these are speculative, extravagant, and almost unnatural opinions." Who knew to what such notions might lead?

The legal aspects of the Divorce Bill were passionately exciting to lawyers, and its general trend was one on which not only the Church but every individual in the land had an emphatic opinion. Mr Gladstone made twenty-nine speeches, some of them of characteristic length, in opposition to a single clause of the Bill; but he was not alone in his excitement. People on the other side were equally moved. Petitions came in to Parliament in shoals, and the Press discussed it widely. Pamphlets appeared by scores, and among the many who felt impelled to take part in the fray was Caroline Norton, the heroine of the Infants' Custody Act.

Mrs Norton was herself, of course, painfully familiar on the whole subject of the marriage laws, and her views carried great weight. "Even now my friends say to me, 'Why write? why struggle? It is the Law! You will do no good!' But if everyone slacked courage with that doubt, nothing would ever be achieved in this world. This much I will do, woman though I be. I will put on record—in French, German, English, and Italian—what the law for women was in England in the years of civilisation and Christianity, 1855, and the eighteenth year of the reign of a female sovereign! *This* I will do; and others who come after me may do more. The feudal barbarity of the laws between Baron and Feme may vanish from amongst us." [1]

Caroline Norton had no particular interest in the main provisions of the Bill, and, like so many others, she ridiculed the wider reforms of which some people were thinking. She repudiated the "ill-advised public attempts on the part of a few women to assert their 'equality' with 'men,'" and made fun of the "strange and laughable political meetings (sanctioned by a chairwoman) which have taken place in one or two instances." All she wanted was to secure that if a woman was obliged to leave her husband she might resume possession of her own property, or at least of her own future inheritance and earnings; and this she was able to achieve. These amendments to the Bill were brought forward by Lord St Leonards,[2] and with their incorporation the ground was cut away from the other reform. If injured wives were protected, what did uninjured wives want with their property? It was a useless and unnecessary fuss over nothing. The *Saturday Review*, always a violent enemy to the Women's Movement, expressed this opinion very neatly. The proposal "set at defiance the common sense of mankind, and would revolutionise society. There is besides a smack of selfish independence about it which rather jars with poetical notions of wedlock." And so nothing was to be done.

[1] *English Law for Women in the Nineteenth Century*, by Caroline Norton, printed for private circulation, 1854.

[2] The actual amendments for which Mrs Norton was responsible were: (1) Protection to the deserted wife from her husband's claim to her earnings; (2) making possible the payment of a separate maintenance into the hands of a trustee; (3) allowing a separated or divorced wife the power to inherit or bequeath property as if she were single, though without resuming possession of property owned before or inherited or earned during the marriage; (4) allowing a separated or divorced wife the power to sue and be sued, and to enter into contracts in her own right.

The Marriage and Divorce Act [1] which passed in 1857 was no part of the regular Women's Movement, but it is of considerable importance in the history of the position of women. Although it was somewhat amended in 1858 and again in 1884 and 1896, it remained the basis of the marriage law for a long and important period, and the injustices and inequalities which it embodied represented accurately enough the prevailing opinion during that time.

It laid down, in effect, that any man might divorce his wife for adultery, but that for a woman this ground was not enough. It was "natural" that a man should be unfaithful, and a woman must be expected to put up with it. If, however, the husband added cruelty, or desertion, or other crimes to his "lapse," she might divorce him. And divorced people might legally remarry. The Bill included, too, a provision for legal separation which, if the Courts allowed, might give protection, custody of children, and the payment of a maintenance to the injured wife, as well as the right to possess any future earnings or inheritance which were hers.

When this Act was on the Statute Book it was clear that no further progress with the Married Women's Property Bill could be expected for a considerable time to come. Barbara Leigh Smith and her friends therefore turned their attention to another of the major difficulties of women, namely, the employment problem, which, owing to the growth of the philanthropic movement, was now reaching a point at which it could command public attention.

Before we pass on to this new development, however, we must consider the growth of organised philanthropy, which between the fifties and sixties was so potent a factor in setting free the energies and aspirations of the female sex.

[1] 20 & 21 Vict. c. 85. A clear and untechnical summary of the provisions of this Act is to be found in the *Englishwoman's Journal* for May 1857 (vol. i, p. 186). See also *Women under English Law*, by Arthur Rackham Cleveland.

CHAPTER V

SETTING TO WORK. 1850–1860

The philanthropic movement—Louisa Twining, Mary Carpenter, Baroness Burdett Coutts—Florence Nightingale and the training-school for nurses—The National Association for the Promotion of Social Science and the admission of women to it—Mrs Anna Jameson's lectures—The formation of the "Langham Place Circle," the Women's Employment Bureau, and the *Englishwoman's Journal*—Emily Davies and Elizabeth Garrett take up the cause.

WE have seen how the idea that it was the duty of the rich to give help to the poor grew popular, and how it was exemplified in the lives of certain remarkable and admirable women, and how, after these strong pioneers had marked out the paths, it gradually became "suitable" for young ladies all over the country to dabble in cottage visiting and Sunday School teaching of an intermittent and amateur kind.

These philanthropic occupations were the only trace of the outside world which found a way through the walls of conventional idleness behind which young ladies lived, and it can be imagined with what eagerness the unoccupied yet energetic women of the middle classes seized upon them. They knew vaguely that they lived in a world which was teeming with abuses, and by the fifties and sixties they had begun to feel the stir of the new social and economic theories which were inflaming their brothers. The time for organised effort was at hand; and there were scores and hundreds of women, conscious of unused power, who longed to devote their lives to the Humanitarian cause.

But for all that the cause was good, and for all that the time was ripe, there were still difficulties to be faced.

The poisonous little books of moral maxims, of which there had been such a flood in 1840, continued to appear, and though by 1860 they included a plea for a "moderate and modest" engagement in philanthropy, they were still an unsatisfying diet for the young. "A grown-up daughter ought to nurse her mother if she is ill; or teach her little brother to read," and when these occupations failed her, so that she could see nothing "at once important and undoubted to do," she was "to dress as well as she can, and to play on the pianoforte." [1]

The force of this ideal of life was tremendous; and it was none the less strong for being absolutely absurd. It is worth while, therefore, to look at the ideals which were held up before the young women of the sixties carefully, and to make the effort necessary to take them seriously, because they were a real obstruction to the Women's Movement in its early days, and one which it needed true courage to overcome.

The basis of them all was the prevailing ideal of family life. The constriction and monotony of women's lives were justified and, as it were, hallowed by the notion that they were the guardians of the sacred hearth, the keepers of the holy places of men's lives, the home-makers.

This ideal, which is of course one of the primitive conceptions of mankind, covered with an almost religious sanction a host of petty tyrannies, and it was this strong and stubborn sentiment which made change seem positively wicked.

The sanctity of the home did not really depend upon the daughters sitting all together in the drawing-room all the morning doing worsted work and making wax flowers; but somehow they were made to feel that it did. Family life did not perish if one of them went skating with her brothers, nor did their father's heart break when one of

[1] *My Life, and what shall I do with It?* by an old maid (Miss March Phillips), reviewed in an article in the *Edinburgh Review*, 1860.

them read an unauthorised book. But the grip of convention was so strong, and so much entangled with parental "feelings," that to outrage it in any respect seemed a sin. Young ladies suffered terrible agonies of conscience over every forward step. The fear of being "unladylike," or, worse still, "unmaidenly," was a genuine anxiety, and almost everything agreeable appeared to be either one or the other. To ride to hounds, speak to a young man, to think for oneself, even to own a dog, were matters for hesitation, and the dreary timidity of feminine thought was such that the very problems which the new philanthropy was attempting to tackle were for the most part unmentionable.

All these cobwebs of difficulty had desperately practical results. How could a woman be useful to a philanthropic cause when her time was never certain to be at her own disposal, when she could not take a walk—much less a railway journey—alone, and when she could not ask a fellow-worker to visit her unless that fellow-worker happened to be not only a girl, but also a member of a family with which her own was already acquainted? Against these and a thousand similar troubles the first steps of organisation had a hard fight; and, indeed, every aspect of the Women's Movement was more or less hampered by them for nearly fifty years. It is only since the War of 1914–1918 that its traces have finally become dim.

It was not, of course, quite so barbaric in every household. By the middle of the century the number of people who held slightly more reasonable views about the functions of women was increasing, and some few girls were already reaping the advantage of modern ideas. Ruskin, friendly as he was to the Women's Movement, thought that the function of women in the world was "to understand and perhaps to help the work of men," [1] and thought no further; but that was already a long step upon the road.

[1] *Sesame and Lilies* (1865).

In the fifties and sixties there were still an enormous number of girls who had not even this ideal, and who were so completely defeated by their surroundings that their will to "do something" died away before the difficulties of the adventure. As Emily Davies used to say, "It was indeed no wonder that people who had not learned to do anything could not find anything to do." Some of them grew sillier, more trivial, and more scatter-brained as their lives went by, until they grew to be creatures fit for the inferiority they had accepted. Others grew morbid, giving way to exaggerated enthusiasms, whimsical tempers and peevishness, and all sorts of nervous disorders of mind and body, drowning in a wealth of petty grievances the remembrance that they were wasting their lives. But there were others, bolder or more fortunate, who, in spite of the pangs of their consciences and the remonstrances of their friends, pushed out into the fray. They carried with them of course the early Victorian flavour which tinged their age. It was in black silk gowns, corsets, crinolines, and elastic-sided boots that these intrepid ladies began to turn society inside out; but, with a pat here and a whisper there, circumspectly and in ladylike fashion they succeeded.

Louisa Twining and Mary Carpenter were typical examples of women inspired by the new ideals; and both achieved so much, and left such lasting organisations behind them, that their work should be briefly mentioned here.

Louisa Twining, the originator of Workhouse Reform, was born in 1820 of a well-to-do professional family, and she had an extended education, and all the "advantages" proper to her station. Her father was an enlightened man, her home was happy; and there was nothing to drive her into active work except her vigorous temperament. She was actually led into her life's work by very ordinary means, namely, by visiting an old nurse of her family in the parish of St Clement Danes. Louisa went often to see her nurse, and soon made friends among the old lady's neighbours.

The slum homes, the ill health, and the appalling conditions they passively endured shocked Louisa profoundly, and at first she was glad when one of these poor friends of hers took refuge from it all in the Strand Union Workhouse. Her relief was shortlived, however, for one day she went to visit there and discovered that life was even more horrible in the workhouse that it was outside. The housing was almost as bad, with underground dormitories overcrowded and ill ventilated, and there was hardly any classification of inmates. In the bare and dismal wards the idle and the vicious were herded together with the aged and the well conducted, and all alike fed on bad and sometimes nauseating food, repulsively served. The sick were ill-cared for, children with infectious diseases shared a bed with those suffering from accidents, and all alike were nursed by inmates who were incapable, epileptic, or even blind, half-witted and drunken, and entirely without authority over their charges. There were no washing arrangements, linen was sometimes not changed for sixteen weeks, and in every physical respect the workhouse was a repulsive abode. Even worse to Louisa's eyes, however, was the lonely monotony of the life. The only available occupation (and that was eagerly sought for) was making shrouds and coffins, and the listless look of people who had no variety—save, perhaps, when the parish hearse arrived to take someone away—weighed upon her heart. Again and again she went to visit the miserable place, and was so touchingly welcome that she thought to expand the treat. She applied, therefore, to the master for permission to bring friends with her, only to be told that "unpaid and voluntary efforts were not sanctioned by the Poor Law Board." Louisa, for all her early-Victorianism, was not to be daunted by a phrase of this description. Putting on her best bonnet and hailing a cab she proceeded alone to Whitehall to interview the Poor Law Board, though as the cab trundled along she trembled in her seat. But the porter at the office door was kind and reassuring in 1853, even as office-porters are to-day. "You need not be afraid, ma'am; you will find they are very nice gentlemen indeed," he assured her.[1] And so she did. Nevertheless, it needed a year's wait and a good deal of peaceful penetration and another visit to Whitehall before the permission was gained; and then it was only on condition that everything was carried on gently, and without fuss or disturbance.

The thin end of the wedge was all that was needed, however, and in a year or two a regular Workhouse Visiting Society was functioning all over the country, and ladies with kind hearts were carrying snuff, tobacco, tracts, hymn-books, and spectacles to the aged poor. They were doing more, too, for they were questioning the organisation they found, and talking and writing about what was indeed a scandalous state of affairs; and among them there were women who noticed that the regulations were made and the whole thing managed without the help of "the female sex."[2] Louisa Twining herself realised the absurdity of the position more and more clearly as time went on, and presently she carried the "very nice gentlemen" with her, and in 1875, after twenty years' work, the Act enabling women to be Poor Law Guardians went through Parliament and came into force.

Nor was the Poor Law the only instance in which philanthropy led straight to the demand for women's rights. Ragged schools, and, above all, rescue work, taught the same lesson, and the women whose hearts and souls were spent in comforting and mending the outcasts of society naturally turned to an examination of its customs, and as naturally

[1] *Recollections of Life and Work*, by Louisa Twining, 1893.

[2] "I have sat in the Infants' Ward," wrote Frances Power Cobbe, "when an entire Board of about two dozen gentlemen tramped through it for what they considered to be 'inspection'; and anybody more helpless and absurd than those masculine 'authorities' appeared as they glanced at the little cots (never daring to open one of them) while the awakened babies screamed at them in chorus, it has seldom been my lot to witness."

grew indignant at their own powerlessness to alter the evils of the world.

Mary Carpenter was one of these.[1] She was born in 1807, and had the advantage of an education in the boys' school her father conducted; and although when she was young she was "somewhat slow to countenance any innovation in the recognised sphere of women's work," her passionate desire to secure reform led her on little by little until she was an active and ardent feminist. She opened her first ragged school in the slums of Bristol in 1846; and by 1851 she was writing papers on the prevention of delinquency, and the next year she could not refuse the invitation to give evidence before a parliamentary commission. Two years later she found herself agitating directly for various measures in Parliament, including a new Industrial School Bill and a grant for Ragged Schools, and as time went on she was drawn more and more actively into work which was public and parliamentary and anything but "feminine" and "retired."

The devoted lives of Louisa Twining and of Mary Carpenter are but examples of what was the common aspiration. "To do good to the poor" was the dream of the period, and like all dreams it was by some translated into activity and by others into words, while others still, the romantic and the inert, left it all dreamlike and untried. For such as these the fascinating career of Miss Angela Burdett afforded endless encouragement, and many a girl must have spent many an hour in the delightful task of imagining what she would do if there came her way an inheritance of a couple of million pounds.

The magical fairy-godmother of philanthropy who inspired these visions was born in 1814, and before she was of age she had unexpectedly inherited the great Coutts fortune from her step-grandmother.

Very energetic and intelligent, and very well brought up,

[1] *Life and Work of Mary Carpenter*, by J. Estlin Carpenter.

this girl took her wealth very seriously, and the life she built up for herself was a monument of early Victorian virtue.

In the first place she cultivated all the learned society in Europe, entertained every foreigner of distinction, and made her friends among the scientists, the politicians, and the church dignitaries of her age. Although almost every unmarried man who came near her proposed to "the richest heiress in Europe," she thought little of marriage, and preferred to go her own way, unassisted, in the spending of her vast wealth. The ways she took were multitudinous, and ranged from the details of slum charities to the endowment of Colonial bishoprics. She built a fleet of fishing sloops in Ireland, and model dwellings in the East End, and churches in Westminster; she gave bells to St Paul's and prizes to costermongers' donkeys; she founded homes for Art students and sent goats to farmers; she secured lifeboats for Brittany and drinking-fountains for dogs; presented fossils to universities and cotton gins to Nigeria; she paid for the ordnance survey of Jerusalem and provided protection for aborigines, and plants for Kew Gardens. In all these multifarious affairs she insisted on taking an active part,[1] and her personal intervention was experienced alike by the boys of the Shoeblacks' Brigade and by the managers of her banking house. Among the multitude of her affairs, the women's causes, as they grew to organised shape, claimed her attention mainly in their philanthropic manifestations. The stream of her benevolence went on for nearly sixty years, and from being the ideal of young lady's dreams she grew to be almost a public institution. Her hospitality extended more and more widely; 2500 guests dined with her one night, and the peasants in Turkey began to receive the evidences of her care. There seemed no limit to the

[1] See *Baroness Burdett Coutts*, a sketch of her public life and work prepared for the Chicago Exhibition, 1893, by order of Princess Mary Adelaide, Duchess of Teck.

range of her benevolence. In 1871 she was raised to the peerage as the Baroness Burdett Coutts of Highgate and Brookfield, Middlesex, an honour bestowed by Queen Victoria in recognition of all this benevolence; and it is interesting to note that this is one of the very few examples of a peerage bestowed on a woman for any other service than that of being mistress to a king.

Another philanthropist, not so well known to the sheltered dreams of young ladies, but closer in sympathy with the active feminist women of her day, was Anne Isabella Noel, the deserted and unfortunate wife of Lord Byron.[1] This lady, in spite of her matrimonial troubles, was rich and energetic, though neither so rich nor so energetic as Miss Burdett Coutts. Like her, she built and endowed and assisted the charitable and educational schemes of her friends, among whom Mary Carpenter, Harriet Martineau, and Anna Jameson were to be found. As in the preceding generation, so now, the pioneer women drew together and sought each other out; though, in the case of this unhappy lady, there seems to have been a strong element of emotional disturbance in her friendships which is not to be found in those of Mary Somerville or Maria Edgeworth.

While all these philanthropic ladies were learning by experience the need for women's emancipation, another force appeared which gave them fresh sanction, namely, the example and the approval of Florence Nightingale.

When this lady returned from the Crimea in 1857 she was greeted with a storm of popularity such as no woman had ever evoked in England before. The whole country rang with her praises, and the great and the humble alike longed to do her honour. A huge fund was raised and placed at her disposal; and there was hardly anything she could have asked for which would not have been conceded. What she chose to ask for was a training-school for nurses. Florence Nightingale was not greatly changed by the

[1] See *Biographical Sketches*, Harriet Martineau.

experience she had been through. She knew now, even better than before, what it was she wanted; she realised the difficulties of reform and understood who and what were the dragons in the path. But just as in her girlhood nothing had turned her from her purpose, so now in her maturity she remained implacable. There must be work, active and arduous work, before reforms could be secured; and there must be training, training, and more training still, before anything effective could be done. Women must bite hard upon the realities of life, if they were to be of any use as "saviours."

These views of Florence Nightingale, which were not really palatable to most people of that time, were forced on them by her determination. The heroine of the Crimea could not be disregarded; and when to her prestige and the power of her popularity was added her iron determination, even convention must give way. And so a breach, of the most public and important kind, was made in the old superstitions. After the Nursing School had been set up at St Thomas's Hospital, no one dared any longer to say that the feminine instinct alone sufficed for the care of the sick, or to think that women could afford to dispense with discipline.

The Nursing School took a long time to establish, and the trials and difficulties which Florence Nightingale had to overcome were many and exasperating. The women themselves, the material in which she had to work, were fearfully disappointing. Time and again Florence raged against their lack of determination, their lack of pertinacity, their easy-going folly. Time and again, as we have seen, she stormed against them. But always she held on, for the faith that inspired her was unchangeable. There must be male and female "saviours" if the world was to be saved.

The early days of the nursing movement came at the moment when "the principle of association" was being widely discussed. In every direction, and particularly in philanthropy, groups for special purposes were coming into existence and the old personal efforts were expanding into more elaborate shapes. The formation of the National Association for the Promotion of Social Science in 1857 was the result of this tendency, and this body quickly became the centre and the mainspring of the Humanitarian movement. Lord Brougham was the president, and all the great lights of the day gave their support: Lord Shaftesbury, Lord John Russell, Charles Kingsley, and the rest. One of the most remarkable features of this association, the one that makes it important to our purpose here, was the fact that from the very first women were admitted and even welcomed to membership.[1] They attended the meetings, sent papers to be read, Florence Nightingale contributing one to the first meeting, and they even went so far, a year or two later, as to read their own writings themselves. They took part in the discussions which followed even when they were public discussions, and they were allowed to eat, and not merely to look on, at the public dinners.

The formation of this body, and their own admission to it, gave a tremendous impetus to the activities of public-spirited women. At the sessions of the association they met each other, they compared difficulties, they saw and gained the attention of public men, and they devised plans and gathered courage for fresh efforts. They ventured, too, to discuss their own position on these friendly occasions, and papers on "The Woman Question" were read at the early meetings and taken with a most encouraging seriousness. Nowadays, when every week sees more conferences than the hours will hold, and when every effort is organised to excess, it is hard to realise how tremendous an encouragement and how real a help such meetings then were. They

[1] "Social Science Congresses, and Women's Part Therein," by Frances Power Cobb (*Macmillan's Magazine*, December 1861).

must have seemed to the women of the day like the dawn of a new era; and so, in fact, they were.

Many plans which ultimately bore fruit were first discussed at these meetings. Louisa Twining's Workhouse Visiting Association was one of these, and the Ladies' National Association for the Diffusion of Sanitary Knowledge was another. This body, which was the forerunner of all sorts of public health developments, began by the distribution of simple tracts on Fresh Air, Perambulators, Tight Lacing, and the like, and found they were desperately needed, for the public ignorance of hygiene was at that time colossal. Besides these two purely feminine activities, the Ragged School movement, Rescue Work, and the vast ramifications of organised philanthropic effort which grew up in the next twenty years all owed their first shapes to this association, and there is much that is most interesting and instructive in its history. For our purpose, however, we must leave the miracle of the Humanitarian movement on one side, noting only that, with its every forward step, a larger and larger number of women were drawn out of their idleness and into contact with the realities of life. What concerns us here is that nearly all these women, as they realised the evils of society, grew dissatisfied with the powerlessness of their own sex, so that quite a short probation in this school was enough to produce feminists by the score; for the world was too palpably lop-sided.

This process, however, though it worked effectively upon public opinion, was slow and indirect. The women social workers, even when they were most indignant at their own position, were generally more indignant still at the other evils of society, and even as the objects of philanthropy they were content to see their own sex come last. Almost all the early charities were intended to help men; and as late as 1866 kind-hearted ladies said to each other that "it is only natural that women should suffer, but when men are exposed to privation it is hard indeed." It is, therefore, quite clear that a more definite and direct form of organisation was required before the Women's Movement could be said to have begun.

This direct organisation had already come into existence in 1855, when Barbara Leigh Smith had called together a committee to collect petitions for the Married Women's Property Bill. But her committee had at no time been large, and its formal existence had melted away when the chances of proceeding with the Bill were destroyed by the Marriage and Divorce Act of 1857. Nevertheless, the agitation had brought a large number of active and like-minded people into touch with each other, and the original effort soon produced new results. People who agreed over this one point found they agreed over a dozen others, and a circle of friends had grown up to whom the Cause was a burning reality. For the most part this group consisted of young women: Bessie Rayner Parkes, Mrs Fox, Adelaide Anne Proctor, and Barbara Leigh Smith herself; but there were one or two women, older, and of much more standing than these, who gave active support to their ideas. One of these was Mrs Howitt, the writer of tales and poems,[1] and another was Mrs Jameson. In 1855 and 1856 this lady gave two drawing-room lectures which were entitled "Sisters of Charity" and "Community of Labour," which created a real sensation in literary and philanthropic London. They were published and widely read, and their plea for the co-operation of men and women in setting right the evils of society came at exactly the right time. Moreover, Mrs Jameson was exactly the right person to give them. She enjoyed a literary and artistic reputation which made her the idol of thousands of young ladies. Her books on pictures, on Shakespeare's heroines, and on the principles of Art were exactly what the period admired, and with their

[1] Her best known work begins:

"Will you walk into my parlour?
Said the Spider to the Fly."

elegant culture and their earnest feelings, and their sentimental philosophy, they had penetrated even into the most conventional homes. When she, therefore, came forward as the champion of the new cause the effect was prodigious.

Anna Brownell Murphy had been born in Dublin in 1794, and after going through the usual governessing experiences, she had married in 1825 a Mr Jameson, who seems to have been a plausible but selfish man, and turned out to be a very unsatisfactory companion, so that after several years of unhappiness his wife separated from him. Gifted with great personal charm and a certain literary ability, she turned to authorship for her support and won an almost instantaneous success.

Anna Jameson had more in her head than the artistic enthusiasm which filled her books. She was profoundly moved by the stir of social conscience which was going on around her and saw, with an almost desperate passion, the waste which was involved in the untrained lives of women. Wherever she went on the Continent in her pursuit of Art and culture, she sought out also the sisterhoods, the nursing establishments, and the charitable works of women, and when the time came for her to speak publicly of these views she brought a wealth of illustration and a store of real experience to her task.

After the success of Mrs Jameson's lectures, the little band of friends began seriously to discuss plans for furthering their ideas. The field was wide—philanthropy, education, law, custom—but that did not daunt them at all. The point to consider was what would be the most effective first line of attack, and, like all such groups before or since, their dream was the publication of a paper. In October 1856, six months after the Married Women's Property Bill had failed, Bessie Rayner Parkes came across a harmless and ineffective periodical "edited by ladies for ladies" which was for sale, and at once they began to imagine what they could do with such a paper; and the more they thought the more eager they became.

The most influential and wealthiest of the group was still Barbara Leigh Smith, whose many friendships brought her into touch with the world of journalism and literature, and enabled her to seek advice from Harriet Martineau, George Eliot, and all sorts of distinguished people. And Barbara threw herself into the plans with enthusiasm, and came to the conclusion that the first thing for them to attack was the wage-earning position of women. While the slow business of getting their paper started was going on, she plunged at once into this subject and wrote a pamphlet on "Women and Work," which immediately called forth a flood of criticisms and comments in the ordinary Press. This pamphlet was neither as clear nor as well arranged as her summary of the property laws, but it showed forth as great an evil, for the economic situation of women, particularly in the middle classes, was outrageous.

The approved view of the world was that the women of the middle class were not wage-earners, and ought not to have an economic situation at all; but the facts of life were different. The census of 1851 had exposed the comfortable fiction, for all who cared to look at it, and Barbara and her friends looked long and earnestly. They saw lamentably few openings for women and far too many workers in each. They saw the evil results of overcrowding, the low pay, the broken health, the frequent insanity among governesses, the shocking conditions of needlewomen. They foresaw, too, that there was worse to come now that sewing-machines were beginning to be used, and they knew that it was urgent that something should be done. The only help that they could see lay in the finding of new outlets for female labour, and in this belief they set hopefully about the making of new suggestions.

Women should be clerks, they said, and shop assistants, or doctors, or nurses—anything in fact that they were competent to do; and the world mocked and even howled at the absurdity of the idea. Had they quite forgotten that women's job was to get married? They had not forgotten it; indeed, at this very time Barbara was herself falling in love and marrying the French Doctor, Eugène Bodichon, whom she had met in Algiers; but what was the good of talking of husband and home to the 876,920 surplus women who inhabited England, not to speak of the other million and a half whom necessity, in spite of home, forced out into the labour market? Something more than governessing and needlework was needed to support these people.

All this seemed crude and fantastic in 1857. "If this is a fair sample of what a lady who boasts to have made the subject her own is likely to publish," wrote the *Saturday Review*, "we are afraid that the sex is not really so developed as we had supposed." And yet these very suggestions, extraordinary as they were, marked out the courses which events were actually to pursue, and indicated the solution towards which to-day we are still slowly approaching. But progress seemed far enough off at that date. The *Saturday Review* voiced a very general opinion when it said that the number of workers had nothing to do with the rates of wages. Governesses were ill-paid, not because there were so many of them, but because they did their work so badly. "Married life is woman's profession; and to this life her training—that of dependence—is modelled. Of course, by not getting a husband, or losing him, she may find that she is without resources. All that can be said of her is, she has failed in business and no social reform can prevent such failures." "Are women redundant?" asked the serious Press at the same time, and the answer was frivolous in the extreme. If they were, it was because the silly creatures would not marry. And if, after all, women really were found to be too thick on the ground, let them be exported to marry overseas! It needed only a little courage and a big scheme, and all the redundant ones could be landed in the colonies, and a good thing too! Away with all this nonsense of trying to make the single life remunerative and pleasant for women! Its only upshot would be to make marriage a matter of "cold philosophic choice," and then, of course, it would be "more and more frequently declined." And what would happen to the home? Besides, why could they not become domestic servants? These happy creatures "fulfil both essentials of woman's being; they are supported by and they minister to the comfort of men. . . . Nature has not provided one too many."

Views such as these only stimulated the little band to further efforts, and every hostile article brought them new recruits. The project of the paper grew and expanded, and in 1857 the first number of the *Englishwoman's Journal* appeared. Offices were set up and immediately they became a hive of activity, from which the same little group of people set on foot a dozen different but kindred enterprises.

One of their number, Miss Isa Craig, became assistant secretary to the Association for the Promotion of Social Science, and this surprising and revolutionary appointment, together with the fact of the admission of women to the meetings, gave rise to a great deal of mockery in the Press. "There are decided advantages in this Universal Palaver Association . . .," wrote the *Saturday Review*.[1] ". . . It must be remembered to Lord Brougham's credit that he is the first person who has dealt upon this plan with the problem of female loquacity. . . . It is a great idea to tire out the hitherto unflagging vigour of their tongues by encouraging a taste for stump-oratory among them. . . . Lord Brougham's little *corps* of lady orators, preaching strong-mindedness, gives a new aspect to the Association's presence. . . . We heartily wish the strong-minded ladies happiness and success in their new alliance; and do not doubt that they will remember to practice the precept of one

[1] 14th June 1862.

of their debaters 'not to mind being thought unladylike.' It is always better not to mind that which is inevitable."

The young ladies, and the old ones too, *did* mind being thought unladylike, and many were the tears and heart-burnings over such comments as these. Yet all the same their work went steadily on. For, after all, duty was more important than reputation, and reform could not be achieved in secret.

The connection with the Social Science Association was of the greatest value to the "little corps of lady orators," who had determined to preach strong-mindedness. It enabled them to secure the attention and criticism of famous men, and to bring their theories, their experiments, and their experiences before the very parliament of social causes; and from the publicity they so secured, scores of valuable new recruits came in. They not only gave, but they also received instruction at these early meetings, and they were quick to learn the lessons of organisation.

They set up the first Women's Employment Bureau, which rapidly developed into the Association for the Promotion of the Employment of Women. Then there came the Ladies' Institute with its reading-room and small club, out of which grew classes for governesses, book-keepers, and secretaries; then followed the Educated Women's Emigration Society, and a dozen more; and for all of these they were able, through the Social Science Association, to find distinguished and important patrons. The *Journal* dealt with all these things. It supported, of course, the movement for the higher education of women, which was now under way, and which we must consider separately;[1] it gave expression to the arguments for women doctors, who were at this time first mentioned; and it dealt with everything which could be connected with the Women's Movement with a moderation, a seriousness, and a tact which deserved the utmost praise. Among other things it published for

[1] See chap. vii.

some years the reports of the working of the new Divorce Act, which were for the first time revealing the miseries which some women had been enduring without possibility of redress. "The crowded state of the Divorce Court shows what an enormous amount there was of matrimonial misery," wrote the *Times* in 1859; but it was not the object of the *Englishwoman's Journal* to harp on matrimonial misery. The point they watched for, and continually brought out, was the extent to which married women were employed in work. "Almost every aggrieved wife who had sought protection (in the Courts) has proved that she supported her household and has acquired property by her effective exertions." This was the point they desired to drive home; and with the weight of facts they proved it. Yet it was another quarter of a century before the Married Women's Property Acts were passed.

The usefulness of having an "organ" was soon seen. Provincial young women came across stray numbers of the *Journal*, and finding their own thoughts at last set forth, they wrote enthusiastically to the editors. When they could they hurried to the office in London, and some of them stayed permanently to help in the work. Jessie Boucherett was one of these, and she has described how she came expecting to see some dowdy old lady, and found herself in the midst of young women who were well dressed, beautiful, and gay. It was not only helpers who came as a result of the publication of the *Journal*, however; there were also the people who needed help. Unemployed governesses and women seeking advice came wandering in, and each one in her helplessness added fuel to the fire of the great purpose. Articles, suggestions, speeches, schemes, enterprises, and societies all took their inspiration in those three small rooms, in which there was a constant coming and going of crinolines. Why should not women be compositors, they asked? And forthwith one of them, Miss Emily Faithfull, went out and founded the Victoria Press and they printed the *Journal* there. Why should not women do law engrossing? An office was opened at once and filled with women workers. Why should not women be hairdressers, hotel managers, wood engravers, dispensers, house decorators, watchmakers, telegraphists? Out! Out! Let us see if we can make them do it! Why does the school of design threaten to exclude them? We must have a petition at once; and the Royal Academy, why does it not admit women students? We must knock politely on its doors. And then there were the swimming baths in Marylebone, why were they not open to women? Did the manager say that women did not want to use them? Nonsense, of course they did. If thirty women came would they be opened? Very well, thirty women should come; and every Wednesday afternoon the young ladies trooped away from the office to help to stir the face of the waters. Nothing must be let slip, be it small or great, in the campaign they had begun to wage.

The records of these early years of organisation are full of life and spirit. Under the stiff pedantic language, where pay was "remuneration" and swimming a "natatorial pastime," and public speaking "oratorial exhortation," there runs a current of pure youthful enthusiasm and gaiety. Augusta Webster, for example, for whom admission to the Art School in South Kensington was secured, nearly dashed the prospects of women art students for ever by being expelled for whistling. But they recovered from the blow and set to work to organise a Society of Female Artists of their own, and proceeded as gaily as ever.

Barbara Bodichon, with her golden hair, and Adelaide Anne Proctor, with her endless jokes, whisked in and out of the office, and nothing discouraged them for long. How they laughed when Louie Garrett (the eldest of the Garrett sisters) came in to tell them about the hairdresser! She had been having her hair washed and took the opportunity to ask the man who did it if he did not agree with her that it was a suitable trade for women. "Impossible, madam!" the man had cried in horror, "Why it took ME a fortnight to learn it."

How angry they all grew when the watchmakers' and the gilders' Trade Unions refused to allow girls to be apprenticed, and how they enjoyed it when *Punch* poked fun at crinolines! They were free and confident and happy, and many of them were young; and they had got hold of a living idea, and the world was moving in the right direction.

Pitiful cases came before them, of course, in hundreds. Miss Parkes, in a paper before the Social Science Congress of 1862, told how she had had 810 applicants for a post which carried a salary of only £15 a year, and advertisements such as *Punch* pilloried were often to be seen. "Wanted," they ran, "a young lady who has had advantages, for a situation as governess. To sleep in a room with three beds, for herself, four children, and a maid. To give the children their baths, dress them and be ready for breakfast at a quarter to eight. School 9–12 and half-past 2–4, with two hours' music lessons in addition. To spend the evenings in doing needlework for her mistress. To have the baby on her knee while teaching, and to put all the children to bed. Salary £10 a year and to pay her own washing." That was the sort of thing which made them sad; but such things made them also more determined. There were 24,770 governesses in 1851; and this was the way the majority of them lived! Other openings and other professions must be found, for this state of affairs could not be tolerated an instant longer! And then there were the dressmakers, still as wretched as when they were first noticed, working sixteen hours a day and making for 10d. garments which sold for £5. Something must be done about them too.

As time went on the little office in Langham Place saw many sad sights. Women who had been cheated and women who had been ill-treated came to its doors, and many others who had been thrown without training or education or money upon an unkind world. These dreary, listless applicants brought their "culpable resignation" to the Employment office, and with unwearied energy its secretaries tried to put courage and common sense into their hearts. But it was an uphill task. It was difficult enough to find opportunities of training for these ill-equipped and discouraged women and to find openings for them in any new directions, but the passive resistance of the clients themselves was even more insurmountable. They were so timid that they often refused to give their names, and they shrank back in horror from the notion of seeking new work. If a woman did anything at all to earn money she lost caste; and the women who found their way to Langham Place were terribly anxious about this. As governesses they felt some little rags of their gentility remained to them. But as physical instructors, or wood carvers, or lecturers, they must surely cease to be ladies. And after years of the severest privations in the sacred cause of keeping up appearances they could not understand the new ideal and the new hope which was presented to them. Again and again they turned away and went back to their hopeless tasks, rejecting the help which was offered.

It was not all discouragement in those years, however. Four great occupations which have since employed millions of women were opening, for there was a growing demand for shop-assistants, clerks, telegraphists, and nurses. The first two occupations were opening without external pressure, because of the great expansion of trade and business and the cheapness and docility of female labour. The nurses, too, needed no help from the little office, having an advocate more powerful than any other alive. And the telegraphists had begun their work almost as soon as the invention had been completed and before there had been time to organise any opposition to their employment. But the workers in Langham Place did not care how the doors opened, so long as they stayed ajar. The great thing was to widen the field. The rest, they felt sure, would follow.

In 1859, when that hotbed of feminist plots, the offices in Langham Place, had been open but a few months, two new recruits came in whose influence on the Women's Movement was to be enormous. These two were Emily Davies and Elizabeth Garrett. Both these girls were the right material, from the Langham Place point of view. They both belonged to liberal-minded families, and had had education above the average; and though they both looked meek and gentle, they were unusually strong in mind and character.

Emily Davies, the elder of the two, was born in 1830, and, like so many of the other reformers of the time, she was a clergyman's daughter. She lived the life and had the opportunities usual for such girls, with parish work, a little teaching, a serious effort at self-improvement, and that contact at second-hand with a University which the wider opportunities of their brothers usually afforded them. Emily's brother, Llewelyn, was her firm friend and supporter all through her life, and it was through his appointment in 1856 to a London parish that her first introduction to the world of social reform and women's rights came about.

Llewelyn Davies had been only a short while in London before he became a friend and follower of Frederick Maurice, and when Emily visited her brother she too was naturally drawn into the same inspiring circle. Among the many things which these people were planning for the betterment of the world, the improvement of the position of women was one, and this cause at once attracted not only the interest but the passionate adherence of Emily. She did not as yet see what share she could herself take in the great work, for she was tied by many family claims, and in 1858 she was sent out to Algeria with her brother Henry, who was seeking health in a warm climate. Even in Algeria, however, Emily found the Cause, for she met and made friends with Mme. Bodichon, and thereby immensely widened her knowledge of what was already being planned and attempted.

The feminism which took so deep a hold of Emily Davies' life was not, however, the result of these outside influences. She was at all times a person of strong opinions, and long before she had met any of these congenial people she had begun to feel a deep resentment concerning the subjection of her sex. Outwardly she was a quiet and sober young woman, very small and gentle-looking, and apparently the least dangerous of mortals; but inwardly she was firm and unyielding to an astonishing degree, with her heart and her will obstinately and undeviatingly set upon the Cause.

Elizabeth Garrett was six years younger than Emily Davies. She was the second of the daughters of Mr Newson Garrett of Aldburgh, and like her sisters she was following the public movements of the time with deep interest and vehement partisanship. Mr Garrett was, in name at any rate, a Conservative; but he was so radical and enterprising by temperament, and so wholly original in his thoughts, that no label could have described him adequately; and when in course of time his daughters became prominent in the Women's Movement they found him ready to approve and to help them.

Elizabeth was sent to Miss Browning's school at Blackheath, and through friends whom she made there she first met Emily Davies. They liked each other at once, and the friendship which existed between them had an enduring influence upon both their lives. Elizabeth left school at fifteen, and after a tour abroad she settled down at home with no special tasks to occupy her beyond those which naturally arose for an elder sister in a large and affectionate family. She soon began to feel that she could not live in happy idleness all her life and must find something definite to do, and when she and Emily first came in contact with the Langham Place Circle that feeling was intensified. The possibilities which the feminist ideals opened before them enchanted them both; something deep in their natures responded to the call, and they went back to their homes with a new hope and determination in their hearts.

There is a story of them at this time which may not be true in fact, but which is very characteristic of Emily Davies, and which perfectly illustrates the confident frame of mind in which they approached their tasks. Emily, the story runs, went to stay with the Garretts at Aldburgh, and at night the two friends sat talking together by Elizabeth's bedroom fire. Millicent Garrett, then quite a small girl, sat nearby on a stool, listening, but saying nothing. After going over all the great causes they saw about them, and in particular the women's cause, to which they were burning to devote their lives, Emily summed the matter up. "Well, Elizabeth," she said, "it's quite clear what has to be done. I must devote myself to securing higher education, while you open the medical profession to women. After these things are done," she added, "we must see about getting the vote." And then she turned to the little girl who was still sitting quietly on her stool and said, "You are younger than we are, Millie, so you must attend to that."

CHAPTER VI

RIGHTS AND PROPAGANDA. 1860–1870

Election of John Stuart Mill in 1865—The Kensington Ladies' Discussion Society—The petition for Women's Suffrage presented in Parliament, 1866—Formation of Provisional Suffrage Committee in London—Miss Becker forms committee in Manchester—Debate on J. S. Mill's amendment to the Reform Bill—Reconstituted Suffrage Committee in London—The effort to prove in the Courts that women were already enfranchised—Adverse judgment, 1868—Early meetings and country propaganda—Second reading victory, 1870—Further progress barred by opposition of Gladstone.

In 1865 John Stuart Mill received an invitation to stand for Parliament for the City of Westminster. In reply to this invitation he explained that he held somewhat unusual views on the subject of elections. He thought that both canvassing and the spending of a candidate's money in order to be returned were wrong, and announced that he could not consent to do either. He also made it clear that he was not prepared to undertake any local business if he were elected, but he set out plainly the subjects for which he would work, among which Women's Suffrage held almost the first place. Contrary to his expectations the voters of Westminster accepted these conditions and renewed their request that Mill would represent them, and it can be imagined with what eagerness the various groups of Radicals and Feminists watched the contest. A fund was at once raised to defray the expenses of the election, and a committee of ladies came forward to assist his return. The workers at Langham Place were, of course, among the first to be active, and Mme. Bodichon, who always proposed innovations, hired a carriage and covered it with placards, and in this carriage she and Emily Davies and Bessie Parkes and Isa Craig drove about Westminster, testing the novel joys of election excitement. "We called it giving Mr Mill our moral support," wrote Emily, "but there was some suspicion that we might rather be doing him harm, as one of our friends told us he had heard him described as 'the man who wants to have girls in Parliament.'"

The respect which Mill's character and integrity inspired was strong enough to survive this suspicion, however, and Mill was triumphantly returned in 1865.

In this same year a Ladies' Discussion Society had been founded in Kensington, which attracted about fifty members. It consisted chiefly of those who had been interested in the agitation for opening the local examinations to girls;[1] Mrs Manning was its president, Miss Emily Davies its secretary, and among its members were Miss Helen Taylor, Miss Sophia Jex-Blake, Mme. Bodichon, Miss Beale, Miss Buss, Miss Frances Power Cobbe, Miss Elizabeth Garrett, and Miss Wolstoneholme. The Society met four times a year, and its first discussion, in May 1865, dealt with the limits of parental authority, and was led by Elizabeth Garrett. Academic as the subject seems to-day, it was intensely practical to the young women of the sixties whose parents were so often bent on restraining them, and it did not seem at all out of keeping with the subject of the second meeting, which was "Should Women take Part in Public Affairs?" Mme. Bodichon took a prominent share in this discussion, and her paper on the suffrage led to an animated meeting. When, at the end, a vote was taken, it was found, to everyone's surprise, that nearly all the fifty were strongly in favour of women's political activity, even to the extent of the franchise. Encouraged by this discovery Mme. Bodichon's customary enthusiasm broke out, and she wanted to found a regular Women's Suffrage Committee forthwith. Emily Davies, however, tried to hold her back. Not that Emily Davies did not support the suffrage; it was part of

[1] See chap. vii.

the great impulse of her life, and was dearer to her than almost anything else. But she feared that if any formal organisation were set up it would be impossible to keep extremists from joining it, and that the result of any violent statement of the case might be to injure the education movement, which at that date was in a critical, if hopeful, stage.

The appearance of Huxley's *Lay Sermons* in this year, however, which made public his support of Women's Suffrage, was a great encouragement; and Barbara was not easy to keep in check. In April 1866, when a Reform Bill was imminent in Parliament, she went to Mill and asked him what he advised. If they could get up a petition for Women's Suffrage, would he present it? For her part she thought the time had come.

Mill was delighted to see that the movement was taking shape at last. If they could get a hundred names, he said, he would certainly hand the petition in; but anything less would probably do more harm than good.

Mme. Bodichon was as much delighted with Mill's advice as he had been with her question. She hurried back to Emily, who, in view of the concrete suggestion for immediate work, withdrew her opposition, and they called in Jessie Boucherett, Rosamond Hill, and Elizabeth Garrett, and formed the first Women's Suffrage Committee.

They were not perfectly new to the job of collecting names for petitions, since some of them had had experience in the Married Women's Property agitation ten years before; but their path was not quite plain for all that. The first difficulty, which was to grow much more serious later on, lay in the nature of the demand they were to make. Should they ask for votes for all women householders who fulfilled the necessary qualifications, or should they only ask for those of them who were unmarried? Emily Davies was afraid they might be "a little too definite." She pointed out that to include the married women explicitly would be to raise a wholly unnecessary storm; but Mill would have nothing to do with any abatement of equality, and in the end a form of words was found which, while it demanded equality, was capable of both interpretations, and so could be signed by all supporters.

For a fortnight the little committee worked, delighted with the distinguished and respectable signatures which came in, and enjoying themselves to the full. Millicent Garrett, who had married Henry Fawcett the year before, was still too young to sign, but Florence Nightingale, Harriet Martineau, Mary Somerville, Josephine Butler, and 1498 others did so, and, as Mill said, it was a thing he could "brandish with effect."

On 7th June the great day came. Barbara Bodichon was ill, but Emily Davies and Elizabeth Garrett took the bulky package and made their way to St Stephen's. They were very shy as they went in, but by good luck they at once met Mr Fawcett, who went off to find Mill. Meanwhile the two emissaries waited in Westminster Hall. There was only one other female creature to be seen in the place, an old woman selling apples, so they made their embarrassed way to her side, and with her connivance hid the petition under her stall. When Mill came it was pulled out with much laughter, and they told him with pride and joy how many and what distinguished names there were, and how wide had been the support they had found.

This little Petition Committee was the first of all the Suffrage Committees to be set up, but it was soon followed by others. In the autumn, after the first petition was handed in, the Social Science Congress met in Manchester, and Mme. Bodichon seized the opportunity to read a paper on the enfranchisement of women. No doubt there were many of the "already converted" among her enlightened audience; but there was also one quiet, plain, and severe-looking woman to whom this was the first introduction to the subject. This was Lydia Becker, a feminist by nature, and a woman of unusual political insight, who until that moment had never thought of public work at all, but who had been busy with astronomy, botany, and such other scraps of scientific learning as came the way of females at that date. Mme. Bodichon's paper was "an era in her intellectual life"; and from that moment until the very day of her death she remained plunged wholly in the Cause, in which, as will be seen presently, she became a very central figure.

About the time that the Social Science Congress was meeting in Manchester, the original petition committee in London formed itself into a provisional committee of thirteen, with a regular treasurer, Mrs Peter Taylor,[1] the wife of the Member for Leicester, and with Emily Davies as its secretary.

Emily, however, was afraid that the connection of her name with suffrage work might injure her advocacy of education; so almost at once she persuaded Mrs J. W. Smith, the eldest of the Garrett sisters, to act as secretary, and after her death in 1867 Mme. Bodichon took her place.

This committee busied itself in collecting more petitions, and it had hardly begun operations before, in the January of 1867, a similar committee came into existence in Manchester, with Miss Lydia Becker as its secretary, to help in the good work. In Edinburgh, too, although a regular committee was not set up for some months, there were active suffragists collecting signatures, and by the time the Reform Bill came on in May two petitions of over 3000 names had been presented, besides one from 1605 of the women householders whom Mill's amendment, if it were carried, would turn into electors.

Mill's action in bringing about the first Parliamentary

[1] Clementia, daughter of John Doughty, married Peter Alfred Taylor in 1842. They were Unitarians, cousins of the Mallesons and the Cortaulds, and friends of W. J. Fox, Mazzini, and all the Radicals of the day. Aubrey House, Kensington, where they lived, was a hotbed of movements. Mrs Taylor was particularly interested in negro emancipation, and adopted and educated a negro girl who ultimately became a doctor. She must not be confused with the Mrs Taylor who married J. S. Mill.

debate on Women's Suffrage was in his own opinion "by far the most important public service" which he was able to perform in the House of Commons. It was certainly a most remarkable achievement, for not only did he raise the question to the rank of a serious reform, but his own introduction of the subject was of such a nature that not one of the silly and frivolous speeches which so often accompanied the discussion of anything relating to women in the House of Commons made an appearance.[1] His opening speech, indeed, was one of those sincere and deeply pondered utterances which the House has always respected; and even the most thoughtless or antagonistic of his hearers was startled into respectful attention. After he had set forth the main claim, based on justice and on the fundamental principles of the British constitution, Mill turned to the more human aspects of his case. "I know there is an obscure feeling," he said—"a feeling which is ashamed to express itself openly—as if women had no right to care about anything, except how they may be the most useful and devoted servants of some man. . . . This claim to confiscate the whole existence of one half of the species for the supposed convenience of the other appears to me, independently of its injustice, particularly silly. For who that has had ordinary experience of human affairs, and ordinary capacity of profiting by that experience, fancies that those do their own work best who understand nothing else? . . . Is it good for a man to live in complete communion of thoughts and feelings with one who is studiously kept inferior to himself, whose earthly interests are forcibly confined within four walls, and who cultivates, as a grace of character, ignorance and indifference about the most inspiring subjects, those among which his highest duties are cast? . . .

[1] Mr Henry Fawcett said that he had heard M.P.'s speaking of this Bill beforehand, and anticipating such fun in the debate that they gave up dinner-parties to be present at it.

"It is said that women do not need direct power, having so much indirect, through their influence over their male relatives and connections. I should like to carry this argument a little further. Rich people have a great deal of indirect influence. Is this a reason for refusing them votes? . . . Sir, it is true that women have great power. It is part of my case that they have great power; but they have it under the worst possible conditions, because it is indirect, and therefore irresponsible power. . . . But at least, it will be said, women do not suffer any practical inconvenience, as women, by not having a vote. The interests of all women are safe in the hands of their husbands, and brothers, who have the same interest with them. . . . Sir, this is exactly what is said of all unrepresented classes. The operatives, for instance: are they not virtually represented by the representation of their employers? . . . Is not the farmer equally interested with the labourer in the prosperity of agriculture? . . . and generally, have not employers and employed a common interest against all outsiders, just as husband and wife have against all outside the family? And what is more, are not all employers good, kind, benevolent men, who love their workpeople, and always desire to do what is most for their good? All these assertions are as true, and as much to the purpose, as the corresponding assertions respecting men and women. Sir, we do not live in Arcadia . . . and workmen need other protection than that of their employers, and women other protection than that of their men. I should like to have a return laid before this House of the number of women who are annually beaten to death, kicked to death, or trampled to death by their male protectors; and, in an opposite column, the amount of the sentences passed, in those cases where the dastardly criminals did not get off altogether. I should also like to have, in a third column, the amount of property the unlawful taking of which was, at the same sessions or assizes by the same judge, thought worthy of the same amount of punishment. We should then have an arithmetical estimate of the value set by a male legislature and male tribunals on the murder of a woman . . . which, if there is any shame in us, would make us hang our heads. . . ." For the first time those who listened to this speech of Mill's were brought face to face with the real implications of this perfectly new subject; for the first time they caught a glimpse of the determination and the passion which underlay the demand for an alteration in the position of women, and for the first time they understood that it was no joke, but a big social change which was in question. Most of them disliked and feared the whole subject, and having faced it for an hour they turned away their thoughts and would not look at it again; and when the vote came to be taken there were but eighty to support the amendment. But for all that the debate was justly regarded as a great triumph; for the first step forward had been taken, the challenge had been thrown down, and the Cause had been advanced into the political lists.

The infant suffrage societies drew much encouragement from the result. With eighty parliamentary friends, and with the ready response which they were meeting on all sides, they believed that the final victory could not be far off. Next year, or at most the year after, the thing would be done. This was the belief in 1867.

This optimistic view was perfectly false, and it was not shared by Mill, nor by those men who had any political experience; but the women held it strongly, and it was natural enough that they should. They had never before done any political work, and, being intelligent and disinterested themselves, they assumed that if a cause was just, and demonstrably just, as this was, it must quickly prevail. Moreover, they moved almost entirely in the select Radical circles where no bitter opposition was to be found, and meeting each other over and over again they rather forgot that there was a vast public outside with which they had no contact. Satisfactory numbers of new converts came in, and they did not notice that these came almost all from the same section of society, but thought they were making magnificent progress. They were aware, of course, of an undercurrent of laughter, and of the opposition of such papers as the *Saturday Review*; but they had themselves so low an opinion of the value of the quarters from which this laughter and opposition issued that they could not think it of much account. The formidable mass of hostility which really existed was hidden from them. They did not know that thousands upon thousands of their fellow-countrymen honestly regarded their cause as impious and immoral. They did not understand that the more clearly they represented their vision of a new free world for women, the more surely they arrayed against them the selfish and self-interested among men and the sheltered and lazy among women. They did not realise how preposterous and subversive their whole conception seemed, but continued to believe that because it was just it must soon be popular. And so they were filled with hope.

Even for a short campaign it was important to organise nationally, however, and the provisional London Committee was dissolved and reformed again on a wider basis in June. The reason for this dissolution and reformation was in reality political, and was due to the first appearance of an internal difficulty which was to recur again and again during the course of the movement. The fact that a Women's Suffrage amendment had come forward in the House, and that it had been supported by men of various Parties brought out the divergences of view among the committee members. Emily Davies, always very cautious as well as very wise, attached the utmost importance to Conservative support, and therefore wanted to proceed by taking one small step at a time, so as not to alarm public opinion. Most of the active suffragists, however, were extreme Radicals, to whom this policy was highly uncongenial; so it was amicably agreed among them that a separation of effort would be wise. Miss Davies set up and for some time controlled a Suffrage Committee in Kensington, which seems to have been rather inactive on principle, and which at one time accepted a donation given on condition that it would abstain from action for the rest of the year. Before long Miss Davies' absorption in educational work drew her away from this committee, and the Kensington Society lapsed altogether.

The others, meanwhile, were called together by Mrs Peter Taylor, and on 5th July 1867 their reconstituted committee met at Aubrey House, Kensington, with Miss Frances Power Cobbe in the chair, and Mrs Henry Fawcett among the members, taking up then for the first time the task which Emily Davies and her sister Elizabeth had allotted to her when she was a child.

The first name chosen for the society was "The London Society for Obtaining Political Rights for Women," but this was almost immediately changed to "The London National Society for Women's Suffrage," and the first business was to be the establishing of close co-operation with the societies which had just come into existence in Manchester and Edinburgh, and which were on the point of formation in Birmingham and Bristol.

An interesting and characteristic letter from Mill appears upon the minutes at this time.

"Though I highly approve (of the change of name and national work)," he wrote, "and think it of the greatest importance, I had nothing whatever to do with originating it, but it was entirely and exclusively my daughter's. . . . It is desirable that the minutes of the society should not contain anything positively incorrect, and especially anything tending to keep up the vulgar idea that women cannot manage any important matter without a man to help them. You know how utterly false this supposition would be in the case of the present movement. . . ."

It seems to have been Mill's view that no men should be admitted to the committee at all, but, assuming the independence he so much approved of, they disagreed with his opinion, and from the first a considerable number of men took part in the work. At that date it was usual, when men and women were on a committee together, for the men to do all the talking, but in these early suffrage groups neither the men nor the women were of that kind. They practised, as well as believed in, equality, to the great advantage of their cause.

Although a great deal of help came from the co-operation of men, it was natural that the greater part of the detail and of the executive work should be done by the women members, and their inexperience gave rise to many difficulties. Very few of them could give continuous or regular work, and they were always going away at critical moments. Some of their committees were so large that no business at all could be accomplished; in other places they were so small that the minutes recorded that "at the committee meeting summoned for October only one lady arrived." Often they did not know how to reach an effective decision, so that the minutes read, "A discussion ensued, but nothing was quite decided upon"; and at other times they held up all the business by requiring the secretary to read to them *all* the correspondence which had come into or gone out of the office since they last met. "This," as the minutes said, "has been treated by some of our public men as unreasonable and ridiculous," as indeed it was. But they had a grand storm over it none the less. All sorts of matters of policy arose, of course, upon which they differed acutely; there was one proposal, seriously mooted in 1867, to ask for a separate constituency for women, so that the grant of the franchise should not lead to family quarrels. Only one woman in a thousand, its supporters said, would venture to vote against her husband's views, and this plan would solve the difficulty!

The danger of serious disagreement over this was not great, but there were other more substantial differences which arose from the attempt of the various societies in different parts of the country to co-operate with each other. The London Committee had not been formed two months before this trouble showed its head. "We are of opinion," wrote two of its members, "that it would be impossible to BENEFIT by the other Societies without also sharing in the DISADVANTAGES which unadvised acts of any of them might produce"; and with this cryptic utterance the two ladies withdrew. Who or what their fears were aimed at does not appear on the minutes, but it is probable that this was the first hint of the storm over Josephine Butler's Campaign which was presently to split the movement in two.

These matters of internal organisation, absorbing as of course they seemed to those involved in them, were not the real essence of the work. Curiously enough, the essence of the work in the first year of real organisation was quite different from the propaganda and arguments which the movement settled down to at a later stage. It consisted in the effort to prove that women were not disfranchised, and that it was perfectly legal for them to vote as the law already stood.

The originator of this hopeful idea was Mr Chisholm Anstey, and he based his belief partly upon Lord Brougham's Act, which laid down that wherever the word "man" occurred in parliamentary statutes it was to be read as including woman, but still more upon historical researches into the ancient legal rights of females.[1] He claimed that in feudal times the right of appointing parliamentary representatives went with property, and not with sex, and he discovered many curious and interesting records of the occasions when female landowners and the freewomen of certain towns exercised these functions. There was the

[1] For details of these cases, see *British Freewomen*, by C. C. Stopes.

famous Anne Clifford, Countess of Dorset, Pembroke, Montgomery, and Baroness of Westmorland, who not only claimed and exercised all ancient rights belonging to her titles, but also resisted the suggestions of the Secretary of State, and nominated her grandson to be Member of Parliament in 1667; there was Dame Elizabeth Copley, who signed the indenture in 1628, and there were many more. And as they listened to these cases the Suffrage Committees became filled with excitement. The matter was a plain question of justice; the right was theirs already, and all that remained was to resume it, and put it into immediate practice.

While this discussion was going on a case occurred in Manchester which greatly encouraged and stimulated them all, namely, the case of Mrs Lily Maxwell. By some accident this woman's name slipped on to the register of Parliamentary voters, and, a by-election occurring at that time (1867), she went to the poll and recorded her vote. It so happened that this woman was just exactly the sort of person whom the suffragists would have selected for a test case, if the matter had rested with them. She was a widow, supporting herself by keeping a small crockery shop, and she had most decided and positive political convictions which she was delighted to express. Moreover, these convictions led her to vote for Mr Jacob Bright, who was a great supporter of the Cause in the House, and so it was with the utmost satisfaction that Miss Becker accompanied her on her adventure. The actual event passed off without incident, save that "three cheers" were given for the "heroine of the occasion" by the men who happened to be in the polling-booth at the time; but, of course, the suffragists made as much of it as they could, and took it for a good omen.

Immediately after this event, Miss Becker set to work to get a large number of women to claim to be put on the register, and a house-to-house visitation of female householders was arranged. The consequence was that revising barristers were confronted by shoals of these ladies claiming what they believed to be their rights. Mr Chisholm Anstey was himself a revising barrister, and the claims which came before him, as well as a number of others in different parts of the country, were allowed to stand. In most places they were questioned, however, and an appeal to the courts was the natural and proper result.

For this case the supporters of the women's claims took an immense amount of trouble, and owing to the great importance of the result which might derive from it, it attracted attention all over the country.

The 5346 women householders of Manchester were the first to be heard, and their case, which was known as *Chorlton* v. *Lings*, came on before the Court of Common Pleas on 7th November 1868. The counsel for the women were Sir John Coleridge and Dr Pankhurst, and, as the *Times* said in reporting it, "a number of ladies who appeared to take an interest in the question were in the gallery. A lady, said to be Miss Becker, sat in the jury-box, and was, of course, much and favourably observed."

The argument of the case need not be rehearsed here. It was long and erudite, but it was unavailing. The judges, on the following Monday morning, gave against the claims, and held that "every woman is personally incapable" (in the legal sense). Owing to the fact that the matter was one of public importance, no costs were awarded to either side. There remained a large number of other cases dealing with county franchises, and with freeholders, and with women whose claims had not been objected to by returning officers. Dr Pankhurst made a desperate effort to get these cases heard. "It is so great a subject," he said, "there is so much to urge . . . it involves so vast a mass of material." But there was "laughter in the court," and the judges would not hear him. The decision was given, and the matter was at an end.

The next morning the *Times* had a leading article on the

subject much less obnoxious than many which appeared years later :

"As we cannot affect a decent sorrow at the result, it might be thought more becoming that we should say nothing at all. But we are apprehensive that silence in this case might be considered more offensive even than a shout of victory . . .

"The contention that women, being liable to taxation, must also be entitled to a share in representation, might justify women in a rebellion, but not a Court of Law in adjudging a privilege to them which no law, customary or statutory, can be shown to have conferred."

Even while the leader-writer was at work in Printing House Square, Miss Becker had begun to organise the rebellion which he referred to. But it was to be a peaceful, constitutional rebellion.

"I had made arrangements," she wrote, describing these events, "that immediately the decision was given, a note from me asking every candidate in England and Wales to support a Bill to establish Women's Suffrage should be despatched. The ladies of our Committee and others undertook the writing of eight hundred notes, and I telegraphed from Westminster Town Hall 'Post your letters' as soon as I left the court. Most were sent off that night, so the first note of agitation throughout the country sounded simultaneously with the announcement of the decision."

Even yet, however, the members of the committees were not really discouraged. Some, Miss Becker and Mrs Fawcett among them, foresaw that the struggle would be long and difficult, but to many it still seemed obvious that the thing had only to be put plainly before Parliament for their Bill to pass. They looked, therefore, to the new Members who were at that moment being elected to redress the decision of the courts.

John Stuart Mill lost his seat, which was a severe blow to their hopes, but there were other friends left in the new House, and to these they turned. Early in 1869 Miss Becker asked Mr Jacob Bright to get into touch with Mr Russell Gurney and to consider the parliamentary situation. This was duly done, but the result was a reference back to the societies for more widespread propaganda.

"Our movement is now in a stage to demand greater effort than we have hitherto been able to accomplish," wrote Miss Becker. "We cannot hope for immediate, perhaps not even for speedy, success—and ultimate success can only be accomplished by a long course of systematic and persevering agitation. We have to tread the paths that other causes of progress have done before us—the Anti-Corn Law League, the Reform Movement. . . ."

This was undoubtedly true, though somewhat discouraging. However, the young committees took up their burden courageously, and began to formulate their plans. The first step must be to spread the organisation over the country, they felt, and to make their principles known. Mrs M'Laren and Miss Mair in Edinburgh, Mrs Osler in Birmingham, the Misses Priestly in Bristol, and a dozen more began to work in earnest. Over 18,000 pamphlets were issued, but they soon realised that something more direct was required, and the question of meetings arose.

Up to that date hardly any women had spoken in public at all. A few bold spirits had given "lectures," and one or two had read papers before Social Science Congresses, and Miss Becker had arranged a real public meeting in the Free Trade Hall in Manchester the year before, at which the Mayor had taken the chair, and she herself had been among the speakers. But even she, intrepid as she was, had admitted to being "unnerved," and all the other ladies, earnest as they were, were appalled at the prospect of entering the rough and tumble of political meetings. However, the thing had to be done, no matter what individual suffering and distress it imposed upon them, and the thing was done.

Drawing-room meetings were the first step, and these

were alarming enough, but public meetings had soon to follow, and in July 1869 the first London one was held in the Gallery of the Architectural Society in Conduit Street. It was not in itself a formidable gathering, for the hall was filled with supporters, and almost everyone in the room was known to almost everyone else. Mrs Peter Taylor was in the chair—the presiding of a woman was another startling novelty—and she was supported by a crowd of distinguished speakers, enough, as we should think in these days, to have supplied half a dozen meetings. There was John Stuart Mill, Charles Kingsley, Professor Fawcett, John Morley, Sir Charles Dilke, Mr Stansfield, and *six* others, one of whom was Mrs Fawcett, who made on that occasion the first public speech of her life. It all went off splendidly, and everyone was thoroughly pleased. The new campaign was launched.

Delightful as the actual occasion was, however, this new style of meeting did not escape unfriendly comment. The newspapers for the most part gave this particular meeting serious reports, but many people were profoundly and honestly shocked by the thought of mixed speaking. One gentleman, a Member of Parliament, took occasion to drag into one of his own speeches the fact that "two ladies, wives of Members of this House," had recently disgraced themselves by speaking in public, and he kindly added that he would not "further disgrace them by mentioning their names." The ladies in question bore up quite cheerfully under his censure, and neither Mr Fawcett nor Mr Peter Taylor challenged him to fight; but the attitude of mind which his words revealed was a very common one at that date. Although it undoubtedly stirred some of the suffragists to laughter, and others to anger, it was not an attitude calculated to encourage women to come forward for this new service; and, indeed, in the beginning, women speakers were hard to find.

It was one thing to speak at such a gathering and in such company as had been assembled at the Architects' Hall, but it was far more difficult to go out into country places and break new ground. This, however, had now to be undertaken, and a number of volunteers came forward for the unwelcome task.

In those days, before the Reform Bill of 1884, constituencies sometimes consisted of a single small town, and in consequence one successful meeting might be enough to influence one Member. There was no fear of the meetings failing for lack of audience, for everyone crowded to see the novel sight of a woman speaking in public, and only the ultra-timid stayed away. Nervous and anxious chairmen found it necessary to assure their audiences that the ladies were quite respectable, but sometimes there was no chairman to do this, and no one who could be persuaded to sit on the platform at all. The meetings themselves were doubtless very different from what the audiences had expected, and the impromptu votes of thanks which were moved at the end were often a little curious. They frequently referred to the "heroism" of the speakers, and were sometimes extended to include the husbands who had been so good as to spare their wives to come away and speak on this occasion!

It was undoubtedly very hard work for these first speakers, and very agitating work too. They hardly knew whether the female voice could carry in a large hall, and the nervous strain of being so very peculiar must have been great. Then, too, their anxiety for success must have been acute, and the uncertainty of their reception very wearing. On the other hand, it must have been much more entertaining than public meetings have since become, more full of novelty and excitement and of the sense of real adventure; and the fact that the meetings were always successful and their voices always audible must have been a recurring delight.

There was another great compensation for the hard work, and that was the friends whom the speakers made all over the country. While it was still so new—and indeed right on to the very end of the agitation—the sense of understanding and sympathy which springs up among the supporters of an unpopular cause was very sustaining; and the comfort of being sheltered in the congenial and comfortable homes which were open to them made these parts of the early speaking tours a very pleasant memory to the bold adventurers. Many, too, were the jokes which these "heroines" enjoyed as they went on their adventurous way, and many the comic tales they related to each other. Some of them were young and beautiful, and others were rather less young and much less beautiful; and there was much quiet manœuvring over the attempt to modify the manner, and still more the appearance, of the fierce ones. It cannot be denied that among these brave and devoted women there were a few who were not only plain, but positively uncouth to the outward eye. They were entirely unconcerned as to their looks and did not realise at all that other people were given to judging by appearances, and that their best and most cogent arguments might be unavailing if presented by a lady in thick boots, untidy hair, and a crumpled dress. There were not many such among them, but the real existence of one or two was enough to give rise to the legend of the strong-minded and rather hirsute female with spectacles and large feet who figured so freely in the comic Press for a quarter of a century or more. This legend was not good for the Cause, but all the same it enhanced the success of those other far more numerous speakers whose appearance was the exact reverse—the lovely Miss Ashworths, for example, Mrs Fawcett, Miss Rhoda and Miss Agnes Garrett, Lady Amberley, and the rest. When an audience expected to find a fierce and strident virago, and found instead a young lady whose voice, dress, and manner were not only quiet but exquisite, then indeed they were startled to attention; and when these young ladies began to develop their theme with the power and eloquence of Rhoda Garrett, or with the wide sweep of thought of Mrs Fawcett, then the lesson went home. The memory of those early meetings stayed with many of those who attended them as long as they lived, and the light which then dawned upon them grew into an unfaltering conviction. New adherents came in from every meeting which was held, and the effort brought a great return.

It was not all success and plain sailing, however. Miss Becker watched over the new committees as they were formed with anxious care, even though she hoped that "like a newly-married couple they will best settle to their work if left to themselves"; but sometimes the hopeful converts slipped out of her hands. "My efforts to find someone at Coventry to take up the question have not been successful. The lady to whom I last applied wrote that she considered our zeal overforward," the Birmingham secretary reported, and Lady Amberley sometimes told a similar tale. After a meeting she had taken at Stroud she [1] wrote to Helen Taylor most gloomily: "I had no sympathy with me at all. . . . Amberley was the only supporter I really had, and people expressed surprise to me afterwards to see that a woman could lecture and still look like a lady! . . . I hope Mr Mill will be pleased at my having made the effort and taken my share of ridicule which falls to the lot of women who advocate this cause. I hear I was made great fun of at the Carlton, and we had insulting anonymous letters; but one must make up one's mind to some disagreeables for the sake of one's opinions." And after all the meeting had done good. A fortnight later she was able to report, "I find that it has stirred up Stroud, and I have got twelve people for a Women's Franchise Committee." But it was hard work.

"I shall be so glad to see you," she wrote another time,[2] "for I have been thrown into such low spirits by being very much laughed at at Gladstone's party the other night,

[1] Letter to Miss Helen Taylor, 26th May 1870.
[2] Letter to Miss Helen Taylor, February 1871.

as my poor little committee somehow found its way into the London papers. I should not have minded for myself, because a woman can always turn it off, but they told me I made Amberley so ridiculous that I diminished any influence he might have—that whenever his name was mentioned it made people smile, and such-like pleasant things. . . . I wish I never saw anyone but you and your friends."

Neither she nor Lord Amberley paid any attention to this opinion, however. "I tried to get Lord Henry on the committee," she reported about the same time, "but he only snubbed me very much, wondering how I could dream that any of HIS FAMILY could sanction such a thing; that the word Women's Suffrage was revolting to him, and that he really thought I must be chaffing. It will come on such people as a thunder-clap or perhaps worse yet," she comforted herself, "if they don't get used quickly to the march of events."

Unfortunately it was the suffragists who had to get used to it. In 1870, before the country propaganda had been much developed, a second opportunity had arisen to test the feeling in Parliament, and the upshot of that testing was the downfall of all their hopes of immediate success. Mr Jacob Bright secured a day for the introduction of a Suffrage Bill, and Dr Pankhurst drafted it with care, and after a serious and dignified debate on 4th May its second reading was carried by 124 to 91. But matters ended there. In the committee stage Mr Gladstone brought out his determined opposition, and the majority melted away. "It would be a very great mistake to carry this Bill into law," he said, and though he gave no reasons the whole tone of the House changed forthwith, and when the second vote was taken the hostile majority was 106.

So ended the early hopes of parliamentary success. The women realised at last the feebleness of the individual support they had won, and the extent of the opposition they had to overcome. They set themselves in earnest, therefore, to change the public opinion of the country, and took up their organisation with new zeal. Yet even so they did not realise how long it was to be before another favourable vote would be secured in the House of Commons,[1] or that forty-eight years would have to pass by before even the first instalment of their demand would be conceded.

[1] The next parliamentary victory was in 1885, when a second reading was carried without a division, it being known that the Bill could go no farther. After that no favourable majority was secured until 1897.

CHAPTER VII

THE REVELATION OF IGNORANCE. 1848–1868

The pioneer schools for girls—Miss Buss and Miss Beale—Emily Davies secures the opening of the Oxford and Cambridge Local Examinations to girls—The Schools Inquiry Commissions Report in 1868.

WHILE John Stuart Mill was bringing the cause of Women's Suffrage into prominence among Radical thinkers, and while Barbara Bodichon and her friends were advocating that married women should have control over their own property, and also that there should be extended opportunities of employment for women, the foundations upon which the whole breadth and force of the Women's Movement were to depend were being slowly constructed. And these foundations were, of course, secondary and higher education for girls.

To trace the development of the organised movement for women's education we must go back to 1848 and 1849, when Queen's College and Bedford College for Ladies had been opened.

In the first year Queen's College had had two hundred students, women of all kinds and all ages. The majority of them had been teaching before they applied for the college course, and most of them took up the same profession when they had finished it, although many of the pioneers who branched out into other work were there as well. George Eliot and Barbara Leigh Smith, for example, were at Bedford College, and Sophia Jex-Blake and Octavia Hill at Queen's. But these colleges were primarily intended for the training of teachers, and it was not only the scarcity of other work, but also the deliberate encouragement of the lecturers, which sent out the pupils to this task. Moreover, they needed little stimulation; the deplorable state of girls' education provided a cause for which it was easy for anyone who had caught but the dimmest glimpse of the new ideals of the Women's Movement to feel a missionary zeal, and the young women who were rejoicing in their own new knowledge went forth with high hearts to spread the light.

In these days, when education for girls has become so much a matter of course, and when education for everyone has become so much more fully organised, it is difficult to realise how it can ever have been a pioneer subject. Nevertheless it is true that when these early students set out to found real secondary schools for girls they faced a multitude of difficulties.

The first of these was, of course, the lack of capable teachers, and, though this was a diminishing difficulty, it was very acute at the outset. The second was their almost complete lack of capital to invest; and it was many years before this ceased to be a practical hindrance to the new movement. But perhaps the worst trouble of all was the timidity, if not the actual hostility, of parents. The prevailing notion still was that girls must be prepared to achieve matrimony in a difficult and overcrowded market; and how would arithmetic do this? As a mother said, when urged to send her daughter to one of these schools, "You can't send a girl into the drawing-room repeating the multiplication table." So why should she trouble to learn it?

The enthusiasm and tact of the first head mistresses, and the eager support of their pupils, gradually broke down this opposition in the neighbourhoods where the new-fangled schools came into being; but it was inevitable that they should begin on a small scale, and that a heavy burden of anxiety and hard work should fall upon the venturesome ladies who founded them. The young women who were taking up this side of the Women's Movement were afraid neither of anxiety nor hard work, however, and they had enthusiasm and energy enough to carry them through to success.

The first of these dangerous schools to appear was the North London Collegiate School, founded by Miss Buss in 1850; and the second was Cheltenham College, founded in 1854 and taken over by Miss Beale in 1858.

These two, Miss Beale and Miss Buss, were the first of the long list of able women who have devoted their lives to lifting the load of ignorance and inefficiency from the girls of the country, and their place in the Women's Movement is consequently one of very great importance.

Both of these women were school teachers first and foremost, and in spite of the immense volume of administration and public work which the success of their ventures and the development of their cause imposed upon them, both stuck to their class-rooms almost all their lives. The double task was only accomplished by the sacrifice of all their leisure, and by the devoting of every atom of their strength to work. "I have never known leisure," wrote Miss Buss, and indeed she never did; and until she was an old woman she had probably not found so much as one unappropriated half hour.

Frances Mary Buss was born in 1827, and when she was just fourteen she began to teach in a school which her mother was maintaining. At eighteen she took over the responsible management of this school, and she continued to manage it until at twenty-eight she founded the North London Collegiate School. In 1848, when she was twenty-one and while she was still in the first school, she entered herself as a pupil at Queen's College, though of course she could only attend the evening classes. At that date omnibuses did not run in the evening, so her attendance involved a long walk to and fro; but nothing daunted her enthusiasm. Night after night she plodded into Harley Street, and night after night she sat up over her books till the small hours, entranced by the studies to which she was at last beginning to find her way; and morning after morning she rose early to carry on almost single-handed the work by which she earned her daily bread. Later, when her new school was in existence, she worked no less strenuously, devoting not only her time but also all the profits she might have made out of the school to its further development. She felt, as Emily Davies expressed it, "that if one had only a personal interest in the matter it would be impossible to persevere," the work was so "horridly disagreeable" at times. "But we are fighting for people who cannot fight for themselves." Miss Buss herself expressed the same thought. "The terrible sufferings of the women of my own class for want of a good elementary training have more than ever intensified my earnest desire to lighten, ever so little, the misery of women brought up 'to be married and taken care of' and left alone in the world destitute. It is impossible for words to express my fixed determination of alleviating this evil—even to the small extent of one neighbourhood only."

With this aim to inspire her, Miss Buss threw herself into the task of forcing up the standard of girls' schools, and did not flinch before the lack of teachers, the lack of funds, the doubting parents, the hostile Press, or the hampering and clogging atmosphere of popular ridicule. She intended to give her girls sound teaching, physical exercise and outside examinations, and she did give them these things, in the midst of a world which derided them all and thought them dangerous, masculine, and unnecessary.

Dorothea Beale, the other great pioneer of the moment, was some years younger than Frances Mary Buss, and she did not begin her teaching so early. Her own education was built upon what she called "the noxious breed of catechisms," and except for teaching herself Latin and Euclid by helping her brothers with their home work, she had not studied much before she went to Queen's College. After a year there, however, she became one of the tutors in mathematics, and for six years she taught this subject, with great profit to herself. She left in 1856, after protesting that the lady visitors and tutors were allowed too little share in the management, and went to a school for the daughters of clergymen at Casterton. This was the school to which Charlotte Brontë and her sisters had been sent, and which, under the name of Lowood, is so ruthlessly and painfully described in *Jane Eyre*. At the time when Dorothea Beale began to teach in it, the arrangements were, perhaps, a little less miserable than they had been thirty-two years before. But the system was not essentially altered, and everything about the place was just as Miss Beale could not bear to see it: dull, monotonous teaching, bad discipline, with plenty of punishments and no prizes, and a tone throughout which she thoroughly disapproved. The standard of education was far from high, and she herself was expected to teach an impossible number of subjects. Scripture, arithmetic and mathematics; ancient, modern, and church history; physical and political geography, together with English literature, grammar, and composition would have seemed more than enough by themselves, but to these were added also French, German, Latin, and Italian, and it is no wonder that Miss Beale was conscious of ill success and discouragement. Being what she was, however, a violent reformer, Miss Beale could not long remain in such a place and in such a position without trying to change the whole concern, and the result was friction, suffering, and finally dismissal. "It was a year of great and painful strain, but excellent experience," as she said herself long after. But it was a hard training.

Soon after this, however, Miss Beale's real opportunity came, when she accepted the post of Principal to the girls' school at Cheltenham which had been started four years before. This school, at the time she took it on, was steadily dwindling to failure, and for the first few years she had a terribly anxious time. If she stuck to her beliefs, and made the standard of work high, then it seemed as if the whole thing might disappear altogether; and yet she could not abandon her convictions. She had therefore to find a way round, as in the case of the Euclid lessons she wanted to give. "It might have been the death of the College," she wrote, "so I had to wait for the tide. I began my innovations with the introduction of scientific teaching, and under the name of physical geography I was able to teach a good deal. This subject was unobjectionable, as few boys learned geography."

Everything Miss Beale wanted to do seemed dangerous, and it was several years before she was able to make the changes in time-tables and hours and examinations which she had at heart. But in the end she, too, triumphed, and by and by her school began to grow and to flourish exceedingly. In 1864 the first boarding-house in connection with Cheltenham College was established, and since that date it has always been one of the foremost girls' schools in the country; and the training college for teachers which she opened in Cheltenham in 1877 was later moved to Oxford and developed into St Hilda's Hall.

While these two women were making a beginning of the modern secondary education of girls, many other influences were at work in the same direction, and many other pioneers were pushing ahead and attacking other parts of the same problem.

There were, and indeed had long been, isolated experiments in education, and the number of these which included girls now greatly increased. One of these was started in London by Barbara Leigh Smith in her energy and her enthusiasm, and conducted partly by her, but chiefly by her friend Miss Whitehead (afterwards Mrs Frank Malleson), and for some years this school was very much the centre of the thoughts of that same group of people who were later occupied in forwarding the first steps of the Women's Movement in other directions.

This school was unsectarian, co-educational, and exceedingly modern; the pupils were taken to museums and picture-galleries, and were taught to think rather than remember, and its unconventional character attracted a great deal of notice. Garibaldi's sons were at one time among its pupils, and all that group of Radicals which included Mill, Carlyle, and Mazzini knew of and discussed its plans. Miranda Hill at one time thought of being a teacher there, and her sister Octavia wrote to her to assure her that "You would find Mme. Bodichon and Mrs Malleson delightful people to work under; you would have such power to carry out what you thought best." However, Miranda did not go there, for Frederick Maurice, who was her guide in such matters, disapproved of its lack of religious teaching; and in the end she and her sisters started another educational experiment of their own, namely, a combined workroom and school for poorer girls, which in its way was as novel and interesting an experiment as the other.

It would be possible to describe a considerable number of enterprises such as these which were being set on foot between 1850 and 1860 by those who were connected with Queen's and Bedford Colleges; but for our purpose here it is enough to remember that there was a steadily growing body of serious and educated women to whom girls' schools were a cause which stood first and foremost, and who were seeking to work out the principles by which that cause was to develop.

In point of time the next definite attack which was made upon entrenched prejudices in this matter was the struggle for medical education and the effort to gain admission to the universities which grew up alongside it. This movement really began as early as 1860, and as it progressed it inevitably had important reactions upon the question of secondary education. It was, however, in one way a quite distinct movement, and it has therefore been treated separately in Chapter IX.

The demand for good secondary education for young girls, of course, implied the need for higher education for those who were to teach them; but there were at the beginning a great many people who favoured the one while they looked with horror upon the other, and therefore the Secondary and the Higher Education movements, although actually interdependent, were technically distinct. They really moved along side by side until the time came when the normal course of things was established and the schools fed the universities, which in turn supplied the teachers for the schools. But they were not regarded as one and the same by the general public; and the few far-sighted leaders who understood what was going on had many anxious and difficult decisions to take upon the tactics of their two campaigns.

In all matters relating to education the chief arbiter of tactics and the chief organiser of campaigns soon came to be Emily Davies. From the very first she had seen the Cause in its widest terms, and the more she thought on the subject the more clearly she saw it as a vast social change whose various parts must be advanced in their proper sequence and arranged in relation to the whole movement. Surveying the field thus, she decided that the first requisite and foundation of progress must be wider and better education for women; and for this reason, and not because she was by her own nature a scholar, or even a great lover of the young, but only because she was a passionate feminist, she turned her abilities to its service.

Her first efforts were directed to helping Elizabeth Garrett in the early steps in her career.[1] This had brought her, of course, against the solid wall of opposition which every university presented to every woman who asked to be examined in any subject; and from this opposition grew the inflexible determination she formed to break down that wall. In 1862, when she and her mother came to live in

[1] See Chap. IX. For a fuller description of these adventures, see *Emily Davies and Girton College*, by Barbara Stephen.

London, she was able to set to work in earnest, and she found much to help her. The subject of women in relation to the universities had already been much discussed owing to Miss Garrett's various unsuccessful attempts to secure a degree, and in this year, 1862, Frances Power Cobbe raised it again in a paper before the Social Science Congress. For a week or two she was "the subject of universal ridicule," as she noted, but the laughter faded away before the next popular sensation, and the serious consideration of serious people remained. A committee to secure the admission of women to the university examinations was formed, with Emily Davies as its secretary and mainspring, and this committee found that they had more friends than they had expected among the professors, and especially the younger men at several universities.

Now Emily Davies, extreme and obstinate as she was in her thoughts, was remarkably cautious and tactful in her actions. She obtruded none of her ultimate intentions, and was an adept at carrying along with her all who would move a little, though they feared to move far. When, therefore, the idea arose of trying to secure the admission of girls to the recently instituted Oxford and Cambridge Local Examinations, she eagerly welcomed it.

"I do not care so VERY much for (the examinations) in themselves," she wrote to a confidential friend, "because I think the encouragement to learning is most wanted AFTER the age of eighteen. It seems likely, however, that if we could get these examinations it would be a great lift towards getting the University of London." Publicly she said nothing of this; and in 1863, after a great many interviews and the writing of a great many letters and memorials, the Cambridge Syndicate agreed to an experimental plan. The examination papers were to be handed to the committee, who were themselves to be free to organise the affair and to make their own arrangements with the examiners for the correction of the papers.

This permission reached the committee a very short time before the examination was to take place.

"Our breath was quite taken away on Saturday," Miss Davies wrote to the same friend as before, "by receiving quite unexpectedly a favourable answer from the Cambridge Syndicate to our application. I fully expected that they would politely get rid of us by saying it was 'beyond their powers.' It has thrown us into dreadful agitation. We have only six weeks to work up our candidates, and who can expect them to come up on such short notice? . . . We shall look unspeakably foolish if we have no candidates after all."

In this difficulty strenuous efforts were made. Circulars were sent out broadcast to the girls' schools, bringing back many curious and disheartening answers from the mistresses.

"Some of the schoolmistresses' letters are almost illegible and very funny. One is afraid that the examinations will foster the spirit of confidence and independence which is too common amongst girls of the present day. I fancy girls must be excessively insubordinate by nature or they never would have a grain of spirit left, after going thro' school training."

The end of it all was, however, that ninety-one girls turned up, and the fresh difficulty of finding accommodation, chaperonage, and escort through the streets for so many was also surmounted. The examiners had been most kind and friendly, and had not refused to correct the papers; friends and supporters had come forward with the money necessary for the expenses, and all that organisation could do had been done. There remained, however, the core of the matter, the examination itself. What would the girls contribute to the affair, and how would they acquit themselves?

The results were eagerly expected, and when they came they proved to be exactly what was most useful for the Cause.

The girls did fairly well in some subjects, but they failed wholesale in arithmetic. "It was clear," wrote the examiner in this subject, "that this was due to lack of proper instruction." Even Miss Buss's candidates showed this same fault, and the want of an external standard by which to judge the schools was most clearly demonstrated. The movement for providing good secondary schools thus received a tremendous impetus, and a large number of new and useful friends were made for the Cause.

The next step, of course, was to make this examination privilege permanent, and to put it on a formal and not a private basis. To this end the committee staged a special meeting of the Social Science Association, to which Mr Tomlinson, the secretary of the London centre, was invited to come "to testify (if you can conscientiously)," as Miss Davies put it, "that everybody behaved properly, and nothing alarming or scandalous happened at the experimental examination. . . ." A number of other Cambridge men were invited, "especially enemies, to give them a chance of being converted." To make the chance of this greater, Emily Davies took great care to secure some well-dressed and good-looking young women to fill up the front row. She anxiously inquired of her friends whether any of the audience "were strong-minded looking," and pointed out that Miss Garrett at any rate looked "exactly like one of those girls whose instinct it is to do what you tell them" (though here appearances were terribly deceptive!). This meeting went off well, and it was followed by a considerable discussion in the Press and in academic circles, and by several special lectures and pamphlets. The problem, later to become so acute, of whether the same or a modified form of higher education was suitable for girls and boys, made its appearance, but a good measure of agreement was found for the view that the same thorough teaching of the elements, and the same general programme of education was desirable, at any rate up to the age of fifteen or sixteen—the age at which the Cambridge Local Examinations were normally taken. This was not by any means universally admitted, however; and even where it was, the plan of testing the results by open examination was still often opposed. It was seriously urged at Cambridge as an objection that the examination would "give rise to so many jokes," and the Liverpool centre expressed the view that it would be exposed to so much ridicule that the most promising boy candidates would cease to present themselves at all. Another widely held objection was that a dangerous spirit of rivalry between boys and girls would be brought into existence, and some of the real friends of the movement shared this fear. Miss Beale was one of these, and she expressed her opinion in terms which no modern feminist would now subscribe to. "Let me say at once," she wrote in a paper before the Social Science Congress in 1865, "that I desire to institute no comparison between the mental abilities of boys and girls, but simply to say what seems to me the right means of training girls so that they may best perform that subordinate part in the world to which, I believe, they have been called." Acting upon this belief Miss Beale refused to send up any of her girls as candidates for the first examinations, and in this she was supported by Miss Hannah Pipe, another of the pioneers among head mistresses. Miss Pipe, indeed, saw a different danger. Her view was that the girls would be overexcited, overworked, and crammed at the expense of their "health of body and peace of mind." The weight of opinion was on the other side, however. A large memorial was collected by Miss Davies (and she took care to include a great many "ladylike ladies" as well as educational experts among the signatories), and in 1865, after much anxious canvassing in the university by Professor Fawcett, Mr Markby, and other friends, the Senate confirmed the Report of the Syndicate by 54 votes to 51, and the Local Examinations were officially thrown open to girls.

While all this was going on other efforts in the same

direction had been carried forward, and Emily Davies herself had discovered and had won an outpost as important as the examinations themselves, namely, the inclusion of the education of girls in the scope of the Schools Enquiry Commission. This commission had been set up by the Government in 1864 to inquire into the "whole subject of middle-class education," but it seemed at first as if the education of girls was not included in this definition. It was not so much excluded as overlooked in the original designs of the commissioners, and when Emily Davies began her approaches to them she found them, not unfriendly, but a trifle surprised, and perhaps more than a trifle bored at the prospect of making such an arduous, but relatively unimportant addition to their labours.

After prolonged correspondence with the commissioners individually, Miss Davies came to the conclusion that some more formal step must be taken, and she rapidly organised one of her influential and well-selected memorials. This had the desired result, and she had the additional satisfaction of hearing that the assistant commissioners who were to be sent out to make the investigations were interested in the affair, and that the secretary of the commission, Mr Roby, was anxious to secure her help and co-operation in making the enquiry a success.

Until then no one had had any means of finding out what was the real state of things in girls' schools. Everyone knew, from their own observation, that they were liable to be "frothy and superficial," inefficient and pretentious; but exact information about them did not exist. "It is exceedingly difficult to visit such establishments," wrote Mme. Bodichon in a paper before the Social Science Congress in 1860. "They are *private*, and I have found the mistresses exceedingly jealous of inspection, most unwilling to show a stranger (and quite naturally) anything of the school books, or to answer any questions." But now this was to be overcome, and the sub-commissioners would have the right to make thorough inquiry and to make their reports upon full knowledge. Miss Davies, being allowed to be behind the scenes to some extent, was indefatigable in making suggestions, and it was owing to her that J. S. Mill, Huxley, and Mark Pattison were called as witnesses. "I should like to have Huxley examined about the brain," she wrote, "because the physiological argument is constantly used, and people believe it"; and of other distinguished men she added, "I don't think they know anything, but they might be primed." At her suggestion, too, Miss Buss and Miss Beale were called, and she herself gave evidence in November 1865, on the same day as Miss Buss.

Intrepid and positive as both these ladies were, they were horribly nervous on this occasion. It was almost the first time that a woman had ever been heard before a Royal Commission of any kind, and they were much afraid of doing badly. Miss Davies quickly regained her composure, however. "Seven people asking questions are not so bad as one alone, and they were good-natured and encouraging to the last degree," she wrote. "We were both nervous, but I had some success in concealing it. . . . After I had given my evidence, and was being regaled with claret and biscuits in Mr Roby's room, Mr Acland came hurrying in with 'This witness is not so self-possessed as the other,' and asking me to go back to support Miss Buss. She was almost speechless with nervousness, but managed to give good answers to questions."

Curiously enough this nervousness of Miss Buss was as effective in its way as Miss Davies's collectedness. "We were all so much struck by their perfect womanliness," said one of the commissioners. "Why, there were tears in Miss Buss's eyes!" Nothing could have been more reassuring.

Stage-managing the commission, like stage-managing the examination, was one thing, but the report was another; and since, of course, Miss Davies was not herself a commissioner, this matter was beyond her control. However, it soon became clear that it would go all right. Almost at once Miss Davies noticed that "there was a great ferment going on about the education of women," and that "it is most useful to have (the assistant commissioners) going about, stirring up and encouraging the schoolmistresses," and even if the report had been bad, a great deal of good would have been done. But the report was not going to be bad. So many of the commissioners were "sound," and so conclusive was the evidence which had been put before them, that the only real question was how far they would go in the right direction.

When the report finally appeared, in 1868, it was the very thing to carry on the good work. It assumed at the outset that the education of girls was a matter of the utmost importance, and while carefully avoiding any comparison of boys and girls, such as might alarm the critics, it gave evidence for its belief in the capacity of girls to be taught, and of their eagerness for instruction. It went on to describe the rotten state of the existing arrangements.

"It cannot be denied that the picture brought before us of the state of the middle-class female education is, on the whole, unfavourable . . . want of thoroughness and foundation; want of system; slovenliness and showy superficiality; inattention to rudiments; undue time given to accomplishments, and these not taught intelligently or in any scientific manner; want of organisation . . . a very small amount of professional skill, an inferior set of school books, a vast deal of dry, uninteresting work, rules put into the memory with no explanation of their principles, no system of examination worthy of the name, a very false estimate of the relative value of the several kinds of acquirement, a reference to effect rather than to solid worth, a tendency to fill rather than to strengthen the mind. . . ." All this was clear and unescapable; and then the cause was as plainly exposed. "The two capital defects of the teachers of girls are these:

they have not themselves been taught, and they do not know how to teach."

For all their plain speaking, the commissioners were not prepared to be very extreme. They approved the Cambridge Local Examinations, though they called it a bold step to admit girls to "the very same examination as boys"; but they were careful to express no opinion as to whether higher education and training for teachers should follow identical or modified lines for women, and they cautioned the advocates of the new ideas not to expect too much success.

"We have had much evidence showing the general indifference of parents to girls' education, both in itself and as compared to that of boys. It leads to a less immediate and tangible pecuniary result; there is a long-established and inveterate prejudice . . . that girls are less capable of mental cultivation, and less in need of it than boys; that accomplishments and what is showy and superficially attractive are what is really essential for them; and in particular that, as regards their relations to the other sex and the probabilities of marriage, more solid attainments are actually disadvantageous. . . . It must be fully admitted that such ideas have a very strong root in human nature. . . ."

Even if those who cared for girls' education must "be prepared for a larger proportion of failures," however, they were still advised to persevere, and the whole tone of the report was just what the pioneer educationalists found most helpful. Moreover, the practical proposals of the commission in regard to endowments, which led to the passing of the Endowed Schools Act, were of the utmost importance.

"It is certainly a singular fact, and one not by any means admitting of an easy explanation," the commissioners said, "that with these few exceptions NO PART of the large funds arising from endowments for the education of the middle classes is now, or has been for a long time past, devoted to so important a purpose as the education of girls and young women. . . . The appropriation of almost all the educational endowments of the country to the education of boys is felt by a large and increasing number both of men and women to be a cruel injustice." [1]

The publication of a report such as this, and the gradual introduction of the reforms it suggested, led in a remarkably short time to a complete revolution, not only in girls' schools, but in the whole outlook of the public towards them. There were still difficulties and hindrances ahead, and there was to be a fearful controversy over university education; but with the publication of the report of 1868 the preliminary battle was won, and the rest was bound to follow. If nothing else had been done in that decade it might still have been almost enough, for when the girls trained in the new way should be grown up, more workers and more enthusiasts were bound to arise among them. But much else was done, as we shall see in the following chapters; and the new generation, when they took over the Cause, found that Miss Davies and her fellow-pioneers had smoothed a great deal of the way before their feet.

[1] Sir Josiah Fitch showed that girls were admitted to charity schools but not to grammar schools, and gave as an example Christ's Hospital, where 1192 boys were being prepared for the universities and 18 girls for domestic service. He described how he himself had reminded an intending donor of £10,000 for scholarships that his scheme was drawn up for boys only. The man replied that he had not deliberately excluded girls, but that it had not before occurred to him that they could want higher education.

CHAPTER VIII

THE SIEGE OF CAMBRIDGE. 1866–1873

Attempt to secure admission to London University—Emily Davies plans a real women's college and forms her committee, 1867—North of England Council for Higher Education of Women formed—Anne Jemima Clough—The clash between the two schemes—Miss Davies takes a house at Hitchin and six students enter in October 1869—Early difficulties of the students and the examination uncertainty—Local lectures to women in Cambridge early in 1870—Students coming from other places, and house taken for them by Mr Sidgwick in October 1871—Miss Clough takes charge of this house—First students from Hitchin pass Little Go in 1870 and get informal permission to take Tripos papers in 1873—All three of them pass.

WHILE the Suffrage Cause was getting under way and passing through its preliminary disappointments, the problem of securing university education for women came into public view, and grew to be a "Cause" as difficult and as enthralling as the other.

Tennyson had published "The Princess" as early as 1847; but when the Queen's College came into existence in the following year it had been singularly unlike the imaginary picture he had drawn. Some of the aspirations of the Princess Ida were indeed cherished by the young women who flocked to the lectures; but at first there was nothing so revolutionary as a residential college in prospect, and the soft sentimental moonshine of the poem was absent from the real affair. None of the feminists of that or any other moment wanted to shut women away from the society of men; that was left to Mrs Grundy and the conventional chaperones. But still, even in the early fifties, there were some who cherished in secret the idea that one day a real college might exist, where there would be university life and true university standards for women. Barbara Bodichon had been one of these; but while the ordinary education of girls was in such a sorry plight it had seemed to be quite unattainable, and for many years she made no serious efforts for its foundation. One or two isolated attempts were made in the early years by people connected with Queen's College to secure admission to London University, but they met with no success at all, and it was not until 1866 that the subject of university education for girls came out into the light of day.

In this year, when the Local Examinations for girls had just been safely secured, Emily Davies began to turn her thoughts towards the really higher education which she privately thought so much more important to the Cause. When she looked about to see what could be done she perceived that the time was almost ripe for a forward step. A great many new friends had been revealed by the preliminary agitation, and so much support had been found for the first examination privilege that she ventured to approach London University once more and ask whether the Matriculation Examination could not now be thrown open. But this was more than London was as yet prepared to grant. After a great deal of talking, and a lot of earnest and pompous discussion, the Senate decided that the best thing they could offer was a special women's examination, of an easier standard than matriculation, which could take its place for females (though, of course, it would carry with it none of those university privileges which the real thing conferred upon men). Miss Davies and her committee at once rejected this offer. "I am afraid," she wrote to one of the Senators, "that the people who are interested in the education of women are a thankless crew. . . . They do not consider a special examination any boon at all, and will have nothing to do with it. . . . We are really obliged to Convocation for their kind intentions in offering us a serpent when we asked for a fish, though we cannot pretend to believe that serpents are better for us."

The reason why Emily Davies and her committee regarded this offer as "a serpent" is easily understood. If women were to have special examinations and special standards of their own, there was no doubt that these would be regarded as inferior, and would in fact be so. The possibility of testing themselves against the real standards of the world would be gone, and however good the work a woman might do it would inevitably be stamped as "only a woman's," and so would not ever be judged on its merits.

It was, of course, just this possibility that women would test themselves against the ordinary standards of men which those who offered the "serpent" wished to avoid. Not that they feared the competition of women; far from it. What they feared was the effect upon women of the rough jostling with men in the intellectual world. They feared that it would for ever destroy that special and peculiar bloom which they regarded as woman's greatest charm, and take away that valuable, intangible "superiority" of women which they now appeared so unaccountably to be disregarding. Women were, and must be kept as creatures apart, sheltered from the harsher forms of arithmetic, as from the discoveries of medical science, and not allowed to contaminate themselves, even though they wished to do so. They might indeed have a better education than they had hitherto been allowed; it would keep them happy, and would doubtless do them good. But it must stop short of being quite the real thing, for that would be dangerous and unsexing.

This point of view was anathema to Emily Davies, but there were men and women among the advocates of higher education who had no such violent objection to it. They had faith that the result of any kind of improved education would be the demand for more; moreover, they did not wholly approve of the existing system, and believed that it would be wrong to impose an apparently dying classical tradition upon a new set of victims. These were the educationalists proper, who valued learning for its own sake, and who did not subordinate it to any other cause. What they wanted for girls was teaching, and ever more teaching, spread out into wider and wider circles and taking the broadest possible lines of experiment. They felt it right to try everything which offered any hope of improvement, and to reject nothing which seemed to promise any help. These people, therefore, accepted the special women's examination and were not afraid of the consequences. The results must be what they would.

These two ways of thinking were not always incompatible, and the special efforts to which each gave rise went along more or less harmoniously side by side. People who held the one view were often able to support the work of those who held the other, and, though in the innermost heart of the movement the cleavage was well understood, it was not blatantly obvious to the outside world. For the field was distressingly wide, and there was room for all.

When Emily Davies failed to secure the opening of London University to women she was disappointed, but not daunted. If the universities would not help them, then they must help themselves; and she turned her energies and her thoughts towards the planning of a separate college of her own, which was to be truly academic and quite independent, though, if possible, it was to be connected for teaching and for examination purposes with some existing men's university. As early as 1866 this dream had begun to take shape, and in that year she began to talk about it and to begin that cautious "sounding" of suitable supporters which was the first step. As she conceived it, the new college was to be an institution which should provide for young women the same things which Oxford or Cambridge provided for young men. It was to give "instruction and discipline," advanced lectures, and examinations of the Pass Degree and Honours standards. The supervision and control ("just so much as would be practised by a wise mother") was to be in the hands of the Mistress and resident teachers; there were to be active games ("not too violent or straining") and country rambles; the students were to have opportunities for companionship or solitude, each with a small sitting-room to herself, and, as Miss Davies said, "of all the attractions offered by the college life, probably the opportunity for a certain amount of solitude . . . will be the one most welcomed by the real student."

Those to whom she first mentioned this dream were startled "at the magnitude of the enterprise," but, on the whole, people seemed very friendly, and before the end of the year the scheme was concrete enough to be described in a printed pamphlet. In January of 1867 Emily Davies was able to send a full account of her plans to Mme. Bodichon.

"Now that the scheme is about to be brought down from the clouds," she wrote, "it seems necessary to make some sort of a statement about it. . . . The best plan seems to be to have a rather large general committee of distinguished people, to guarantee our SANITY, and an executive to do the work. . . . If we can get Lord Lyttleton, who has the reputation of being rather High Church, to be our chairman, and Lady Goldsmid to be the treasurer, I think the comprehensiveness of the scheme will be pretty well guaranteed. The next question will be how to set about raising the money. We are told that we ought to ask for £30,000 at least. . . . It is not a large sum, considering that there is to be but one college of this sort for Great Britain, Ireland, and the Colonies, and considering how easy it is to raise immense sums for boys' schools. But considering how few people really wish women to be educated, it is a good deal. Everything will depend, I believe, on how we start. If we begin with small subscriptions a low scale will be fixed, and everybody will give in proportion. . . . What we want is a few promises of large sums, to lead other people on. . . . I am anxious that the building should be as beautiful as we can make it. As we cannot have traditions and associations, we shall want to get dignity in every other way that is open to us."

This letter displays Miss Davies' methods and her plans very clearly; but the actual progress was not so fast as she hoped at first. Still, things did move forward. The schoolmistresses in particular were most encouraging. "What they say," wrote Miss Davies, "is that they think the girls will want to come to the College, and that if girls set their hearts upon a thing they can generally persuade their parents." Before long she was able to write to Mme. Bodichon to report progress.

"We had an exciting debate over the College project" (on the Examinations Committee). "Lady Goldsmid, who could not come, wrote to say that she could not make up her mind to take any part at present. She thought we had better wait till the ferment about the franchise is over. Mr Gurney sent word that he could not give his adhesion till he knew more about the domestic arrangements and how the young ladies were to be looked after. Mr Hastings said he would do anything he could do for us, and then went away. (He had an engagement.) . . . Miss Bostock opposed, Mrs Wedgwood hesitated, Mr Tomkinson and Mr Clay were very strongly in favour. Mrs Wedgwood asked whether we thought young women would like to go from home to College, and then our side had to admit that the weak point of our scheme was that the girls would want to come and would hate to go home. . . . Mr Clay and Mr Tomkinson are almost too strong on our side and too determined to make the College a paradise. They insisted that the girls should breakfast in their own rooms (instead of all together like a school), as if the whole thing depended upon it. . . . It was amusing to hear them talk about the examinations. They evidently thought the ordinary degree examinations, which we are going for, rather beneath their notice."

It was not long after this that Miss Davies began to get her general committee together, and she took care that it should include only a minimum of people who were known to be supporters of "Women's Rights." She wanted to put forward only names which "would be likely to win the confidence of ordinary people," and for this reason Mme. Bodichon herself did not at first join the committee. When it was suggested that a number of professors from Cambridge should be added, Miss Davies, who of course welcomed them heartily, could not help regretting their youth. "I suppose," she wrote to Mr Tomkinson, "they are all young men, and our committee is, I am afraid, rather deficient in the due proportion of age and experience. If we could get a few more old ladies like Lady Stanley of Alderley, who has six grown-up daughters and a multitude of grandchildren, they might counterbalance the levity of young Cambridge."

By the end of 1867 this carefully selected general committee had come into being and the small executive had begun to try and collect funds. They had had some success in securing the prominent and dignified people whom Miss Davies thought it so necessary to enlist, but they also had a good many rebuffs. Sir Charles Lyell had objected to a plan which involved young women "entirely quitting the parental roof"; Dr Pusey had "violently opposed" the whole affair, and Mrs Gatty and Miss Charlotte M. Yonge, who might have done so much to make the idea popular, had feared the result "upon the tone and manner of women of such publicity as is proposed." Miss Yonge, indeed, went so far as to say that girls "always hurt one another in manner and tone" if brought together in large numbers; moreover, she said, "superior women will teach themselves, and inferior women will never learn more than enough for home life," so there was no need for anything to be done. George Eliot, on the other hand, welcomed the plan enthusiastically; but then George Eliot's support was of no use in reassuring the public about the absolute respectability of the affair. And, notwithstanding the general committee, the mere idea of a female college was received everywhere, as Lady Augusta Stanley put it, "with shouts." In spite of this, however, the scheme went on and a little money began to come in—not, indeed, the £30,000 Miss Davies had first mentioned, but a little here and a little there, mounting up to a total of £2000 by the summer of 1867. In the autumn of that year Miss Davies read a paper on the college before the Social Science Congress, that familiar starting-point of new enterprises, and the immediate result was an outbreak of ridicule and hostility in those parts of the public Press which liked to raise a good old-fashioned laugh. Other newspapers noticed it too, and with them the respectable committee served a good purpose. As the *Times* said, "The names which have been subscribed for the proposal demand for it at least serious consideration," and the general conclusion seemed to be that since the experiment had been launched it was bound to go on.

During the two years when these preparations were on foot, however, a second set of experiments had been started which aimed at the same object, namely, the provision of university teaching for women, and about 1868 the two schemes began somewhat to clash with and confuse each other. These other efforts centred, not in London, but in the north of England, and they were carried out by those people to whom Miss Davies' old friend "the serpent" was more or less acceptable. The leader of these adventures was Miss Anne Jemima Clough, a lady who in her own way was to be as much the organiser and mainspring of the Higher Education movement as was Miss Emily Davies herself.

Neither Miss Davies nor Miss Clough at all resembled the popular idea of a strong-minded pioneer of women's rights, but Miss Davies had at any rate some of the expected qualities. You could not meet her without feeling the definiteness and the strength of her determination and the hard quality of her will. Miss Clough, on the other hand, gave a completely different impression. At first sight you would think she was a lady who did not know her own mind, though in fact there could not have been a greater mistake. She had plenty of original and interesting schemes, and knew well what she wanted, but she did not care for "causes" or things which seemed doctrinaire, and was not at all anxious to express her views in general terms. She worked for education because she believed in education, not because it was a part of the Women's Movement, and consequently she was more ready to be experimental and to depart from the established tradition than Miss Davies was. Moreover, as she saw the world, it was made up, not of theories or movements, but of individual people for whom she felt acute and almost unlimited sympathy, so that she looked upon what came before her in personal and practical terms. The natural thing, as she saw it, was to interest other people, and to let them make what contributions they could to building up a new enterprise, and she was more apt to put forward her ideas through others, even if they were altered a little in the process, than to insist upon her own way.

Anne Jemima Clough was born in Liverpool in 1820 and spent a good deal of her childhood in America, where her father's business interests took the family. Her family lived at Charleston, in the south, and as they always intended to return to England they had not really taken root there, and the influences of Anne's childhood were in her home circle. When she was sixteen they returned and settled again in Liverpool, and from that time onwards the influence of her brother Arthur was an important factor in her development.

Arthur Clough was one of the favourite pupils of Dr Arnold of Rugby, and he caught up with eagerness the liberalism of the moment. This combined with his own scrupulous sincerity to produce an outlook on life which found a ready sympathy in his sister's mind. "I do believe," she wrote after his early death, "that in secret, unknown places, the foundation-stones of much that is wise and good are still left standing"; and certainly she, who knew and loved him, was able to "build up some goodly structures thereon."

His sister was, however, a very distinct personality, and she worked out her own ideals and transmuted them into efforts which were severely practical. She had no regular intellectual training, and turned for criticism and advice to her brother's greater instructedness; but her opinions were her own, the fruit of her own thinking. She was quiet and apparently diffident, and had not by nature or training any great power of logical or even clear expression; but, like others of her day, she knew from personal experience how great was the need for women to have occupation and education to fit them to do their work in the world, and without often saying so in words she devoted her life to securing these things for them.

During the interval between her girlhood and the beginning of her efforts to set up lectures for ladies in 1866 she had considerable personal experience of teaching. She lived with her parents, first at Liverpool, and later, after her father's death, at Ambleside, and in both places she opened small schools. She did all she could to make herself efficient, and at one time went to London to get training at the Home and Colonial School, and studied educational methods wherever she could. Though she was unmethodical, she was a very stimulating teacher, and took the deepest interest in the work. After her mother's death she came to live in the south, and began to work out schemes for the improvements which her own experience had suggested to her. At this time, between 1862 and 1866, she made the acquaintance of Mme. Bodichon, Miss Emily Davies, and Miss Buss, and others of those who were already at work in this direction, and in March 1866 she was one of the twenty-five ladies who attended the first meeting of the Schoolmistresses'

Association which Miss Davies had founded to break down, if possible, the isolation in which these women were working.

All these things added to her own deep interest, and made Miss Clough think that her most useful contribution might lie in the organisation of education; and in this same year she published a paper in *Macmillan's Magazine*, in which she suggested that there should be a special Board, largely consisting of university men, to regulate the education of girls, and that it should among other methods arrange for lectures in different parts of the country, by university lecturers, for the elder girls and for older women. This idea was, of course, the same that James Stuart put forward a year or so later as regards working men, and it was ultimately embodied in the University Extension movement.

Miss Clough was not content with putting forward her idea on paper, but in 1866 she went back to Liverpool to see if she could not get some of her old friends there to help in carrying it out. The first person she sought out was Mrs Butler, whose husband was at that time Principal of Liverpool College, and both of them were at once interested. Mrs Butler, indeed, was a powerful and delightful supporter, and she and Miss Clough set out to attack the problem of the education of women in the north of England together. The plan they wished to pursue was that of having university lectures for ladies of a regular and systematic kind; but the difficulties seemed almost too formidable to overcome. Neither Miss Clough nor Mrs Butler were in the least daunted by opposition, however, and in the course of the next year they got together a considerable band of people, mostly schoolmistresses, who were ready to join in the new experiment. For simplicity and economy they decided to arrange the same course of lectures for a number of neighbouring towns, so that one lecturer could supply them all, and an organisation called the North of England Council was therefore formed, of which Mrs Butler was president and Miss Clough secretary, to carry out the business and raise the necessary funds.

As in most pioneer movements, the scheme was experimental, and no one knew at first just what would happen. Mr James Stuart, then a young don at Cambridge, agreed to come and lecture on Astronomy in October 1867, and for months beforehand anxious ladies went about the four towns where he was to appear, canvassing schoolmistresses and others, and wondering in their secret hearts whether they would not themselves prove to be the only people who would attend the courses. Their fears were completely unfounded. The lecture-rooms were crowded with five hundred and fifty diligent and interested students; the circulating libraries had to order wholly new consignments of books, and the editions of several scientific works were abruptly sold out. Mr Stuart had proposed to set aside some time after each lecture for the answering of questions, but he found that it was considered to be "improper" for young ladies to ask questions of, or be asked questions by, a young man. He arranged, therefore, to have his questions printed, and offered to correct written answers, and thus, as he put it, "all the dangers attaching to personal intercourse" were avoided. But Mr Stuart had expected at the most to get some thirty sets of answers; he got three hundred, and was hard put to it to get them all corrected in time for the next lecture.[1]

The popularity and success of the lectures need not have surprised anyone, novel as the idea was. For the demand for advanced education was genuine, and these lectures met a real and crying need. They had the advantage over the college scheme that they were available for women who could not possibly undergo a full three years' course away from home, and also that they could be attended by teachers who were already at work. They were therefore easier to develop once the beginning had been made,

[1] *Reminiscences*, by James Stuart.

and they expanded rapidly. So widespread was the demand for them, indeed, that the enterprise presently grew out of all recognition, and before very long it merged into the University Extension Scheme, which included both men and women.

Besides the local lectures the North of England Council struggled to get advanced examinations for its students, and being of those who had no particular fear of Miss Davies' "serpent," they petitioned Cambridge to grant them a special woman's examination suited to the requirements of the students they were instructing. This petition was granted in 1869, and this, too, grew out of its original shape in a very short time. Five years after the woman's examination was established, men candidates were admitted to it, and it became the "Higher Local Examination" and took its place in the scheme of extra-mural teaching which the universities were about to organise and encourage.

This development, however, was not apparent in 1869, when the petition for the woman's examination was granted, and in consequence the whole affair was regarded by Miss Davies with the utmost suspicion. She feared—with some justice—that the local lectures and the women's examinations were drawing away possible support from her college project, and, what was even worse, were prejudicing the claim which she meant to make in the future for women to have degrees.

"I have heard," Miss Davies wrote to a friend, "that (Miss Clough) is pressing the scheme (of a woman's examination) expressly on the ground that it will be specially adapted to women's needs. I have known this all through, but it has not hitherto been necessary to dispute about it. Now, however, the question is being put: Do practical, thoughtful, and working women want degrees and a common standard, or is it only the clamour of a few fanatics and women's rights people? . . . You see it won't do to blow the trumpet with an uncertain sound. It only leads to misunderstandings, and the misunderstandings reappear at Cambridge. . . ." She still feared the serpent's tooth; and when she found that most of her own committee were wobbling in their minds, and inclined to doubt the wisdom of the straight and narrow path of equality, she was a good deal perturbed.

"My impression is that (the woman's examination) will be used as an excuse, but that we shall carry all our points in the long run. In the meantime, it is no doubt doing harm both in absorbing interest and energy and stirring up strife. . . . To have our best friends employed in working a false scheme would be a great injury. People so easily get to love the thing they are working at, and think it the best thing possible. . . ."

Miss Davies, however, had determination and skill enough all by herself to override any number of doubtful colleagues, and before any other movement had grown too strong, or had filched away too many of her followers, she had brought her dreams into practical existence and had called into being a concrete and tangible institution round which to rally their loyalty and support.

Before this could be done, of course, there were long and anxious consultations over finance and over every sort of practical matter, as well as over the conflicting theories. Could they afford to build, and if so, where? Was it possible to take a band of young women and to settle them down in a university town such as Cambridge, without turning the whole place upside down, and bringing the whole scheme of the college to disaster? The more adventurous spirits saw no insuperable difficulties in the way, and nearly all the Cambridge residents on the committee were in favour of making the attempt; but Miss Davies overruled them all. Though she was, perhaps, more ambitious and more confident of ultimate success than any of the others, she was also more anxious to be careful at the outset. It is true that she was ready to claim for the college that it would "aim at no higher position than, say, that of Trinity College" (a degree of humility which, as the *Times* said, could not be considered excessive), but she was also very genuinely afraid of anything which might savour of advanced or unladylike behaviour on the part of the first students. If the new experiment was to succeed—and succeed it must—then the remotest possibility of any social criticism must be avoided. Young ladies who went to college must be at least as carefully guarded and chaperoned as young ladies who stayed at home. "The smallest indiscretion on the part of any student would be disastrous." And in a university town how could indiscretions be avoided? The mere existence of unattached young ladies would seem an indiscretion in the Cambridge of the sixties—that Cambridge where Leslie Stephen could spend all the years of his undergraduate life without speaking a word to any female creature save his bedmaker—where Fellows of colleges had to resign on marriage, and where the intercourse which went on among the professors' ladies and those of the Heads of colleges was ludicrously formal and severe. If they were to try to start in such surroundings, Miss Davies felt, they would be foredoomed to disaster. Parents would never allow their daughters to come, or if they did it would only be on conditions as to supervision and chaperonage which would destroy all freedom and peace. The girls would be beset by invitations, by undergraduates, by worries of every undesirable kind, and their quiet hours of study would be gone. It was not to be thought of for a moment.

Although Miss Davies induced her committee to take this view, she recognised that some connection with Cambridge was necessary, since the lecturers, and if all went well, the examinations and in time the degrees would come from that university, and so she persuaded them to fix upon a site at Hitchin, half-way between London and Cambridge, for the great adventure. In spite of her own desire for a permanent building, however, she had to be content with a hired house, funds being alarmingly low, and Benslow

House was taken and prepared for the opening session of October 1869.

Once more, as at the time of the first Local Examination, Miss Davies had fully completed the preparations and the stage managing of the new venture, and it remained for the unknown young women to provide the substance, the justification, and the success. It was with some anxiety, though with more hope, that Miss Davies now began to correspond with schoolmistresses and with the few isolated candidates of whom she had heard. What would be the motives, and the spirit of the students? And how would they acquit themselves in the ordeal to come? The day when she first encountered "a real girl, who is definitely preparing for college" was a day of great importance.

The prospective students were themselves even more uncertain of what lay before them. Their motives, of course, were not all the same. Some perhaps were moved, as Miss Davies herself was moved, by the desire to improve the conditions of the women who were to come after them; others, of course, were inspired by the love of learning, and by an innate and irresistible mental curiosity. Far more common, however, was the feeling that the existing limitations of their lives were intolerable, and that the college offered a way of escape. Whatever their motives, however, they all faced the same difficulties and problems, and they all reached Hitchin through opposition, discouragement, and ridicule. There were apparently no parents at all, in 1869, who welcomed the idea of sending their daughters to college. Even those who were supporting the plan did not propose to send their own daughters to incur the peculiarity of being female undergraduates, and it was only with the utmost difficulty that the "real girls" materialised at all. "I am more and more impressed with the difficulties of conscience in the way of young women, as I hear more about them," wrote Miss Davies. "They think they ought not to urge their own wishes against those of their parents, who, as

Miss E. says, 'don't see the use of learning such a lot.'" Moreover, the financial difficulty also stood in the way, and though friends of the college offered two scholarships there were many more than two who needed them. In spite of every hindrance, however, twenty-one candidates presented themselves for the entrance examinations, sixteen of whom passed, and six, the maximum number there was room for, were actually admitted. "I have been seeing more of the students," wrote Miss Davies, "and like them much. Those we are sure of are all past twenty, and look like discreet young women. They seem, too, inclined to be good-natured about their accommodation, which is fortunate, as we shall certainly be cramped INSIDE. . . . I get delightful letters from the students. There is not one as to whom there need be the least fear that she would do anything foolish."

This last statement was, perhaps, rather over-optimistic, but at any rate it was with good hopes that the college opened, and that the pioneers took up their residence. The great experiment was begun.

Two years of somewhat difficult and anxious work followed, made anxious not by any unexpected folly of the students, but by the peculiar difficulties of the undertaking. The lecturers, who had to come by train from Cambridge, could not come as often or stay as long as the students wished; they found pupils who were some of them brilliant, and much more mature than the ordinary undergraduate, but who were all of them exceedingly ignorant of the elements of the subjects they wanted to study. It seemed to lecturer and pupil alike that the grind which was necessary to prepare for "Little Go" was almost a waste of time, and Miss Davies had a difficult task in keeping the studies upon the orthodox lines. She had, however, determination enough to control both lecturers and students, and in December 1870, five second-year students were ready for the test of the University Previous Examination.

Here, as usual, a fresh anxiety arose: would the university agree to examine the women? If permission was refused, the whole college would be destroyed; and yet there was no telling what they would do. When the answer came it proved to be of the usual non-committal nature, with which Miss Davies was already familiar; the university said it had no power to examine the women, but that there was no objection to private arrangements being made with the examiners. They, on being applied to, proved to be willing to look over the papers unofficially, and so for the moment all was well—or at least as nearly well as anyone expected. The students—trembling a great deal—and Miss Davies, quite equally nervous, went to Cambridge, and after some days of agony the ordeal was at an end. All five had passed in their Latin and Greek, and the two who had taken mathematics as well had also succeeded. It was a tremendous relief.

The studies were not, however, the only difficult things about the little community at Hitchin, where everything was experimental and new. Miss Davies was not in residence, but she was the governing spirit, and in her determination to make it really collegiate she made some arrangements against which the students were inclined to rebel. There was one fatal day when they gave a theatrical performance of selected scenes from Shakespeare which almost broke up the harmony altogether. Some of them on this occasion dressed as men—and although, of course, there was no audience but themselves, Miss Davies was seriously alarmed. They were breaking out into the foolishness of which she had thought them incapable—and the reputation of the college was at stake.

This terrible matter was composed, after much heart-burning and anxiety, and the students agreed to abandon what they felt to be their rights for the good of the Cause; but the committee began to think that the time for some change in the arrangements had come. The number of students was slowly increasing every year, and the house at Hitchin—even with the addition of some tin huts in the garden—was uncomfortably cramped. Moreover, it was clear from the theatrical outbreak, if from nothing else, that the students needed more outside interests and more contact with the world than was possible with the college as it was. And the question of building was again revived. As before, a strong and united effort was made to persuade Miss Davies to agree to moving into Cambridge, and as before, she stood like a rock against it. The expense and inconvenience of being so far away were, however, exceedingly strong arguments, and after prolonged discussion a sort of compromise was reached and land was bought at Girton, two miles from Cambridge, where, although funds were deplorably low, building was at once begun.

In 1870, when this decision was taken, two miles seemed a considerable distance. It was enough, Miss Davies believed, to give the necessary feeling of safety to parents, though it was not so much as to be a hindrance in matters of lectures and work. It was still true to say that the college was not in Cambridge; and yet it was near enough to provide the modified contact with university life which the students seemed to require. Everything, therefore, was satisfactory except the funds, which came in very slowly. However, Miss Davies wrote and spoke and pleaded, and finally a loan was raised in order that the start might be made. And meanwhile the students remained cramped rather uncomfortably in Benslow House, awaiting their new college buildings.

While this infant college was fighting its way, and while Miss Davies was striving to stamp her ideals and her purposes quite clearly upon it, there came an important development from the other camp of educationalists. The local lectures were flourishing and were much in demand, and Mr Henry Sidgwick, who was one of their firmest friends, conceived the idea that Cambridge itself ought to be one of the centres in which these lectures should be given. There were young women in Cambridge, he noticed, just as much as in Leeds or Liverpool; and for them lectures would be very easily procured. In 1869, therefore, he asked Mrs Fawcett, who was then living in Cambridge, whether a discussion on this project might take place in her house. Both she and her husband were of course delighted with this plan, and accordingly it was in their drawing-room that the first arrangements were made. When the tea came in there came also their little daughter, Philippa, who trotted about among the guests and said nothing; and no one realised that they were at that moment founding a college, and that in course of time that little girl would herself achieve one of its brightest and most resounding triumphs.

The scheme for local lectures in Cambridge was immediately popular, and they began in the Lent term of 1870, just one term after the college at Hitchin had been opened. Eighty ladies attended the first courses, and before the end of the year others from a distance were asking if they also might be admitted.

Several friends of the movement, including John Stuart Mill and Helen Taylor, subscribed money to give scholarships to these girls, but the problem of how they were to be lodged was a difficult one. A hall of residence was considered, but as there was no money available to open it the Lectures Committee did not think it feasible, and for the moment nothing was done. Every term, however, the applications for admission to the lectures increased, and by the autumn term of 1870, three girls actually came to Cambridge and were lodged with friends in order that they might attend the lectures. The demand still grew, and in the summer of 1871 Henry Sidgwick decided, upon his own responsibility, to make some provision in Cambridge for the accommodation of the students. He gave up his own summer holiday, and with the money so saved he took a small house in the town, over which he persuaded Miss

Clough to preside, and in which, in the autumn term, five students were received; and in this small and unpretentious fashion Newnham College began.

The house was crowded and uncomfortable, and the living was very plain indeed. The students did some of the housework, and had but one sitting-room between them. They had no garden, and of course no games, and the only things which were pleasant to them were the work —for which they had come—and the friendly intercourse with the band of lecturers and helpers which had gathered about the Cause. These, though real pleasures, were solemn ones for young people at the best, and even in regard to these they were severely restricted. For Miss Clough, conscious of all the criticism and hostility which was directed against the experiment, was rather overwhelmingly careful of their manners and behaviour. They had to be met at the station when they arrived, and seen off when they left— this, of course, was only to be expected if young ladies were to travel alone at all; and all the time between arrival and departure they had to be carefully chaperoned. At lectures, Miss Clough, or some other devoted lady, had to sit patiently knitting, and all their social invitations had to be most carefully supervised. They were, in short, hedged in with excessive "womanliness" against which some of them were inclined to rebel. But they were enthusiastic for their work, and they understood that they were pioneers upon whose success the future might depend; and they were, after all, of the generation when young women expected little personal freedom; and so, in spite of some friction, and much anxiety, nothing went wrong, and their "discretion" was completely vindicated. The presence of a small collection of young women students in Cambridge did nothing either to cause a scandal or to disrupt the university, and all was well.

By the next autumn term the number of students had doubled, and a charming old house on "the Backs" was found, in which they were much more comfortably installed. There, with a garden, and with the variety which space and larger numbers ensured, a collegiate atmosphere began to grow up of its own accord. The restrictions in regard to intercourse with Cambridge were of course maintained, and Miss Clough still tried anxiously to persuade the students to modify any eccentricity of dress or behaviour; but, in their happiness and their new interests, they could bear these things better. The numbers still increased, and in the next year, although a second house holding seven more was taken, there were still a large number to be accommodated with friends in the town.

It was clear that further expansion was again required, and in 1874 the decision to build at Newnham was reached.

Before this was done, however, Mr Sidgwick had made an approach to Miss Davies, and when the move from Hitchin was being discussed by the College Committee, he had suggested the amalgamation of the two schemes. The old difference of principle, however, still stood in the way. Miss Davies still feared the "serpent" as much as ever, and the Cambridge group could not agree to her terms. They despised and opposed both the compulsory Greek of the Little Go and the existing Pass Degree Examinations for men, and they could not consent to see them fastened upon women; moreover, they thought it only reasonable, in these early days, to encourage special arrangements and special courses for exceptional girls. They did not insist upon the strict limitation of the length of time spent in college before the final examination (in which matter Miss Davies always carefully adhered to the university rule). Their feeling was that, with students so untaught, a longer course of preparation was perfectly legitimate, and in the case of girls knowing no Latin or Greek, and yet aiming at a Classical Tripos, it was positively essential. They also freely admitted students who were working for no Tripos at all, so long as their work, even if it cut across the orthodox lines, was good in itself, and profitable to the student, and they were prepared to take students for a year or even less. The differences of outlook were thus wide and profound, and neither side could conscientiously compromise. "I am sure it is generous inconsistency," wrote Miss Davies to Professor Sidgwick, "and not cruel mockery that makes you say you are willing to help us, when your scheme is the serpent which is gnawing at our vitals. It glides in everywhere. As soon as any interest is awakened, people are told there is something else, as good or better, and which does not ask for money. I daresay it does not end in their doing much for the lectures, but it is enough to hold them back from doing anything for the college. We meet this hindrance at every step, and lately it has seemed to me that it bids fair to crush us. However, we are not going to give in yet."

So the two colleges went their separate ways, interfering with each other, indeed, in so far as they made calls upon the generosity and help of the same people, but helping each other in reality. For the lecture scheme rapidly increased the supply of teachers for the schools, and the schools sent pupils to the college; and the college in its turn opened the way to the regular university course. There was indeed ample demand, and ample room for both.

While these material developments of the two schemes were taking place, the central question of the Tripos Examinations came up for decision. The first students from Hitchin, who had taken their Little Go at the end of 1870, were hoping to take their Finals in the summer of 1873, and, in preparation for this event, some friendly members of the university brought a Grace forward in the Senate, proposing that the Tripos Examination should be formally opened to women. This, however, was rejected, and it became doubtful whether, in the face of it, the girls could be examined at all. Much anxious and difficult correspondence ensued, at the end of which Miss Davies, by mingled firmness, conciliation, and argument, secured the same limited sanction which had been given to the Little Go, namely, the permission to hold a private examination on the same papers, and to make unofficial arrangements with the examiners for the marking of the results. The whole thing was precarious in the extreme, and depended on the goodwill of the individual examiners; and up to almost the last moment the college authorities were not sure that their candidates might sit. However, the students went on with their preparations, suffering every kind of agony of nervousness and apprehension, and well aware that the attention of the whole country would be turned upon the results. There were only three of these girls, Miss Woodhead, who was taking the Mathematical Tripos, and Miss Cook and Miss Lumsden, who were doing Classics. The last had only succeeded in clearing the Previous Examination out of the way that same year, and consequently had had practically no time to specialise; but, nevertheless, her teachers thought she might venture on the trial. Her description of the occasion reveals some of its terrors.

"How well I remember the first morning at the University Arms. We settled down in our sitting-room, pen in hand, expectant of the paper, while Miss Davies knitted away steadily by the fire. I can hear the click of her needles still! But minute after minute slipped away and still, until a whole hour had gone by, no paper came.

"Miss Davies said nothing, but she must have despaired, for she knew, though she had considerately hidden it from us, that some of the examiners were dead against admitting us to the examination at all. For my part I grew desperate —had the examiners at the eleventh hour refused the paper? When at last the messenger came, he had, it appeared, been sent first to a wrong address. My nerves were all in a quiver and work was almost impossible. . . . That morning was the worst bit of the week, and it settled my class, a Third, while Miss Cook took a Second."

Miss Woodhead also took a Second, and with this success the aptitude of women for higher education seemed at last to be established. It was true that the arrangements at Cambridge were unofficial, and that no degrees were available, but a precedent had been secured, and there was good reason to hope that further progress would follow. The Cambridge Local Examinations, after being unofficially allowed, had been regularised, and with every year they were growing more popular. It was, therefore, natural to suppose that the higher examinations would follow the same course, and after this date both Girton and Newnham felt free to expand as rapidly as their funds allowed in order to provide for the ever-increasing stream of eager students.

CHAPTER IX

WOMEN DOCTORS. 1858–1873

Elizabeth Blackwell lectures in London, 1858—Elizabeth Garrett decides to be a doctor—Her early difficulties—Secures qualification by Apothecaries' Examination in 1865—All British qualifications now carefully closed against women, and foreign degrees not recognised for the British Medical Register—Sophia Jex-Blake determines to break this down—Goes to Edinburgh, 1869—The prolonged struggle with the university—The Hope Scholarship—The Riot at Surgeons' Hall—The libel action—The case between the Senatus and the women, and the victory of the women—Sophia Jex-Blake fails in her examination—The loss of the Appeal Case—Difficulties of medical students abroad.

CLOSELY related to the movement to secure university education for women was the still harder fight to secure medical education; and the two struggles went on simultaneously. Each, as they proceeded, reacted to some extent upon the other, and of course each drew upon the enthusiasm of the same friends; nevertheless the two things were distinct and separate. It was quite possible for people to approve of the colleges and to abhor the idea of women doctors, and many actually took this line. The opposite course, namely, approving of the doctors but not of the colleges, was hardly possible, and thus it is evident that the medical women had the harder and the lonelier road.

Not only were their friends fewer, but the opposition they met was fiercer. The vested interests of a lucrative profession were even more obstinate than the hoary traditions of ancient universities, and the bold women who first attacked them had a dangerous and difficult task. Moreover, the public, which is the ultimate arbiter in all attacks upon social custom, was much harder to move in this case than in any other. The idea of women doctors was revolting to every sense; it was indecent, dangerous, and brazen, as well as new; and it is therefore no wonder that progress was slow.

Although there had been medical women in several European countries in the Middle Ages, the idea was a completely unfamiliar one in Victorian England, and the first person to bring it into prominence was Elizabeth Blackwell. This pioneer was born in Bristol in 1821, but she was taken to America as a child and found her vocation and her training there. The story of her medical education, and of her early struggles and difficulties, is charmingly told in her autobiography,[1] but since it deals with the American rather than the English movement, it must not be repeated here. A sentence or two, however, may well be quoted from one of her letters, for they give a glimpse of the prospect which lay before those who first entered upon this great career, and mark the wide gulf which lies between the first women medical students and their successors of to-day.

"I understand why this life has never been lived before," she wrote. "It *is* hard, with no support but a high purpose, to live against every species of social opposition. . . . I *should* like a little fun now and then. Life is altogether too sober."

Elizabeth got her degree in America in 1849, and then came at once to Europe where she studied, with varying fortunes, in London and Paris. In London she was on the whole very well treated, and found a number of medical men ready to help her, among them Mr (afterwards Sir James) Paget. She obtained permission to study at St Bartholomew's and was admitted to lectures and welcomed in many directions. Among others, Barbara Leigh Smith and her friend Bessie Parkes sought her out, and through the friendship which naturally sprang up between them she

[1] *Pioneer Work in Opening the Medical Profession to Women,* by Elizabeth Blackwell.

gained admittance to all sorts of interesting circles, meeting Lady Byron, Mrs Jameson, and the Russell Gurneys, for example, as well as scientists like Faraday and the Herschells. At this time, too, she made friends with Florence Nightingale, and more than once she stayed with her at Embley. When in town Florence often came, escorted by her attendant footman, to call upon her in her London lodgings, and the two would sit over the fire discussing life and work and medicine; and it was to Elizabeth Blackwell that young Florence Nightingale confided her hopes and ambitions.

While Florence was wearing through her last years of young ladyhood at home, Elizabeth was back in New York opening a dispensary and gaining experience. But she left behind her in England an idea which was soon to have important developments.

At the moment, however, things looked most unpromising. The ordinary public naturally supposed that women doctors would be odious, unsexed creatures, and even among the more enlightened friends of the woman's cause there were doubts. Frederick Maurice felt it was necessary to dissociate himself and his work at Queen's College from the suspicion of approving of Miss Blackwell. In his *Lectures to Ladies on Practical Subjects*, in 1855, he took care to make this quite clear.

"I hope, by this language, I have guarded myself," he said, "against the suspicion that I would educate ladies for the kind of tasks which belong to OUR professions. In America some are maintaining that they should take degrees and practise as physicians. I not only do not see my way to such a result; I not only should not think that any college I was concerned in should be leading to it; but I should think there could be no better reason for founding a college than to remove the slightest craving for such a state of things, by giving a more healthful direction to minds which might entertain it. The more pains we take to call forth and employ the faculties which belong characteristically to each sex, the less it will be intruding upon the province which, not the conventions of the world, but the will of God, has assigned to the other."

It is probably safe to assume that there were a good many ladies in his audience who did not look upon education as a safety-valve to prevent women from wishing to intrude upon "our professions," and who saw the will of God in an exactly opposite light. But they were doubtless too well behaved to cry "shame," and too grateful for all the good help which Maurice had given them to do other than let this monstrous sentiment pass; and he himself changed his view before long and became one of the supporters of the medical women's agitation. But in 1855 the time for agitating the question of women doctors had not quite come, and the interest in the subject which Miss Blackwell's visit created died down.

Three years later, however, Dr Elizabeth Blackwell returned to London, and her name was placed upon the British Medical Register in 1859.

This was almost the latest moment when it could be placed there, for in the following year the medical profession secured a new charter under which it was empowered to exclude from the British Medical Register all holders of foreign degrees. Thereafter the only legally qualified practitioners would be those whose degrees were British degrees; and Elizabeth Blackwell, with her American and Paris diplomas, would not have been admitted.

This new charter was not aimed at the exclusion of women doctors—who at that time would hardly have seemed worth so much attention; but it had a serious effect upon their progress none the less. For although it was possible for women to study medicine and to qualify in France, Belgium, Switzerland, Italy, and Spain, as well as in some of the medical schools in the United States, the new law rendered these opportunities useless to British women. The only way in which another woman could join Elizabeth

Blackwell as a doctor qualified to practise in Great Britain was by the opening of one of the British schools and one of the British degrees to women.

The bearing of this new law upon the women's cause was not immediately apparent, for the extent of the exclusion of women from British examinations had not yet been tested, and public opinion seemed so much less antagonistic that Dr Blackwell and her friends felt a little more confident than they had felt when she was in England ten years before.

Encouraged and supported by Mrs Jameson, whose own two lectures on the Women's Movement had been so successful, Miss Blackwell ventured to give a series of public lectures on the suitability of the medical profession for women.

"My warm friends, the Misses Leigh Smith, supported by their generous-hearted father," she wrote, "and Miss Bessie Rayner Parkes, interested themselves actively in preparing for the first delivery of my lectures. The Marylebone Hall was secured. Our young friends brought up primroses and other lovely flowers and green wreaths from Hastings to ornament the reading desk, and warmly supported me by their ardent sympathy. On 2nd March 1859 the first lecture was given to an intelligent and appreciative audience, whose interest was warmly enlisted. I well remember the tears rolling down the benevolent face of Miss Anna Goldsmid, who sat immediately in front of me. But the most important listener was the bright intelligent young lady whose interest in the study of medicine was then aroused—Miss Elizabeth Garrett."

It was one thing for Elizabeth Garrett to decide to become a doctor, and quite another to find the way to do it. She had not, indeed, the usual number of home difficulties to overcome. Her father helped and encouraged her in every way possible, and found all the money she needed, but the world outside, in which there was only one American precedent, was very unfriendly. Though she applied to all the hospitals and canvassed all the schools and examining bodies, she found no regular door of entry, and thus the importance of the new charter began to be apparent. Elizabeth was undiscouraged, and in 1860 she went to the Middlesex Hospital as a nurse, hoping both to learn a little, and to prove to the many who doubted her that she could stand the sustained and unpleasant work.

The authorities of the hospital were inclined to treat her request for teaching with amused contempt, but they let her come and do what she could. "I feel so mean trying to come over the doctors by all kinds of feminine dodges," she wrote to Emily Davies, but in a good cause perhaps it was lawful; and at any rate the "dodges," or her quiet perseverance, succeeded, so that she gradually won a way to the lectures, and even to the dissecting-room.

Then, however, her troubles began, for she worked too earnestly and got on too well, and in one fatal examination she won the best marks. This lack of tact resulted in a memorial against her from the male students, and thereafter her attendance at lectures was stopped. Other hospitals to which she applied gave the same refusal, so Elizabeth gave up that line of advance and tried once more to secure teaching outside. The first necessity was to find an examining body which would give her a licence to practise, and at last, after trying them all, she discovered that the Society of Apothecaries was, by the terms of its charter, legally unable to refuse her. Although this was the least satisfactory way of entering the profession, it was at any rate a real licence, and Elizabeth decided to obtain it, hoping, however, at the same time to matriculate at London University so as to be qualified, if the chance ever came, to sit for a full M.D. degree. She worked away, therefore, at her general subjects, but that was of no avail. London University would not let her matriculate because she was a woman. Their new charter was interpreted against admitting women, and although Emily Davies collected memorials signed by Gladstone, Cobden, F. D. Maurice, Mrs Somerville and many more, the authorities would not give way; and so in 1865 Elizabeth Garrett gave up the hope of matriculating and sat for and passed the easy Apothecaries' Examination.

"Two of the examiners told Mr C. that it was a mercy they did not put the names in order of merit," Elizabeth wrote to Emily when it was over, "as in this case they *must* have put me first." It was a mercy, indeed!

Elizabeth was now qualified to practise, and opened a small dispensary for women and children in London, but also decided, with her father's support, to secure a better degree abroad. She obtained permission to sit for the Paris M.D. diploma without living in Paris, and so she set to work to prepare herself. "It is not very easy to work up for examinations amid the distractions of practical work. I am giving up all society in order to keep the evenings free for work, and this saves both time and energy," she wrote to Helen Taylor in 1868, and a year later she had her reward.

"I think you will be glad to know that I passed the second of the Paris examinations this day week," she wrote in June. "The subjects were surgery and pathology. Each candidate had to perform two operations before the judges and a crowd of spectators, and then to go through a long *viva voce* examination. Two men were examined with me. One of them passed in the *bien satisfait* class, as I did, the other was three degrees lower, in the *passable*. I can do no more till November, as there is a long vacation, but I shall be ready then for the third and fourth, and I hope also with the thesis in the interval. I have chosen 'Headache' as its subject. I had to find a subject which could be well studied without post-mortem observations, of which I naturally can have but very few in either private or dispensary practice; and I wished also to take a *large* subject, one that demanded some insight into the harmony which exists between the main physiological functions."

Elizabeth Garrett succeeded in the third and fourth examinations and her thesis was approved, so that by 1869 she had qualified for and had received the Paris M.D. degree, and, in virtue not of this but of her Apothecaries' license, had put her name upon the British Medical Register.

All through the prolonged effort which led to this result, Emily Davies had been Elizabeth Garrett's prime counsellor. She had organised the attack on London University, and had done everything that a friend could to help her on her way. She had kept a stern eye, too, upon Elizabeth's behaviour, and more than once she had remonstrated with her upon the "levity" of her conduct! "It is true," she wrote to the newly-fledged M.D. in 1870, "that your jokes are many and reckless. They do more harm than you know."

The need for appearing at all times intensely solemn and conventional weighed heavily upon all these adventurous young women. By nature they were more inclined to hate the restraints of the time than any of their contemporaries, but they well knew that if they wanted to gain their wider ends they must give way on smaller matters of dress and behaviour, and they were constantly trying to keep each other within bounds. Elizabeth Garrett, in spite of her own reprehensible tendency to make jokes, worried over the way some of the other medical students dressed. "I do wish the Ds. dressed better," she wrote to Emily. "She looks so awfully strong-minded in walking dress . . . she has short petticoats and a close round hat and several dreadfully ugly arrangements. . . . It is abominable, and most damaging to the cause."

Important as the matter of outward observance undoubtedly was, it was presumably not the way the women students dressed which caused the English Medical Schools to take fright, as they did after Elizabeth had secured her Paris degree. Their mere existence was enough for the purpose; and when it was found that four other young women had passed the preliminary examination of the

Apothecaries' Society in 1867, this had seemed so ominous that steps were taken to put a stop to the invasion, so that by the time they were ready to qualify it had been made legally impossible. Elizabeth Blackwell and Elizabeth Garrett were thus the only two women on the British Medical Register, and seemed likely to be the only two there ever would be. For every British door was shut and the foreign examinations led nowhere.

The position seemed almost hopeless. There were a number of other young women who had embarked on the same course, but their chances of a British qualification were gone. They could still, indeed, obtain degrees in France, Germany, Italy, Switzerland (where there were no women native to the country who wanted them), but it would do them no good when they came home. Several of them, however, pursued this course, and in the early sixties learnt their profession abroad and returned to England to practise, in spite of having no licence, and to press their claims. But it was a thoroughly unsatisfactory position for them to be in.

Another parallel effort was made about the same time to establish a women's school for obstetrics only. The Feminine Medical Societies which were started in London, Edinburgh, and Birmingham backed this plan. They officially disowned the movement for full qualifications for women, and urged only that midwives should be properly trained and women "accoucheuses" given an opportunity to practise. A few of the supporters of the women doctors' movement approved this plan, hoping to pass on from training in gynæcology to the full degree; but the majority of them greatly distrusted any half-way measure, and Florence Nightingale herself, though not particularly sympathetic towards women doctors, objected to the proposed obstetrical training as not being of sufficiently high standard.

This movement came to nothing, therefore, and the deadlock about women doctors continued. Elizabeth

Garrett's success, however, and the agitation which was never allowed to die away, had brought some fresh champions into the field. The two existing regular women doctors carried on their work, and proved in practice what women could do, and before very many years had gone by the effort to obtain qualification was again renewed.

This second fight began in the year when the college at Hitchin was first opened, and the champion who arose to lead it was Sophia Jex-Blake.

This remarkable woman was born in 1840, and even as a child was stormy, tumultuous, and unmanageable. In 1858 she went to Queen's College, where she became a lecturer in mathematics in the following year. At this time she fell in with the band of earnest philanthropists which gathered round Frederick Maurice, and she had no thoughts of studying medicine. Education was her life's work, she felt; she would qualify as no other woman had yet qualified, and have a school better than any yet known. She threw herself into the task, spent a year in Germany teaching there, and then set off alone for the United States to study the schools and colleges in that country. This journey, however, altered her plans, for in Boston she fell in with Dr Lucy Sewell, one of Elizabeth Blackwell's early followers, who had opened a dispensary for women and children in that town. Sophia was quickly admitted to intimacy in the young doctor's household, and as she watched the work and helped with the accounts and organisation she became enthusiastic. With her parents' consent, therefore, she determined to study medicine for herself, and settled in New York, where Dr Elizabeth Blackwell undertook to help her on her way. She had hardly started her studies, however, when her father died; and at once Sophia hurried back, abandoning her prospects and her friends at the call of her mother and her home.

Sophia might abandon her prospects, but she could not abandon her work; almost at once she began her assault upon the entrenched fortress of the medical profession in her own country.

The first thing, of course, was to settle upon the most likely university, and in the inquiry she now made she found many helpers. Dr Sidgwick of Cambridge, Mrs Butler of Liverpool, and most of the other supporters of the Higher Education movement were interested in her plans, and with their help she investigated the lie of the land "to see if I can poke in anywhere." The most favourable —or perhaps least hostile—place seemed to be Edinburgh, where Professor Masson offered very strong support, and in March 1869 a resolute if rather anxious young woman set out, entirely alone, to conquer an absolutely strange town and its ancient seat of learning.

At first she seemed to the authorities harmless and quiet enough. An educated, self-possessed young woman, with a clear knowledge of what she wanted, an agreeable low voice and dark hair—there seemed nothing very ominous about her. She wanted rather an odd thing, namely, permission to attend the lectures given to medical students; but she would soon tire of that; and one by one the majority of the medical professors capitulated, and the permission she sought was obtained.

Her troubles, however, were now begun, for the constitution of Edinburgh University was a complex affair, and at least three superior authorities had power to reverse the decision. The first of these, namely, the Senatus, actually endorsed it in 1859; but the University Court, acting on an appeal sent up by the students, reversed it, being, as they said, unwilling to make a temporary arrangement in the interest of one lady.

This set-back was only temporary. No sooner were the facts known than other students came forward, the first to come being Mrs Isabel Thorne and Miss Edith Peachey. These students approached their task with great seriousness and humility.

"I should like to feel sure of success," wrote Miss Peachey, "not on my own account, but I feel that failures now would do harm to the Cause, and that it is well that at least the first few women . . . should stand above the average of men in their examinations. Do you think anything more is requisite to success than moderate abilities and a good share of perseverance? I believe I may lay claim to these, together with a real love of the subjects of study, but as regards any thorough knowledge of those subjects at present, I fear I am deficient in most. I am afraid I should not without a good deal of previous study be able to pass the preliminary exam. you mention, as my knowledge of Latin is small and Euclid still less. Still, if no very extensive knowledge of these is required (and doctors generally seem to know very little of them) I could perhaps be ready by the next examination, and the study of Carpenter at the same time would perhaps be a relaxation. . . . I shall be sorry if my means will not allow me to take a full share of the expenses, but I am afraid I shall not be able to afford more than double the usual fees for a man."

Encouraged by such letters, Sophia Jex-Blake proposed to organise separate classes for the women students, undertaking to pay the university lecturers whatever was required to compensate for the double toil, and she asked the University Court whether, if she did this, they would allow the women students to matriculate and sit for the Degree Examination.

In October 1869 this request was granted, subject only to the university being held to have the legal power to accept women students, and, in great jubilation, five young women set to work on their Latin and their Euclid in preparation for matriculation. All five passed successfully, and a winter of real work followed, enough friendly teachers and lecturers having been found to provide the necessary instruction.

All went well until in March Miss Peachey of the

"moderate abilities and good share of perseverance" committed the same error of tact that Elizabeth Garrett had committed at the Middlesex Hospital. When the class examinations were held she came out third in the list, the two above her being second-year men. This error might have passed unnoticed, had it not been that a scholarship which gave free use of the university laboratory was attached to the first three places. To Miss Peachey—whose opportunities of using any laboratory at all were severely limited—the privilege would have meant a great deal. To the university apparently it would have been destruction, and in the event she was passed over and the scholarship given to the man below her on the list.

This matter was an exciting piece of news for the papers, and a perfect storm of controversy arose, not only in Scotland, but all over England as well. Public opinion was almost solidly in favour of the young lady, but this, in its way, did a great deal of harm. For the university, blamed on every hand, began to wish the young ladies elsewhere, and to regret the day when they had opened their door so much as an inch.

The young ladies, it must be admitted, enjoyed the situation, and it was well that they could have some pleasure, for there were storms ahead.

One full year of study had gone by and the more or less harmless preliminary work had been mastered, and now the heart of the difficulty, namely, the anatomy class and the practical work in the Infirmary, lay before them. To the first of these they were admitted, but over the second a whole series of difficulties arose. Their application had to be considered by the managers, and for some time the decision was in doubt, the majorities being so narrow that the vote swung backwards and forwards several times. While the controversy aroused by this application was going on the men students organised a petition against the women, and with this added "argument" the pendulum swung finally against them.

Delighted by the success of this intervention, the students now decided to drive the women out of the anatomy classes too, and it was widely believed that their intervention was directly instigated by those of their medical teachers who objected to the idea of female doctors.

However that may have been, the students only too eagerly seized on the chance of a "rag," and on the 18th of November 1870 the "Riot at Surgeons' Hall" took place.

The object of the young gentlemen was to prevent the ladies from entering the building. They massed up in the street at the hour of the lecture, and when their five opponents appeared they began to sing and shout and jostle and throw mud, and finally they slammed the great doors of the courtyard in their faces. The young ladies—whatever their feelings might have been—preserved a perfectly calm demeanour, and made as if they noticed nothing whatever. They walked quietly forward to the gates, in which presently the janitor succeeded in opening a small door, and they passed through and into their class-room without a word.

Inside, as well as outside, pandemonium reigned. The class-room was full of noise, and it was long before the professor succeeded in turning out of it a band of intruders, who had forced their way in. He had hardly achieved this, and began to lecture, moreover, before the door opened again, and a sheep was pushed hastily in, with shouts and laughter from outside. "Let it stay," said the angry professor, "it has more sense than those who sent it here"; and the demonstration went forward, though it is doubtful if the women students were able to summon for it the attention they normally commanded, even though Sophia Jex-Blake noted in her diary that "we passed rather a good examination."

When it was over the professor urged the young women to go away by the back door, but this they refused, and, escorted now by a band of friendly young men, as well as by a howling mob, the police, and a horde of street urchins, they walked silently home.

This affair, even more than that of the Hope Scholarship, brought public sympathy to the ladies and discredit upon the university. The students gained nothing when they explained the sheep incident by saying that they understood the inferior animals were not to be excluded, and feeling now began to run very high. As they walked through the streets the women students had to face annoyance for months to come. They were followed by groups of offensive young men who shouted foul abuse at them, sometimes "using medical terms to make the disgusting purport of their language more intelligible,"[1] but the distress which this caused them only drove them more seriously than ever to their work. "Each fresh insult is an added incentive to finish the work begun," Miss Peachey wrote. "I began the study of medicine merely from personal motives; now I am also impelled by the desire to remove women from the care of such young ruffians." The will to disregard these troubles was with them all, and the strength to ignore them; but their suffering was great. For, advanced and self-reliant as they all were, they were still young women of their date and period. Thirty years later one of them confessed that she would still walk miles out of her way rather than pass the gates of Surgeons' Hall, for the shame and the humiliation were with her still.

The next step after this commotion was another attempt to secure admission to the Infirmary. An election of managers was to take place, and a list favourable to the women had been put forward. Sophia Jex-Blake, in common with the other subscribers to the institution, attended to elect them, and, in common with others, she claimed her right to speak.

She spoke well, with her clear voice and her brave carriage, but she did not speak wisely. The hindrance, the insults,

[1] Letter from Miss Peachey to *Scotsman*, 2nd July 1870.

and the opposition had bitten too deeply, and she committed the error of allowing her indignation to be seen. "I will not say that the rioters were acting under orders, but . . . this I do know, that the riot was not wholly or mainly due to the students at Surgeons' Hall. I know that Dr Christison's class assistant was one of the leading rioters, and the foul language he used could only be excused on the supposition I heard, that he was intoxicated. I do not say that Dr Christison knew of or sanctioned his presence, but I do say that I think he would not have been there had he thought the doctor would have strongly objected to his presence."

Dr Christison at once rose up. ". . . I appeal to you, My Lord, whether language such as this is to be allowed in the mouth of any person. I am perfectly sure that there is not one gentleman in the whole assembly who would have used such language in regard to an absentee. . . . I wish that this foul language shall be put an end to." The Lord Provost did not consider that foul language had been used, but requested Miss Jex-Blake to withdraw the word "intoxicated." Miss Jex-Blake was quite ready for this. "I said it was the only excuse for his conduct. If Dr Christison prefers that I should say he used the language when sober, I will withdraw the other supposition."

All this, however, although it relieved the feelings, did not advance the cause: the favourable managers were not elected, the women's application was twice again refused, and, to cap it all, Dr Christison's assistant brought an action for libel.

The case came on in May 1871, but owing to the legal advice she had received, Sophia Jex-Blake did not plead justification. All evidence tending to prove the presence of the assistant at the riot was therefore disallowed, and the jury found her guilty, but with damages of one farthing only. To this, however, the judge added the costs, which amounted to nearly £1000, and although it afterwards transpired that the jury had expressly intended to free her from costs by their verdict, she was left with this heavy bill to meet.

Friends, however, sprang up on every side to help her, and money came in by small and by large amounts from total strangers in all parts of England and Scotland, so that in a very short time more than enough was subscribed.

Public sympathy and support were all very well, but the actual crux of the affair, namely, the position in the university, was going backward. The first Professional Examination was now in sight, and according to the technical regulations the women who had been allowed to attend only the "extra-mural" or private classes were not qualified to sit for it. A petition to the Senatus to waive this irregularity was refused, on the ground that there was no legal power to set it aside; and on the very day before the examination was to take place the fees were returned to the young women, and they were told they might not sit. Sophia Jex-Blake, in spite of the storm she had just come through, was undaunted. She sent a solicitor's letter to intimidate the Dean, threatening him with a personal action for damages, which caused him to give way under protest. It was in this atmosphere that the three of them sat down to their papers—and all three passed!

Troubles of a different kind then fell upon the little band of students, for to the despair of their leader no less than three of the five became engaged to be married in the same autumn of 1871; and although two of these returned later to their chosen profession, the interruption was a sore blow. Three new recruits appeared at the same time, but these, although immensely welcome, introduced a new complication. For now two sets of private classes had to be arranged and paid for, and a threefold fight undertaken: for matriculation, for the first Professional Examination, and for the right to work in the hospital.

Matters looked so unhopeful at Edinburgh that Sophia Jex-Blake thought of trying again at other universities, and the anxious canvassing of chances began once more. However, after another prolonged struggle with the Infirmary managers, in which the votes were scrutinised several times, and appeals to legal powers were plentifully made, the coveted permission was granted, and the remainder of the first set of students were actually admitted to the Infirmary in December 1872.

The first Graduation Examinations now came in sight, and a formal appeal was sent in to the Senatus, which kindly replied that it was willing to offer the ladies a "certificate of proficiency" but had no power to give them a degree. As they could not practice medicine on a "certificate of proficiency," the offer was merely derisory; but the women, with the wisdom of their bitter experience, offered to waive the question of graduation, pending an appeal to the courts, provided arrangements for their regular instruction and examination might go forward, and this proposal was accepted.

They then, on their own initiative, took the legal steps necessary to settle the disputed point, and the case came on in July 1872, judgment being given for the women.

The Senatus appealed against it, and matters were in that state when the autumn examinations again came round.

It was Sophia Jex-Blake upon whom fell the whole brunt of presenting the case, as well as of arranging the lectures, raising the fees, and organising what university support was to be had. Her days and nights were filled with anxiety and toil, her thoughts were occupied with petitions, legal precedents, and all the intricate technicalities of her task. Nevertheless, she felt she could postpone her examination no longer, and sat for it in October of that year. And when the results came out she had failed.

To the medical student of to-day a few failures seem almost an inevitable part of the arduous task of getting qualified; but to the pioneers of the early years failure was a dreadful thing. It seemed almost a crushing blow, and was all the worse in this case because Sophia could not believe her papers had been fairly judged. But whatever the setbacks, her purpose held firm.

Curiously enough this failure in the examination, which of course obtained a wide publicity, acted as a spur to the movement. Her friends rallied round her closer than ever, and one of them, Agnes M'Laren, a niece of John Bright, who had hitherto devoted her energies to suffrage work, now decided to throw in her lot with the medical students.

The appeal meanwhile was pending, but matters did not look very hopeful, and the weary search for other possibilities went on. They tried once more at Newcastle, Durham, Birmingham, St Andrews, and elsewhere, though without a vestige of success, so that some of them decided to qualify abroad, with a view to practising at home even though not on the register.

This course involved its own troubles. There was first the difficult question of *where* to go, and the uncertainty whether Paris, Berne, Montpellier, Bologna, or any of the other possible places gave degrees which were well thought of in England. Then followed the language difficulty; but as this depended only on themselves for its overcoming, the young women students made little of it. More serious, however, was the family disapproval from which nearly all suffered, which increased the strain and worry tenfold. To these they added several material troubles: the difficulty of finding clean and respectable lodgings in a foreign town, the danger of ill-health which went with overwork and worry, the pinch of narrow means, and the isolation and loneliness of exile.

"You will be glad to hear that I have passed my exams," wrote Agnes M'Laren to Helen Taylor in 1877,[1] in a letter which is typical of many, "but I am sorry to say that I did not do well. I knew the subjects on which I was examined perfectly, and had the examination been a written one would have answered the questions put to all the candidates. As

[1] MSS. papers of Helen Taylor. (London School of Economics.)

it was, I was extremely nervous and unfortunately showed it by the shaking of my voice and my hesitancy. Unfortunately I had for examiners men I had not seen before and whose classes I had not attended, and so did not so well understand what they said. I expect everyone is very much disappointed with me. The Hall was, of course, crowded—and I was the first one called on, which took me by surprise, as the Secretary told me my name was the last on the list and that this would give me the advantage of hearing the examination of the other candidates. You know I always told you I should do badly, but I did not expect to be so nervous, or rather did not expect to show it so much. . . . I don't believe they were unfair to me at all. They made me more nervous by telling me not to be frightened, but I suppose this was meant kindly, as also the calling me up first. I am far more sorry for the sake of other women than for my own. . . . My father disapproved of my studying medicine, feeling, as so many men do, that though it was right for others it was not right for their daughters."

In some places the difficulties were even greater. The medical examiners in Brussels distinguished themselves by trying to embarrass the women candidates with grossly and deliberately indecent questions publicly addressed to them; and here and there the men students adopted a similar method of annoyance. The women suffered acutely under this form of persecution, but it made them so angry that they became even more determined to carry on; and none of their difficulties really daunted them at all. They stuck to the self-appointed tasks, and one by one they secured their qualifications; and then they came home, to join their strength to the little band of fighters there, and try to force open the firmly barred doors of medical education.

But their help seemed unavailing. The appeal was decided in favour of Edinburgh University, and against the women in 1873, and voluntary admission anywhere else in Great Britain seemed unobtainable. Other methods would have to be tried, and other methods were accordingly adopted after this date, and, as we shall see in another chapter,[1] the end was not so far off as it seemed. All the different parts of the Higher Education Movement were strengthening each other by breaking down the opposition of public opinion. The universities and all the other vested interests seemed almost unshaken, but the general public was getting used to the new idea. And when once this great ally was converted, the young women were not to be stopped. Time, as well as justice, was on their side.

[1] See Chap. XIII.

CHAPTER X

THE C.D. ACTS. 1870, 1871

The women's protest against the regulation of prostitution, 1st January 1870—Josephine Butler—Her decision to take up this crusade—The violent opposition it aroused—The Colchester election of 1870—The Royal Commission of 1871.

By 1870, as we have seen, the woman's rights idea had really begun to move in many different directions. Few people as yet saw the new movement as a whole, and of those who did some were thoroughly frightened by its implications; but still there was evident and marked progress. Among those whose interests were philanthropic, the old notion that personal charity was enough for women had given way, and now even the small private enterprises and the unofficial organisations which had sprung up in the fifties and sixties were beginning to seem inadequate. The dreams of the new generation were turning towards more responsible work, and the idea that it might be possible for women to influence policy and administration, and even to share in local government, set their thoughts racing in a new direction. It was, of course, many years before these hopes were at all widely realised, but as time went on Royal Commissions, Bills before Parliament, and the by-laws of local authorities began to enter the minds of philanthropic ladies; and after that date problems of poverty and destitution emerged for them from the stage where individual cases were their only concern to that in which wholesale prevention or collective remedy could be considered. Among those whose interests were educational an even greater change had taken place. The existence of girls had, as it were, been discovered, and schools which really intended to teach them something more than accomplishments were multiplying fast. Young women also were just beginning to be heard of as possible students, and for hundreds and hundreds of them throughout the country the magic doors of learning were opening. Public opinion was obviously and decidedly moving towards better and longer education for the female young, and they were thriving upon the change.

From that moment the empty listless hours of young ladyhood were doomed, and the life against which Florence Nightingale had so violently protested was destined to disappear. Not that there were not still, and for many years to come, binding, cramping, and deadly conventions holding women back from their free development; nor that there were not still hundreds and thousands of girls who were taught to believe that the new ideas were wicked, shameful, and unladylike; nor that there was not still a laziness, an insipidity, and a frivolity about the lives of women of the leisured classes against which it was exceedingly difficult to rebel. All these things persisted and in a measure persist still, because of the economic dependence of women in which they had their rise. But in 1870 they were already doomed to extinction, for new energy was making way against them. With every year which passed, with every school which opened, and with every woman who found a place for herself in the world of affairs, the old nonsense shrank back. For the march of the Women's Movement had definitely begun.

All this, however, good and helpful as it was, touched but a small part of the problem. The position of women involved more than the education of the daughters of the well-to-do, and more than an outlet for the energies of the women of the middle classes. It involved more even than their enfranchisement, or their economic liberation, great though these causes were. For the position of women was rotten in ways which had never yet been considered and hardly even mentioned; ways so terrible to society, and so humiliating, that the whole world had conspired to cover them with silence; and under the cloak of that silence the physical, social and civil liberties of innumerable women were quietly but effectively destroyed.

In 1870, whatever may be the case to-day, it was undoubtedly true that the fair outward structure of society was built up over a foundation of cruelty and oppression, over the vice, the bribery, the drunkenness, and the filth of the underworld. In one section of society there stood the sacred hearth and the inviolable family, and there women were, in theory, sheltered and respected, not so much for themselves as because they were the centre of the home and the guardians of the "honour" of their husbands. In the other section there were women, too, equally necessary, but very differently regarded. These women were not honoured either for themselves or for any other thing. They were exploited, bullied, and ill-treated, cooped up in the brothels of the great towns, condemned to a dreadful life and an early death, but "tolerated," and under the "protection" of the police.

These two worlds existed side by side, but the women of the one had no contact with the women of the other. Men could, and did, pass freely between them, but for women there was a great gulf fixed. If they were "respectable" they might not even know of the existence of prostitutes, or of the problems which their existence created. For these victims of society had no claims upon and no relationship with the virtuous woman. It was contamination for her to touch them, or even to know of them, for they were outcast.

Yet, in spite of the convention of society, prostitutes were women; and, moreover, all their evils and misfortunes came from this very fact. It was actually because of their sex that they were outcasts, not because of their behaviour.

The men who did as they did, and who shared their vice and their degradation, were not dealt with in the same manner, nor held in the same disgust. The double moral standard allowed to men what it forbade to women; and it was from this root that the worst of the evil grew.

Hardly anyone realised that this was so. Lecky, for example, in his *History of European Morals* (1869) [1] described the existence of prostitution in terms which assumed its necessity. "There has arisen in society," he said, "a figure which is certainly the most mournful, and in some respects the most awful upon which the eye of the moralist can dwell. That unhappy being whose very name is a shame to speak; who counterfeits with a cold heart the transports of affection and submits herself as the passive instrument of lust; who is scorned and insulted as the vilest of her sex, and doomed for the most part to disease and abject wretchedness and an early death, appears in every age as the perpetual symbol of the degradation and sinfulness of man. Herself the supreme type of vice, she is ultimately the most efficient guardian of virtue. But for her, the unchallenged purity of countless happy homes would be polluted and not a few who, in the pride of their untempted chastity, think of her with an indignant shudder, would have known the agony of remorse and despair. On that degraded and ignoble form are concentrated the passions that might have filled the world with shame. She remains, while creeds and civilisations rise and fall, the eternal priestess of humanity, blasted for the sins of the people."

There had been before 1870 one or two thoughtful men and women to whom this view had seemed repellant. The monstrous hypocrisy and the flagrant injustice had troubled them, and there were some small groups of people who had tried to improve the position. The Churches, too, taught the doctrine of equal and unchanging morality, and preached virtue to men and women alike. The main efforts of all

[1] Vol. ii, p. 299 (chap. v, "The Position of Women").

these people, however, had always been directed towards the reformation of "the fallen"; and they had been unable or unwilling to try and face the problem in its relation to the State. The system and its underlying assumptions were taken for granted; the thing was to snatch, if it might be, some brands from the burning, and to lessen the number of those who fell under its evil sway.

Those few people who cared at all about this awful subject therefore busied themselves with rescue work, and the world at large forgot evils which were apparently so inevitable, so ancient, so well concealed. Society did very well on the whole. It was no use stirring up mud.

On 1st January 1870, however, this calm was broken, for on that day the Members of the House of Commons received, almost without warning, a serious and solemn protest against the existing laws concerning the regulation and control of prostitutes. This protest, which bore the names of scores of well-known ladies, was a staggering document; and when its publication in the Press was followed by the formation of a Ladies' National Association for the Repeal of the Contagious Diseases Acts, the matter grew serious indeed. It was a "revolt of the women," and no one knew how it was to be met.

The first reaction of the political and social world to this new development was indignation. Society was not merely shocked, it was outraged; and the usual opinion was that the women who could touch such questions, and espouse the cause of such "creatures," must themselves be vile or mad. The storm of hostility which arose against the reformers was unparalleled in bitterness, and nothing was too harsh to be believed.

The band of workers against whom this fury was directed were not unprepared for its onslaught. They had not plunged light-heartedly into the dreadful business, but had already counted the cost, and the reception of their first move, and the outcry in the world at large, shook them not at all. They were prepared to suffer hardness, for they knew they had a righteous cause.

The Women's Protest of 1870, though it burst so suddenly upon the country, was the outcome of long years of preparation. The story of this preparation, as of the crusade which followed it, is closely bound up with the story of one woman's life, and the two are best told together. For, although there were other people treading the same path, and although there were other elements at work tending in the same direction, yet she was without question the chief inspirer and the chief influence of them all. It was her fight, as it was in the end her victory; and without her it might never have begun.

Josephine Grey was born in 1828, in the border country of Northumberland, and she passed her girlhood among the wholesome influences of the quiet countryside. Beautiful and gifted, and very much loved, Josephine had no outward troubles; but in her own soul she was deeply and at times painfully moved by the thought of sorrow and suffering and wickedness. She laboured and agonised in her own heart, and she prayed often. She found no easy solutions for the riddle of human sin, but her religious faith sustained her, and when she married George Butler she found in him a companion with whom to share her difficulties, her anxieties, and her faith. Outwardly their course of life seemed plain. They lived in Oxford, and they had friends and interests and children, and a thousand good and worthy things to do. Josephine was very delicate, too, and had not strength for much work, and yet she felt always that there were such difficult and terrible things in the world, that she could not be wholly at peace. The thought of vice and of the miseries which it entailed lay, as it were, in the background of her thoughts troubling her. Every instinct in her whole being revolted against the conventional view of sex morality, and she prayed much in her own heart. She suffered, even to agony, and laboured long and passionately to understand what was her duty in the matter; and more than once, as opportunity came their way, she and her husband sheltered and protected women who had fallen into the abyss.

In 1864 a terrible misfortune overtook the Butlers. They had moved to Cheltenham, where Mr Butler had been appointed Vice-Principal of Cheltenham College, and it was there that their only daughter was killed in her mother's presence by a fall from a staircase. This dreadful calamity nearly crushed Josephine, and it left a lasting mark on her whole nature. But it neither shook her trust in God, nor weakened her feeling that she must devote herself to the hardest and most appalling work. On the contrary, it intensified these impulses, and when her husband became Principal of Liverpool College, and they moved to that city, she began to seek out the outcasts from society, to visit prisons and workhouses, and to occupy herself with the "fallen" of her sex, driven, as she said, by the longing to find some pain keener than her own, and to meet people more unhappy than herself.

The first result of her visits to the oakum sheds, the quays, and the hospitals was to draw down upon her head an avalanche of miserable but grateful womanhood. With her husband's full co-operation Josephine opened her home to as many of these destitute people as she could, and it was soon crowded with friendless and unfortunate girls, many of whom she nursed until they died. As the numbers who came to them soon grew too large for their own house to hold, the Butlers took another near at hand, and opened a "House of Rest," and after a time this developed into a refuge for incurables, and was taken over and supported by the town.

All this work, absorbing and important as it was, still seemed to Josephine to touch but the edge of the problem. The state of public morals, the impenetrable indifference of the world, were not to be changed by rescue work, however widespread or beneficent. And Mrs Butler, as she grew to know more and more intimately the full sweep of the problem, felt more and more clearly that broader remedies must be found. Still she prayed, and still she suffered, shrinking back from the course which began to seem her duty, and dreading the task to which she felt she was called. It was a time of bitter inward preparation, but at last her decision was made, and in 1869 she was ready to come forward. The call she believed was the voice of God; she must go out and uphold the cause of the betrayed and the fallen, though it should take her into the wilderness alone.

When Josephine Butler made this decision, and when, with her husband's help, she began her onslaught upon the conventions of the world, she had to face not only the scandalised indignation of society, but also the laws and police regulations of the country; and it was this last fact which gave her the basis of her crusade. The laws recently introduced and rapidly extending, which regulated the lives of prostitutes, offered a concrete object to attack, and this opposition became the rallying cry for all those who took part in her crusade.

The system of the State Regulation of Vice originated in France under Napoleon, and early in the nineteenth century it had spread through many other European countries. England was slow to adopt it. It was said, indeed, that the matter had been considered by the Government early in the reign of Queen Victoria, but that Lord Melbourne had not been able to face the thought of taking such an Act to the young Queen for signature; and nothing was actually done until the first year of her widowhood, when she was giving less attention than usual to public affairs. Whether this is true or not, and whether it was that the Queen thus unconsciously protected the rights of her female subjects, or whether it was because of the inborn dislike of the English people to coercion and abridgments of liberty, it remains certain that no regularised system of licensing brothels and dragooning prostitutes was established before 1864; though, after a beginning was once made, several amending, or rather extending, Acts slipped through Parliament.[1]

The system, as it existed at the time when Mrs Butler first began to work against it, was in force in military and naval centres. It provided that all women living within certain areas were liable, on police accusation, to be declared "common prostitutes," and as such they were bound to undergo periodical medical examination. Refusal to submit to this was punishable by repeated terms of imprisonment, while acquiescence was, of course, accompanied by a total loss of reputation. According to the official view, the inspection was required to check the danger of contagious diseases; and although, of course, it was applied only to women, it was assumed that where it was enforced the sexual immorality which was thought essential for soldiers and sailors might be considered "safe."

Mrs Butler was not the only person to disbelieve in and to detest this point of view. Her final impulse to action came from an appeal which reached her in 1869 from a group of medical men, and long before that date other protests had been made. In 1860, when a commission had considered the subject in connection with the provision of brothels for the army in India, Florence Nightingale had given emphatic evidence against it, and a little later Harriet Martineau had contributed a series of indignant articles to the *Daily News*. The Rescue Society, and a group of Nonconformist ministers had protested against the first introduction of the system, and had repeated their protest at every extension. These forces, however, were not enough to break down the deliberate silence of the world, and for five years after its first appearance the system had its way, and naturally began to build up a set of official interests which sought to extend it wider and wider, until it might well be expected to creep over the whole country.

[1] The dates of these Acts were 1864, 1866, 1868, and 1869.

This was the state of affairs when Josephine Butler came to her decision, and with her entry upon the scene the whole aspect instantaneously changed. There were hundreds of women who had been uneasy, and yet afraid; and there were thousands of working-men who had instinctively loathed and dreaded the whole idea. These people now found a leader, and one, moreover, of such moral courage, such practical sagacity, such unquenchable energy, and with it all of such saintly and spiritual nature, that they could all follow her without question. And, accordingly, early in 1870 a storm of opposition to the Acts rose in the country whose like had never been seen before.

The first practical step which Josephine Butler took was to make an appeal to working-men. She took the train to the nearest large centre, Crewe, and there, without previous preparation, she spoke to the railway men. She had no idea what her reception would be; but it surpassed any hopes she could have entertained. The men not only agreed with her while she spoke, but they came to her afterwards and discussed further action. There was a group of them there who had served an apprenticeship in Paris, and who thus knew the full force of the danger which was threatening the morals of the country; and with their help an organisation of working-men rapidly sprang up all through the northern counties to oppose the Acts.

Josephine Butler was not content with this, encouraging and helpful as it was, but immediately she set on foot that "Revolt of Women" which led to the presentation of the first petition to the House of Commons. In this part of her crusade there was far more difficulty than there had been among the working-men. First of all the majority of the women whom she approached were wholly ignorant of the question, and so much afraid of it that they did not wish to listen. They were so shocked, so terribly upset by the very broaching of the subject, that it was hard to make any progress at all. There were, of course, a great many of whom this was not true; there were brave and devoted women who came at once to her side, and who faced the opprobrium which followed without flinching. But by far the greater number drew their skirts away. Some were frightened by the effect which would follow their joining in the agitation. Some saw that their friends would desert them, and feared that their husbands' interests might suffer if they mixed themselves with such a disreputable affair; others hated the whole subject and were obstinately convinced that only harm would come of discussing the matter at all. The authorities must be right, they felt; and, dreadful as it was, it was no concern of theirs. There were many others besides who were positively roused to indignant anger by the agitation; they felt that there was something wicked in bringing the subject up publicly at all, and the more serious were the efforts to convince them the more passionate did their opposition become. Friendships were broken and families were divided; and the storm which swept through the earnest society of the country was unparalleled. It was, of course, made all the more difficult by the fact that every trace of the controversy had to be concealed from the eyes of all the younger women. The letters and protests, the pamphlets and the documents, were regarded as positively indecent in most of the households to which they were sent. They were carefully hidden away, if not burnt outright, lest anyone should get hold of them, and each time that public mention was made of the crusade the indignation of the "respectable" flamed higher.

Within the ranks of the regular Women's Movement this same cleavage of opinion was to be found. Practically all those who were working for education felt wholly unable to touch this new crusade at all. It is true that both Mrs Butler herself and Professor James Stuart continued to work for both causes, and that no harm but only good resulted; but there were not many who were in a position to do the same. Head mistresses and teachers of all kinds had to be exceedingly careful, and the danger of injuring instead of helping the causes they had at heart seemed very acute. This difficulty troubled those who were working for Women's Suffrage,[1] and although a certain number of them disregarded the risk of confusing one unpopular cause with another even more notorious and detested, and therefore came out openly on the abolitionist side, the majority felt obliged to leave this crusade alone.

Since it was to be expected that those who believed in either of these reforms would find it easier than other people to believe in the other, this tactical division which separated them was a serious loss to both, and during the early years of the movement for the repeal of the C.D. Acts it cut off many sources of strength and encouragement from Mrs Butler and her followers.

There were other people from whom they might have hoped for support and from whom they did not get it, and these were the new women doctors who were just struggling into existence. Dr Elizabeth Blackwell was strongly opposed to the Acts, but most of the others took the official medical view and believed that, unpleasant as the Acts were, they were necessary for the health of the districts, and were effective as protection against contagion. They could have known little of what they were talking of, for of course no hospital appointments were open to them, least of all those in which venereal diseases were treated, and they had had throughout their training the greatest difficulties when studying this particular branch of their trade; but all the same their lack of support was a grievous blow, and one which was especially depressing.

In spite of all difficulties, however, the band of supporters which gathered round Josephine Butler grew steadily. Besides Professor Stuart, who gave invaluable help from the first, there were the two Mr Mallesons, Mr Henry Wilson of Sheffield, Mr Hopwood, M.P., Mr Jacob Bright, and many

[1] See Chap. XIV.

more.[1] Mrs Butler was one of those who make friends wherever they go, and even a few moments in her company left an impression which lasted a lifetime. She seemed different from everyone else, and her goodness and her sincerity evoked instant veneration. The force of her reasoning too, combined with her wit, her beauty, and the charm of her personality, made an extraordinary effect on those who met her, so that she seemed almost irresistible. Men and women were drawn to her at first sight, and their loyalty and love helped them to bear the persecution and the ostracism which following in her footsteps involved. They suffered, many of them, in a measure which corresponded very nearly with the hostility of their opponents; but that did not turn them back. The harder the task, the more evident the need that they should do it.

Not long after the presentation of the Ladies' Protest, the repeal agitation came to public notice in a new and even more startling fashion. Mrs Butler decided that it was necessary to raise the issue at the by-election which took place in Colchester in 1870, and the events of that contest were so unprecedented that its fame spread all over the country.

Sir Henry Storks, the Government candidate, was a military administrator who had himself enforced the Acts when Governor of Malta, and he was wanted at the War Office for that very reason. Colchester, the seat which he proposed to represent, was a military centre, and one of the places where the Contagious Diseases Acts were in force; and it was, therefore, an easy matter to raise the issues

[1] The list of workers in this movement is a long one, but the following women who came into the work in the early days must be mentioned: in Belfast, Miss Todd; in Bristol, the Misses Priestman, Miss Tanner, Miss Estlin; in Colchester, Mrs Marriage; in Edinburgh, Mrs Bright M'Laren; in Leeds, Mrs Ford and her daughters; in Manchester, Mrs Bright and Miss Wolstenholme, and in Newcastle, Mrs Clark. At a later stage Mr Dyer, Mr Gillett, and Mr W. A. Coote came into the movement and devoted almost their whole lives to the cause, and Mr and Mrs G. W. Johnson, Mr and Mrs Sheldon Amos, and Mr and Mrs Percy Bunting gave enthusiastic and invaluable help.

of their repeal during the course of the election. It was an easy matter to raise it, but it was not easy to lay it again; for with its emergence into the daylight there came an outburst of ferocity and physical violence on the part of the supporters of the system which did more to alarm the country about the significance of the Acts than years of propaganda could have accomplished.

The events of that election were dramatic in the extreme. Mrs Butler and her friends were attacked by mobs, and went in danger of their lives. The inns which sheltered them were surrounded and the innkeepers so threatened that they were forced to turn their visitors out into the streets; and many times they escaped only by disguising themselves from the mobs which were pursuing them. The halls in which they held their meetings were rushed by gangs of rowdies, and in one instance a loft was set on fire while Mrs Butler was speaking within. The police were unable to protect them and, indeed, hardly made the attempt, and the situation became very serious indeed. All the clamour and disorder which went on, however, served to bring home to the citizens of Colchester the nature of the interests which Mrs Butler was attacking, and the worse the violence became the more definitely the serious voters of the town came round to her views. They knew for themselves what the effect of the system was in their own town, and they now saw what sort of supporters it collected, and as the election progressed the people began to see clearly what was on foot. Working-men and working-women began to talk seriously to each other about the subject of regulated prostitution, and day by day more of them understood the issue. Sir Henry Storks, who honestly believed that the Acts were good and useful, damaged his own cause most seriously by saying that if he had his way he would like to bring the wives of soldiers as well as the inmates of the brothels under the control of police and medical regulation; and the free people of Colchester took alarm. When the poll was taken the

Government candidate was roundly defeated, and there was no question but that it was on this one issue alone.

The result of this election was the most remarkable political triumph ever achieved by a woman, and it marked a turning-point in the history of the crusade. Now that the reformers had dragged the subject out from the silence and obscurity in which it had been covered, and had made it resound not only in the drawing-room of the respectable middle classes, but in the lobbies of the House of Commons, it was necessary for something to be done. Within a few months a Royal Commission to inquire into the administration and operation of the Acts was appointed, and pending its report no further effort to extend them was proposed.

The commission was composed of Members of Parliament, soldiers, doctors, clergymen, and administrators, and there was, of course, no suggestion that any woman should be a member of it. But advocates and opponents of repeal were represented in fairly equal numbers, and witnesses were called on both sides. One of the most important of these was John Stuart Mill, and in answer to the questions of the chairman he set out in the clearest terms the constitutional principles involved. "I do not consider (such legislation) justifiable in principle," he said, "because it appears to me to be opposed to one of the greatest principles of legislation, the security of personal liberty. It appears to me that legislation of this sort takes away that security almost entirely from a particular class of women intentionally, but incidentally and unintentionally, one may say, for all women whatever; inasmuch as it enables a woman to be apprehended by the police on suspicion and taken before a magistrate, and then by that magistrate she is liable to be confined for a term of imprisonment, which may amount, I believe, to six months, for refusing to sign a declaration consenting to be examined."

This threat to the personal liberty of all women was indeed the basis of the demand for repeal; and its presentation by such a man as Mill carried great weight with the commissioners.

Mrs Butler, when she was called in 1871, intensified this impression, and added another to it. It was a very unusual thing for a woman to be in such a position, and the occasion was, as she said herself, a formidable ordeal. She was the only woman present before a large assembly of Peers, Bishops, Members of Parliament, naval and military experts, and doctors; her questioners were many of them hostile, and the subject was serious and difficult. "It was distressing to me," she wrote, "owing to the hard, harsh view which some of these men take of poor women, and the lives of the poor generally. . . . I felt very weak and lonely. But there was One who stood by me. I almost felt as if I heard Christ's voice bidding me not to fear"; and in that faith she spoke.

Her evidence corresponded with, and went farther, than Mill's. She said, in reply to questions, that for fifteen years she had devoted her leisure to these unhappy women; that she had had five of them living in her house at one time, not as servants, but as friends and patients. She had sought them in brothels night and day, in their homes and in the streets, in the workhouses and the Lock Hospitals. . . . She urged that the industrial question was all important. "Economics," she said, "lie at the very root of practical morality." The want of industrial training and good openings was one cause of their downfall, and another was the crowding and want of decency in their homes. She urged several specific reforms: that seduction might be punishable by law, that legislation should deal equally with men and women, that the bastardy laws should be amended and the C.D. Acts totally repealed; but she maintained that the evil could not be reached by legislation alone. There should be equal laws to check solicitation in the streets by either sex, but the law must be aided by moral influences acting upon both men and women.

The impression which Mrs Butler made upon the commission was profound, and it was all the greater because of the contrast between her and some of those who came to defend the Acts. One of the commissioners, Mr Rylands, described her evidence in the following words: "I am not accustomed to religious phraseology, but I cannot give you any idea of the effect produced except by saying that the influence of the spirit of God was there."

The commission finished its labours in 1871, and its report was unanimously in favour of the immediate discontinuance both of compulsory medical examination and of the imprisonment of suspected women; and these were the very essence of the regulation system. Several of the members of the commission, who had formerly supported the Acts, were brought to change their opinions by the evidence they heard, and not only signed the report but publicly announced their adherence to the other side. The Rev. F. D. Maurice was one of these, and also Mr Charles Buxton, M.P., and Sir W. James. From every point of view it was a resounding victory, and though Mrs Butler and her friends did not make as much of it as the suffragists of later years would have done, it comforted and strengthened their hearts.

The commission also reported unanimously in favour of the raising of the age of consent from twelve, where it then stood, to fourteen, but neither this nor the condemnation of the C.D. Acts was enforced. Thirteen years went by before action was taken to check the operation of the Acts, and an agitation even more sensational and startling was required before the age of consent was altered.[1] Nevertheless, the report of the Royal Commission gave the reformers a position and a standing much surer than they had had before, and the work of converting public opinion went steadily forward.

It is not necessary to trace the whole of the campaign in

[1] See Chap. XI.

detail, nor to follow its ups and downs. It was primarily a moral, and not a political movement, and although it aimed at a political object, and triumphed in the end by the passing of an Act of Parliament,[1] it accomplished a far more widespread change than the Repeal of the Contagious Diseases Acts, more widespread even than the International Vigilance movement which sprang from it. For it changed the whole basis of sex morality and swept away a multitude of shams. When Mrs Butler came forward in the cause, a double moral standard was not only tolerated but widely upheld; before she had been working a year that comfortable assumption was upset. Not that there were not still innumerable men and women to support it, not that it does not to this day influence and bias the judgment of society, but its hold on thoughtful and serious people was destroyed. Thousands of those women who were the guardians of the conventions and social conditions of the country were awakened to the inconsistency, the evil, and the flagrant injustice of the old idea; and once that awakening had come there was no going back. People remained, and still remain, as unmoral, as thoughtless, and as prone to evil as before; but the burden of the blame was no longer heaped upon one sex alone, and the matter began to assume truer proportions. With that slow but inevitable shifting, the position of women in regard to sex questions began at last to improve. The old silence and the old timidity began to die away and honest thinking and free discussion became possible. And the movements for the freedom and the rights of women along every other line grew stronger as that change took place.

[1] See Chap. XI.

CHAPTER XI

LEARNING THE JOB. 1870–1900

Progress in municipal affairs—School Boards and Poor Law Guardians—The development of organised philanthropy—The Salvation Army—Catherine Booth—The repeal of the C.D. Acts, 1883—Mr Stead's crusade—His imprisonment—Progress of social legislation—Guardianship of Infants' Act, 1886—Case of *Jackson* v. *Jackson*, 1891.

WHILE the suffrage societies were learning their political lessons, while the industrial women were beginning their organisation, and while the women doctors and university graduates were consolidating their gains, another field of public work had been opened to women which still further advanced the whole cause.

In 1869, without opposition, and even with the approval of the Government, the municipal franchise was extended (or, as Miss Becker put it, restored) to women ratepayers. Mr Jacob Bright was the mover of the amendment by which it was done, and as Miss Becker wrote to Mme. Bodichon, "The question passed through the House without a dissentient word, causing surprise and excitement of a quiet sort and much pleasure to the real friends of the Cause." After a little anxiety about the House of Lords, which caused her to write a few reasonable and reasoned letters to Lord Salisbury and other influential members of the Government, the Bill was passed into law, and no one seemed to realise that it was "the thin end of the wedge."

In the following year Mr Forster's Education Act brought the School Boards into existence, and enabled women not only to vote for but also to be elected to serve upon these bodies. At once the suffragists seized upon the opportunity of doing practical public work, and Miss Becker in Manchester, Miss Flora Stevenson in Edinburgh, and Miss Davies and Miss Garrett in London, were all successful candidates at the first elections. Miss Garrett, indeed, secured a larger majority than any of the other Londoners or than any municipal candidates had ever had before, winning 47,858 votes in spite of the fact (or perhaps because of the fact) that she was by that date that most alarming and outrageous thing, a female medical practitioner.

The work of the new School Boards was very heavy and exacting, but it was just the work which most deeply interested those pioneers of the Women's Movement, and when a few years later Miss Davies and Miss Garrett felt themselves unable to stand for re-election because of the pressure of other occupations, there were other women to come forward and take their places. From 1870, indeed, begins the long tale of detailed work, carried out by an increasing number of disinterested and devoted women in connection with local government, at first as members of School Boards and as Poor Law Guardians (the first of whom to be elected was Miss M. C. Merrington in 1875), and later (after they had become eligible) as County and Borough Councillors.

This part of the Women's Movement was not pushed forward without much effort and labour. Month after month the *Englishwoman's Review* and the *Woman's Journal* (the two "organs" of the Movement) published articles and appeals upon the subject, and many and many a quiet and unwilling lady was remorselessly pushed out by an awakened sense of public duty to do things which she hated and loathed. The mere fact of standing for election—even so dull and quiet an election as that of a Poor Law Guardian—was enough to fill the Victorian female with dismay; and the companionship, the work, and the knowledge which followed election were at first exquisitely distasteful. Nevertheless, women came forward in increasing numbers, and they soon began to find that there was a reward and a satisfaction in what they were able to achieve. At no time were there enough women on any one Authority to make as much effect as they wished; as Miss Davies said on her retirement, "we were willing to do our best, but when it is remembered that the Board has consisted of 47 gentlemen and 2 ladies it will not be a matter of surprise that the two ladies have proved incapable of doing their half of the work." Yet even so, few in numbers, and handicapped by the existence of considerable prejudice against them among a large proportion of the ratepayers and many of their colleagues, they undoubtedly managed to hasten and advance that reform of local government organisation and particularly of educational organisation which was at that time in progress. The days of Bumbledom were passing, and the new Local Authorities were in the main inspired by the active humanitarian spirit of the day; and though red tape and ancient custom and even corruption still held back progress, the presence of capable, disinterested, and daring women among the elected bodies acted as a stimulus to the side of the reformers. Not, of course, that they were always "progressive" in the technical political sense—though it must be admitted that they had a tendency in that direction—it was rather that they were original and progressive in thought, unhampered by Party feeling, quite unafraid of difficulties and misrepresentations, and wholly and even passionately concerned with what they believed to be the welfare of the community. Measured in numbers, their influence might be thought to have been small; but the value of this part of the Women's Movement to the development of national life was nevertheless of considerable importance.

In 1871 the Local Government Board was created, and two years later Mrs Nassau Senior was appointed under it as the first woman Poor Law Inspector. It was not till 1888 that County Councils came into existence, but in that year Lady Sandhurst and Miss Cobden were returned to the London County Council by good majorities, and Miss Cons was chosen as an Alderman. The Act expressly sanctioned the voting of women ratepayers, but nothing was said in it about eligibility for election, and objection was at once raised to their taking their seats. The case was taken to the courts, and after delays and appeals it was decided against them. Bills were then introduced to regularise the position, and the L.C.C. itself petitioned Parliament five times to be allowed to keep its women members; but all in vain. It was not until 1907 that the "Qualification of Women Act" was passed, by which they were rendered eligible for County and Borough Councils and for the offices of Chairman and Mayor—though it was expressly stated that where women held these offices they should not thereby become Justices of the Peace. The first woman Mayor to be appointed under this Act was, most appropriately, the first woman who had been elected to the School Board thirty-seven years before. In choosing Mrs Garrett Anderson for this post in 1908, her native town of Aldburgh did honour both to itself and to her; and even the anti-feminists could not but be pleased.

This striking proof of the success of the local government side of the Women's Movement seemed to come about naturally and without effort. It was, however, the result of long years of agitation which had gone before. All through the lean years of the Suffrage Movement, from 1884 to 1906, this aspect of affairs had been kept to the forefront, and it was not until the greater excitements of the suffrage agitation overshadowed it that it passed into the background. This was, of course, only natural, and to be expected, and would perhaps hardly be worth mention were it not for the fact that the anti-suffragists, when they came into belated existence in 1909, took the matter up with such vigour. They seemed to think that only those who rejected the wider demand had the sense to realise the opportunities for usefulness which already lay open to the female sex; but they were late in the day. The early supporters had pushed open the door, and, in point of fact, they had already marched in.

While some of the bolder and more adventurous women were nerving themselves for public work, a far greater number had been plunging into the various philanthropies which during the sixties and seventies and eighties were multiplying rapidly. The Social Science Association had done its work well, for the number of its offshoots was legion, and the hosts of societies which are now familiarly known by their initials were beginning to take their place in English life.

Ever since the beginning of the century philanthropy had been, as we have seen, an emancipating activity for women; and now, with the more extended organisation and the wider sweep of the Humanitarian movement, this influence became even more powerful. It is unnecessary here to enumerate all the new organisations which came into existence to reform the world and its ways. They covered an immense field, stretching from the welfare of soldiers, sailors, and domestic servants to the conversion of savages and heathens, and including, by the way, prize-fighters, orphans, and lunatics; they were directed towards "furthering the claims of humanity and religion," and they aimed very high; but most of them show, to modern eyes, a curiously limited benevolence, and their importance to the development of society has been largely different from that expressed in their aims and objects. The multiplication of charities, and the wide interest in reform which accompanied them, did not lead to the immediate improvement of the whole world, but it did lead first to the co-ordination and arrangement of the charitable organisations, and from this there followed the scientific study of the problems of poverty.

We must not trace this development further here, interesting as it is. What concerns us is the feminist by-product of the expansion of charities, which the leaders of societies generally either overlooked or disliked, but which was quietly piling up results in the most unexpected places.

The Girls' Friendly Society, for example, is a case in point. This society was founded in 1874 for the purpose of looking after working girls, particularly those in domestic service. It was avowedly a "Handmaiden of the Church of England," and drew into its work clergymen's wives and religious ladies all over the country. Many of its members must have hated the whole idea of the Women's Movement, and looked with dismay upon their entry into public life. We can indeed draw from the speeches and addresses delivered at its gatherings a fine indictment of the whole feminist idea, and a wholehearted restatement of the case for the submission and subjection of women. Nevertheless, even the early leaders of the G.F.S. when faced with the problem of managing a huge and growing society realised that their old individual ways must be changed. In 1879, when the society had already 30,000 members, the need for rules for the conduct of public business was discovered. "About this time," one of their workers tells us, "we began to find out that there were such things as 'Rules of Procedure' which governed all meetings held by men! We made enquiries among our gentlemen friends as to what these rules were. To our astonishment and utter perplexity we found that no two people gave the same answer and that these rules, though of untold antiquity, were unwritten and wholly traditional! . . . Never shall I forget the feeling of hopeless perplexity that weighed upon one at that time, while realising more from day to day the immense importance of these rules. Someone told us there were such beings as 'experts' in drafting rules, but we sought for them in vain."

In the Metropolitan Association for Befriending Young

Servants, an undenominational society for the same purpose as the Girls' Friendly Society, a similar perturbation arose, when, in 1877, men were first introduced as members of the committees. "It was much against the feelings of some of the oldest and best members . . . and those of us who had most advocated the admission of men to the Council can remember still the consternation caused by the yards of red tape, the forms that seemed to us brought from the Circumlocution Office and invented for the consumption of time that they brought with them. However, no one now for a moment, I suppose, doubts the wisdom of the move."

These difficulties seem a little absurd to the present generation, and they look perhaps a trifle dull and useless too. We may even be tempted to imagine that the ladies who lost their tranquillity by worrying over resolutions, amendments, previous questions, standing orders, and parliamentary procedure were wasting their time, and would have been as well occupied with the fancy work and the afternoon calls they were forsaking. But it was not so. Even these dry and arid matters thrilled and palpitated with interest for the ladies of the day, and the joy which they got from them was unbounded. For, unlike the fancy work and the calls, philanthropy carried the sense of being worth while; something good and concrete, something, above all, impersonal to themselves, was its ultimate object; and to have the power of working for a cause was a new and thrilling and satisfying experience for the female mind.

The popularity and success of these organisations was indeed so great that by the end of the seventies it had become fashionable, almost to the point of necessity, for wealthy women to engage in charitable work; and, while the more thoughtful worked seriously and in an organised manner at lasting reforms, the more foolish took a mania for "slumming." A pet charity was at that date almost as much a part of the equipment of a smart lady as was a rope of pearls. She had to have her own "poor"—costermongers, orphans, newspaper boys, flower girls, match-sellers, crossing-sweepers or something of the sort—and even if the amount of good she did to the recipients of her charity was small, there was still some benefit to herself. For, however frivolous and limited her work might be, it was always a widening of her experience beyond the drawing-room of her own home.

While these activities were modifying the outlook and widening the horizons of the rich, a religious and philanthropic movement was gathering way among the poor which we must consider in greater detail, and that was the Salvation Army.

This body, which came into formal existence in 1875, exerted a most tremendous influence upon the position of women, and the practical example of sex equality which it displayed did more than millions of arguments to destroy the suspicion and the prejudice of the poor.

It is impossible to consider this or any other aspect of the Salvation Army's work without considering the lives of its founders, William and Catherine Booth. They devised and created it, founding it upon their own vehement and passionate beliefs; and their own lives are so intimately bound up with it as to be one and the same story.

These two remarkable people were married in 1855, but even before then the woman question had been settled between them and settled on the advanced side. William Booth, although of his own accord well disposed to grant the "equality of woman as a being," had had some slight hesitations about the practical consequences, but Catherine had stamped them out. She had vowed never to marry a man who did not fully share her position in this matter, and by prayer, argument, and persuasion she brought the young Methodist preacher completely to her side. And once there he never looked backwards, but went on whole-heartedly, as she did, to the extremest practical consequences of their joint belief.

Catherine Mumford was born in 1830. She was delicate and always in wretched health with spine, heart, and lungs all out of order and no energy save that of the spirit. But of that she had enough and to spare. For Catherine was passionate, vehement, and desperately determined to know the Lord's will and to follow it. She was one of those who burn with the longing for righteousness, and when after much struggle and prayer she grew clear in her beliefs, they came to her as absolute and unfaltering convictions. From that time forwards her path was plain. Outwardly, to the world's eye, her troubles were many and her problems and difficulties great; but in her innermost heart no doubts or hesitations existed. She knew the Lord's will, and all that remained was to fulfil it.

Catherine married when she was twenty-five, and had eight children in quick succession. When four of these were born, and the eldest not yet five, she began her preaching; and from that moment until her death, thirty years later, her life was filled with the rush and drive of a revivalist's work. Her body, always a "poor old troublesome affair," as she called it, was mercilessly subdued to her will. Again and again she would go from her sick-bed to her pulpit, would preach for hours with power and conviction, and then fall fainting from the strain. But these things did not hinder Catherine or abate her zeal. The hard edge of her character, which she turned upon the ungodly, was turned also upon herself. For the Lord had work for her to do.

Catherine Booth was not one of those to whom public ministration came easily. She had had to wrestle and fight with the shrinking of her nature for years before she brought herself to make her first public prayer; and she suffered a perfect agony of distress the first time she saw her name upon the hoardings. With long years of evangelistic work, of course, this reluctance grew less, but she was never able to preach without effort and great strain, over and above the weakness and failing of her body. In addition to this, as the Salvation Army grew in size and importance, a volume of work fell upon her which was almost incredible. Her correspondence was enormous, the problems of organisation which she alone could settle multiplied, and the scale of her duties widened from year to year. With it all, however, Catherine remained undismayed; she was a mother, watchful and careful of her children; a wife, helpful and devoted to her husband; a notable housekeeper and a pleasant, friendly, humorous, and eminently practical woman.

That all these qualities should be combined in one person may seem almost an impossibility, yet it is one of those impossibilities which have often occurred and which will continue to occur so long as flaming spirits are born into this world.

We have no need here to consider the basis of Catherine Booth's religious work, nor the broad lines of her theology. A personal devil, a literal hell, and the possibility of sudden "conversion" were all of the essence of her faith; and these things made a simple and comprehensible appeal to the neglected and the outcast, for whom the Army chiefly worked. Neither the faith nor the success of the Army is our present concern; the part of it which is relevant to our purpose is the fact that in its ranks, from the very top to the very bottom, absolute sex equality has always prevailed.

"As the Army refuses to make any difference between men and women as to rank, authority and duties," the regulations run, "but opens the highest positions to women as well as to men, the words 'woman, she, and her' are scarcely ever used in orders, 'man, he, his' being always understood to mean a person of either sex unless it is obviously impossible."

The principle outlined in this instruction, which, of course, was implanted into the rules by Catherine Booth, has been faithfully and honestly followed. It aroused, of course, a great deal of opposition in the early days, and caused repeated storms and protests, and was a stumbling-block to many; but the General and his wife stood firm, and it was never modified in any way. The worst of the trouble arose, indeed, from the ranks of the Army itself. The subordinate male officers resented being placed under the orders of a woman, and tried in all sorts of ways to get out of a position which convention told them was undignified and unworthy of their manhood. But the discipline of the Army was firm. Those who did not like its ways were free to leave it; but while they remained, its rules and principles must not be set aside. They could take it or leave it; and for the most part they took it with a good grace.

Even if the principle had been bad and had proved ineffective in practice, Catherine Booth would probably have stuck to it and gone down, and let the Army go down, with these colours flying. But the very contrary was the case. By liberating the energies of the women who joined them, by using their ministry and their gifts, the Army more than doubled its strength. It grew and prospered amazingly. "It may only be a coincidence," as W. T. Stead said,[1] "but if so it is a curious one, that the year (1875 when this principle was adopted) marks the beginning of the phenomenal expansion of the Salvation Army." Certainly it was a phenomenal expansion, for within twelve years it was employing nearly 50,000 officers, and was spending an annual income of over half a million pounds.

The effect of this concrete evidence of the practical working of sex equality upon the progress of the Woman's Movement cannot be measured in Acts of Parliament, or in any other tangible shape, but it had its influence both upon "the man in the street" and the woman "on the streets." While the regular feminist organisations were attending to the politicians, the educators, the philanthropists, and the men and women of the professional classes by meetings, pamphlets, arguments, and the like, the Salvation

[1] *Life of Catherine Booth*, by W. T. Stead.

Army was carrying through the slums an object-lesson which was much more easy to understand. The Hallelujah lassies were not consciously preaching feminism; they were looking for souls to be snatched from sin and damnation, they were wrestling with drunkenness, vice, and degradation; but as they went about their business they taught the other lesson too, in that quiet and practical fashion which best carries conviction.

Through the seventies, eighties, and nineties, therefore, the movement was steadily gaining ground by the increase of favourable public opinion. It was still a good joke to allude to strong-minded, unsexed, and blue-stockinged members of the shrieking sisterhood, but little bits of the ideals of these ladies were actually finding their way into the laws and customs of the country, and the general public was, slowly and unconsciously, getting used to the general feminist idea.

In 1870, just at the time when the suffrage committees had divided over the question of the degree of their connection with Mrs Butler, the workers in her crusade had first embarked upon the international side of their cause, and she herself had begun those visits to the Continent from which a widespread organisation was to follow. She did not neglect affairs at home, however, and the campaign against the Acts was continued with unabated vigour. In 1874 Gladstone's Government went out of office and thus freed Mr James Stansfeld, who had been a member of it, to come out publicly on their "Abolitionist" platforms. He stood forward boldly on their side in the House (thereby ruining for ever his own political prospects); and after that date no extension of the Acts was even proposed. It was one thing to check their spread, but a harder one to secure their repeal; and for session after session Mr Stansfeld and the others battled against the mighty force of official parliamentary obstruction. At last the opportunity for a straight decision on the question was secured, and in 1883

Mr Stansfeld brought forward his resolution condemning compulsory medical examination and the whole system of state-regulated prostitution.

Mrs Butler and her co-workers were desperately anxious about the result. "We have arranged," she wrote to her son, "for a great meeting of prayer; we shall hold it close to the House of Commons during the whole debate, and all night, if the debate lasts all night. Some of our parliamentary friends counselled this course, saying that it was well that all the world should know with what weapons and in whose name we made war, even if they scoff at the idea, as of course so many do." When the night came this prayer-meeting was duly held, and a very strange and moving sight it was. A large hall in the Westminster Palace Hotel was packed with women—ladies in their evening-dresses kneeling beside outcasts from the slums of Westminster, many of them in tears, and all beseeching Heaven to guide their rulers into the paths of justice. Mrs Butler came and went to and fro between this gathering and the House. "I felt ready to cry," she said, "but I did not, for I long ago rejected the old ideal of the division of labour, that 'men must work and women must weep.'" It was no time for tears while there were still words which might be spoken and prayers which might be said. In the meeting-room an old lady from America rose from her knees. "Tears are good," she said, "prayers are better, but we should get on better still if behind every tear there was a vote at the ballot-box," and all the women in the room agreed with her words.

When at last the division came, the result was a victory for the crusaders; and from that day the operation of the Acts was suspended. Three years later, in 1886, the formal Repeal followed, state regulation of vice disappeared from the statute book, and the definite objective of the crusade was won.

All was by no means settled and put right by the Repeal of the Contagious Diseases Acts, however. The position of women in regard to sexual matters was still profoundly unsatisfactory, and in particular the protection offered by the law to girl children was lamentably incomplete. Although the Royal Commission of 1871 had recommended a change, the age of consent was still only thirteen, and the business of "procuring" was quite openly practised, and could not legally be proceeded against. If a child of thirteen entered a house of ill-fame of her own accord (even though she knew nothing of its character or of the existence or purpose of such houses) she could then be violated without any possibility of redress; the act of entering its doors was legal proof of her consent to what might take place within. The houses where this occurred, and the men and women who made their living by the traffic were well known to the police, but since it was all perfectly legal they could make no attempt to bring it to an end.

A commission of the House of Commons, which had reported on the White Slave Traffic in 1881, had led to the drafting of a Bill to amend the Criminal Law, but nothing more than its formal introduction took place. The Bill was strongly opposed by a group of members who argued that attempts to legislate upon the subject did nothing but harm, and that those who supported them were visionary, impractical, and did not know the world. The supporters of the Bill—the same, of course, as the supporters of the Abolitionist Crusade—carried little weight, and in this matter they had not got behind them the driving public opinion which Mrs Butler had mobilised. The subject was so horrible, and its details so revolting, that few people cared to think of it at all. And session after session the Bill was blocked, and the evil continued unchecked.

In the summer of 1885 the supporters of the Bill saw its chances vanishing once more, and decided to make a supreme effort to save it, and the method they chose was exposure in the public Press. Mr Benjamin Scott, the City Chamberlain, and Mrs Butler went to W. T. Stead, then

Editor of the *Pall Mall Gazette*, and begged him to save the Bill by publishing the facts of the situation, and Stead, as soon as he understood the full urgency and difficulty of the situation, undertook the task. Stead's methods were dramatic. He first made an inquiry into the vices and crimes of the underworld, and when he was clear as to the facts and the state of the law, he devised a plan which would show them up in their luridness. He went to the leaders of the religious bodies and secured their approval, and he asked Mrs Booth for the practical help which the Salvation Army was so well qualified to give, and then he proceeded to carry his plans into effect. With the aid of a woman who had once been the keeper of a brothel, but who had been converted and reformed by the Salvation Army, he found a mother who was willing for the sum of five pounds to sell her daughter, a child just over thirteen, and he had this girl brought to him in a house of ill-fame, and kept there for a night. She was, of course, carefully guarded the whole time and protected from harm, and the next morning she was taken away to Paris and put under the care of a woman officer of the Salvation Army; but the transaction had been carried through in all seriousness, and its possibility and its legality were manifest.

The next day Stead began to publish his indictment in the *Pall Mall Gazette*, under the heading of "The Maiden Tribute of Modern Babylon," and the storm which he thereby roused exceeded even his own anticipations. Everyone in London, and, by the next day, everyone all over the English-speaking world, read the articles. They were the one topic of conversation, the one interest of the whole week. Cabbies spread out the sheets on the tops of their hansom-cabs, and newsboys fought with each other for a supply of copies to sell. The office of the paper was fairly beseiged, and so great was the demand that the supply of paper ran out and more had to be hastily commandeered. Everyone read "The Maiden Tribute," but almost everyone disapproved of it and cried out against its publication. The rest of the Press came out with a blaze of indignation, not against the crime and the vice that Stead was exposing, but against Stead himself for putting it into words. The world was shocked and shaken, and the foundations of all public decency seemed to be cut away when such things could be done, and such things said in the cause of public morals.

Day after day the articles followed each other, however, driving home the facts to the eager, the horrified, the scandalised, and the serious alike, and on the fifth day the Criminal Law Amendment Bill, which had waited for five years in obscurity, was rushed through its second reading. The real public had been successfully aroused and its force was overwhelming. Nor did the pressure stop with the passing of the second reading; all over the country the mass of well-meaning and orderly citizens met and demanded the immediate completion of the Bill, and in another month all its remaining stages had been cleared out of the way, and it had passed into law.[1]

The passage of the Act of 1885 secured Stead's main object, but the storm he had raised did not die down with this victory. He was attacked from all sorts of different angles, as a seeker after notoriety, a purveyor of indecent literature, and a maker of money by sensation; but the thing which really tripped him up, and which enabled his enemies to get a sentence of imprisonment passed against him, was the fact that the procuress who acted for him had secured the consent of the girl's mother and had paid the money to her, whereas in law the mother was not a legal parent and it was the father alone who was legally entitled to negotiate such a sale. Curiously enough it came out,

[1] The Criminal Law Amendment Act of 1885 raised the age of consent to sixteen, made procuration a criminal offence, and the penalty for assault on a girl under thirteen either whipping or penal servitude. It also gave certain rights of search in houses used for immoral purposes, and made it possible to put children under the custody of guardians appointed by the court.

at a later date, that the girl was illegitimate, and had been, therefore, under the mother's control and not the father's all the time,[1] but this was not known when Stead was arrested, and the supposed illegality of his contract with the mother was the chief reason why, a few months after the Act was passed, Stead and his helpers, when brought to trial for abducting the girl, were condemned to imprisonment for various periods; and Stead's portion of this "punishment" was three months.

"I cannot find words to say how I honour and reverence you for what you have done for the weakest and most helpless among women," wrote Mrs Fawcett to Stead on the day that his sentence was passed, "I always felt that by some legal quibble you might be tripped up, as it were; but this is nothing; your work will stand. . . . If gratitude and honour from myself and many hundreds and thousands of your countrymen can help you at this stress, I want you to have that help." These words, and the fact they stood for, did bring comfort of course; and it was much needed. Stead suffered greatly under his imprisonment, especially until his friends had secured his removal from Millbank to Holloway, where he was well treated; and he tormented himself with the thought that he might have managed his plot better and have avoided the trial and the punishment he had brought upon his helpers. But the great thing was that the public had been roused to the evils and dangers of the case, and that real and solid reforms had been won. The National Vigilance Association was founded in this same year, with Mr W. A. Coote as its secretary; and henceforward it was certain that the enveloping blanket of silence would never again completely cover over the criminal vice which lurks in the great cities of the world.

The safety and honour of women and their protection

[1] Children born in wedlock were entirely in the power of the father. Children born out of wedlock were said to be *filius nulli* and were under the control of the mother, who was alone liable for their support.

against commercialised vice and state regulation were not the only aspects of their sex position which received attention during the years we are considering. Women can be victims and prostitutes and also wives and mothers; and all these capacities arise from the fact of their sex. The positions of married and unmarried mothers, of the wives and the "kept women" were very different under the law; but the Women's Movement extended to cover them all; and even at the time when these outcast and unfortunate women seemed the centre of attention, the "sheltered and protected" were not forgotten.

The technical fault upon which Stead had been convicted gave some prominence to the state of the law in regard to mothers; but their absence of rights in their legitimate children was generally assumed to be natural. In 1886, however, a small advantage was won for them and a Guardianship of Infants' Act was passed, which laid down that upon a father's death a mother should become the guardian, or at least a joint guardian of her children. From that date it was no longer possible for a man to leave his children wholly away from their mother, and she secured a possibility of appeal for custody to the courts. The work which Mrs Norton had begun was thus carried a step further, and the position of mothers considerably improved. But matters were still far from satisfactory or just.

Married women, as we have seen, were without their free property rights until 1882; but there were other disadvantages connected with the state of matrimony which were alleviated at other times. The Divorce Law of 1857 had opened the possibility of divorce to women in cases where there was adultery plus desertion or cruelty on the part of the husband, and in 1869 the courts for the first time held that "restraint and confinement" constituted legal cruelty for this purpose.[1] The old theory that on marriage the woman became the property of her husband was severely

[1] Decision of Lord Penzance, 1869.

shaken by this judgment, and the extensions which followed in the course of the next few years weakened it still further. In 1878 a wife was enabled to secure separation, with custody of her children under ten years old, if her husband was convicted of aggravated assault upon her, and the limits to his legal rights of abuse were thus laid down.

In 1884 matters went farther, and the Matrimonial Causes Act put an end to the penalty of imprisonment for refusal to comply with a decree for the restitution of conjugal rights (on the part of either party), and established the convenient fiction that such a refusal was equivalent to desertion.

In 1886 the Married Women (Maintenance in Case of Desertion) Act enabled a woman to proceed at law for a contribution to maintenance without first going to the workhouse, and the framework of legal redress for matrimonial abuses was raised.

It was as yet far from complete, however, and the old tradition died hard. It was not until 1891 that a married woman's personal freedom was finally safeguarded. In that year a Mr Jackson, whose wife had left him, obtained a decree for the restitution of conjugal rights. She refused to obey it, and one Sunday as she was leaving Church with her sister he seized upon her and with the aid of two other young men he forced her into a carriage and drove her to his house, where he imprisoned her. The wife's friends brought an action for Habeas Corpus, and, after long argument, and much quoting of precedents, the decision was in her favour.[1] Henceforth a woman was a legal, as well as an actual person, free to go where she pleased, whether she was married or not.

Many minor disadvantages still weighed upon the married woman, however, which only time and enfranchisement were to redress. But the worst of the old abuses were extinguished, and by 1900 British women were, in the main,

[1] *Jackson* v. *Jackson*, 1891.

free, both in their persons and their properties, their minds and their consciences, their bodies and their souls. They were still politically outcast and economically oppressed. Many of them were still under-educated and over-flattered, too much despised and too much admired; but the number of those who were seeking for the new road was increasing, and the Women's Movement was nearing its height.

CHAPTER XII

WOMEN MUST WORK. 1860–1890

The development of women's employment—The custom of low pay for women—The opposition of the men workers—The learned professions—Women's work in factories—The attitude of the feminists—Their intervention in Parliament against regulation based on sex—The Cradley Heath Nail- and Chain-makers' Deputation, 1887—The Trade Union attitude—The formation of women's unions—Mrs Emma Patterson, the attitude of the Trade Union Congress—The men at last support the women's unions—Women's Trade Union League formed, 1889.

WHILE the Women's Suffrage question was passing from hopefulness to temporary eclipse, another more complicated aspect of the Women's Movement was developing, and as it did so it revealed new problems and new dangers. The matter of women's employment had been in a bad case in 1857, when Barbara Bodichon had opened her little office in Berners Street, but at least the line of progress had seemed clear. Women were then shut out from an enormous number of ways of earning a living, and the obvious course had been to batter at the doors and get in. By 1890, however, the problem was a wider one; the battering was still needed, indeed, for a multitude of possible careers were closed, but there was another element in the situation which had now to be reckoned with, namely, rates of pay. And this was no easy problem to tackle.

During the thirty years which had followed the establishment of the Society for the Promotion of the Employment of Women great changes had taken place. Nursing had developed enormously, and by 1891 there were 53,057 women, the great majority of whom were definitely trained for their job, who were supporting themselves in this profession. Teaching, too, employed a huge number of women. The census of 1861 had shown 80,017 female teachers, but by 1891 the number was 146,375, and since by that date the standard of qualification had considerably risen, this figure measures both the increase in teachers and the spread of girls' education.

The most striking expansion of employment, however, had occurred in the commercial world. In 1861 there had been 17,568 women shop assistants, but they numbered 29,166 only ten years later, and their increase accelerated after that date. On the clerical side the figures were even more striking. There were no female clerks or secretaries mentioned in the census returns of 1861 and 1871, but the figures, which were 5989 in 1881, rose to 17,859 ten years later.

The expansion of the field of women's work which these figures mark was not confined to these occupations alone. In every direction—though not so quickly in industry—the employment of women was increasing, and nowhere was a decrease to be found.

This large extension of wage-earners was, to some extent, accounted for by the rapid increase in the population, and in part by the general rise in the prosperity and business of the country; it was, however, also closely connected with the new stirrings of ambition and independence which education and the Women's Movement between them were stimulating among the younger women, and opportunity thus coincided with desire. The valuation which the new class of women put upon their work, and the maximum of independence which they desired, were not as yet very exorbitant. Girls were satisfied to earn just a little money, and to have just a shadow of freedom in the seventies, eighties, and nineties of the last century; and, having no acquaintance with economics, they did not realise what troubles they were bringing upon themselves by the docility and gratitude with which they accepted low rates of pay.

The greater number of these new entrants into business lived at home, at any rate when they first began to work, and they were, therefore, not called upon wholly to support themselves. A small contribution to the housekeeping from the daughter was a great boon in families where she had been expected to be a dead weight upon the income, and the pay which the typists and the shop assistants received not only made this possible but allowed a little tiny margin to the girl herself, to spend on the independence and the "fun" which she craved. Those of them who were not in this sheltered position, of course, found that wages based on these standards were all too little for their bare needs; they skimped and scraped to keep themselves alive, they lived on "a glass of milk and a bun," and bravely set up the false and pathetic tradition that a woman does not need to eat so much as a man, and can live in comfort upon a fraction of his pay.

During the years when these evil habits were growing up there was no one to advise the new workers. The Trade Union Movement was too busy with the multitudinous industrial problems to have attention to spare for other fields, and the feminists were still pushing against closed doors, and were too eager to see women introduced to new work to boggle at the terms of their introduction. They did, indeed, make formal protests about equal pay, and tried to keep the idea forward; but they could not find it in their hearts to advise women to stand out for wages they were certain to be refused, nor would the women have listened to them if they had! Miss Davies and Mrs Garrett Anderson made an effort in 1872 to persuade the London County Council to adopt equal scales of pay for men and women school visitors, but they totally failed. The men were started at rates from £80 to £100, and the women from £50 to £70. And at these rates there were few men and hundreds of women to accept the work.

There is no doubt that the cheapness and the "docility"

of women greatly facilitated their employment in all the avocations which now opened to them. Employers said this quite openly. An official of the Post Office put it clearly in 1871. "We get a better class of women for the same pay," he said; "they are more patient under routine, less liable to combine, and leave often on marriage when their pay would be increasing." From the employers' point of view nothing could be more excellent.

From the point of view of the men workers, however, there are other things to be said. Although in that period of prosperity and expansion there was not a present danger of unemployment, yet a tendency to try and keep the intruders out was distinctly to be seen. Mr Frank Scudamore introduced women for the first time into the Post Office, and when they were taken on in the Savings Bank Department in 1872, there was almost a riot at St Martin's-le-Grand. The controllers and all the staff united in protests against what they declared to be the "grievous dangers, moral and official, which are likely to follow the adoption of so extraordinary a course!" The indignation meetings of the staff actually led to the abandonment of the experiment, and the forty dangerous females who had been engaged were sent about their business. In the next year, however, the Postmaster-General tried again, and advertised eleven vacancies. The fact that he had 2000 applicants, although the starting wage was 14s. a week, is evidence that, for all the improvement that was going on, the available avenues of women's employment were still considerably choked up.

Among teachers the tendency for the men to resist the "encroachments" of the women was also to be found. In 1867 a deputation of parochial school-masters urged upon the authorities that some additional allowances might be provided for them by means of a reduction in the salaries of the school-mistresses, and in 1879 the Birmingham Education Authority was temporarily forced to discontinue the employment of women as teachers of small boys because the men teachers raised such an outcry about the "encouragement to immorality" which it involved!

In spite of these and many other examples of the expression of the men's hostility, it is true to say that among the professional and middle classes the opposition did not find very effective utterance. Where they were highly organised, as among lawyers and doctors, it was evident enough; but elsewhere they had no way of voicing their feelings. Individual men might sneer at the self-supporting women, and attempt to hold back their own daughters with a heavy hand; but the gradual invasion of shops and offices went steadily on, and they were unable to stem the tide.

Among the learned professions the fight was fiercer. As we have seen, the medical women had to force their way against the bitterest opposition, and, had they added undercutting to the crime of being women, they would have fared even worse. Fortunately, however, they did not make this mistake. From the very first they demanded, and received, the same scales of payment, and succeeded in holding their own on equal terms. The medical women had special and particular arguments to back up their claim, and they had won because there was a well-defined work for them to do. In the legal world, however, there was no such clear case for female practitioners, and the barristers and solicitors easily kept them at bay. A society was indeed founded in 1879 "to promote knowledge of the law, and to consider the abilities and disabilities of women as to the practice of law in any of its branches," but it made no headway at all. The Inns of Court clung tightly to their privileges, and kept the women out. The Army, the Navy, and the Church, of course, were not so much as considered. Even the most advanced feminist hardly thought of attacking these strongholds, and they were left undisturbed. Little bits of progress appeared in other directions, however, some of them owing to the efforts of the Women's Employment

Society, and others—spontaneous manifestations. The Slade School of Art opened its doors to women in 1872 (although only on condition that they did not study from the nude), and the examinations of the Pharmaceutical Society were available in the same year. Journalists began to multiply. Mr Stead employed one in a high position on the staff of the *Pall Mall Gazette* in 1882, and, what was more, he paid her what she would have had if she had been a man; and by 1895 there were sixty women members of the Institute of Journalists. The assistant teachers in the new High Schools set a wholly new standard of affluence for governesses by earning from £80 to £100 a year. Nursing extended and increased, the training schools of the big hospitals were always full, and the magnificent work organised in Liverpool for the nursing staffs of Poor Law Infirmaries began to spread over the country. The Midwives' Institute was founded in 1881, and an effort to improve the standards of that calling began. The chief reform which the midwives desired was the introduction of an official register; but this was bitterly opposed by the British Medical Association, which succeeded in staving it off for many years. The doctors were afraid that if midwives were trained and registered they themselves would be less often called in; and the doctors were so powerful and so well organised that, in spite of the cruelty of this obstruction (which, of course, they disguised under specious arguments), they had their way. In numerous other directions, however, the field of employment widened out. Swanley College for gardening was opened in 1892, and though the choice that lay before the non-manual worker was still limited, and the pay barely enough to live upon, the old miserable state of affairs was undoubtedly improving.

It was still true, of course, that girls were almost wholly untrained, that they were half ashamed of earning their livings, and that they neither expected nor desired to undertake important or responsible work; they acquiesced in the fatal system of lower pay, they half agreed with those who maintained that they did not deserve more, and they neither resented nor combated the opposition of their male colleagues. But economic necessity was driving the girls out, and the old prejudices and the old taboos were slowly and quietly breaking down.

This was the trend of affairs in the middle classes during the thirty years preceding the close of the century, but in the working classes rather different conditions prevailed. The same difficulties existed, of course. Economic pressure drove women to the factories, as it had done ever since the Industrial Revolution first began, and their own meekness, the opposition of the men workers, and the traditions of ages held them back and restricted their scope. Employers wanted them because they were cheap, and as far as these general factors went, the situation was the same in all ranks of employment. But by 1870 things were no longer fluid in the industrial world. Laws and hard-and-fast customs were beginning to govern the skilled trades; the unions had managed to make an end of individual bargaining, and everything was more closely watched and more sharply defined than was the case in the commercial and semi-professional fields.

We cannot describe here in any detail the position, numbers, or rates of pay of the female factory workers of the seventies, eighties, and nineties. The innumerable variations of detail, the constant development of processes, and the fractional fluctuation of wages are matters which were of untold importance to the women whom they directly affected, but which can now fall into their places as straws indicating the direction in which the wind was blowing.

The main tendencies of the period in regard to female factory workers seem to have been conditioned by three factors, the first of which was the operation of legal restrictions and measures of state control and protection, the second the rigid demarcation and other customs imposed upon the trades by the policies and inclinations of the Trade Unions, and the third the employers' habit of paying women very low wages. All three of these important factors were imposed upon women's industry without reference to the wishes or opinions of the women concerned; they were enforced for what was thought to be the greatest advantage of the country as a whole, and the women workers, unorganised and inarticulate as they were, would have had no way of expressing their views, even if they had had any views to express.

The organised feminists, however, were not in this condition. They had views upon the matter of industrial employment for women, and they expressed them freely; and, although they could not include any large number of working women within their ranks, they felt themselves as well able to pronounce upon the questions as the Members of the House of Commons or the male workers. Indeed, they felt themselves rather better able to form a judgment than these other sets of people, since they were neither open to pressure from the voting strength of employers or workmen, nor themselves in any way competitors of the people for whom the regulations and restrictions were made.

The intervention of the feminists in the matter followed only the first two lines: the line of legal enactments, and the line of Trade Union organisation, for wages seemed too difficult to touch. In both the directions in which they did move the feminists were almost wholly unsuccessful, but their attempt and their failure are nevertheless of considerable interest and importance.

Their intervention concerning the laws affecting women's work began in 1873, and is still continuing (though in a somewhat different form) at this day. As we saw in Chapter III, the Ten Hours Act of 1847 (which was further extended and completed in 1850 and 1853) regulated the hours of employment of women and young persons, but, except through its consequent results, it did nothing to control the employment of men. When this law was first passed there was no feminist organisation in existence to express an opinion upon it, nor were the women workers themselves organised in any way, or able to make their own views known. If they had been, it seems probable that they would have been frightened of the change lest it should injure their powers of earning wages, though at the same time they would certainly have longed for the relief of shorter hours. At any rate they had no opportunity of saying anything, and the Act was passed, and became part and parcel of the industrial structure of the country. The employment of women at night, and in trades involving night work, ceased to be a possible experiment, and—after Government inspection had become a reality—it was no longer attempted. As those who had promoted the Act had hoped, it had its repercussions upon the employment of men. Although there were many exceptions, it gradually came to be the custom to employ men only for the same standard day as was legally imposed upon women, and their possibilities of unlimited overtime were checked, and bargained for, by the Trade Unions, whose increasing strength established a parallel form of protection for men. There were great differences between the two forms of protection, however; the one which protected the women was imposed on them without their consent; it was entirely inflexible, and infringements of it were punishable in the courts, so that not even the most special circumstances would warrant its relaxation. The other, which was the result of the men's own combination, was a much more adaptable affair. The male workers in different trades could, and did, adjust their demands to the necessities of the different trades, and, owing to the fact that the agreements were voluntary, and not enforceable at law, they could be freely modified on either side. Both systems had their disadvantages; but the fact that no agitation arose on the part of the men for legal enactments to reinforce their bargains about hours seems to indicate which of the two forms of protection they themselves preferred.

The women, of course, were different. They were women in the first place, which made their affairs of less moment; and then they were unorganised. Except in the textile trades, where their position from the first had been a strong one, the women of the factory population were not admitted to the Trade Union movement, and so the possibility of voluntary self-protection for them did not exist. In the labour opinion of the period legal protection was all that the women could expect.

In 1873 an inquiry of the Home Office into the matter of factory hours was held, and a report was adopted recommending further reduction of women's hours from sixty to fifty-four a week. This proposal was embodied in a Bill which came before the House the same year, and it was then that the opposition of the "feminists" appeared. Professor Fawcett argued so strongly and so urgently against the Bill that it was dropped and lost to view. In the following year a small Bill amending the existing Act came forward, and this gave an opportunity for the position to be stated again. Mr Fawcett, therefore, moved that, over and above the matters included in this Bill, a clause be inserted freeing women from the operation of the hours' provisions of the Ten Hours Act, and putting them on an equal footing with men workers in this respect. His argument was unavailing, but it is worth while to restate it, as it represents the point of view which was held by the official Women's Movement. He maintained that protection imposed upon one set of workers alone amounted to discrimination against them; that because they were not free to work the same hours as their competitors, women were shut out of opportunities of employment which would otherwise be open, and that their freedom of choice, and of bargaining, was thus unduly restricted. He naturally desired to abolish abuses in the number of hours worked, and did not advocate a longer working day for women; but he believed that they could protect themselves by organisation, as men did, and that this was a more just, more effective, and less dangerous form of protection than a legal rule applied to one sex alone.

Mixed with these observations and underlying them there was, of course, the individualist doctrine. The Radicals of the seventies and eighties hated all infringements of individual liberty from their hearts, and for this reason the form of equality in industrial legislation which they preferred was an equality of liberation from State interference. But the tide of opinion was setting more and more towards State control of the conditions of work, and it is conceivable that if they had pressed for an equality obtained by the equal restriction of men they might have achieved their objects. As it was they failed; Mr Fawcett's amendment was lost in 1874 and lost again in 1878, and the legal restriction of women's hours remains to this day.

One little concession they did gain, namely, the exclusion of "home workshops" from the operation of the Factory and Workshop Act of 1878; but this exception, standing by itself, unsupported by the general practice of the trades, proved most unfortunate. The women employed in "home workshops" were even less susceptible of organisation and less capable of self-protection than the other women workers, and the freedom which was won for them turned out in practice to be nothing but a freedom to be sweated and overdriven. Whether this would have been the case if the whole amendment had been won we cannot tell; but it seems probable, in the light of modern developments, that it would, and that the substance underlying the feminist case could have been best secured by the early imposition of restrictions upon men, and not their removal from women.

After the Parliamentary defeat on the Factories and Workshops Act, no other opportunity to raise the question of hours arose; but there was another occasion on which the "feminists" intervened in an industrial question, and this time with greater success, and that was the case of the Mines Regulation Amendment Act of 1887.

Women had been forbidden to work in mines in 1842,[1] but the prohibition had not extended to work at the pit-head, and a considerable number of women had continued to be employed there, shifting and grading coal and loading trucks. In 1874 there were nearly 12,000 women and girls so employed, but the number was decreasing, and by 1886 there were but 5568.

When a Government Bill appeared in 1887 to amend the regulations in force in the mining industry, an attempt was made to shut these women out from their occupation, on the ostensible ground that it was "unhealthy and immoral," and, moreover, "undesirable for women." The women concerned, however, protested vigorously against all these accusations, and their health was so remarkably above the average that the first of them was clearly fantastic. The case was taken up with the greatest sympathy by the suffrage societies, who held protest meetings and wrote to the papers, and took all the other customary steps to bring pressure to bear. At the same time also an attempt was made to fix by law the weight of the hammers which might be lifted by the women nail- and chain-makers. If this were done it would restrict the women to the smaller work and seriously interfere with the employment of a great many of them, and at Cradley Heath, where a large number were employed, there was intense excitement and anxiety. The suffragists took up this matter earnestly, and Louisa, Lady Goldsmid, paid the expenses of a deputation of women who desired to come from there to lay their case before the Home Secretary, Mr Matthews.

They were escorted to the Home Office by Mrs Fawcett and Lady Goldsmid, and as soon as they got into the room the Home Secretary began to explain to them that a certain important medical officer had reported to him that the

[1] See Chap. III.

heavier hammers would be prejudicial to their health, especially those who were of child-bearing age. A very stalwart-looking woman immediately exclaimed, "I ha' had fourteen children, sir, and I never was better in my life." Mr Matthews expressed polite satisfaction, and again quoted the doctor, whereupon all the nail- and chain-makers exclaimed in chorus, "He's dead, sir!" as much as to say, "He's dead and we are alive, so we needn't bother about him any more." The Home Secretary then asked very politely if one of them would describe exactly what happened in the course of their work, and the stalwart one again spoke up and said: "The manager, he come down in the morning, and he say he want fourteen sweat of chain before the afternoon." Here Mr Matthews interrupted: "I beg your pardon, I don't quite understand?" and another woman explained, "Fourteen 'undredweight she mean, sir; c-w-t. sweat, you see"; and then the explanation proceeded without further interruption, the women from time to time asserting that limiting them to the lighter hammers would restrict their wage-earning power, which they much resented. Mr Matthews was most polite and kind throughout, and as the deputation was talking it over among themselves outside, one of the women turned to Mrs Fawcett and summed up their impression of the Home Secretary: "It's very 'ard upon the pore gentleman," she said, "to 'ave to make the laws, and not to know nothing about it."

Whether it was the effect of this deputation, or, as he claimed in the House, the "pore man's" own unaided judgment, the upshot was that the amendment excluding women from the pit-brow work, and the regulation preventing the use of the heavier hammers, were not proceeded with; and for the moment the women were allowed to continue their work undisturbed.

These occasions were the chief ones upon which the feminists tried to intervene to improve the position of industrial workers in relation to the law; but it was not the only way in which they tried to help them. The legal position of women workers, although it is the easiest to explain, is not by any means the most important of the factors governing their working lives; customary restrictions, and the subdivision of industry into men's and women's work is a far more considerable matter, and on this complex and difficult ground the feminists dared to tread—only to be warned off with indignation by the spokesmen of the men's Trade Unions.

The truth of the matter was, in reality, that the "feminists" and the Trade Unionists were talking and thinking at cross purposes. The feminists were thinking of industry not as it was, but as it ought to have been in respect to women. They saw that the customs and segregations and lower wages of the women workers resulted in their exclusion from the skilled processes, and they believed that this meant not only hardship to women, but also a waste of natural ability, and an uneconomic use of labour and brains. The men, on the other hand, took industry as it was, and thought chiefly of the dangerous results which might follow from change; they regarded women as necessarily unskilled, almost casual labour, and believed them to be a menace to their own precarious standard of life, and a dangerous class of blacklegs whose whole industrial existence was a mistake. Starting from these divergent premises, the two policies could not fail to clash. The men's very genuine fears were put aside by the feminists as plain sex selfishness, while the ideals of the women were derided as middle-class ignorance by the men; and it is only within recent years that they have begun to draw within sight of agreement.

In actual fact, moreover, there was some justification for both views; and they very quickly began to clash with each other. The trend of industry between 1870 and 1900 was such that the conflict between men and women was apparent. In spite of the traditional customs, in spite of the hostility of the men and the obedient apathy of the women workers, "encroachments" were constantly taking place, and in all the light metal trades (cycle, chain, nail, bolt and rivet, etc.), as well as in tobacco and a dozen other industries, unskilled women were being taken on in place of skilled men, at half or less than half their rates of wages.

This transformation was not possible in any trade which was itself stable as regards method of production. So long as conditions remained unchanged the women would refuse to do "men's jobs," or, if they were willing, the men would refuse to work beside them. But when the job itself changed, when new machinery, new subdivision of processes, and new objects of manufacture were introduced, the employer was able to put in an entering wedge, and the custom was circumvented.[1] And in most cases the employer was eager to do this, because of the immediate reduction in the wages' bill which he could thus ensure.[2]

This process went on steadily and perpetually, and the only way in which the men tried to meet it was by resistance. The certainty of undercutting was so terrible, and the economic pressure so great that they opposed the employment of females as much as they could, refused to work with them wherever they had any hope of success, and tried hard to drive them down to as small a number of trades, and as small a number of processes within those trades, as they

[1] "Usually the women perform some branch of work which is wholly abandoned to them by the men ; and they refrain, whether willingly or not, from engaging in the branches monopolised by their male rivals. The line between the two classes is often subtle enough, and it varies from place to place. Moreover, whatever the dividing line may be in any particular locality at any given time, it shifts with almost every change in the industrial process ; moving, too, nearly always in the direction of leaving the women in possession of an ever larger industrial field."—Sidney Webb, *Problem of Modern Industry*.

[2] "In the inquiry into wages one of the outstanding facts elicited was, that whenever women had replaced men the former always received a much lower wage, and that this wage was not proportionate to the skill or intelligence required by the work, but approximated to a certain fixed level—about ten shillings to twelve shillings a week. The wage that the man previously received gave no criterion as to what the woman would get."—*Women's Work and Wages*, Cadbury, Matheson, and Shaw, 1906.

could secure. Their motives for this policy were comprehensible enough, but unfortunately they did not state them clearly. Instead of justifying themselves by their own needs, they sought for a moral justification, and ardently preached the doctrine that women "ought not" to be in industry at all, and that their "proper place" was at home. Whatever there may be to be said for this doctrine in the abstract, it was useless to preach it to the working women of the end of the nineteenth century. Fate and society had so arranged the world that nearly four millions of women had to work or starve; and preaching was of no avail.

The feminists, of course, were infuriated by this line of argument. They claimed that women should have the opportunity to do as they liked; that home and work were not, or at least ought not to be, alternatives, and that in any case it was for women themselves, and not for men, to make the choice. Moreover, they remembered the disproportion in the numbers of men and women, and while they might perhaps have had sympathy for the real motives of the men, they had nothing but contempt for their preachings.

In these circumstances they adopted the course which, as things have developed, has proved to have been the wisest line of progress. For they set to work to organise the women, and began to encourage a Trade Union movement among them.

The woman who first started Women's Trade Union organisation was herself both a working woman and a feminist, and at first she got her main support from outside the Trade Union world. Emma Patterson was born in 1848, apprenticed to a bookbinder in her youth, and married to a cabinetmaker at twenty-five. She was secretary both to a working-men's club and to a Women's Suffrage Society, and at one time worked with Miss Emily Faithfull in connection with the Victoria Press. She went to America in 1874, and there she saw women's unions in existence, so that she became fired with the hope of founding similar bodies in England. On her return she interested Charles Kingsley, Harriet Martineau, and a number of other "middle-class" people, as well as a few "real" Trade Unionists, in the idea, and with their help she launched a society called the Women's Protective and Provident League, in 1875. Under this general title a number of little struggling unions came into existence among the women dressmakers, upholsterers, bookbinders, artificial flower-makers, feather-dressers, brick-, lace-, paper-box and bag-makers, glass, tobacco, jam and pickle, and small metal-workers, rag-pickers, shop-assistants and typists. These little societies were exceedingly unstable; they sprang up and melted away with great rapidity, and Mrs Patterson and her friends soon realised that the task they had set before themselves was one which was appallingly hard. Then, as now, the women workers were difficult to organise because of the very things which made their organisation so necessary. Their low wages, their unskilled status, their youth and helplessness, the overcrowding of their employments, and their own tendency to stay but a short time at their work all rendered them very unstable material; and yet each one of these causes was by itself an argument to prove the necessity for their organisation.

The difficulties which Mrs Patterson met with were made no easier at the outset by the attitude of the men's unions. For several years her application for admission to the Trade Union Congress was refused as that of "some middle-class ladies," and after it had been conceded she found that, although she herself was treated with the utmost personal courtesy, she could get but little support for her views. She held the same opinion that Professor Fawcett was urging upon the House of Commons, namely, that women workers were hindered and handicapped by the protective legislation which was imposed upon them, and she wanted to see the Factory Acts amended so as to restore to women the freedom that was enjoyed by men. Mrs Patterson's speeches on this point were listened to by the Trade Union Congress, and she was allowed to put her amendments to their resolutions on Factory Laws; but when it came to voting, she and her two women companions found themselves alone; as the spokesman of the parliamentary committee put it in 1877, "it was natural for ladies to be impatient of restraint at any time . . . (But men) had the future of their country and children to consider, and it was their duty as men and husbands to use their utmost endeavours to bring about a condition of things when their wives should be in their proper sphere at home, instead of being dragged into competition of livelihood against the great and strong men of the world."

How Mrs Patterson's heart must have sunk as she listened to phrases such as these, and heard the passionate applause with which they were greeted! How she must have longed to make them see that women too "had the future of their country and children to consider," and that it was for that very reason that she wanted to end the overcrowding, the sweating, and the restrictions of the women workers! But she could not get the men to understand. Their attitude resembled that of one of the very early Trade Union Congress delegates whom Mrs Butler and Mr Stuart had tried to convert to Women's Suffrage. They had argued that the grounds for asking for the vote for women were exactly the same as those for asking for the vote for working men, and this delegate, who was a miner from Wigan, had listened attentively. "I agree," he said, "that the arguments for women are the same as the arguments for men. The only difference is that in the case of working men these arguments apply, and in the case of women they do not apply." [1]

In spite of this unsympathetic attitude of the men's unions, Mrs Patterson struggled on at her uphill task, and preached the ideal of co-operation to working women

[1] *Reminiscences*, by James Stuart.

wherever she could find an opportunity of interesting them; inside the Trade Union Congress she continued to preach the feminist doctrine whenever she could find a loophole to bring it in, but after the passing of the Act of 1878, when it was no longer possible to hope for an amendment of the law, she changed her demands. Since regulation and protection were to be enforced, she said, it was necessary that there should be women among the Government inspectors, and she therefore moved that the Congress ask for their appointment. This proposal met with some opposition as tending to make their main demand ridiculous, but it was accepted by the mass of the delegates and carried in 1878. The next year when the Congress came round, the same resolution (without the women) appeared on the agenda, and Mrs Patterson again moved her amendment and again carried it. A year later exactly the same thing took place, and so again and again. Every year the committee struck the amendment out of the resolution, and every year the women delegates moved, and the Congress agreed to put it in again, until at last the president expostulated—not with the obstinate committee, but with the persistent women! "Feminine unreasonableness and obstinacy," he said, "were superabundantly proved"; but even this did not daunt the women, and at last after twelve years the committee gave way, and included the demand in the official form of their resolution.

Mrs Patterson did not live to see this, or any of the other results of her work, for she died in 1886. She left behind her a movement which was as yet young and small, and which was beset with every kind of difficulty, but which was one desperately called for by the needs of the time. The undercutting of the men by the women still went on, and there seemed to be almost no limit to the possible subdivision of processes, so that at last the men grew really afraid. In 1889, after the work of organising the women had been going on for fourteen years, they came to the conclusion that they had better give it some real support. In that year, therefore, they definitely adopted the policy of helping the women to organise, and plans and agreements were made to that end. The Protective and Provident League was turned into the Women's Trade Union League, and members were passed into it by a great many of the existing Trade Unions. Local branches of the men's unions wrote to its office when there were opportunities of special organisation among women, and there began to be signs of progress. The motives of the men were perhaps a little discouraging to the women. "Please send an organiser to this town," was the sort of message which arrived, "as we have decided that if the women here cannot be organised they must be exterminated." Yet even so it was better than the uncompromising hostility which had gone before. New agreements were now made, to which the women had some slight chance of being parties, by which the work in several of the trades was parcelled out; and though in these agreements the women invariably got the worst of it, still they got a trifle more than they would have had alone. They entered upon the path of collective bargaining, and here and there, as a crisis arose, a union would spring up, a fight would be fought, and a little advance recorded. When the fight was over the organisation usually fell to bits, and it seemed as if the whole thing would have to be done over again; yet all the same, inch by inch, a trifle of real progress was established, and the Women's Trade Union movement came to life.

Mrs Patterson's work was carried on and extended by Mrs MacDonald, a woman who combined in a remarkable measure the gifts of wisdom, sympathy, and enthusiasm. Margaret MacDonald was one of those pioneers whose work for the women's movement was invaluable. She opposed the "feminists," indeed, on some points of policy, and devoted herself mainly to improving the conditions of working women, and to strengthening their position within the

Labour Party; but she was one with them in her aims and ideals, and in her enthusiastic support of the Suffrage. After her death in 1911, however, the gulf between the feminists and the leaders of the labour women widened. Each, indeed, approved of the aims of the other, and shared the same ultimate ideal; but their paths towards it diverged, and labour women felt themselves both stronger and safer in alliance with the labour men than in the company of the suspect middle-class women. From this date, therefore, the two movements officially diverged; and though the strength of each added to the strength of the other, and though both were signs of the advancing political status of women, the actual organisations were distinct and separate, and few of the same people were to be found working actively in both.

CHAPTER XIII

EDUCATIONAL PROGRESS. 1870–1900

The spread of education—The London School of Medicine for Women and the victory of the women doctors—Degrees granted at London University and refused at Cambridge—Philippa Fawcett above senior wrangler in 1890—Progress at Oxford.

It is necessary to dwell in some detail on the three decades after 1870, even though the events of that period were less exciting and sensational than those which came before and after. For these years marked the development out of the pioneer stage, and were therefore the real testing-time of the vitality and soundness of the movement. It is comparatively easy for a revolutionary idea to win a few adherents and to make a preliminary stir and commotion, but it is not until it has survived the broadening process that it gathers force enough to count in the political or social world; and it was exactly this broadening and solidifying which was now going on in regard to the freedom of women. The movement had so many sides that cross currents flowed into the general stream from them all, and each was able to contribute a little to the whole. The people who granted one part of the women's claim were predisposed to tolerate, or at least to listen to, the others, so that progress began to be cumulative.

In this respect education, as was only natural, was the most effective, and after 1870 it began to make very rapid progress. The bitter opposition which had met the pioneer schools and colleges was dying down, and the necessary but undramatic task of expansion was what was now required. For this purpose a society, called the National Union for

Improving the Education of Women, came into existence, and this and the School-mistresses Association and the colleges at Girton and Newnham all played more or less smoothly into each other's hands.

The leading spirits of the new organisation were Mrs Grey and her sister Miss Sheriff. These two ladies realised that there must be a great many schools of the new type if the full experiment of education for women was to succeed, and in 1872 they formed a regularly constituted company, the Girls' Public Day Schools Company. By this device they secured money for the building and equipping of the new schools, and by good management and enthusiasm combined the enterprise was made to pay its way. In the first five years of its existence this company founded and equipped fifteen schools, and these were later followed by seventeen others, all of them schools of the new type where a real and solid education was available for a cost of about £15 a year. These schools, which of course had an immense influence upon all the private schools in the districts where they appeared, were not set up without difficulty. At first there were protests from neighbours, objections from landlords, and hesitation and timidity from parents. Teachers, too, were not easy to find, and the money difficulties were always present. But the friends of the scheme were devoted and generous. Mrs Grey herself was able to speak and to write most effectively, and she had a way of phrasing her ideas which stuck in the minds of her hearers. Those parents who heard her say that girls educated under the old system were "not educated to be wives, but only to get husbands" were likely to think that sentence over afterwards, and thought of that kind led to conversion. Moreover, Mrs Grey had many important friends, and she was able to draw Huxley and F. D. Maurice and Mark Pattison and Leslie Stephen and Professor Seeley, and Mr Cowper Temple and Mr Bryce, and dozens more into her net; and their support was invaluable. So, too, was that of the Dowager Lady Stanley of Alderley, who was a member of the council from the beginning; and her friend, Miss Mary Gurney, gave not only support and money but also daily devoted service to the task. These schools, and the hundreds of imitators which naturally followed on their success, carried forward the work of the original pioneers, and made the education of girls a reality. After the first, it was not at all an exciting movement; the slow beating down of ancient prejudice, the perpetual struggle with recurring difficulties, and the gradual widening out of a new idea is a process not capable of dramatic development. But the fact, the solid result of it all, remains profoundly important. For with the wide spread of sound teaching for girls, and with the growing up of a generation of women educated not to catch husbands but to live sensibly, the whole attitude of society towards the female sex began to change. The Women's Movement was still a long way from being popular or triumphant; its advocates were still considered cranks and oddities, but the ordinary average women, for whose benefit the whole thing primarily existed, were rapidly moving in the right direction. They were stepping out of the shadowy sentimentalities in which they had for so long been entangled, and were entering the same world as men; and when once they had done this the thin edge of the wedge was in place.

One of the most direct and immediate results of the spread of good secondary teaching for girls was, of course, that the demand for higher education increased. More girls knew that it was available, more of them had their ambitions roused, and, perhaps most potent of all, more parents realised that a college-trained girl would have a secure means of livelihood as a teacher. The remedy which F. D. Maurice and his friends had devised in 1848 was at last taking effect, and the profession of governess was raising its standards. The pay was not good, but it was a marked improvement on that of the earlier period; and, with all these elements at work, the applicants for admission to the colleges steadily outran the accommodation.

At Cambridge, after the success of the first Tripos candidates in 1873, the position steadied to a precarious balance. Each year the girls secured examination by the favour of some of the examiners, and, though sometimes there were refusals, enough friends were available to prevent a breakdown. Many of the lecturers, too, were very helpful indeed, and took great trouble and pains to help the women students. By 1873 twenty-two out of the thirty-four university professors at Cambridge were admitting women to their lectures, and sometimes the girls (properly chaperoned, of course) were allowed to attend these lectures in the class-rooms of the men's colleges. The teaching of the science students presented greater difficulty, since the Victorian sense of propriety would have been outraged if the girls had worked in the same laboratories at the same times as the young men; but Mr Philip Main, of St John's College, came to the rescue. He obtained the necessary permission, and by getting up very early and taking the girls before breakfast, he was able to give a double set of classes, and so help them on their way. This kind of generosity met the women's colleges in rather greater quantity than the obstruction, and it was immensely cheering; indeed, without it the experiment never could have succeeded. There is a long list of "Benefactors" to whom the cause of women's higher education owes its existence, and the professors who refused fees for teaching the girls, or returned them into the college funds, and those who gave their time and leisure to the work of establishing the new venture stand high upon it.

In actual bricks and mortar the colleges were not as yet very well supplied. The students from Hitchin were moved into their new building at Girton in the autumn of 1873, but it was not by any means ready for them. There were few doors, and hardly any windows; the grounds were merely heaps of builders' rubbish, without trees or even fences, and the whole thing was raw and unfinished and uncomfortable. Miss Davies was acting as mistress at this period, but even she, with her indomitable enthusiasm, could not make the place seem anything but unattractive. However, the students, though they grumbled and revolted a bit, cared intensely for their work, and in course of time the place became habitable. Money, however, was terribly scarce both there and at Newnham; and what little there was had to be devoted to more and more accommodation. In 1876, when thirty of the Newnham students were living in their own Hall they still had twenty in an extra house in the town, and twenty-five more lodging with friends. Every penny which could be scraped together was set aside for building, and the amenities had to be postponed.

The students for whom all this effort and enterprise was undertaken were, in those early days, almost unbelievably satisfactory. There were none of them who had come easily, and they were therefore without exception earnest and sincere in their desire to make the most of their chances. Many of them were older than the average undergraduates, and all of them had been differently trained. Some were almost wholly self-taught, others had had special, if lopsided, advantages, and they brought together the most varied experiences and abilities. Their work was original and often brilliant; there was nothing conventional about them, either in the preparation they had had, or the way they studied. And the results they achieved reached an exceedingly high average. Indeed, like the early medical students, they did almost too well; and when Miss Creak passed both the Classical and the Mathematical Triposes in 1874, opposition was by no means diminished.

However, the fact that women were doing well did of course help the movement on the whole. The fact that females could profit by advanced education was no longer in dispute, and a new line of attack was now brought out by the opponents. This was that women could submit to higher education, and could expand and cultivate their minds, but that by doing so they inevitably destroyed their bodily health, and made themselves incapable of "performing their functions as women."

This line of attack was launched about 1874, and began with the publication of an article by the famous mental specialist, Doctor Maudesley. Great perturbation was caused in the opposite camp, and Mrs Garrett Anderson was enlisted to answer him. She was in considerable difficulty, however, for it was extremely important that she should write nothing which would "offend people's sense of decency and modern refinement," and yet she had necessarily to refer to matters of sex and physiology! With great skill she and the other champions of the young women shifted the ground. They said (with perfect justice) that it was not brain work, but lack of physical development which injured women, and they started a sort of counter-agitation in favour of games and gymnastics, which not only diverted the attack but had in itself far-reaching results upon the health and development of the girls of that and every succeeding generation.

In the early seventies, when this movement began, the dress which young women wore was fantastically unhealthy. Tight lacing and long skirts between them made rapid movement next door to impossible, and the conventions which forbade games and sports were amply reinforced by fashions in boots, sleeves, waists, and draperies. Even in the new schools there were no organised games and no gymnastics before 1876, and only the most wild and adventurous people had so much as heard of "Callisthenics." However, once the idea was set going it travelled rapidly; and in its triumphant progress it swept out of the way the silly notion that study or physical exercises unsexed women.

While matters were progressing more or less smoothly in the High Schools, and at Cambridge, the affairs of the medical students were less prosperous. After the adverse decision of the High Court in the matter of the Edinburgh appeal,[1] it became clear that the voluntary admission of women students to that seat of learning was most unlikely, and Sophia Jex-Blake and her companions were forced to look about them for other ways of achieving their ends. Many of the women students had given up hope of a British qualification, and had gone abroad to complete their courses there, but this did not commend itself to Miss Jex-Blake. She was determined to break down the disability at home; and her determination was no light matter. If the universities would not do the right thing of their own free will, then they must be forced to do it against their will. Parliament, as the only authority which could coerce them, was the only hope; and to Parliament she accordingly turned.

Sophia Jex-Blake had rather more influence, and rather more encouragement when she began her attack upon the legislature than when she had gone by herself to Edinburgh in 1869, but for all that it seemed a difficult task. The autonomy of universities was a matter as jealously guarded in the seventies as it is to-day, and a frontal attack upon them seemed to have little chance of success. There were, however, two less direct ways in which something might be accomplished, and in consultation with the friends of the movement in London it was decided to try them both. The first was to secure a Bill specifically conferring upon the universities the power to admit women, and the second was to secure a Bill recognising foreign qualifications in the case of women doctors. Neither of these plans gave quite what Sophia wanted; but the success of either would have been a step in the right direction, and might have led to further developments. The first Bill was, therefore, drafted and introduced at once, and it was backed by Mr Stansfeld, Mr Russell Gurney, Mr Cowper Temple, Dr Cameron, and Mr Orr Ewing.

[1] See Chap. IX.

Parliamentary procedure is always slow, and while waiting for something to happen, Sophia Jex-Blake set to work upon another effort, namely, the forming of a special medical school of their own for women students.

This enterprise was perhaps even more alarming and tremendous than her first attack upon Edinburgh. As before, she was almost single-handed. She had only a few hundred pounds of money, and only a few medical men to approve of her plan. The *Lancet* was still maintaining that "women's sphere in medicine should certainly be limited to carrying out the desires, and implicitly obeying the dictates" of male doctors, and there seemed little help to be had. Mrs Garrett Anderson and Miss Blackwell—who were practising in London—were both doubtful whether the right time had come for so bold a step; and to make matters worse, Sophia herself committed another of her serious indiscretions, and damaged her own cause just at this critical moment.

What happened was thoroughly characteristic. The Press comments upon the women medical students had continued to trickle on through the daily Press, and from time to time the fact that Miss Jex-Blake herself had failed in her examination was unkindly referred to. Now abuse was a thing she could well understand, and she paid no attention; but some of her admirers and followers were less impervious, and one of them, made angry on her behalf, wrote a letter explaining and excusing her failure, pointing out the difficulties under which she had worked, and the immense burden of affairs which at the time she had been carrying. Though Sophia could bear abuse, she could not bear pity; and when she saw this injudicious attempt to defend her she broke down. In a letter which was published in the *Times* she allowed it to be seen that she did not believe that her failure had been genuine, and that she thought her examination papers had been unfairly judged. Huxley, who had been one of the examiners, answered the letter; and Huxley was, of course, one of the firm friends of women's education, so that the scandal was great, and poor Sophia was condemned by friends and foes alike. The storm of criticism which she raised against herself was tremendous, and it was not an atmosphere favourable to her chance of founding a separate school in London.

But Sophia cared little for atmospheres, and without paying heed to any of the hostility she rushed her plans through. In September 1874 she actually took the house in Hunter Street which has now developed into the London School of Medicine for Women, and instantly moved in; and with plumbers and plasterers still about, she got the first class together.

Elizabeth Garrett Anderson, when she saw that the thing was in being, at once decided to give it all the help she could; she joined the staff in the first autumn, and the adventure was launched.

A school was all very well, but a hospital in which to practise was even more important, and an examining body willing to grant a degree was the most essential of all. Yet when the school opened both these were lacking! In 1875 a loophole was discovered which seemed to offer hope in the matter of an examining body. The Midwifery licence —which obviously could not be held to be closed to women —was found to have the same legal status as the licence of the Royal College of Surgeons, and to entitle its holder to be placed on the Medical Register. It was a power which had never been used, but its legal foundation was solid, and in the following year three of these persevering women applied for examination. They were accepted, but, having accepted them, the whole Board of Examiners at once resigned; and with no examiners, no examination was forthcoming! By this step the women were checkmated again, and though it involved the complete and eternal cessation of the Midwifery Board, the authorities evidently held it was cheap at the price.

It would have needed more than this to stop Sophia, however, and in point of fact this was the last of her reverses. No progress was being made with the Foreign Qualifications Bill, but in August of this same year, 1875, the Bill enabling universities to admit women if they so desired was accepted by the Government and passed into law, and victory began to come into sight. Edinburgh, though now able, was still unwilling to admit the troublesome females, but Edinburgh was not the only medical school in the Kingdom. King's and Queen's College of Physicians in Ireland consented to examine and grant medical degrees to women, and with that agreement the struggle was at an end.

Sophia herself took her own degree first in Berne in 1877, and in the same year proceeded to Dublin and was re-examined there. She passed successfully this time, and put her name thankfully and a little triumphantly upon the Medical Register of Great Britain, feeling, perhaps, as if all the work in the world were done.

After this everything suddenly became easier. The Royal Free Hospital in the Gray's Inn Road agreed to admit the students from the Women's Medical School, though it was necessary to secure substantial promises of money for a considerable number of years ahead, to guarantee it against loss of revenue from such an unprecedented step. Sir James Paget was exceedingly helpful in all this, and many other friends came forward, and prospects began to brighten. London University agreed to admit the women medical students to the examinations, and the road to British qualification was clear. The fight was over and the victory was won.

It was not only the medical students who were now welcomed by London University, but also students of every other kind. The Enabling Act was followed in 1878 by the grant of a new charter to the university, and this charter surpassed the hopes even of the most optimistic of the women concerned in higher education. Miss Sophie Bryant was with Miss Buss in the gallery of the Senate when the Chancellor, Lord Granville, made the announcement, and, as she said, it was a thrilling moment. "The concession was unexpected," she wrote, "and it was so perfectly complete. There were no reservations in it, no locked doors, no exclusion from rights in the government of the university, or from eligibility to any of its posts. The time for experiment was over, and the test had been approved; the time for half measures was over too." The faith of the pioneers had been justified in their works.

Almost at the same time that the "half-measure" system seemed to be passing away in London, however, it was making a beginning in more conservative Oxford. There had been a few lectures on somewhat the same lines as those which led to the formation of Newnham College in 1866, but these had come to an end, and had been re-started in 1873. This second time the lectures were an immense success. The ladies of the university town flocked to hear them, and a great many of the able and prominent men supported them. Mark Pattison and Professor T. H. Green were perhaps the most active, but there were many more. Jowett was a friend, Ruskin gave the scheme his blessing, and Professor Nettleship, Canon Scott Holland, Arthur Sidgwick, and Arnold Toynbee all gave steady support. All through the seventies, when Oxford was talking of Italian art, of working-class movements, settlements, the pre-Raphaelites, Browning, and the higher criticism of the Bible, it was talking also of the education of women; and many of the young Oxford ladies, such as Mrs Creighton and Mrs Humphrey Ward and Mrs Arthur Johnson, threw themselves into the fray with enthusiasm. In 1877 they first began to talk of the possibility of a hall of residence for the young women, and it soon became apparent that there were two quite distinct ideas of how such a hall should be managed. There was a strong and influential group of supporters who felt that it was of paramount importance that such an enterprise should be definitely connected with the Church of England, and there was also another set of people who felt clear that it should be wholly undenominational. The two parties made what some called an "unholy alliance"; that is to say, they agreed not to quarrel with each other, and two halls were set on foot at the same time, and grew up together. The undenominational one, which was named Somerville, after Mary Somerville the astronomer, chose for its first principal Miss Shaw Lefevre, and followed a course very similar to that pursued by the colleges at Cambridge. The other, which was named Lady Margaret Hall, followed the same lines, with perhaps a slightly greater degree of caution and anxiety at the outset. The Rev. E. S. Talbot, afterwards Bishop of Winchester, who was one of those chiefly instrumental in founding it, suggested that the first principal should be Miss Elizabeth Wordsworth, the daughter of the Bishop of Lincoln, and the sister of the Bishop of Salisbury. As he truly said, no other name "could have been a greater protection against any charge of rashness in our attempt"; and yet no other lady could have so brilliantly carried it forward. Miss Wordsworth was not at all like either Miss Davies or Miss Clough. She had very little enthusiasm for "women's rights," and was far more interested in religious questions. When considering whether to accept this offer she received some rather curious encouragement from her brother. "If I thought your not going would put an end to the whole thing," he said, "I should say, 'Don't go'; but as I don't suppose it will, I think you had better accept." If it was in this spirit that his sister went to Lady Margaret Hall, however, her doubts must soon have departed; for under her direction the college grew and developed exceedingly. At first, as was natural, the students were very much hemmed in with restrictions. They might not walk into the town alone, even if it was only to buy a bun; they might not go to coachings or lectures without a chaperon, and everyone was anxious that they should "dress carefully and have gentle manners," so that they were conscious of being watched with anxious solicitude; but time and experience modified all these things, and this college followed the same lines as the others.

When the first women students arrived in the autumn of 1879 there were no college lectures open to them, and none of the preliminary ground of passing examinations had been cleared. The success and decorum of the first students reassured the authorities, however, and in 1884 most of the honours schools and examinations (though not the degrees attaching to them) were opened to the women students.

The formal recognition of the right of women to do the degree work (without getting the degree) was conceded at Cambridge a few years earlier. The calm progress of the women students had been interrupted in 1880, when Miss Scott of Girton made another of the errors of tact to which the women students were prone, and secured a place in the Mathematical Tripos list equal to eighth wrangler.[1] By itself this would not have been so bad, but it had the natural and, to orthodox university minds, the unfortunate result of making the women more uppish than ever. Public attention was turned again to the anomalous position of women at Cambridge, and a memorial to the Senate was set on foot in Newcastle, asking that women should be

[1] The eighth wrangler of this year, with whom Miss Scott was bracketed, was George W. Johnson, already a convinced believer in the Women's Movement. Mr Johnson, both then and later, was an active worker in Mrs Butler's campaigns, and he supported all the different parts of the movement. With his wife he wrote a life of Josephine Butler, and just before his death in 1926 he completed an historical account of the Women's Movement (see bibliography). He followed Miss Scott's later mathematical work with interest, and always strongly resented the disadvantages of her position compared with his own; in 1896 he wrote to the *Daily News* to champion her as follows: "Sir, Your paragraph in to-day's *Daily News* as to lady wranglers is not quite correct. As long ago as 1880, in the days when Girton and Newnham students were examined 'by courtesy,' Miss Scott of Girton was bracketed eighth wrangler, thus obtaining the first lady wranglership, a higher place than Miss Longbottom has gained this year. I write this in justice to Miss Scott, who is absent in America.—Yours faithfully, Her Bracket."

recognised and admitted not only to the examinations but also to the degrees of the university. The authorities of the women's colleges were somewhat alarmed, particularly at the request for degrees, which they felt had not the ghost of a chance of success, but of course they could not refuse to make their views known once the agitation had been started, and early in the summer of 1880 a syndicate was appointed to examine the question. This syndicate recommended the regularising of the informal examinations, but not the granting of degrees; and the matter came to a vote in the Senate in February 1881.

The friends of the women naturally regretted the decision about degrees, but welcomed the main proposal, and every precaution which could be devised was taken to ensure its success. A special train was chartered to carry back to town those voters who were Members of Parliament, so that an important division should not keep them away; and circulars, broadsheets, and memorials suitable to every type of opposition were sent out. As the time grew near the fears of the supporters melted away; their strength was greater than they had supposed, and before the actual voting took place it was clear that their opponents were discouraged. In the event most of these abstained from voting, and the "Graces" were carried by 351 votes to 32. After that the uncertainty about the examinations was over, and the colleges, secure in the right to test their students by the standards of the honours degrees, could turn with fresh energy to the task of accommodating them. Another ordeal awaited them, however, and this time it was of their own seeking. In 1887 Miss Agneta Ramsay of Girton secured a first class in the Classical Tripos, and none of the men of that year was placed higher than in the second. Had she been a man, therefore, she would have been the "senior classic," and once more public attention turned towards the position of the women. Miss Davies thought that on the whole this was a favourable moment to raise the degree question again, and accordingly did so, in spite of the fact that Dr Sidgwick and the others connected with Newnham advised strongly against it. The matter came before the Senate in 1888, but by a majority of eight to seven they refused even to appoint a syndicate, and the matter dropped. This defeat was a great disappointment, even to those who had expected it; but two years later an event occurred which comforted them, even though it led to no immediate alteration in the position. In 1890 Philippa, the daughter of Professor and Mrs Henry Fawcett, and the niece of Elizabeth Garrett Anderson, sat for the Mathematical Tripos Examination. There was no one who might be held to be so truly a product of the Women's Movement, no one who was more fully its representative in the new generation, and her success or failure were thus of particular importance. It was known in Cambridge that she was going to do well, but the college authorities hardly dared to express the full extent of their hopes. When the results came out, however, they saw them all fulfilled, for Philippa Fawcett was placed "above the senior wrangler," thus winning the most famous mathematical honour in the world. Gone now were the arguments that women were incapable of advanced abstract thought; gone was the notion that arithmetic was too severe for females. Nothing more appropriate or satisfactory could possibly have happened, and the rejoicing which found expression in bonfires in the Newnham garden was echoed all over the country.

To add to the perfection of this event Miss Alford of Girton was, in the same year, bracketed with the senior classic. Thus both colleges shared in the triumph, and both the great university subjects were conquered, and the women students vindicated to the full.

In spite of these resounding successes the degree question was not raised again at Cambridge. The governing bodies of the two colleges meant to get full recognition in time; but for the moment they were satisfied with the substance of education, and with the knowledge that the dreams of the pioneers were well on their way to fulfilment. London University had granted women full membership in 1880, and all the new provincial universities which were springing up were following this lead; and Oxford and Cambridge would have to come into line in due course. It seemed better to wait until it should come without struggle or bitterness rather than to fight again so soon.[1]

Although the principle of higher education for women was now conceded, there remained a great deal of practical work to be done. The actual numbers of girls who were able to secure education were still pitifully small, for the total of the residential students at Oxford and Cambridge together was under two hundred in 1882. College Hall, a residential hostel for women students, was opened in London in that year, and efforts of all kinds were made to increase the actual places available for students; but the funds of all the colleges were in a most meagre state, and everything had to be done on the narrowest possible scale. There was not much harm, perhaps, in plain living when it went with high thinking, but it was more serious that the scholarships were few and scanty, and the prejudices of parents by no means overcome. It was generally assumed that a girl who had been to college would not know "how to talk to a guardsman," and consequently would never get married; and fathers were distinctly reluctant to spend money in order to make their daughters alarming to young men, and unlike other people. Moreover, it was believed that even if they

[1] It is interesting to note that the degree question was raised at Oxford in 1909 by no less a person than Lord Curzon, the President of the Anti-Suffrage League, when he became Chancellor of the University in that year. Lord Curzon warmly advocated the reform, but took care to point out that " there is all the difference in the world between giving women an opportunity of increasing and improving their natural powers, and granting to them a share in political sovereignty." No action was taken upon his recommendation at that time. A short time previously Dublin University had offered to give degrees to the women qualified at Oxford and Cambridge, and a considerable number took advantage of this opportunity.

did not break down in health, they would become eccentric in dress and appearance, and generally fall out of step with their home surroundings.

It must be admitted that these fears were sometimes well founded. In order to protect themselves against the ridicule which they faced in going to college at all, some of the students of the eighties developed a rather aggressively earnest manner, and were less patient of the small change of social intercourse than their parents desired them to be. Their clothes, too, sometimes underwent surprising changes. In the time of the "greenery yallery" æsthetic movement many a country parsonage must have suffered a shock when its daughter returned from under the shadow of her ancient seat of learning in flowing robes embroidered with large, yellow sunflowers, while a little later stiff collars and hard hats produced the same effect. For the most part, no doubt, the students avoided these extremes, and were as unremarkable to the outward eye as anyone could wish; but the existence of a few eccentrics was quite enough to give rise to a legend, and the legend died hard. As the body of old students grew, however, and as they passed out into the world and did their work therein, they gradually blotted it out. The college girl was found, on trial, to be still a normal woman, better trained, perhaps, and with wider interests than her predecessors, but not more alarming, even to guardsmen, than the others. Some of them became very learned and very distinguished; some of them became very domestic and very quiet; some of them pushed out into new fields at home and abroad; some of them threw themselves into causes, philanthropies and good works; and the majority of them became teachers, in their turn to spread abroad the knowledge they had secured. But all of them, whatever they made of their lives, were glad of the education they had been granted; and as their number increased so did the prejudice against them die down.

There was indeed a little flutter of the old opposition and ridicule at the beginning of the nineties, but it had an out-of-date flavour even then. The immediate cause of it was the fashion of tight lacing and trailing skirts, then very much in vogue. Although the majority of the "advanced" women took great pains to keep their appearances as close to the prevailing fashions as was needful to escape remark, there were some who revolted against this particular form of torment, and dressed themselves with an affectation of mannishness which occupied the comic Press a great deal when it appeared. Tailor-made coats and skirts, stiff collars, and hard round hats must have been almost as uncomfortable as the tight lacing; and in any case they made no headway against long skirts, and soon disappeared from public notice.

In 1902 the question of the admission of women to learned societies was raised, when Mrs Hertha Ayrton's name was suggested to the Royal Society. Counsel's opinion was taken, to the effect that it would not be legal to elect her without a new charter, and the matter therefore dropped; but the Linnean Society in the following year applied for and obtained a new charter and admitted women. In 1895 the same question came up to the Royal College of Physicians and the Royal College of Surgeons. The former refused to admit women, though the latter welcomed them, and the anomalies of their position increased. Each exception as it occurred made the position more absurd, yet there seemed little prospect of any general or wholesale change. Oxford, when it admitted women to the examinations, excluded theology, medicine, and law (the three chief directions in which University studies might lead directly to professional appointments), but in 1895 an exception was made in favour of Miss Cornelia Sorabji, who was preparing for legal work in India. It thus became clear that the exclusion was based not so much on any inherent impropriety as upon the desire to reduce competition; but it continued all the same. Little advances were apparent here and there, and individual victories were won; but along the whole line progress, though it undoubtedly existed, appeared to be very slow.

CHAPTER XIV

THE DECEITFULNESS OF POLITICS. 1870–1900

The suffragists settle down to steady propaganda—The tone of opposition in the House—The effect on this cause of Mrs Butler's crusade—The first quarrel among the suffragists—Death of J. S. Mill—The question of the married women's vote—Second reading defeats in 1875 and 1876—The suffrage societies reunite—An amendment to the law of Married Women's Property, 1870—Continued propaganda on this point, and the success of a complete measure in 1882—The Reform Bill of 1884 and Mr Gladstone's success in throwing the women overboard—The effect of this upon the suffragists—The formation of women's Party organisations, and their effect upon politics—The second quarrel among the suffragists, and the separation of the Liberal from the non-party women—Death of Miss Becker, 1889—The period of deadlock and discouragement.

IN 1870, when the Suffrage Bill was definitely blocked, the suffrage workers at last realised what was before them. They had, so they thought, proved their case to the intelligent and won over a majority of Members of Parliament, and yet their Bill had been defeated, and they saw that their task was really hard. The fact of the matter was that the subject was too important, and the change too fundamental to be carried through without the genuine conversion of public opinion; and, realising this at last, they settled down to systematic propaganda. The municipal franchise was extended to women ratepayers in 1869,[1] but in the course of the following years there is little in the Suffrage Movement proper which is of dramatic interest. A monthly paper, *The Women's Suffrage Journal*, was founded and edited by Miss Becker, and papers, pamphlets, and all the minor parliamentary tactics of an unpopular cause succeeded each other month after month. But although the meetings

[1] See Chap. XI.

grew steadily in number, and the petitions multiplied, and the number of adherents increased, the parliamentary deadlock continued. There were always friends of the Cause in the House, and these friends tried by every possible device to bring the subject forward, and to get a full-dress debate. But the passive resistance of Government after Government, and the steady hostility of the rank and file, made this a very disheartening task. After 1870, indeed, whenever a private Member's opportunity arose to bring the matter forward, whether by Bill or by Resolution, the whole tone of the House was not so much hostile as facetious. The opposing speeches elicited a good deal of that distinctive laughter which greets jokes on the subject of sex, and some of those jokes themselves went near to the limits of parliamentary decency. The Hon. Member[1] who drew the moving picture of a female Prime Minister busy with her accouchement, while the female Solicitor-General eloped with "a mere male," was, however, only considered to be amusing. Another Member, speaking in 1870, remarked that he "did not like to see women enter into competition with dancing dogs, to show their wonderful powers in doing things which it is not expected they will do"; and even *Punch*, usually most friendly, could not resist observing that "those who want women's rights want also women's charms."[2]

Against such a tone it was difficult to make headway; and if that had been the only difficulty it would have been serious enough. But, of course, there were other more respectable elements of opposition as well. "Man in the

[1] Earl Percy, May 1873.

[2] It was not only in Parliament that the subject aroused mirth. The *Accrington Times* of 13th April 1872, for example, reveals the reaction of municipal authorities. " Local Board Meeting : Amid considerable laughter the Clerk announced that he had received a communication from the National Society for Women's Suffrage, wanting the Board to adopt a petition in favour of female enfranchisement. Mr Bell : You must get Miss Becker to come. Mr John Haworth : I move that all women stop at home and mind their own business (laughter). The Chairman : Can you manage to keep your own at home ? (laughter). No reply was given and the subject dropped."

beginning was ordained to rule over women," one Hon. Member maintained, "and this is an Eternal decree which we have no right and no power to alter." Against this belief no headway whatever could be expected, and it was much the same with those numerous stupid and honest gentlemen who believed that to give the vote to women would bring the homes of England to ruin, and who thought that it would lead to the "unsettling, not to say uprooting, of the old landmarks of society," and were convinced that it would "unsex" women, "contaminate" them, "drag them down to our own coarse and rough level," and "defile their modesty and purity." These gentlemen shared the views of the *Saturday Review*, which declared that "It is no small thing that half the human race should habitually take a purer and more sentimental view than those who have to do the dirty work." They were unaware that it was they, and not the suffragists, who were taking the "sentimental" view!

Apart from considerations of theory, however, there was a practical aspect of the proposal which weighed heavily against the Suffrage Bill, and that was the complete uncertainty as to what its effect on Party politics would be. The Liberals were convinced that women would vote Conservative, and the Conservatives felt sure that they would vote Liberal; and neither side cared enough about the matter to take this appalling risk.

In the early seventies, when all these various objections were at their height, the existence of Mrs Butler's crusade added yet another to them. The two movements were separate and distinct, but it was known that a large number of people supported them both. In particular some of the parliamentary champions of the suffrage, such as Mr Jacob Bright, spoke openly in the House of Commons in favour of the repeal of the Contagious Diseases Acts; and mere mention of this subject was enough to rouse conventional Members to fury. "The agitation," they maintained, "was a disgrace to the country, as it flooded gentlemen's breakfast tables with abominable literature, not addressed to themselves only, but also to their wives and daughters." [1] They were not going to "sacrifice their manhood," make a revolution in Society, and "amend the laws of creation" at the bidding of a handful of narrow, factious, noisy and indecent fanatics, and the more the crusade was heard of the more bitter the opposition to the suffrage became.

The various Women's Suffrage Committees, of course, were fully aware of this difficulty; it caused much heart-burning among them. The majority of their members, though by no means all of them, were in sympathy with the objects of the new campaign, but they could not help seeing that the unpleasant notoriety which was gathering about it was damaging their other cause. Moreover, there were quite a number of their own supporters who disagreed with Mrs Butler, and even a few who thought the matter too painful and improper to be mentioned. It was, therefore, clear that the two movements must be kept officially separate, and that the suffrage committees as such must not take part in the crusade.

This decision was obvious, but the matter by no means ended there. For how could movements supported by the same people be kept separate? Miss Rhoda Garrett, for example, who was the most effective of all the early suffrage speakers, was an officer of the Repeal Society; and it was difficult to see how she could be dissociated from either movement, especially as they both wanted her so much. And even if the women speakers could have managed their dual rôles, how could the same parliamentary leaders act for both movements without causing hopeless confusion? This difficulty arose in the minds of all the committees, and in London, which was, of course, the political centre

[1] Mr Osborne Morgan, Debate on Women's Disabilities Removal Bill, May 1872.

of both movements, matters came to a crisis. While some of the suffragists thought that so long as the actual societies were kept separate there was no harm in the same people supporting them both, others felt that this course spelt ruin to the suffrage; and a tremendous sending of letters to and fro began among the committee members. There were strained sessions, votes of censure, private indignation meetings in drawing-rooms, and a great deal of heat and agitation. Although the language of these Victorian ladies was severely restrained, the feelings which they expressed ran very high, so that before long there came the inevitable split, and two suffrage organisations came into existence. "The principle upon which we have taken our stand," wrote one of the parties in their official minute book, "is of careful avoidance of even apparent mingling with any other agitation. . . . We hold it to be important that no person conspicuously engaged either as officer or lecturer in some other agitation now proceeding, to which we will not further allude, should hold any conspicuous place in the movement for women's suffrage." And so, shutting their eyes tightly to "the agitation to which we will not further allude" this group stuck strictly to their own reform, and tried by being very respectable to counteract the terrible doings of their former colleagues.

Looking back, from this distance of time, when both causes have been successful, and the heat and fury has gone out of them both, this crisis in their affairs does not seem very important. If we are to record the history of the movement, however, we must not pass too lightly over the points of tactics and of procedure which had such supreme importance from year to year in the actual development of the campaigns. It is true now, as was indeed true then, that the agitations for the repeal of the Contagious Diseases Acts and for the enfranchisement of women were both parts of the Women's Movement, and that they were of necessity intimately dependent upon each other; yet it is also true that they did not gain from close association, and that there was more strength at the time from separation. This was the opinion of John Stuart Mill, of Mrs Fawcett, and of Miss Emily Davies, the first two of whom were themselves strongly in favour of Mrs Butler's views; it was the opinion of the ordinary rank and file member, and of the public at large, but there were many active workers who did not share it, and both schools of thought found plenty of supporters.

This first split in the ranks of the suffragists occurred in 1871, and both branches of the old London National Society went on their way. The seceders, who were those supporting Mrs Butler, took the name of the Central Committee of the National Society, while the others kept their old name; and the public was perhaps not sufficiently interested to become confused between them. No serious difficulties arose until 1874, but in that year it became necessary to re-appoint the parliamentary leader, and the divergence of views between the two sections threatened to lead to a public and most unedifying rupture. While the General Election was in progress the old London Committee let it be known that they would no longer consent to be represented by Mr Jacob Bright, because of the way in which he was coming to be identified with "the agitation to which we will not further refer." If he were so chosen, the committee said, they would feel it their duty to make a public protest; and the consternation which this threw into the other camp can be imagined. Accusations of ingratitude, of folly, and of every other political mistake were freely exchanged, but, fortunately for the harmony of the movement, Mr Jacob Bright lost his seat and the storm blew over.

The death of John Stuart Mill, in 1873, was a terrible blow to the suffrage workers. He was the chief exponent of their doctrine, and the judge of all their problems. His faith and his advocacy had launched the movement upon the political sea; and when his guiding hand was taken from them, the committee felt lost indeed. They missed him as a champion, as an adviser, and as a friend; and no one ever arose to take his place.

The Cause, however, had to go on. A new parliamentary leader had to be chosen to replace Mr Bright, and the committees had to resolve their difficulties as best they could. Nor were these long in coming upon them. Mr Forsyth, Member for Marylebone, was the new parliamentary leader, and this gentleman, though a convinced suffragist, had not been much associated with the movement before. When he came to look at the Bill he had undertaken to father, he could not bear the uncertainty about the voting of married women which had been deliberately inserted into it. Mr Forsyth was a lawyer, and he was a Conservative; and before the committees knew what he was about he had inserted a proviso definitely excluding married women from the operation of the Act if passed. The commotion which arose in the suffrage ranks was tremendous; and perhaps it was strengthened by the passions roused and unsatisfied in the previous quarrel. Accusations of bad faith—which were called in the language of the day "unworthy aspersions"—followed close upon arguments about law and tactics, and poor Mr Forsyth doubtless thought that he had fallen into a hornet's nest. The whole thing was slightly fictitious, since all parties agreed that, whatever the terms of the Bill, married women would, in fact, be deprived of any votes to which they might be entitled by the operation of the coverture system which still governed their legal position. But though this point doubtless appealed to the Conservatives and carried weight with them, it had no effect at all in moderating the fury of the Radicals. To them the theory was important; they looked for the speedy disappearance of the coverture system, and were profoundly opposed to the inclusion in their Bill of anything which seemed to bolster it up. They felt, moreover, that to demand anything less than equality was to betray their own cause, even though of course they recognised that they might for a time have to accept some compromise. But they were determined to claim nothing short of full equality, and in consequence there were protests, resignations, indignation meetings, and great turmoils in all the suffrage camps. Mr Forsyth was anxious to allay their fears if he could, but he believed that his proviso would increase the chances of carrying the Bill and would make matters easier within his own party. All that he could do by way of compromise, therefore, was to substitute the words "no woman under coverture" for "no married woman" in the actual text. This ingenious turn of phrase satisfied most of the malcontents; but, after all, a whole year had to go by before the Bill could come up for discussion. And when it did, it only got so far as to be defeated on second reading.[1]

For three years Mr Forsyth led the parliamentary forces, and then in 1877 Mr Jacob Bright returned to the House. By this time the fire and fury had gone out of the opposition to Mrs Butler's crusade, and the tactical considerations which had split the London National Society had ceased to be important. When, therefore, Mr Forsyth passed the Bill back to its old leader no protest was made, and Mr Bright was able to take up his familiar task once more. The fatal proviso was quietly dropped out of the Bill, but there was no better parliamentary result. In 1878 the Bill was talked out amid an uproar, and the only change which appeared in the situation was that the opponents of the measure thought it worth while to organise themselves into a parliamentary committee "for preserving the integrity of the franchise."

In 1878 Mr Jacob Bright fell ill, and retired from the House of Commons, and the leadership passed to Mr Leonard Courtney. The first act of this general of the forces was to call together all those who had divided upon the question of the Contagious Diseases Acts, and forcibly

[1] April 1875 and 1876. Adverse majorities 35 and 87.

reunite them again. The solid ground of their differences had melted away, and there was no valid reason for separation; but, of course, as always happens with human undertakings, vested interests (of the most innocent nature), and personal animosities (of the most ladylike kind) had grown up. Honorary secretaries were unwilling to give up the arduous tasks of writing letters and keeping minutes; honorary treasurers clung to the privilege of making up deficits out of their own private purses; committee members did not like the idea of sitting round the same table together, and Mr Courtney's task was hard. He was, however, a young man full of hope and courage; and he fairly forced the warring committees to amalgamate, and to present a united front to the enemy.

After this reunion the organisation of local suffrage societies went steadily forward, and for a few years no drawback of any kind was encountered. Miss Helen Blackburn, who had become secretary to the Central Committee in 1874, acted for the united Committee, and Miss Becker carried on the parliamentary work and edited the *Woman's Suffrage Journal*. Lectures were given in many new towns and everything went well. Popular support, indeed, became very nearly popular enthusiasm, and when in 1880 Miss Becker devised the plan of holding large mass meetings for women only, her daring innovation was justified. In Manchester, London, Edinburgh, Bristol, and other big towns, these meetings were more than successful, and the working women who thronged to them showed that they wanted enfranchisement no less than the ladies who addressed them. The hopes which had been damped ten years before rose again, and were encouraged by the grant of Women's Suffrage in the Isle of Man, so that the Reform Bill, which the Liberals were known to be preparing, was expected to mark the end of the fight. Meantime, however, there were other things than suffrage which had to be attended to, and of these the most fundamental was the winning of property rights for married women.

The agitation for this reform had been simmering on ever since 1855, and in 1868 a Bill had squeezed through the House of Commons by one vote, only to be lost amid the mazes of parliamentary procedure. In 1870 a comprehensive Bill came forward again, with better fortune, and this time it got as far as the House of Lords. In that place, however, it suffered a complete transformation, and when it came back to the Commons again it was not at all the same Bill. Instead of putting women upon a free and reasonable footing, and granting them the possession of their own wealth, the truncated Bill only allowed them to keep possession of what they earned for themselves. Everything else, whether acquired before or after marriage, belonged, as before, to their husbands.

The new proposal, incomplete as it was, was an advance. It was that useful instrument, the thin end of the wedge; and it was more. For it was a measure which was to redress the worst of the hardships and scandals with which the advocates of the Bill had long urged their case, and which would effect the most obvious practical reforms. And that was doubtless why the Lords chose to keep it, and to reject the rest. They did not care in the least about the theory of equality (unless and in so far as they found it comic). They were not a bit upset at the idea that a man should be the legal owner of his wife's property, but they did respond to the argument that a woman was hardly used if, while she worked to support herself and her children, the man who had deserted or ill-treated her could step in and take away the money she had earned, and sell her household goods behind her back.

The supporters of the married women, realising that the Bill gave them something which was urgently needed, accepted the Lord's amendments, and the Bill passed into law in 1870. But even while they rejoiced in the immediate practical results they were also discouraged. Not only was the position in which married women were left "utterly absurd and intricate," [1] but the possibility of ever getting matters put right appeared to be cut away from them. The adventitious aid of "hard cases" was gone, and nothing remained but the bald, unpalatable principle for which they stood. The "organs" of the movement, which had called attention to individual injustices for many years, were thrown back upon theoretical argument, and it soon grew clear that it was not going to be easy, or even possible, to get enthusiastic popular support among men for the remains of their claim. Those who were honest and kindly, as most men are, could see no reason why their wives should cease to trust them with their money; and those who were neither honest nor well-intentioned objected to the Bill from other motives. It was a bad subject for agitation; and yet, of course, it was absolutely fundamental to the cause of feminism, and could never be allowed to drop. In this difficulty Mrs Jacob Bright came forward as a leader. With the help of Miss Lydia Becker, Miss Wolstonholme (then the head-mistress of a school in Manchester), Mr and Mrs Peter Taylor, Doctor and Mrs Pankhurst, Mrs Venturi, Sir Charles Dilke and others, she formed a special committee and proceeded to work upon the sense of justice of Members of Parliament. Popular agitation was not discontinued. Petitions were circulated and signed, but the main effort was directed towards the Members of Parliament themselves.

A most important element of support came from the trading community. The law was so confusing, and the possibilities of fraud so great, that the Mercantile Law

[1] A curious and illuminating example of the intricacies and absurdities of the law affected the Suffrage Society in London in 1879. A legacy of £500 was left to this committee, and one of their members, Mrs Whittle, was appointed as trustee. It then appeared that since she was a married woman she could not act in that capacity, and another lady Mrs Lucas (who happened to be a widow) had to be appointed.

Conference took the matter up. As they said, they were not concerned with "the hardship sustained by married women," but only with their difficulties with their own creditors. "This state of law is a constant source of loss and annoyance to tradesmen," said the solicitor of the Law Association for the Protection of Trades, "and such an alteration as would make women the owners of their own property, responsible for their own debts, would greatly increase the safety of trade transactions."

Mrs Jacob Bright thought, quite rightly, that the theoretical case, backed by arguments such as these, was good enough, and that popular agitation would be an unnecessarily roundabout and slow procedure. She and her other committee members, therefore, gave a large number of small dinner-parties, and used a great deal of individual argument; they interested lawyers and won many friends, and in one form or another they managed to bring the question forward a good many times. The knotty problem of whether a woman's savings bank deposits were her own made quite a stir in the world, and one after another the anomalies of the Act were brought to light. In spite of the discouraging facts that in 1873 the House was counted out six times when their Bill came on, and that it was postponed seventeen times more, even when its second reading had been secured, little bits of improvement made their way through Parliament. A wife's property was made liable for pre-nuptial debts in 1874, a married woman's earnings were safeguarded in Scotland in 1877, but the real matter moved slowly. The heart of the objection was clearly put by Lord Fraser in 1881, when the House was in committee upon one of the Scottish Bills. "The protection which has been thrown around a married woman already is sufficient," he said, "and why she should be allowed to have money in her pocket to deal with as she thinks fit I cannot understand." Nevertheless, Mrs Bright and her friends (who could understand this proposal) went on persuading and explaining, and in

1881 a full Married Women's Property Act was passed for Scotland, which, in 1882, was extended to England, Ireland, and Wales; and the difficult job was done.

The success of this measure of justice was tremendously encouraging to the agitators of the Women's Movement, and it came at the time when their hopes of winning the suffrage were rising high.

The General Election of 1880 had resulted in the return of a considerable majority of Members favourable to Women's Suffrage, and it had also been marked by a new development within the Liberal Party, namely, the passing of suffrage resolutions at Party meetings, large and small. In 1883 Mrs M'Laren (John Bright's sister) and Miss Jane Cobden (Richard Cobden's daughter) went as delegates to the great Reform Conference at Leeds, and when this conference enthusiastically passed their resolution, it seemed that the great majority of the Liberal Party was ready to agree to the inclusion of women in the forthcoming Reform Bill. Another internal difficulty, however, showed its head this year. The Married Women's Property Act was now in force, but the coverture system was not thereby destroyed, and it was uncertain whether married women would or would not be legally entitled to vote under a clause enfranchising them "on the same terms" as men. In these circumstances the old division of opinion reappeared, and when the parliamentary leader (now Mr Hugh Mason) framed his resolution ambiguously, in accordance with the policy of the committees, the extremists fell into despair. Again the protests and passions reappeared, again the resignations and the storms arose, and once more a separate organisation was set up, with a committee and officers of its own. Mrs Jacob Bright and Mrs Pankhurst supported it, and its headquarters were in the North of England, but it does not seem to have attracted the affiliation of any of the existing local societies.

These storms and differences of opinion were not of great

moment to the progress of the Cause itself; the world at large knew little of them, and cared less, and a laughing reference to "women quarrelling among themselves" was the worst that resulted. Nevertheless these early differences and the steps taken to compose them are of importance to the history of the movement. Had they not existed, and had there been nothing but harmony and unanimity, the movement would not have been really alive. It was by experiencing in their own internal affairs the rough and the smooth of political life, and by going through the ordinary vicissitudes of public business, that the early suffragists learnt what politics really were. They were slow to learn, being confirmed idealists; but bit by bit, through the very quarrelling which they tried so hard to avoid, they gained their experience; and the larger their organisations grew the more exactly did they mirror the difficulties, the faults, and the virtues of national affairs.

The internal troubles of the suffragists in 1883 were soon overshadowed by their outward fortunes, for in the following year the Reform Bill was introduced, and their great opportunity arrived. It arrived, but it passed them by, for Mr Gladstone was Prime Minister, and Mr Gladstone did not like the idea of Women's Suffrage. His Bill, therefore, when it appeared, contained no mention of women, and, what was even more serious, he let it be known that the Government would resist any amendment which would insert them. In vain did the suffragists point out that women's position would be made worse by the further extension of the franchise to men; in vain did they appeal to the definite and categorical election promises. The Prime Minister had said that women would overweight the Bill, so overboard they must go. Party loyalty was stronger than promises to non-voters, stronger than conviction itself, and when the division came 104 of the Liberal Members who were pledged supporters voted against the

Women's Suffrage amendment, which was thereby roundly defeated.[1]

The result of this vote was serious to the last degree. It was evident, even to the most optimistic, that it must be years before another change in the franchise laws could be expected. By the inclusion of the agricultural labourers the male population was now very fully enfranchised, and the impetus for pushing democracy farther appeared to be spent. If a Women's Suffrage Bill was to come it must stand on its own feet, backed only by the sex injustice; for men, so it seemed in 1884, had now got all they could want.

To those of the women's leaders who were politically minded this appeared as a serious drawback, as indeed it was. But there was another calamity, even more serious, which appealed to the leaders and to the rank and file as well, and that was that they had lost faith in their parliamentary friends. Some few, of course, had been staunch; three Cabinet Ministers had walked out of the House rather than vote against their convictions, and a small number of Liberal Members had resisted the Party Whip; but what were these among so many? A deep distrust of the Party machine sprang up in the ranks of the suffragists, and that distrust never died away. The action of Mr Gladstone and his followers in 1884 was but the first of a long series of similar betrayals, and made a rent in the prestige of the Party system from which, in the eyes of those who cared for the suffrage, it never entirely recovered.

In 1884, however, this hardly mattered at all. There were not a great many suffragists, and in any case the politicians did not care what they thought; if they chose to reject the Party labels they could do so; it was their own loss.

This official indifference did not last long, however, for about the time of the passing of the Reform Bill a change

[1] The figures were: for the amendment 135, against 271.

came over the methods of British electioneering, and women sprang of a sudden into a usefulness which made their adherence to the Parties a matter of considerable importance. This development, which had in the end a profound influence upon the progress of the Women's Movement, was the result not so much of any political awakening among women, or of any desire on the part of politicians to enlighten them, as of the passage in 1883 of the Corrupt Practices Act. Before this date canvassing and the other subsidiary work of elections had been done by men specially engaged and paid for the job, and, with the exception of a few of the candidate's relatives, no women had taken part in the affair at all. After the passing of the Act of 1883, however, all this changed. The work had still to be done, but might no longer be paid for; and what was more natural than to discover that, after all, it was women's work? A whole new technique of election machinery came into being, and with the appearance of the volunteer women workers the modern type of electioneering began.

So successful and so eager were the women who were allowed to take a share in this new work that the Parties soon saw advantage in permanently securing them, and within a very few years the Primrose League and the Women's Liberal Federation made their appearance. The former body, which set up its Women's Council in 1885, made no pretence of wanting the women's help in any but practical affairs. The object of the league was to support the Conservative Party as it was; no power of initiating, or even criticising that policy was vested in the league, and its paraphernalia of dames and garden parties was more effective in enlisting the great force of social snobbishness than in adding to the intellectual strength or representative nature of the Conservative Party.

The Women's Liberal Federation, similarly, was called together by Mrs Gladstone "to help our husbands," and the same stamp was intended to be put on it. The Radical ladies, however, were less easy to manage, and before very long dissension and ideas crept in among the members, and wrought considerable havoc, especially when the Women's Suffrage question again became acute. In 1893, indeed, this became so burning a question that a new body, the Women's Liberal Association, sprang from it, and the two existed and flourished side by side, the one supporting all Liberals because they were Liberals, and the other supporting only those who were pledged to the Suffrage Cause in return.

After the Home Rule Split in 1886, another body, the Women's Liberal Unionist Association, came into existence. The women who composed this organisation were very active indeed, not only in support of their own leaders, but in social questions of all kinds, and a great many of those who later played important parts in securing reforms got their training in its ranks.

Apart from anything they won for the Suffrage Cause, the mere existence of these political associations did a great deal for women. The old notion that the "rough and tumble" of elections was unfit for women could not survive their universal employment as canvassers, and the mere fact of their taking part in such activities, from however personal or obedient a reason, awakened the canvassers themselves. For twenty who worked away as they were told in blind loyalty to the views of their men-folk, there was probably one who began to think for herself; and every such an one sooner or later became not only a convert to the suffrage idea, but a centre of propaganda. They remained on the whole more or less faithful to the Party which had awakened them; for it was not until many years later that the exodus of suffragists from the Party ranks really began; but, in the new sphere to which they had been summoned, they proved their utility; and by so doing they broke down the ancient belief that politics was exclusively a "man's job."

The blow which the Reform Act of 1884 dealt to the

Suffrage Cause was a hard one, and the societies staggered under the shock. Although many of the leaders and supporters abandoned their former innocent faith in politicians, there were others who resisted this feeling, and refused to admit it. The feminists who, by reason of their family connections, or of their individual convictions, were unwilling to doubt the good faith of the Radical Party, took up its defence with aggressive vigour. The thing to do, they maintained, was to work for Women's Suffrage within the Liberal Party. This, the obvious and traditional Party of reform, was the real hope of the Cause, and the disappointment they had just experienced must only spur them on to fresh efforts in the same field. It was fruitless to be bitter and despairing; wiser to keep their faith intact and win their triumph without losing their loyalty. These people believed in all sincerity that the Liberals were the only people who would ever give women the vote; they thought that the course they were recommending was their only hope; and they urged their view with all the more earnestness because it seemed at the time so unlikely and impossible of success.

The existence of this body of active and undiscouraged Radicals among the suffrage societies at once caused trouble. A battle as fierce, and almost as acrimonious as the previous storms, began to be waged, and once more pamphlets, letters, resignations, protests, and memorials began to fly about among the members. The point at issue, as it narrowed down, came to be whether or not local branches of the Women's Liberal Federation were to be accepted for affiliation to the Central Committee of the Suffrage Societies; and after three years of divided councils the breach came.

It appeared in London that the Party section were the strongest. After an earth-shaking annual meeting which raged for three and a half hours, their new rules were carried, and the divergent minority, headed by Mrs Fawcett and

Miss Becker, walked out of the hall. Henceforward there were two Central Suffrage Societies in London, each with their contingent of branches in the country. The old one, which had now changed its rules and its officers, kept the old name and the old premises; the new one, which stuck to the old rules and personnel, had a new name and a new office. Both were lodged in Westminster, within a short distance of the House; both included the words Central and National in their titles, and both had parliamentary committees; but for all the confusion of the situation, no inconvenience seems to have been felt. Both societies grew and expanded after the split; both raised more money and did more work than before, and neither maligned the other. It was rather a stiff test for the political capacity of the leaders, but they survived it, and continued to attach more importance to their common cause than to their differences of opinion.

While this was happening in London a similar divergence of opinion was, of course, going on in all the big towns. It is not necessary here to disentangle all the varying means which were taken to resolve the trouble; they were interesting and even amusing, as differences of opinion among people of strong character and intellect are apt to be; but they had no permanent bearing upon the progress of the movement. Some of the provincial centres held with the new rules, and some with the old; but all alike were still faithful to the Cause, and still continued to push their propaganda wherever they could. Although the years from 1884 to 1897 were comparatively inactive, the Suffrage Bill twice came to a vote in the House of Commons, being passed on second reading in 1885, and defeated in 1892.[1] But these parliamentary occasions were of little significance. Everyone knew that the Bills had

[1] In 1885 the Bill was passed without a division, but it was understood that it would go no farther. On 27th April 1892, Sir Alfred Rollit's Bill came up for second reading, and the majority against was 23.

no chance of going farther, even if they passed the second readings, and the real effort which the suffragists made was to introduce the idea into current political thought. Women's Suffrage Resolutions were passed by the National Liberal Federation and the National Reform Union Councils, as well as by the National Union of Conservatives and Constitutional Association Councils again and again, and in this direction matters seemed to be progressing.

During these years between the passing of the Reform Bill and the close of the century, it became apparent, bit by bit, that the effort to win the suffrage through the Liberal Party alone was unavailing. In spite of the loyalty of a strong section of the suffrage women, in spite of the devoted work of hundreds of others within the Party, in spite of the repeated professions of agreement on the part of the conventions and individual Members and candidates, the Party machine was altogether unmoved, and the Party leaders showed not the faintest sign of giving way. The fear that women would vote Conservative, which had prevailed in 1870, held sway in 1880 and 1890, and an absolute deadlock ensued. Although there were exceptions on both sides, it was roughly true that the Liberals, who professed to believe in giving the votes to women, would not do it because they thought they would lose thereby; and the Conservatives, who were expected to benefit, disliked the principle so much that they would not do it either. Moreover, it was a curious fact that in the Liberal Party, where the rank and file of the members professed to support the claim, the leaders were passionately opposed to it, while in the Conservative Party it was the leaders alone who were friendly;[1] and the women, being voteless, could alter neither situation, but got the worst of it in both cases.

In addition to this curious and unfortunate state of affairs, the agitation had begun to grow stale by the middle of the

[1] Compare, for example, Mr Gladstone and Mr Asquith with Disraeli and Lord Salisbury.

nineties. Its supporters, indeed, were as keen and as hard working as ever (it was in the nineties that Mrs Fawcett was obliged to make a rule not to speak at more than four meetings a week, or more than one a day), but the enthusiasm of supporters was not enough. The agitation had been going on so long that the Press and the public were tired of hearing of it. Nothing was happening in Parliament, or anywhere else, to give the subject a news value, and the arguments were, of necessity, the same as they always had been. And so a regular Press boycott set in and the dead period of the movement came on. Drawing-room meetings, pamphlets, lectures, resolutions, and all the rest were of no avail; and though the societies steadily expanded they made little other headway, and the winning of the vote seemed in the early nineties to be farther away than ever before in the history of the agitation.

In 1887, too, the Cause had suffered a terrible loss in the death of Miss Lydia Becker. This lady had been, almost from the first, the chief parliamentary agent of the suffrage societies. Although she always maintained her close connection with Manchester, she spent much of her time in London and edited the *Women's Suffrage Journal* from there. Whenever there was the smallest hope of a parliamentary opportunity she became active, and her direct and explicit letters were as well known to Members as her uncompromising personality. She combined political sagacity with undeviating enthusiasm, and she was therefore widely trusted and respected, in spite of a certain angularity and rigidity of outlook. Indefatigable in work, Miss Becker never thought of sparing either herself or anyone else, and when she died it was as if one of the pillars of the movement had been knocked away. The *Journal* was discontinued, the parliamentary committees became confused, and a phase of temporary discouragement came over the Suffrage Cause.

For the first time, too, an opposition more formidable

even than that of Members of Parliament made its appearance, when in 1889 a solemn Protest against Women's Suffrage signed by a number of well-known ladies appeared in the *Nineteenth Century Magazine*. Mrs Humphrey Ward, Mrs Creighton, and Mrs Sidney Webb were the most important of the signatories, for all these three were well-known as supporters of the movement for women's education, and as being themselves very active in philanthropic and public life. "We believe," their manifesto ran, "the emancipating process has now reached the limits fixed by the physical constitution of women"; and this statement, coming from them, carried great weight. The suffrage societies of course did not let the Protest go unanswered. Throwing aside their internal differences for the time being, the two London groups united to publish an answer signed by many more ladies, as active and as well known as the first; but the damage had been done, and a new argument was presented to the other side. "Women themselves don't want the vote," they could now say; unfortunately it was partly true.

CHAPTER XV

THE BEGINNING OF THE MILITANT MOVEMENT, 1897–1906.

Passing of second reading of a Women's Suffrage Bill, 1897—Reunion of the divided suffrage societies—The new movement among industrial women in the North—The formation of the Women's Social and Political Union, 1903—Its effort to work within the Labour Party—Mr Begg's Bill talked out, 1904—Christabel Pankhurst and Annie Kenney ask questions at Liberal meeting in Manchester, 1905, and are thrown out and arrested and imprisoned—The policy of "interrupting" meetings adopted—Deputation to Prime Minister arrested—Mr Keir Hardie's resolution talked out, and interruption from the Ladies' Gallery—Joint deputation from the suffrage societies to Sir Henry Campbell-Bannerman—His advice is "Patience."

TOWARDS the middle of the nineties the fog in which the suffrage societies had seemed to be working began to clear. New Zealand had granted Women's Suffrage in 1893, and South Australia had followed this example in 1894, and these events provided a refreshingly new argument. The election of 1895, moreover, had shown the return of a great deal more than half the House of Commons pledged to the principle of Women's Suffrage, and although no one but the Party supporters put much faith in election pledges, there was some encouragement in the fact. Miss Edith Palliser became secretary of the Central Society, and an active Joint Parliamentary Committee was set up, whose chief work was to secure that the question should come to a vote in the House. The chances of a debate on a Private Member's Bill were always uncertain, however, and the committee had an anxious task. The enemies of the women made a very skilful use of blocking tactics, and all through the Parliament of 1892–1895 they had succeeded in staving off the hated subject. Mr Labouchere in particular had developed a great flow of loquacity upon the subjects which stood before the Suffrage Bills on the Order Paper, and it was considered a fine parliamentary joke for him to do so. In 1897, however, even his ingenuity broke down, and a Women's Suffrage Bill introduced by Mr Faithfull Begg actually came to a second reading. A monster appeal, arranged according to constituencies, and bearing 257,796 names, was spread out in Westminster Hall, and the Members of Parliament who passed through were unable to escape this reminder of the people to whom they had made their promises. The enemies sent out an urgent whip against the Bill, but the friends sent another in its favour, and when the vote was taken the measure was found to have the substantial majority of seventy-one behind it.

Except for the unchallenged second reading of 1885, this was the first favourable vote since 1870, and it naturally encouraged the suffragists enormously. The societies, which had already been moving towards reunion, now took the matter up in real earnest. The two London societies became one central society, and, with the eighteen provincial ones, grouped themselves in a national organisation of which Mrs Henry Fawcett was the president, and adopted a regular democratic constitution, under the name of the National Union of Women's Suffrage Societies. Although it was some years before the new constitution really functioned smoothly, the danger of divided counsels and separate parliamentary action was at once very greatly reduced, and a fresh stimulus to new activity was provided.

In the House of Commons the further progress of Mr Begg's Bill was obstructed. Mr Labouchere talked at such length about a Bill dealing with verminous persons on the day when the committee stage might have been reached that the chance was lost, and the victory was rendered purely theoretical. However, even a theoretical victory was better than defeat, and the work in the country continued. The

South African War, which followed in 1898, seemed to make the introduction of further measures impossible, and from the headquarters of the union little was done during the next two years. The fact that political rights were one of the chief issues of the war naturally influenced public opinion, however. If the representation of the Uitlanders was important enough for England to fight the Boers for, the denial of it to Englishwomen became even harder to defend; and Mrs Fawcett lost no opportunity of driving this lesson home.

In the north of England at this time a movement in favour of the suffrage arose among the mill hands and textile workers. The last years of the nineties was the time when the question of a political levy was being discussed among the Trade Unions, and when the Labour Representation Committee was beginning its work. The Independent Labour Party was entering the field of practical politics, and the possibility of the formation of an effective political Labour Party began to gain credence among the workers of Lancashire and Cheshire. Among the early members of the I.L.P. there were many feminists. Miss Isabella Ford, of Leeds, was one of the most active of them; and with the hearty support of such men as Philip Snowden and Keir Hardie, the whole body had been brought to include equal rights for men and women in its programme. This support had a great influence upon labour opinion, and it was re-enforced by the attitude of the independent women workers of the textile trades. These women were members of their mixed Trade Unions, and therefore would be called upon to contribute to the political funds if these were raised. They were deeply interested in political questions, and the majority of them strongly supported the new movement for labour representation. Their own position in relation to it naturally occurred to their minds, however, and they began of their own accord to talk about Women's Suffrage. This forward movement among them was encouraged and stimulated by the Manchester Suffrage Society, and Miss Gore Booth, the secretary, together with Mrs Pankhurst (who was at that time a member of the committee) and Miss Reddish, who had herself been a mill hand, became very active indeed, and a petition bearing the names of 67,000 textile workers was sent to Parliament. Their aim was not only to arouse the factory population to support the movement, but also to induce the new Labour Party to give a foremost place on their programme to this subject, and the suffragists therefore assiduously attended local conferences, and brought forward resolutions whenever the slightest opportunity occurred.

But the leaders of the new Labour Party had other ends in view. Some of them disliked Women's Suffrage in itself, and opposed it on its merits, and many others preferred to put forward a demand for full adult suffrage, without stressing the point of the removal of the sex disqualification; and although Mr Keir Hardie and others of the chief spokesmen of the Party induced them to put these objections aside, and to endorse the regular suffragists' demand of "the vote for women on the same terms as it is or may be granted to men," it was only an abstract approval. Women's Suffrage was by no means the thing they wanted to put foremost, or to identify with their movement at the outset. To do so, they felt, would damage their wider claims, and would certainly delay their propaganda; and so, like the Chartists of fifty years before, they held that the women must wait. So long as the resolutions put forward dealt with abstract rights, all was well; but as soon as the suffragists began to frame resolutions which dealt with their own programmes and their own actions, the Labour leaders grew cautious and recalcitrant, and before very long they were obviously tired of the importunities of the women, and were making the fact plain. When this happened, Mrs Pankhurst and some of her co-workers left the Labour Party, as they had left the Liberals, in disappointment, feeling there was nothing more to be done in that quarter. The industrial women did not altogether give up hope, however, and a "Textile and other Workers' Representation Committee" was formed in 1901, which carried on canvassing and open-air speaking for a long time.

The National Union and the Manchester Society gave support and grants of money to these efforts, and in 1903 a deputation was brought to London with their help and introduced to all the friendly Members of Parliament with whom the other bodies of suffragists were in touch. At the same time, too, the Women's Co-operative Guild came out publicly in support of the movement, thus providing a wider backing than the political and middle-class support which had hitherto been the easiest to secure.

In 1904 the idea of running a special Women's Suffrage candidate at an election occurred to the textile workers, and in 1906 this was carried into effect at Wigan, where Mr Thorley Smith contested the seat on behalf of the women's committee. He was unsuccessful, but the event nevertheless made a great impression in the whole district, and brought the matter into considerable local prominence.

The extension of the movement to working women was mainly carried on in the North of England, and among the textile workers. It was only there that the women workers were admitted to Trade Union membership, or were paid anything approaching a man's wage. In the Midlands and the South, as well as in Scotland and Ireland, the women workers were in no position to stand out for their rights, and though efforts to convince them of the justice of the suffrage claim were always easily successful, the contributions of time or money which they could themselves give to the campaigns were pitifully small.

In these parts of the country, therefore, the societies continued to be mainly "middle class," and their work, which multiplied rapidly in the early years of the new century, consisted of petitions, of meetings in drawing-rooms and public halls, and of the continuous questioning of parliamentary candidates. At the headquarters in London accumulations of details now began to appear. The raising of funds assumed a greater importance, a system of making levies on and giving grants to the local societies was worked out, and a number of paid organisers were engaged and sent off into the country. New societies were formed in a great many places, and although in Parliament it was some time before a good opportunity for a discussion was found, the number of friends was seen to be increasing. In 1904 a resolution moved by Sir Charles M'Laren was carried by 114 votes, and in the following year another second reading victory was only averted by Mr Labouchere, who in order to ward off a possible suffrage success distinguished himself by speaking for some hours about the lighting of vehicles.

Progress was steady, if slow, when a new element in the situation made its appearance, and the Women's Social and Political Union shook the whole question out of its familiar ruts, and sent it careering off upon the most chequered and the most brilliant period of its history.

The Militant Suffrage Movement, which attained world-wide celebrity and became a tremendous legend, began in a simple and almost unpremeditated fashion in 1903.

In that year a few of those who had been working among the factory women of Manchester met together and decided to form a new suffrage society, the Women's Social and Political Union. The leader of this group, Mrs Pankhurst, had already been in the Suffrage Movement for many years. When she was quite young she had married Dr Pankhurst, the barrister who had taken part in the test-case of the Manchester women ratepayers in 1868,[1] and she and her husband had both worked for the Manchester Women's Suffrage Committee and the Married Women's Property Committee. They had been active Liberals, but after Mr Gladstone had "thrown the women overboard" in 1884, they

[1] See Chap. V.

had gone out of that Party, and Dr Pankhurst had taken a notable part in the promotion of the Independent Labour Party in Manchester. He had died in 1898, and Mrs Pankhurst had afterwards lost faith in the Labour Party, as she had in the Liberals. She felt that the Manchester Suffrage Society was old-fashioned and tiresome, and chafed against the restrictions which democratic organisation involved. She had once before formed a separate suffrage society at the time of the trouble over the text of the Suffrage Bill, and now she began again, hoping that by a new group something more vigorous than the quiet propaganda of the old committee could be achieved. In 1904 she went herself to London at the time of the expected debate on the committee stage of Mr Begg's Bill, and she listened from behind the grille while Mr Labouchere talked its slender chances away. Below in the outer lobby a few Co-operative women and other sympathisers waited, and when at last Mrs Pankhurst brought the bad news down there was a great deal of indignation. They went out of the House together, a little group of disappointed women, and tried to hold an indignation meeting in the street outside. Mrs Elmy began to speak, and a little crowd gathered, but they were at once moved on by the police, since meetings of all kinds are forbidden near the House while Parliament is sitting. The women walked away, as they were ordered, and being joined by Mr Keir Hardie, the only Member of Parliament who seemed to share their indignation, they went just beyond the forbidden ground and held their meeting. And then and there at that little unnoticed gathering the militant movement began. Patience and trust were abandoned, and indignation and bitterness took their place. The old ways led nowhere, the old friends did nothing, and it was time for fresh enterprise.

The small group of people who at that time composed the new suffrage society had not any obvious ways of influencing public men. They were almost all settled in a provincial city, they had no money and no votes, and they had not even many friends; but they had a burning grievance. For some months longer, indeed, they found nothing new to do, and went on with open-air meetings; but with the collapse of the Government in the autumn of 1905 their opportunity came.

In October of that year the Liberal Party, being on the eve of taking office, held a great meeting in the Free Trade Hall, Manchester. The chief speaker of the evening was Sir Edward (now Viscount) Grey, and his purpose was to lay before the country the programme and intentions of the new Government which was about to be formed.

The Women's Social and Political Union, having decided that a Government measure was the only hope of progress, determined to press for the inclusion of this in the official programme of the Liberal Party, and accordingly they laid their plans to attend this meeting and ask questions. Annie Kenney, a mill hand from Oldham, and Christabel, Mrs Pankhurst's eldest daughter, were given this task, and armed with little cotton banners bearing the words VOTES FOR WOMEN, they made their way into the hall. When the speaking was over, and question time had come, they duly asked what the future ministry's intention in the matter was, but they got no answer. Annie Kenney unfurled her little banner and stood up on her chair to ask again, and a perfect storm of angry cries from the audience was the result. The stewards rushed at her to drag her down, and one of them stifled her voice by holding his hat over her face; and while they were so engaged Christabel rose up and repeated the question. Those on the platform smiled and said nothing, and though at the suggestion of the Chief Constable the question was sent up in writing, no better result was secured. Votes of thanks were moved and passed, and the audience had begun to go out when Annie Kenney rose up again, and once more tried to put her question. This time the uproar was tremendous. Men rushed at her from all sides, and struck and scratched her; and Christabel, who stood beside her, was pulled roughly away. Both girls were seized by stewards, six to each of them, and were carried bodily from the hall and hurled down the steps into the street below. Bruised and shaken as they were, they at once scrambled up and began to hold a meeting of protest, asking why their question had been ignored while all the others had been answered, and making speeches of fiery indignation. Inside the hall, meanwhile, Sir Edward Grey was tardily explaining that he had not answered them because Women's Suffrage "is not, and I do not think it is likely to be, a party question," and so was not "a fitting subject" for that meeting. Sir Edward Grey was, and always remained, a strong believer in the suffrage; he had helped the Cause before, and he was to help it again most notably; but on this occasion he made a mistake of the first importance. His treatment of these two girls, and his refusal to answer a perfectly well-justified question, taken with the outrageous behaviour of the stewards, fired a train of bitterness and anger which carried the new society forward; and it was the insincere attitude of the Liberals, as much as the fighting spirit of the women, which led to the uprising of the militant movement.

The story did not end with the explanation given inside the Free Trade Hall and the protest meeting outside, for the latter had hardly begun before Annie Kenney and Christabel Pankhurst were arrested and marched off to the police station on a charge of obstruction. The next day, when their examination before the magistrates took place, they were both found guilty and sentenced to fines, with the alternative of imprisonment. Both of them chose imprisonment, and were immediately hurried off to the cells, where they remained in peaceful seclusion while the world outside rang with their affairs. The Press of the whole country seized on this happening with avidity. Here was NEWS, thrilling NEWS, involving a future Cabinet Minister, and a cause about which ridicule and cheap joking were easy. With one accord the brawling and the wickedness of the women were deplored, and the leader-writers lamented with sham regret that their cause was put back for ages, and that women had now proved themselves for ever unfit for enfranchisement. Manchester University (where Christabel Pankhurst had already been troublesome by insisting on being a law student) threatened to expel her, and the whole affair was the great preoccupation of the city. Already by this one act hundreds of people, who had never thought about Women's Suffrage before, began to consider it, and though the vast majority of them deplored what had been done, this did not make the result any the less important. A wonderful new weapon, the weapon of publicity and advertisement, was put into the hands of the Women's Social and Political Union, and the leaders at once saw its value.

The organisation had only a few members at the time of the Free Trade Hall episode, and in the General Election which followed they could not do very much. They produced their banners and made another sensational protest at a big Liberal meeting in the Albert Hall in December; and the policy of asking questions at candidates' meetings was continued in the Manchester district, in every case with the same result of riot and disturbance. No more arrests were made, however, and in the storm and stress of an election little notice was attracted, though the hecklers began to be everywhere expected, and the arrangements for throwing them out of the halls were carefully rehearsed. Mr Winston Churchill was at that time contesting a Manchester seat in the Liberal interest. He was generally believed to have made an unsuccessful effort to pay the fines of Annie Kenney and Christabel Pankhurst after the Free Trade Hall meeting (at which he had been present), because of the adverse effect their imprisonment would have in his own constituency, and he had the reputation of being a supporter of the Cause. Moreover, he was one of those who, if elected, would be in the Cabinet, and so his meetings were singled out for particular attention. The old Manchester Suffrage Society, at the same time, was pursuing its accustomed policy of asking for the individual views of candidates, and an instructive little correspondence passed between him and them.

"Madam," wrote Mr Churchill, "My previous attitude towards this question had, like that of many other members of the Liberal Party, been one of growing sympathy; and on the only occasion on which I have had an opportunity of voting on it in the House of Commons I voted in favour of the motion. I cannot, however, conceal from you that I have lately been much discouraged by the action of certain advocates of the movement in persistently disturbing and attempting to break up both my own meetings and those of other Liberal candidates. I fully recognise that these persons are not representative of the serious supporters of the movement, and I can only urge those who do represent them to exert their utmost influence to repress the foolish and disorderly agitation which is in progress, and which, so long as it continues, must prevent me from taking any further steps in favour of the cause which you have at heart."

They answered, of course, that they felt certain he would "recognise that what to many seems mistaken action does not affect the justice of the Cause," but this produced no effect. Mr Churchill was being irritated, and even made ridiculous, and his open hostility to a cause which he had hitherto advocated was the result. A good many other Liberals took the same line, glad no doubt of an excuse for ceasing to pretend to support a cause they secretly disliked; but the Women's Liberal Federation, which had made a belief in Women's Suffrage a test of their support in the previous year, kept many Members straight, and these, together with the minority who really believed in the thing, were enough to secure the return of four hundred Members of the House of Commons pledged to support a Suffrage Bill.

In the early months of 1906 the Women's Social and Political Union transferred their activities to London. Although they had practically no friends there, except Mr Keir Hardie, and no money at all, they were not in the least afraid, but sent Annie Kenney to hire the Caxton Hall and prepare a demonstration for the day of the opening of Parliament. About three hundred women met there while the King's speech was being delivered, and when the news was brought to the platform that there was no mention of Women's Suffrage in the speech, Mrs Pankhurst at once led the whole meeting down the street to the House of Commons. They found the great doors shut against them, and after long waiting and much discouragement, they dispersed to take up what they were beginning to call their "fight" with renewed bitterness.

Their next step was to try and see the Prime Minister, in order to get from him that statement of the Government's intentions which they had failed to elicit during the election. Sir Henry Campbell-Bannerman refused to see them, but this did not deter them in the least, and early in March a small group of women arrived at No. 10 Downing Street. They were, of course, told to go away, but instead of going they put up one of their little VOTES FOR WOMEN banners, and sat down upon the doorstep to wait until the Prime Minister appeared. A good many messages passed to and fro, and the women were finally got rid of on the understanding that their request would be taken to Sir Henry. Subsequent correspondence proved that this was leading them no farther, and a week later they again returned to the charge. This time they were more insistent, and were removed by the police, but were not charged with anything, and were soon released.

While the suffragettes had been sitting upon the doorstep

and making their somewhat importunate demand, the older suffrage society had been proceeding more strictly according to precedent, and very soon after this they persuaded two hundred Members of Parliament, of all Parties, to ask the Prime Minister to receive a deputation. Urged on all sides, Sir Henry Campbell-Bannerman gave way, and stated that on the 19th of May he would see representatives of all the organisations supporting the Cause.

So far the matter seemed plain sailing, but the question of organising the deputation still remained. The task, of course, fell to the National Union, and a series of the most complicated and delicate negotiations began. Although the militants had as yet done nothing more outrageous than interrupt meetings, there was already a great deal of opposition to them in the political world. Their lack of dignity and political manners, and their extraordinary notoriety were rousing protests on all sides, and in April they made a further demonstration which greatly complicated the situation. Mr Keir Hardie had secured a day for the introduction of a Women's Suffrage resolution in the House of Commons, and everyone hoped that it would be carried by so substantial a majority that the Prime Minister would be impressed, and thereby moved to make some favourable announcement to the deputation. There were, therefore, a great many eager and anxious ladies seated behind the grille, and among them was Mrs Pankhurst with a number of her followers. The debate came on, and in due course the first speaker for the opponents got up. It was Mr Cremer, and his speech was in the traditionally jocular tone. "Were they prepared," he asked, "to hand over the government of the country to women, the majority of whom were not bread-winners, and who had not to bear the burdens, and who did not understand the responsibilities of life? . . . He was sometimes described in regard to this question as a woman-hater, but he had had two wives, and he thought that was the best answer he could give to those who called him a woman-hater. He was too fond of them to drag them into the political arena and to ask them to undertake responsibilities, duties, and obligations which they did not understand and which they did not care for. . . . What did one find when one got into the company of women and talked politics? They were soon asked to stop talking silly politics, and yet that was the type of people to whom hon. members were invited to hand over the destinies of the country. . . . Supposing women were members of this House and a division was imminent, what influences would be used by women on men, and men on women in order to secure votes? Every Member knew that a man dealt far more tenderly with a woman with whom he was arguing a point than he did with a man. Women were creatures of impulse and emotion, and did not decide question on grounds of reason as men did."

These remarks, though they were familiar enough to the House, were new to some of the ladies in the gallery, and irritated the members of the Women's Social and Political Union beyond bearing. Their comments were so many and so emphatic that they were heard by the Speaker below. He sent word to the police to be ready to take the ladies out if such a thing occurred again, but as Mr Cremer had by then sat down, nothing further was done. The debate went on, and the time went on too, until 11 o'clock was nearly reached. It began to look as if the resolution was again to be talked out, and the ladies above grew anxious. Just before 11 o'clock, therefore, they began to protest, and cries of "Divide, Divide" rang out from behind the grille, through which, as the Members looked up in astonishment, little VOTES FOR WOMEN banners were seen to be thrust. At once the police rushed in and pulled the ladies out, and the House rose amid angry murmurs. Friends and enemies alike regretted the disturbance, and while some deplored the "shocking outrage," others lamented what they thought was a lost opportunity.

After this, complaints of the behaviour of the militants poured in upon the National Union from all sides. Their executive committee decided "Not to take any public steps in the matter (as it would probably soon be lived down and forgotten), and that the vigorous and combined official action now to be taken would sufficiently show the policy of the Union"; but it was not so easily disposed of. The official action was of course the forthcoming deputation to the Prime Minister, but its "combined" character was seriously jeopardised. The British Women's Temperance Association, The Women's Liberal Federation, and many of the societies of the National Union itself refused to be represented if these dangerous people were to be included, and demanded at least that an undertaking to be of good behaviour should be given. The Women's Social and Political Union on the other hand refused to be left out, and when asked to give an undertaking not to create a disturbance, they held up their heads proudly and would say nothing more than that "there could be no divergence of opinion as to the question of the behaviour of persons in the position of guests in a private person's house."

With this the other anxious ladies had to be satisfied, but no sooner was this difficulty composed than a fresh one made its appearance. The Labour and Co-operative women who were invited to join in the affair held back because their demand was for adult suffrage for men and women, and they feared that this would be compromised if they joined with people who were asking for any limited measure of Women's Suffrage. The National Union was, indeed, asking for the vote "on the same terms as it is or may be granted to men," but it was with the utmost difficulty that they could be brought to see that this formula covered their position.

At last, however, all difficulties were overcome, and on the appointed day the suffragists were duly received.

The deputation, which numbered over 300, was introduced by Sir Charles M'Laren, and led by Miss Emily Davies, and its speakers represented not only all the organised women suffragists and the 1530 graduates, but also 50,000 textile workers, 22,000 Co-operative women, and the 52,000 members of the British Women's Temperance Association. They made out a case which, as Sir Henry Campbell-Bannerman himself said, was "conclusive and irrefutable"; but something more than justice and logic was needed to make the Government act. After agreeing with every word they said, the Prime Minister was obliged to add that he proposed to do nothing at all about it. There were differences of opinion in the Cabinet and in the Party, his hands were tied, and the only thing he could advise the women to do was "to go on pestering," and to exercise "the virtue of patience."

"Sir," cried Annie Kenney, the irrepressible, jumping on a chair so as to be seen and heard, "We are not satisfied!"; and it was profoundly true. It was a mockery to preach patience to people like Emily Davies, who had been working for fifty years; it was idle to mention the word to the mill girls and the working women whose grievances were so immediate and so burning, and it was in the first degree unwise to advise the ardent and reckless militants "to go on pestering"! They went out from that audience, as was only natural, burning with rage. Patience, indeed! They would show the Prime Minister what stock of patience they had! They would show him what pestering was like. By those foolish words the militant movement became irrevocably established, and the stage of revolt began.

CHAPTER XVI

THE GREAT DAYS. 1906–1911

Increase of interest in Women's Suffrage—Effect upon women—The Mud March of 1907—Two forms of suffrage organisation—The N.U.W.S.S.—The W.S.P.U.—Active militant tactics—The hunger-strike—Lady Constance Lytton—The first election of 1910—Formation of the Conciliation Committee—Militant truce and great joint procession—Town Councils petition Parliament—Second reading of Conciliation Bill carried, July 1910—Adult suffrage used to sidetrack votes for women—The second election of 1910—The voters' petition—Conciliation Bill carried again in May 1911—Its chances destroyed by the announcement of the Government Franchise Bill—The League for opposing Women's Suffrage—Formation of many new suffrage societies.

FROM the summer of 1906 onwards the cause of Women's Suffrage began to attract public attention, and not only overshadowed all the other parts of the Women's Movement but became one of the main political subjects of the time. Not that it was in any sense an important parliamentary question as yet; the refusal of the Liberal Government to deal with it officially left the subject hanging in the dim corners where unofficial measures lurk; but outside the doors of Westminster it grew yearly more important. The extraordinary behaviour of the "suffragettes," as the members of the Women's Social and Political Union came to be called, and the ever-widening propaganda of the "suffragists," as the law-abiding section were styled, made it impossible for anyone in the country to be unaware of the existence of the demand; and once they were aware of it, people found it an easy subject to discuss. Everyone in the country felt an interest; everyone knew, or thought they knew, the fundamental differences between men and women, and consequently everyone was ready to have an opinion. No special learning, no abstruse facts nor formidable statistics were required. One could be "for" or "against" with the greatest certainty and ease, and find plenty of simple arguments on either side. One could say that "woman's place is the home," and feel that everything was disposed of; or one could say "two heads are better than one" and feel equally triumphant; and all over the country people began to say one or other of these things.

Plenty of other arguments were used, of course. Those who wanted the reform knew that they were seeking for a tremendous social change, and those who resisted it were equally well aware of the fact; but it was all so human and unpolitical in its implications that there was no one who could not, and did not, have an opinion. Moreover, since the subject of the relation of the sexes to each other is one of perennial interest, and of unlimited personal variation, the suffrage controversy could be twisted to endless domestic purposes; and the discussion raged from one end of the land to the other. Day after day, as the militants provided fresh headlines for the newspapers, the breakfast tables of England resounded with the debate, and the comments flowed out from the domestic hearth to railway trains, smoking rooms, clubs, and public-houses, and wherever men gathered together.

The wide notoriety of the movement had a marked and not unnatural effect upon women. To hundreds and thousands of them, of course, Women's Suffrage was an impious and shocking notion in itself, and the methods used to advocate it appeared scandalous and almost indecent. Among the working women in particular the suffragettes' "brazen" doings, and their carelessness of appearances, seemed outrageous, and for the moment progress among the factory hands was at a standstill. To hundreds and thousands more, however, the thing came as a new gospel; even those who had believed in the Cause before now began to see it in a new light, and an almost religious fervour entered into their support. The first to be affected, of course, were those who had already come into direct touch with some part of the Women's Movement—the girls at college, the women who had shared in Mrs Butler's crusade, and those who were following the developments of the old Humanitarian impulse. Almost all these women would at any time have signed petitions for Women's Suffrage, but, like Florence Nightingale and Harriet Martineau, they would have let it rest at that. They had believed in, but had not cared for suffrage. Politics had seemed to them a remote and comparatively useless matter, important no doubt in the long run, and clearly a thing which should be open to women; but for practical purposes their own work in a settlement, a school, or a philanthropic society appeared more immediate and urgent. In the early years of the century, however, women of this sort found themselves suddenly called upon to defend their belief in Women's Suffrage. All about them people were beginning to discuss the matter, disapproving, jeering, making fun; and as they defended, protested, and argued, their eyes were opened. They saw that this thing in which they had passively believed was after all the key to the whole position. Driven by their own arguments they realised that philanthropy without political power was but a patching up of old abuses; that education without enfranchisement was but selfishness. They began to look at themselves and their mission in the world in a new light, and poured into the suffrage societies all the enthusiasm which they had thought to devote to other ends. These women, the backbone of the new Suffrage Movement, did not see the struggle as the militants did. To them it was not primarily a fight between men and women, hardly even a matter of "rights" at all. What they saw in it, and what they wanted from it, was an extended power to do good in the world. Just as, a generation before, the desire for cottage visiting had driven young ladies to seek a small measure of personal freedom, so now the longing to do a reformer's work in the world sent young ladies to street corners to demand the vote. The development was natural and inevitable; it was the consequence of what had gone before; and the startling advocacy and flaming challenge of the militants did not create it; but they did, undoubtedly, hasten and quicken what was already coming to birth.

With the militant advertisement on the one hand, and the growing enthusiasm of the constitutional forces on the other, women who had never before given a thought to public questions began to be roused, and when once they had accepted the main doctrine they quickly became enthusiastic. They read into the Cause not only what lay upon the surface, but all the discontents which they, as women, were suffering; their economic dependence, their conventional limitations, and all the multitude of trifles which made them hate being women and long to have been men; and they saw in the Suffrage Movement a symbol of their release from all these evils.

The years which followed were the great years of the Women's Movement, when organised societies were expanding with incredible rapidity, when agitation was becoming an exact science, and when the ever-recurring crises seemed to have a glamour greater than the light of common day. The meetings which multiplied in halls and drawing-rooms, in schools and chapels, at street corners, and on village greens, did not seem like the dull and solemn stuff of politics; they were missionary meetings, filled with the fervour of a gospel, and each one brought new enthusiasts to the ranks. It was the flowering time of the Women's Movement; the long years of preparation and slow growth were forgotten, and the Cause seemed to be springing new born from the enthusiasm of the time.

In 1907 the first of the big public demonstrations was organised, and on a very wet and dreary day the "Mud March" of three thousand women made its way from Hyde Park Corner to Exeter Hall with banners and bands, long skirts trailing on the ground, and hearts in which enthusiasm struggled successfully with propriety. In that year the vast majority of women still felt that there was something very dreadful in walking in procession through the streets; to do it was to be something of a martyr, and many of the demonstrators felt that they were risking their employments and endangering their reputations, besides facing a dreadful ordeal of ridicule and public shame. They walked, and nothing happened. The small boys in the streets and the gentlemen at the club windows laughed, but that was all. Crowds watched and wondered; and it was not so dreadful after all. Similar processions were then arranged in Manchester and in Edinburgh, and the idea of public demonstration of faith in the Cause took root.

As the movement went on, the suffragettes and the suffragists alike developed a high degree of ingenuity in propaganda. They managed to turn everything into a suffrage lesson, and their war cry "Votes for Women" cropped up in the most unexpected places. In both camps there were women who devoted their whole lives to the Cause, travelling month after month from one end of the country to another to address meetings, organise election campaigns, collect money, and encourage new support; but besides these, there were others, particularly in the constitutional societies, who advocated the Cause as they went about their ordinary lives. They still lived as they had always lived, among people who knew and laughed at them, and they braved all their conventions by standing up at street corners and in the public parks to address the passers-by. They chalked the pavements and sold their newspapers in the streets, they walked the gutters in sandwich boards, and toiled from house to house canvassing for members, collecting money, and advertising meetings. In their holidays they toured in caravans, setting up stalls in market-places and speaking on village greens, finding on the whole great friendliness, with just that spice of opposition which makes such deeds exciting. The wild reputation of the militants, of course, suggested violent reprisals to the unthinking, and the quiet and orderly meetings of both sections of suffragists sometimes suffered disagreeable interruption. Pepper, mice, rotten eggs, fish, oranges, and other such missiles flew at the speakers' heads, and occasionally there were rather nasty rushes of real hooligans. The women speakers, however, soon learnt the technique necessary to control these silly manifestations. They learnt that to keep their own tempers, to make jokes, and to go on steadily with their business was the sure way to get the goodwill of the crowd, which, in the main, was always tolerant and good natured, and the opposition had thus no power of hindering the campaign. Indeed, the suffragists became so experienced in riots, and so successful in dealing with heckling and interruptions, that they turned to the advantage of the Cause all the difficulties which they encountered; advertisement supplemented argument, and persistence reinforced persuasion.

There were two kinds of effort in the suffrage world, inspired by differing ideals and carried on by rival systems of organisation. The constitutional societies, which were united in the National Union and led by Mrs Fawcett, carried on the regular tradition of the whole movement. They did not regard their work as an attack upon men, but rather as a reform for the good of all, and the next step in human progress. Their newspaper, which existed to promote Women's Suffrage only, was called *The Common Cause*, and it was in these terms that they saw their aim. Their chief effort was the conversion of public opinion, and they felt that this conversion was as important and as much a part of their object as the gaining of the vote itself. Mrs Fawcett, their leader, had seen the whole movement grow; she knew, and she taught her followers to know, that their Cause was part of a development wider even than the change in the position of women itself. Though she watched the progress of the Franchise Bills with the utmost care, and let slip no opportunity to advance them, she was quietly and obstinately convinced that the Cause was bound to triumph, and no set-back, no discouragement, no misfortune perturbed her. When her followers grew too emphatic, or too much discouraged, she rebuked them gently enough but very firmly, and the very quietness of her outlook kept them in check. There were times, of course, when they made extravagant claims and gave utterance to unwarranted views, but she never let these pass unnoticed. One instance, typical of hundreds, will reveal her method. It was at a little meeting in Yorkshire, where an obscure speaker was holding forth upon the virtues of women, their great superiority to men, and the wonders they could accomplish if they were only free. In proof of her argument she adduced Mrs Fawcett's own sister, Elizabeth Garrett Anderson, and declared that it was only since she and the other women doctors had been practising that attention had been paid to the diseases of women and that discoveries in this direction had been made. There was truth in the statement, but the implication was all wrong, and Mrs Fawcett, when it was her turn to speak, quietly put it right. "It is true," she said, "that great discoveries have been made since the days when women doctors were first admitted to the medical profession. For my part, however, I do not believe that women alone are responsible for them. I think that the same spirit which brought women into the profession, the spirit of generosity in men and of enterprise in women, was the spirit which brings progress." There was nothing personal in this reproof, but it is very convincing. The speaker who had made the exorbitant claim got a new glimpse of the meaning of the Cause for which she was working, and the men in the audience whom she had antagonised went away convinced that there was sanity and sense after all in the Women's Suffrage ranks.

Under Mrs Fawcett's leadership the numbers of the constitutional suffragists grew rapidly. As the local societies multiplied they became increasingly democratic in their internal organisation, so that their development was governed by their own council meetings, and their constituent societies took a real and highly expert share in the direction of the movement. Within a year or two they had evolved a technique of democracy inside their own ranks which became in itself an absorbing interest, and the surplus energy which the movement was stimulating among its supporters found vent in this direction. The affairs of the National Union during these astonishing years are not now of much moment; the niceties of by-election policy, the adjustments of affiliation fees, the basis of representation, and the devolution into federations are all matters which are dead and gone; but the spirit which caused them to be of such moment, and the energy which was poured into them, prove at once the vitality of the movement and the practical abilities of its supporters. They were not content that their machinery should be less than supremely efficient, and they were prepared to take, and did take, almost unlimited trouble to ensure the perfection of their own organisation.

As the network of societies spread out, and as the number of their members increased, so did the efficiency of the machine improve. It was so planned and so organised as to be capable of almost indefinite expansion, and by 1910 it had grown to be an amazingly powerful and important political instrument.

The militant society was entirely different. Its propaganda, though directed towards the same end as that of the National Union, rang with quite other notes, with defiance, antagonism and suspicion. "Deeds not Words" was the motto of the organisation, and its deliberate policy was to seek sensational achievement rather than anything else. Its leaders did not scruple to brush aside the ordinary niceties of procedure, and they did not care whom they shocked and antagonised. They distrusted everyone who was not a militant, and laughed at all talk of persuasion. What they believed in was moral violence. By this force, and by the driving power of their own determination, they hoped to turn the Liberals out of office, and to coerce whoever succeeded them into granting their demand. The whole atmosphere of their work was thus aggressive and headlong; it resounded with charges of the treachery and ill faith of their opponents, and was sharpened by sarcasm, anger, and excitement. Moreover, since they deliberately put themselves in the position of outlaws dogged by the police, they were always wrapped round with secrecy and mystification, and planned surprises alike for their followers and for the public. The policy of sensational public protest was not one which left much time for the tasks of self-government, nor was democracy much to their taste. The Women's Social and Political Union adopted, therefore, a purely autocratic system, and entrusted all decisions to their leaders—Mrs Pankhurst and her daughter Christabel, and Mr and Mrs Pethick Lawrence. These people alone decided what was to be done; the others obeyed, and enjoyed the surrender of their judgment, and the sensation of marching as an army under discipline.

In course of time divisions of opinion arose within the organisation, and separate societies were more than once formed from among its members. In 1909 a considerable body, under the leadership of Mrs Despard,[1] broke off and formed the Women's Freedom League—a society which followed much the same policy as that of the W.S.P.U. though it arrived at it by a different line of reasoning, and

[1] Mrs Despard was one of the early members of the I.L.P., and was exceedingly well known both in South London and in Dublin for her work among the poor. She was twice imprisoned. Though the sister of General French, she was during the war an extreme pacifist. In 1919 she stood for Parliament unsuccessfully for Battersea, and in 1927 was expelled from the Irish Free State as a dangerous character.

conducted its affairs in a more regular and democratic fashion. The main body, however, continued on its way, bound together by a loyalty to its leaders almost more passionate than to its cause, and attracting to its ranks not only those of extreme opinions but also those whose natural inclination led them towards drama, hero-worship, and self-surrender. The actual number of adherents of the society was never known. No attempt was ever made to keep a record of those who joined it, and no regular subscriptions were paid. Enormous sums of money passed through the hands of the society, but no full accounts were ever published, and no audited balance-sheet was ever presented; for the Women's Social and Political Union spent no time upon "formalities." All was action! action! As fast as money came in it went out again, spent on flags and banners, leaflets, organisers, meetings, parades, bands, shows, ribbons, drums or even bombs—anything, everything with which to make a noise and a stir, and keep enthusiasm burning and the Cause shining in the public eye.

For the first year after 1906 the militants followed the course they had already adopted; they opposed the Government at by-elections, heckled Cabinet Ministers at meetings, and went on undiscouraged deputations to the men who refused to see them, only to be arrested in the roadway for "obstruction." They grew to be very experienced in such matters, and learnt how to circumvent the police by stratagems and surprises. They arrived in all sorts of guises, and appeared in all sorts of places. Now one would appear as a messenger boy, now another as a waitress. Once they chained themselves to the railings in Downing Street, and so gained time to make some longish speeches before being haled off to Bow Street; another was found chained to a statue in the lobby of the House of Commons, a thoroughly strategic position. They sprang out of organ lofts, they peered through roof windows, and leapt out of innocent-looking furniture vans; they materialised on station platforms, they harangued the terrace of the House from the river, and wherever they were least expected there they were. Again and again they made efforts to see the Prime Minister, who perpetually refused to see them, and their so-called "raids" upon Parliament became a regular feature of their work. They were raids only in a technical sense, for the proceedings of the women were strictly orderly. A meeting in the neighbourhood would be the first step; at this meeting a deputation would be appointed, and eight, ten, fifty, or a hundred women would then file out, either in procession or in small groups, and proceed quietly towards Westminster. As they neared Palace Yard they would be met by cordons of police, sometimes as many as a thousand strong, on foot and on horseback. They would then be ordered to turn back, and would refuse. The crowds which had been following them would close in, and a sort of confused scuffle would follow in which the women were usually knocked about, sometimes pretty severely. They would do no violence themselves, but merely persist in their attempt to go on, and finally, after varying periods of time, they would be arrested. Conviction for "obstruction" usually followed, although the suffragettes argued that the obstruction had been used against them, and protested that they were being deprived of the ancient right of petition. They claimed, moreover, that the responsibility for the disturbances lay with the Government, and called Cabinet Ministers and even the Home Secretary himself as witnesses. The result was, however, always the same; imprisonment for varying terms in Holloway Gaol.

All this was extremely annoying to the authorities, who felt that they were being put into a ridiculous position, and orders were accordingly issued that the suffragettes were not to be arrested, or if they had to be arrested they were not to be charged. This did not suit the militants at all, and they decided that they must at all costs force the magistrates to convict them. The plan of committing technical assaults was accordingly adopted, and Mrs Pankhurst herself led the way by striking Inspector Jervis upon the face at the door of the House of Commons. Her victim perfectly understood why she did this, and admitted it as he arrested her; but from the Press a howl of indignation arose. Screaming, scratching, biting, kicking and yelling were attributed to the militants, and a flood of generalities about the nature of the female sex filled the leading articles, where for the most part it was now maintained that women had proved themselves to be for ever unfitted to vote. The militants paid no attention to this, and a policy of stone-throwing followed, in which shop fronts in Regent Street, as well as public buildings, were attacked.

The change from passive to active militancy, of which this was the beginning, was strongly disapproved of by many of those who supported the cause of Women's Suffrage. The National Union of Women's Suffrage Societies had often before thought the militants unwise in their methods, but now they thought them wrong, and publicly dissociated themselves from their unconstitutional actions. It seemed to many people that the militants made a sort of inverted appeal to the privileges of sex. On the one hand they challenged physical violence, as if they were real fighters, and yet they refused any real contest because they were women. Their talk of being the victims of aggression no longer rang true, and some of those who cared most for the Cause felt that it was being degraded and dishonoured by what seemed the merest sham. Those who were not feminists, and who thought the movement expressed nothing more than a desire to be feeble imitations of men, were of course delighted by the turn of events. They felt that the suffragettes nicely symbolised the absurdity of the whole ideal, and each manifestation of incomplete rowdyism gave them fresh joy.

The militants themselves, of course, had a different view.

They knew well enough that they suffered real violence in return for merely technical offences, and they firmly believed that by their voluntary imprisonments they were advancing the Cause. It belonged to their temperament and outlook to care nothing for what people thought; they despised the constitutional suffragists and laughed at the "antis"; and volunteers followed each other in quick succession to Holloway Gaol.

Once in prison the suffragists by no means ceased to be militant. From the first they had protested that they ought to be treated as political prisoners, and moreover they had made accusations and revelations about the ordinary prison routine which greatly angered the authorities. They now devised a further method of annoyance, and as soon as they reached the cells they refused to eat their food. Forcible feeding was tried in vain; the prisoners struggled so violently against it that the process became actually dangerous, and the prison officials were obliged to let them starve till they came to the edge of physical collapse, and then to let them go. In spite of the severe pain and damage to health which this process involved, scores of suffragette prisoners adopted it, and the passing of sentences upon them became a farce. The officials tried everything they could think of in vain; and sometimes their severities went so far that they took effect upon the public imagination, and roused real anger outside. Such a case occurred when on a freezing night the hose was turned on a recalcitrant prisoner, who was then left all night, wet as she was, in an unwarmed cell. An even worse case, however, occurred in 1910. A year before, Lady Constance Lytton joined the Women's Social and Political Union and suffered arrest in one of their raids. On being taken to Holloway she was declared to be too delicate to endure ordinary prison discipline, as indeed she was; and in spite of her earnest efforts to be treated like the rest she had been taken to the Infirmary and released before the expiry of her sentence. A second time in the same year she was arrested in Newcastle, and a second time accorded the same treatment; and she began to think that her name and her influential friends were the cause. Her third imprisonment, therefore, was undertaken in disguise. Under the name of Jane Wharton she went to Liverpool, and there, by throwing a stone, she secured arrest in January 1910. This time no careful medical examination followed. With the other prisoners she went to the cells, where she began her hunger-strike and was forcibly fed; and it was not until the secret of her identity came out that her condition was noticed. She was then at once released "on medical grounds," but the damage was done. Lady Constance was an invalid from that day until she died, a true martyr to the Cause. And a great many people were furiously and justly indignant.

None of these things seemed to have any favourable effect on the Government, however, and the parliamentary situation remained deeply discouraging. Second readings were indeed secured in 1907 and 1908, the latter of which was successful,[1] but Mr Asquith, who had become Prime Minister, paid no attention. He refused to see or hear anyone connected with the suffrage societies, and pretended to be unable to distinguish between those who were attacking him and his Party and those who were merely pressing their cause.

A second procession, this time 15,000 strong, went through the streets of London, and vast meetings in Hyde Park and the Albert Hall followed; but they appeared to make no impression.

In 1910, however, there was an access of hope. The General Election of January had resounded with talk of Women's Suffrage, and when the Liberal Government again resumed office a really serious parliamentary effort

[1] Those Bills were private Members' Bills, introduced by Mr Stanger in 1907 and talked out, and by Mr (now Sir Willoughby) Dickinson in 1908 and carried by 179 votes.

was made. An all-party committee of Members was formed, with Lord Lytton as its chairman and Mr Brailsford as its secretary, and this committee, which was known as the Conciliation Committee, drafted a Bill such as all sections of opinion seemed ready to support.

The Women's Social and Political Union was persuaded to call a truce to its militancy, in order to give the Bill every chance, and for six months an unparalleled intensity of propaganda was carried on. Huge processions, one of them over four miles long, marched through the streets of London, and these processions were both imposing and beautiful. The women, tired of the tawdry ugliness of cotton banners inscribed with black letters, devoted themselves to making lovely symbolical standards, worked in silk and velvet, and for the time some of the pageantry of the Middle Ages came back to the London streets. The militants, always more extreme about everything, paraded in costume, some on horseback, others representing the professions and occupations of women, or the famous women of the past. With bands and banners the women marched, and thousands upon thousands followed them and crowded into their meetings to hear what it was all about. Twice in one week the great Albert Hall was filled to overflowing, and enthusiasm and hope ran high. Mr Asquith himself unbent so far as to receive a deputation from the constitutional societies, and town and borough councils began to pour in resolutions upon him. Dublin sent its Mayor and public officials in all their robes of State to lay their unanimous plea before the bar of the House of Commons, and 129 other important towns, including Edinburgh, Glasgow, Manchester, Liverpool, Birmingham, and Newcastle, officially supported the Cause. The Conciliation Bill came to the House in July in an atmosphere of expectation, and although the *Times* had published articles against it every day for the preceding fortnight, it passed its second reading by 110 votes. But second readings had been won before; the critical thing was the attitude of the Government, and this seemed hardly changed. Mr Lloyd George and Mr Winston Churchill attacked the Bill on the ground that it was not sufficiently democratic, and no time was allowed for its further progress. Matters now seemed almost worse than before. Indifference and open hostility were one thing, but the obstruction of people who claimed to be friends was worse. All the real supporters of the Cause, whatever their Party, were agreed that the only form of Bill which was likely to succeed was one on the limited "Conciliation" basis. The Labour men, much as they wanted to see adult suffrage on its merits, admitted that it was vain to expect to get votes for women by that road, and not only supported the "limited" measure but forced its endorsement upon their Party. But some of the Liberal friends were not so single-minded. They saw in the adult movement a chance of escaping from the difficulty of having to deal with the questions at all, and accordingly they used the basis of the franchise to sidetrack the whole unwelcome and distasteful affair.

When the second election of 1910 began, therefore, the Liberals had upon their programme a Male Franchise Bill, which might, or might not, be amended so as to include women; if the House did so amend it Mr Asquith said that he would abide by that decision, and this meagre prospect was all that the suffragists had gained.

The leaders of the Women's Social and Political Union were outraged; here was a fine reward for their truce, a fine result of keeping quiet! At a huge and excited gathering in the Albert Hall they called back their promises, and declared war once more. They would fight the Liberals tooth and nail in the election; they would resume their violence and their protests; let the Government look to itself! In pursuance of this decision they interrupted Mr Lloyd George while he was making a suffrage speech to women Liberals, and dogged the footsteps of the Liberal Ministers with even greater pertinacity than before.

The N.U.W.S.S., though exceedingly uneasy at the prospect before them, was not opposing the Liberal Party at the election, but only working to secure the return of individuals of all parties who were true supporters. They decided, however, to try and influence the new Government by a direct expression of opinion from the electorate. Petitions from women had been gathered in their hundreds of thousands, and had been wholly unavailing, but they hoped that perhaps petitions from voters might meet a different fate. They accordingly arranged to attend all the polling stations in the kingdom; and during the snow and sleet of that December election the women stood outside the doors of the sacred booths, asking the voters to support their plea to be allowed to come inside. This petition received three hundred thousand signatures; working men signed it readily, and spoke with kindness to the watchers at the gates; but the Government, as usual, ignored the whole thing. Anyone would sign anything, was the official view, and this great document went, along with its innumerable predecessors, into the official waste-paper-baskets.

When the Liberal Government resumed office for the second time, the problem of the Lords Veto was settled and the Home Rule question was to the fore. Both these great constitutional problems were of kindred nature to Women's Suffrage; both dealt with the elements of democracy, and seemed to be about to be settled in a radical direction; but the voteless women were still left out in the cold. Since the agitation had begun the male electorate had increased from 700,000 to 7,000,000, but nothing was in sight for the women. The Conciliation Bill, indeed, came on once more, and in May 1911 it was carried by a majority of 167; but its further chances were wrecked and its prospects utterly destroyed by the action of the Government, which now named a definite date for its forthcoming Male Franchise Bill. "If it had been (the Prime Minister's) object to enrage every woman suffragist to the point of frenzy," as Mrs Fawcett said, "he could not have acted with greater perspicacity." The feeling of bitterness, of betrayal, and of political disillusionment which arose surpassed anything of the kind that even the most experienced worker in the Cause had ever known, and it was difficult indeed for the Liberal women to hold to their allegiance. Scores of them came out from their Party, never to return, and no one was surprised when the militants began a campaign of even greater virulence and indignation.

About this same time, too, the opposition tried to add fresh fuel to the flames. An anti-suffrage society of ladies had been formed in 1908 under the presidency of Mrs Humphry Ward, and in 1909 a "Men's League for Opposing Women's Suffrage" came into existence. These two bodies amalgamated in 1910, and soon began to afford great delight and comfort to their opponents by the ineptitude and futility of their ways. Every meeting they held was of course largely attended by the faithful, and it was an easy matter to make converts to the Suffrage Cause when the opposite case was plainly put. So invariably was this result secured that some of the younger and more light hearted of the suffragists made a practice of introducing prearranged "anti" speeches into their own campaigns, drawing lots for the privilege of stating the false case. The real "antis" soon saw that a purely negative gospel was not very successful, and they therefore tacked on to it a demand for the increased use by women of the local government privileges they already possessed. The "logic" of their case was that women could properly be entrusted with municipal affairs, while imperial matters were outside their "sphere"; but the two doctrines did not combine very happily together. They had some trouble with their own members, particularly with the imposing array of Peers who were their vice-presidents, since these gentlemen objected just as strongly to the presence of women on borough councils as anywhere else (outside the home); and the spectacle of their troubles was a constantly recurring delight to their opponents. Debates, which were sometimes arranged between the two camps, were an unfailing joy; but so heavily were the "antis" defeated whenever they ventured upon this method of warfare that it became very difficult indeed to persuade them to adopt it.

The League for Opposing Women's Suffrage was not the only new organisation to come into existence at this time. A Men's League for Women's Suffrage was formed in 1909, and about the same time fifteen other societies for the same purpose made their appearance. There was the Actresses' Suffrage League, and the Artists' Suffrage League; the Catholic Women's Suffrage Society, the Church League for Women's Suffrage, and the Conservative and Unionist Women's Franchise Association; the Free Church League, and the Friends' League, the Jewish League, the London Graduates' League, and the Scottish Universities Women's Suffrage Union, and so on, until there was no group of people left in the country for whom an appropriate suffrage society could not be found. The regular National Union added sixty new branches in 1910, and all these societies united in believing that the next year would be a critical year for their cause, and in watching with anxiety for the result of the Government pledge.

CHAPTER XVII

THE REFORM BILL FIASCO. 1911–1914

Preparations for the Reform Bill—Rumours in the House—Militants throw stones—Conciliation Bill defeated, February 1912—New policy of the N.U.W.S.S.—Arrest of militant leaders and conspiracy trial, March 1912—Sentenced to nine months, but released after hunger-strike—Second reading of Reform Bill carried, July 1912—Difference of opinion between militant leaders—Mrs Pankhurst renews militancy—Committee stage of Reform Bill, January 1913—Speaker's ruling that Women's Suffrage amendments are out of order—Withdrawal of the Bill, and offer of Private Member's Bill instead—Offer refused—Militants now begin to destroy property—Passage of Cat and Mouse Act—Mrs Pankhurst sentenced to three years, and defies Act—Repeated rearrests—Death of Miss Emily Davidson—Mrs Pankhurst visits America—Pilgrimage organised by N.U.W.S.S.—Evidences of public support—Bill introduced into the Lords—The outbreak of War.

In the autumn of 1911 the preparations for the Reform Bill, which was to extend the male franchise, began. Mr Asquith consented to receive a deputation from both the constitutional and the militant suffragists, and to them he categorically repeated the promise that his Bill would be so drafted as to admit of amendments including women, and that if these were inserted by the House of Commons he would accept that decision. The Women's Social and Political Union cried out at once that "they were not satisfied," and when they began to speak outside they called his offer "a gratuitous insult to women." The Liberal women's organisations, on the other hand, felt that the franchise was as good as won, and both Sir Edward Grey and Mr Lloyd George were triumphant. The latter was particularly pleased that the Conciliation Bill proposals, which he greatly disliked, had been "torpedoed" by the new offer, but the National Union of Women's Suffrage Societies, though they had hopes, were a little uneasy. And within a few weeks their uneasiness increased. The Prime Minister received another deputation, this time from his friends the Anti-Suffrage League, and to them he said that the inclusion of Women's Suffrage in his Bill would be "a political mistake of a very disastrous kind." At once the rumour began to fly about that the passing of such an amendment would lead to his resignation, and good Liberals were urged and implored in the name of their Party loyalty not to put their leader to the "humiliation" of being obliged to carry out the undertaking he had given.

The precincts of the House of Commons had been closed to women since the militant "outrages" began, but the suffragists knew well enough, even without being on the spot, what was said, and they realised that every kind of report was spread about to poison the atmosphere in which the Conciliation Bill was to come up once more. To complete the confusion the militants chose that moment for one of their most striking exploits. Mrs Pankhurst and two companions broke the windows of No. 10 Downing Street, and simultaneously hundreds of women in other parts of London smashed the plate-glass windows of shop fronts, post offices, and Government departments. One hundred and fifty women were marched off to Holloway for this exploit, and Mrs Pankhurst and Mr and Mrs Pethick Lawrence were held for trial on a charge of conspiracy and incitement to riot. The offices of the Women's Social and Political Union in Clement's Inn were raided by the police, and Christabel Pankhurst, to avoid the misfortune of having all the leaders in prison at the same time, disguised herself and escaped to Paris, from whence she edited the paper and directed the tactics of those in the fighting line at home.

All these events did not tend to produce a very happy atmosphere for the Conciliation Bill; and still further ill-luck awaited it. There was a coal strike in progress at the time, and on the night when the Bill came up, thirteen Labour Members were away from London in connection with it; and all thirteen would have voted for it had they been there. In addition to this misfortune, all but two of the Irish Nationalists, who had previously voted right, obeyed the orders not to imperil a Government which seemed to be in the act of giving Home Rule, and abstained from voting, or transferred their support to the other side. The result was that the division, when it came, showed an adverse majority of 14—and this in the very same Parliament which had carried the very same Bill by 167 votes not a year before!

The fears of the National Union of Women's Suffrage Societies, and the indignation of the Women's Social and Political Union, were now intensified. At the beginning of the year there had been two strings to the suffrage bow. The expectation of a Reform Bill had been used to snap one of them, and it now remained to be seen whether the loss of the Conciliation Bill was going to destroy the other. The Liberal suffragists still remained confident, and the others determined at any rate to leave no stone unturned. Propaganda meetings all over the country multiplied at an astonishing rate, and the National Union of Women's Suffrage Societies alone held more than fifty every night. They were not content with mere propaganda, however. The failure of the Private Member's Bill, and the evident fact that nothing but a Government measure would ever ensure success, led them to strengthen and change the election policy which they had hitherto pursued. Instead of supporting those men who were personally in favour of the Cause, they now supported only those whose Party as well upheld it. There was at that time but one such Party, the Labour Party, and the decision was therefore a difficult one for Liberal and Conservative women to take. The democratic constitution of the National Union, moreover, and its extremely well-organised machinery, made the change of policy a matter of considerable moment. It could not be done at the command of one, or even of any group of leaders; it could only result from real consultation and real understanding in the 411 self-supporting societies which at that time constituted the union. These societies were all represented in proportion to their size at the council meetings, and only by the council could such decisions be taken. The spring and summer of 1912 was thus a time of serious tactical discussion among the women, a time when political principles were weighed against each other, and when the internal affairs of the union assumed an importance to its members greater than ever before. The old days when women were first learning to work together, and when the procedure of public business seemed a mystery, were now long past. The union carried on its business with the utmost efficiency and dispatch. Points of order and rules of procedure became a fine art, and the heavy proportion of irrelevant and tedious speaking which normally attends conferences was absent. Here were hundreds of women, desperately in earnest, fully understanding what they wanted, and thoroughly experienced in putting their case; and the discipline and training which they gave themselves by submitting to their own majority rule improved them year by year. Differences of opinion of course there were, sharp and sometimes heated; but there was no disorder, no splitting into factions, no ill-feeling. Those who won their way were too busy to triumph; those who lost prepared to try again the following year; and all the time the work grew, and the enthusiasm mounted.

The Reform Bill came on for the second reading in July, and passed that stage without alteration. In introducing it, however, Mr Asquith did his best to put a spoke in the wheel of the forthcoming Women's Suffrage amendments. "The Bill does not propose to confer the franchise on women," he said; "the House at an earlier stage of the session rejected with sufficient emphasis the proposal . . . and, so far as I am concerned, I dismiss at this moment as altogether improbable the hypothesis that the House of Commons is likely to stultify itself by reversing in the same session the considered judgment at which it has arrived." That the same House had passed the same Bill by a majority twelve times as large as that by which it rejected it was a point Mr Asquith did not mention, and suffragists grew more uneasy than ever. The Prime Minister was clearly as hostile as ever, and the tactics which had wrecked the Conciliation Bill were likely to recur.

There was nothing to be done, however, but to make the best of the chance, even if it was a slender one, and to this end the suffragists continued their efforts. Money came in freely, and it was possible to organise great and enthusiastic meetings in the Albert Hall, as well as in all the principal towns in the kingdom, in order to secure real support and backing in the struggle which lay ahead.

While the National Union of Women's Suffrage Societies had been expanding and recasting its policy, the affairs of the Women's Social and Political Union had been following another course. The three most prominent leaders had been arrested in March, and tried for conspiracy, and in May they were found guilty, and sentenced to nine months in the second division. This extraordinary verdict disturbed people who were far from sympathising with the militant methods, and caused a great deal of astonishment and indignation. Mrs Pankhurst and Mr and Mrs Pethick Lawrence, though admittedly guilty of exciting their followers to violence, were plainly political offenders, and so much pressure was put upon the Home Secretary that after a few days he gave orders that they were to be removed to the First Division. When this had been done, however, they discovered that the privilege had not been extended to their followers, and as a protest all three of them adopted the hunger-strike. For some time the expedient of forcible feeding was employed by the prison authorities; but the prisoners resisted so violently and struggled so much that this was a difficult, and even a dangerous proceeding; and in due course not only the three leaders, but also the other imprisoned suffragettes were reduced to such a low and dangerous state of health that they were all released.

The release of the leaders took place in the summer of 1912, and after convalescence they prepared to renew their fight. At this stage, however, a difference of opinion arose among them. Mrs Pankhurst, undismayed by her own repeated imprisonments, and by the successive hunger-strikes which she had already endured, was determined that the fight should be intensified along the lines already laid down. Christabel was of the same opinion; to weaken now, they felt, would be to undo all that they had gained. Mr and Mrs Pethick Lawrence, however, disagreed with this view. They did not give their reasons, but a statement signed by all four of them was issued to the Press, which made clear the fact that Mrs Pankhurst and her daughter remained the leaders of the Women's Social and Political Union, while Mr and Mrs Pethick Lawrence separated from them and retained the paper *Votes for Women*.

This second split in the militant ranks was more serious than the first; it marked the end of prudence, and the plunge into greater extravagances of militancy. Christabel, who remained in Paris, was fertile in expedients; her mother, who faced repeated imprisonments and the torment of hunger-and-thirst strikes, was recklessly brave; and their followers, inspired by the ringing articles of the one, and the indomitable example of the other, grew more and more reckless. "I will incite this meeting to rebellion!" Mrs Pankhurst cried at the first meeting in the autumn of 1912. "Be militant each in your own way, I accept the responsibility for everything you do!" With such words she intoxicated her followers, and their passionate admiration and hero-worship gathered ever more closely around her. Large sums of money poured into the coffers of the society; rich women gave hundreds, and unknown friends gave thousands of pounds, and others, carried away by their enthusiasm, threw their very jewels and watches at their leader's feet.

In sober fact, however, the militant movement was now at the end of its importance. The militants did not know it, living as they did in an artificial world of their own creating, where danger followed quick upon danger, and excitement always ran high. To them their work seemed supremely important, and if they faltered or held back they believed that all would be lost. But it was not so. The Press and the public had grown tired of the news of "outrages," and even when these became more serious in character they attracted comparatively little attention. The Home Office and the police were indeed still troubled, and the Liberal Government was still furious, but none of these things mattered very much; for the Suffrage Cause itself had emerged from the darkness of unpopularity, and held the centre of the stage. What people wanted to know was how the matter actually stood, what the Government would do, and what the real prospects were; and the question of methods, which had once been so interesting, faded into insignificance.

The long-expected Reform Bill was approaching. The session of 1912, already of unusual length, had been prolonged, and the Bill was due to be debated in January 1913. In preparation for this event the rumours of a Cabinet crisis revived again, but the friends of Women's Suffrage in the House of Commons did everything they could think of to counteract them. They met frequently to consider the text of the Bill, and the form their amendments would take. It was obvious that there were several different ways in which women could be included, and the different proposals were finally reduced by agreement to three. The first was the equal way, which, if the proposals of the Bill became law, would be practically adult suffrage; the second was the household suffrage way, which would give the vote to women householders and the wives of householders when they reached the age of twenty-five; and the third was the more limited Conciliation Bill way, which would enfranchise only those women who were householders in their own right. It was important that these amendments should not be allowed to block each other, and much time and thought was devoted to the drafting of them, and to their arrangement upon the Order Paper. They were put down in descending order of magnitude, so that those who, like Suffrage Societies themselves, wanted equality but were ready to accept less, might vote for each in turn, while those who only wanted one particular form would have the opportunity to vote for it alone. The three amendments stood in the names of members of the Labour, Liberal, and Conservative Parties respectively,[1] and a great deal of very careful lobbying went on in order that no misunderstanding might interfere with the success of one or other of them. The numbers of women who would be enfranchised under each proposal were estimated, and everything that could be done by the National Union of Women's Suffrage Societies to clear the situation was done with the utmost care. Before any of these amendments could come on, however, it was necessary that the word "male" should be struck out of the Bill, and this permissive amendment, which would not in itself enfranchise a single woman, but which was essential to the carrying of any of the other three, was moved by Sir Edward Grey, the Foreign Secretary, on the 23rd of January. And then there occurred one of the extraordinary accidents which occasionally diversify Parliamentary life; for the Speaker, in answer to a question on another point, made it clear that in his opinion the adoption of any one of the Women's Suffrage amendments would so alter the Bill as to make it no longer the same Bill, and consequently that it would be killed if such an amendment were adopted, and would have to be reintroduced in its new form.

[1] Mr Arthur Henderson, Mr (now Sir) Willoughby Dickinson, and the Hon Alfred Lyttelton.

At one blow all the hopes of the suffragists were thrown to the ground; and by the same blow the Government was shown to have blundered most egregiously. Their own Reform Bill, which they had been discussing for years, which had been read a second time in the previous spring, had to be hurriedly withdrawn, and the public was left to attribute to Mr Asquith and his colleagues either a stupid mistake or an elaborate wickedness. And in either case the women were equally defrauded of their opportunity. Moreover, to make matters even worse, Mr Asquith refused to offer any hope of a Government Bill in place of the one which was withdrawn. He would not even see the people whom he had so completely misled, but he offered, with an air of great magnanimity, to allow time for another second reading discussion of one of those futile Private Member's Bills, seven of which had already successfully and uselessly been secured within four years.

The suffrage societies were furiously indignant. With one accord they refused to have anything to do with the Prime Minister's derisory offer, and demanded a Government Bill. Mr Asquith paid no attention, and when in due course the Private Member's Bill made its appearance it suffered the inevitable defeat. Nothing more was ever hoped for from the Liberal Party. The only prospect of success lay in a change of Government, and to this end the women now devoted their energies.

The fiasco of the Reform Bill, if it enraged the constitutional societies, fairly maddened the militants. They had, it is true, always expected to be "betrayed," but this did not reconcile them to the actual event. Mr Lansbury, who was one of their firm supporters, resigned his seat in Parliament, and sought re-election (unsuccessfully) upon this issue alone, and a form of militancy aimed at the destruction of property followed. The amount of damage which the militants achieved was not particularly impressive, and the pouring of acids into pillar boxes, the cutting of telegraph wires, and the slashing of pictures in public galleries seemed to the public even less relevant to the cause of Women's Suffrage than their former deeds. The militants, however, saw their actions in a heroic light. They set fire to empty houses, they destroyed golf-courses, they threw bombs at churches, and they believed that by so doing they were advancing their cause. In February, soon after the fiasco of the Reform Bill, an attempt was made to burn down Mr Lloyd George's country house, and although it was not proved to have been the work of the suffragettes, Mrs Pankhurst was arrested and charged with inciting to commit a felony. She was tried at the Old Bailey and conducted her own defence, and after a long and exceedingly interesting trial she was found guilty, and sentenced to three years penal servitude. Under the conditions which had hitherto prevailed, this sentence would have been of little importance; for by adopting the hunger-strike she would have been quickly released. But the Home Secretary had grown tired of seeing the sentences treated with contempt by these prisoners, and in his determination to crush down these troublesome women he did not scruple to introduce a new principle into English law. The same Government and the same Parliament which could not find time to attend to the widely demanded Suffrage Bill, succeeded in passing an Act controlling the treatment of suffragette prisoners, which came to be known as the Cat and Mouse Act. This Act, which was actually so framed as to apply only to one class of prisoner, made it possible for the Home Secretary to release a suffragette on a ticket-of-leave when her hunger-strike should have brought her in danger of death; she was then to be allowed to go out of prison to recover, and immediately she was strong enough she was to be re-arrested, without a fresh warrant, and go on with the serving of her sentence, the days of recovery not being counted towards its fulfilment. With this prospect before them, the Government thought, the women would no longer defy the law and make the Courts of Justice ridiculous; they would taste the hard realities of punishment, and cease from troubling. Little did the Home Secretary understand the nature of the people he was dealing with! With all history and all the tale of human martyrdom to guide him, he still fell into the error of supposing that fanatics could be kept down by force, and that those who fought for justice would submit to coercion. But he was soon undeceived.

Mrs Pankhurst was taken to Holloway on 3rd April, and immediately began her hunger-strike; and while she lay in prison awaiting the moment when she would be too ill to be kept longer, her followers outside continued their protests, and scores of them followed her into gaol. By 12th April Mrs Pankhurst was in danger of her life, and on that day she was released on ticket-of-leave for fifteen days. She was taken to a nursing home, and later to a house in the country. More than fifteen days passed, and though the place was surrounded by the police she was not arrested. Towards the end of May she began to recover, and at once announced that she would attend a meeting and speak to her followers. The meeting was fixed, and although, when it came to the point of setting out, Mrs Pankhurst found herself unable to stand, she still determined to go, and was more or less carried down the stairs to a waiting car. The police, however, were waiting too; if she was strong enough to go to a meeting she was strong enough to go back to Holloway, and they carried her off. The second attempt to make her serve her sentence lasted only five days, and on 30th May Mrs Pankhurst, again in danger of her life, was again released.

The next day was Derby Day, and in the midst of all the gaiety and excitement of the race-meeting one of the militant suffragettes, Emily Wilding Davidson, introduced a sudden and tragic note. To call attention to her cause, to testify to its seriousness and its urgency, this woman, who had told no one of her intention, threw herself under the feet of the racing horses and was killed. Her action startled and indeed roused the country. People who sincerely thought that militancy was madness, and who saw no relevancy and no purpose in her sacrifice, could not but be startled by the deed. All over the world people read of it, and all over the world it was known that there were women in England who courted death for the conviction that women should be free.

Miss Davidson's funeral was the occasion of a great militant procession, and the crowds which silently watched it pass through the London streets knew not what to think. They knew this cause to which they were growing friendly, and they knew militants, at whom they were accustomed to jeer; and now they were faced with a martyr, at once reckless and tragic, and they were moved and distressed. It was time that the struggle ended.

Mrs Pankhurst, only a few days out of Holloway, intended to walk in that funeral procession; but once more the police intervened, and she was taken back to prison. There she resumed the ordeal of the hunger-strike, and this time added to it the refusal to touch water, or to sleep. The suffering increased, but the danger-point was reached more quickly, and in three days she again had to be released.

Mrs Pankhurst was not to be daunted by illness or suffering or danger. In less than a month from this release she spoke at a meeting in the London Pavilion, and escaped in safety by the strategy of her followers. For a week the militants played with the police after the fashion of the most flamboyant detective stories, hoodwinking them with disguises, leading them on false scents, and generally making the whole operation of the Cat and Mouse Act ridiculous, and then the prisoner was again secured. For the fourth time the effort to make her serve her sentence was resumed, and for the fourth time she resisted it, and soon had to be let out once more. A few days later she was carried in an invalid chair to a public meeting, and was allowed to speak undisturbed; and not long after that she openly left the country to join her daughter Christabel in Paris. From there she sailed on a French boat to America, to raise money and interest for the Cause; but on her arrival at New York she was held up at Ellis Island at the request of the British Government. When this detention became known to the women's organisations of the United States a perfect torrent of protest was poured out upon the President. The militant movement, which undoubtedly had its drawbacks at close quarters, and which was regarded with very mixed feelings by the majority of feminists in England, did nothing but good in other parts of the world. At the distance of thousands of miles the drawbacks were of no effect, and the courage stood out undimmed by undignified incidents or political unwisdom. The women of America regarded Mrs Pankhurst in no sense as a criminal, and they were determined to see and welcome her. When the President acceded to their protests, and gave permission for her to enter New York, they gave her a perfectly overwhelming reception; and when she sailed back to England she carried with her a considerable contribution for the funds of her campaign.

Mrs Pankhurst was arrested before she landed at Southampton, and took up at once her battle with the police. She faced the horrors of the hunger-strike twelve separate times, and a year after her sentence had been pronounced she had served only thirty days towards her three years penal servitude. Though she was, of course, the most famous of the prisoners, she was not the only one to defy the operation of the Cat and Mouse Act. In 1913 there were 182 other suffragette prisoners, each of whom went through the same terrible experiences, and did her part in proving the futility of the attempt to end legitimate grievances by coercion. The Home Secretary indeed congratulated himself that there were fewer convictions than in the previous year,[1] when there had been 290; but it was a false ground for satisfaction. One hundred and eighty-three women, who were ready to die for the Cause, and who proved it by the dreadful expedient of repeated hunger-and-thirst strikes, meant more than thousands of short imprisonments; and with every release on ticket-of-leave, and with every rearrest, the bitterness of those who belonged to the militant societies deepened.

While these things were taking place among the members of the Women's Social and Political Union, the other suffragists were working in their different fashion. They were no less indignant at the way the Cause had been treated, but their rage and passion expressed itself in other ways. Public meetings became almost incessant; the membership of the societies doubled, new branches formed with amazing rapidity, 39,540 "Friends of Women's Suffrage" were enrolled, and enthusiasm reached and stayed at boiling-point. In the summer of this year, 1913, the National Union of Women's Suffrage Societies planned and executed a great pilgrimage. In the middle of June women set out on foot from the far corners of the kingdom, and, marching with banners and bands along eight main routes, they converged upon London. As they went along they were joined by others living on the routes, and the processions grew daily. At each town and village as they passed they spoke to the people, and the warmth of their welcome and the enthusiasm of their meetings proved beyond question that the country now at last accepted their demand. A few hooligans here and there raised a tumult; but they only marked the contrast more sharply. For the tide of public opinion was turning, had in fact already turned, and the pilgrims began to feel that their task was really done.

When the pilgrimage reached London on 26th July, it ended with a mass meeting in Hyde Park of a size and nature hardly ever seen there before. The organisation, which

[1] See *Hansard*, 11th June 1914.

was carried out by the London Society for Women's Suffrage, was perfect in every detail. Moreover, the huge crowd was not merely gathered to see the fun; it was gathered to support the demonstration; and the suffragists were at last able to feel that their task of converting public opinion was virtually accomplished.

Evidences of public support grew more and more numerous. In a grand pitched battle Mrs Humphry Ward was worsted at a conference of all the social workers and philanthropic societies, and she and the Anti-Suffrage Society withdrew from membership of the National Union of Women Workers (now the National Council of Women). The Church Congress, the Trade Unions,[1] and many hitherto hostile newspapers added their support, and still more new suffrage organisations sprang into existence. In the House of Lords a Women's Suffrage Bill, introduced by Lord Selborne, came up for second reading, and much to the surprise of Lord Curzon and the Anti-Suffrage League, 60 Peers were found to support it. There were, it is true, 104 to oppose it; but in the absence of a Government measure nothing better could have been expected, and the result gave rise to fresh hopes.

But still the Government made no move, and the political impasse remained. The Liberal Party, exasperated by the militant campaigns which had given them so much trouble and made them look so ridiculous, was obstinately blind to the feeling in the country. They seemed to think that severity towards the militants, and indifference towards the Cause would make the whole thing die down, and took refuge in a masterly inactivity.

The only hope of progress appeared to be in a change of Government, and the suffragists knew that it would be difficult to secure this upon their issue alone. Though the

[1] The Albert Hall was filled almost entirely by men in February 1914, when 342 separate Trade Unions sent official representatives, and £5000 was collected by the National Union.

public approved their Cause, it was unlikely that many men would consent to make it a test question; and the people who cared most were without votes. Nevertheless, they were full of hope, and the winter of 1913 and the spring and early summer of 1914 passed in renewed campaigns. They were planning, organising, and expanding; they looked forward to another winter of hard work, and then to an election which might open the door to their triumph, when suddenly upon them, as upon the rest of Europe, there fell the calamity of war.

CHAPTER XVIII

THE WAR YEARS. 1914–1918

Political action suspended—Women's desire to be of use—Expansion of nursing services—Belgian refugees—Unemployment among women, followed by great demand for their work—Difficulties of the employment of women on men's jobs—Their success—The opposition of the Trade Unions—Government orders safeguarding the rates of pay—The munitions procession of 1915—Expansion of munition work—Substitution of women for men in all trades—Women employed by the military and naval authorities and by the air force—Food preservation—The Land Army—War charities—Work for the Allies—The Scottish Women's Hospitals—Swing of public opinion in favour of women—Their own changed outlook.

WITH the outbreak of the European War in August 1914, the Women's Movement, along with all the other political preoccupations of the day, vanished out of sight. It is true that as the war went on they all reappeared, altered indeed, but only on the surface, by the new circumstances; in the early months of the conflict, however, they appeared to be irrelevant and futile matters which had no bearing on the great struggle of the Allies, and which everyone united to forget.

The suffrage societies at once suspended their political activities, and the Government, as soon as there was time for such matters, issued an amnesty to all the suffragette prisoners. Militancy faded away, and no more was ever heard of the Women's Social and Political Union.

The N.U.W.S.S., which had a much firmer life of its own, kept together. On the 3rd of August its committee decided that their strength and their machinery should be turned at once to the service of the country, and should be used to the utmost for the relief of distress caused by the ır. "Let us prove ourselves worthy of citizenship, whether our claim is recognised or not," wrote Mrs Fawcett; and the societies followed her lead. Within the first week of the outbreak of war they had begun, collectively as well as individually, to offer their services to the Local Relief Committees, to the War Office, and to the Red Cross; they had opened emergency workrooms for the women who were thrown out of work, and they had established information bureaux for those thousands of eager, ill-informed, voluntary women workers whom nobody as yet knew how to use.

The confusion of the first months of the war was tremendous. For men the course of action was, on the whole, straightforward, but for women it was perplexing in the extreme. The impulse of vehement patriotism burned in their hearts, and the longing to be of service moved them; but there was little they could find to do. Even the women doctors, when Dr Elsie Inglis approached the War Office with their offer of fully staffed medical units, were told, "To go home and keep quiet," and that the commanding officers "did not want to be troubled with hysterical women." It seemed almost as if the old anti-feminist argument was true, and that in a time of national crisis women were superfluous and irrelevant, passive creatures to be fought for, whose only personal function was to sit at home and weep.

If this was what the civil and military authorities felt in the autumn of 1914, it was not what the women accepted. The Women's Movement had gone too far, and its ideals had penetrated too deeply for any such rôle to content them. They knew they were able and energetic; they knew that they had gifts to offer and help to give to their country; and rich and poor, young and old, spent their time in searching for useful work. It was not long before opportunities began to offer. The expansion of the nursing services, which had to keep pace with the expansion of the armies, absorbed thousands of eager women. The Voluntary Aid Detachments, which had been originated by Miss Haldane in 1909, expanded rapidly, and over eighteen thousand women enrolled in them and began their splendid supplementary aid to the Army Nursing Service. Hundreds of small private hospitals were prepared all over the country, and the Territorial Forces Nursing Service grew from under three to over eight thousand, and Queen Alexandra's Military and Naval Nursing Service from one to ten thousand. Depots for the preparation of surgical dressings, and comforts and appliances for the wounded sprang up in hundreds and were presently organised under the name of Hospital Supply Depots, which, in spite of official disapproval of this method, insisted on delivering their goods direct to the places where they were required. Motor ambulances, too, were endowed and staffed as fast as the works could produce them, and convalescent homes and care of the blind offered an opportunity to hundreds of women eager to "do their bit."

All this, however, only touched the fringe of the female population and by no means satisfied their zeal; and when the Belgian refugees began to arrive in England they were in great demand. The first refugees arrived on 22nd August, and thereafter they came in rapid succession, until there were more than a quarter of a million of them to care for. The task of housing and providing for this enormous number of homeless and practically destitute people was a difficult one; but it was eagerly welcomed by the women of this country. Offers of hospitality, gifts of money and clothing poured in upon the relief committees, and in a surprisingly short time the whole mass of refugees was settled and absorbed into the country.

This was a task for the well-to-do; but the working women were no less anxious to do their share. The first consequence of the war, as it affected them, was widespread unemployment. Within a month a quarter of a million women were out of work, owing to the suspension of trade and the closing down of luxury production, and it was not until many months later that the growing shortage of men enabled them to be reabsorbed into industry. Early in 1915, however, this process had begun, and as the armies grew and the magnitude of the war became apparent, it accelerated quickly. The idea that women could take on "men's jobs" and so release them for actual fighting was easy to understand. It caught the imaginations of the millions of women who were so eager to help, and from all ranks and circumstances they rushed forward to answer the call. Easy as it was to understand, this idea involved some serious difficulties when it came to putting it into practice; and those who, like the London Society for Women's Suffrage and the Women's Trade Unions, had to do with its initial stages were faced with some extremely difficult problems. There were the women, in the first place, eager and enthusiastic, but for the most part wholly untrained. They were willing to do "everything," but they did not know how to do anything, and a consciousness of a power of organisation (which so many of them felt) was not of much practical service in a carpenter's workshop. This difficulty was of course a diminishing one; as training courses and experimental workshops were opened, and as the women were drafted into the new occupations they rapidly found their feet. Their quickness and aptitude were astonishing to themselves no less than to their employers and their fellow-workers. In a few weeks they learnt to perform most unexpectedly difficult mechanical operations, and they turned from being daughters at home, or parlourmaids, or whatever they had been before, into charge hands, tool setters, or factory supervisors, with the utmost readiness and success.[1]

[1] The Annual Reports of the Chief Inspector of Factories and Workshops, as well as the Report of the War Cabinet Committee on Women in Industry, and the Home Office Report on the Substitution of Women for Men during the War (1919) provide detailed accounts of the actual

This adaptability in itself was enough to break down the second of the troubles which had beset their employment at the outset, namely, the reluctance of employers to take them on. At first they had been very much afraid of the change; they had dreaded the influx of unskilled and unfamiliar women, had expected the consequence to be utter dislocation, and had anticipated that it would be impossible to make the new workers of the slightest use. But as the experiment proceeded they found the women skilful, willing, patient; they saw their production go up and their labour troubles diminish; and almost without exception they became enthusiastic for the change. But these very factors of success intensified the third, and greatest, difficulty of all, which came from the opposition of the men. The better the women were, and the more the employers liked them, the less welcome did their men colleagues find them; and their hostility at times seriously threatened the whole experiment, and gave rise to Government enactments and undertakings which increased in complexity and confusion as the war went on.

The ground of the men's hostility to the introduction of women was perfectly natural and comprehensible, inconvenient and troublesome as it proved to be, and greatly as it hindered the efficient conduct of the war. The conditions and rules governing industry had been won as the result of long and bitter struggles by the unions, which were already anxious and uneasy because of the relaxations and changes of process that the war made needful. They had to stand by and see a subdivision of skilled work, to allow of greater output and of the employment of semi-skilled men; they had to acquiesce in the shift system (which had been a bugbear to the unions from the days of the Ten Hours' Day agitation), and they had to endure a speeding up of production wholly

processes where substitution took place, and give a picture of the advantages to the women workers, and the satisfaction of the employers which justify the use of superlatives.

foreign to their normal policies. These things they could just endure, because of the national emergency; but when there was added to them the alarming prospect of all being combed out for active service, while their places were taken by females—then indeed they could bear it no more. It outraged their traditions and their sense of what was right; and, even more strongly, it filled them with fear for the future. Women were blacklegs; they were of necessity "unskilled" in the technical sense of having served no apprenticeship; and if they were brought in, and especially if, when brought in, they did well, where would the men's position be in their "own" trades after the war? Early in 1915, before dilution had really begun, these considerations agitated the men's unions, and they adopted an attitude of passive resistance which bid fair to stop the whole scheme at the outset. The men in a great many factories refused to work at all with the women; they refused to teach them anything, and in the myriads of ways a factory affords they made their lives impossible. In so far as this objection was economic, the Government recognised its force. In March 1915 an agreement was formally entered into with the chief unions concerned, by which the Government undertook to protect the rates of wages, and to ensure the payment of equal piece-work rates to all dilutees (of either sex) if the unions would withdraw their opposition. They further promised to restore, when the war was over, the "pre-war practices" of industry. The great majority of the women concerned were in no way parties to this agreement; they could not be, since they were unorganised and inarticulate; but if they had been, they would doubtless have welcomed, at any rate, that part of it relating to wages. No one, even among the employers, wished to lower the standard of wages while the men were away fighting; and the women were among the first to recognise that they would be unwelcome if they were blacklegs; of course, too, they were dazzled by the possibility of pay double their ordinary rates, and were only afraid that they could not be worth so much. As to the pre-war practices, they gave them not a thought, though to the feminists the absurdity of undertaking to learn nothing by war experiences was fully apparent. However, it was war-time, and everyone had to do the best they could; and so the agreement was made. It was followed, in July of the same year, by a further promise from Mr Lloyd George to safeguard time rates, and by a widely advertised call to women to come forward for munition work. A great spectacular munitions procession of women was organised for him by Mrs Pankhurst (acting now for, and not against, the Government),[1] and thousands upon thousands of volunteers answered the call. But it was terribly premature; nothing was prepared, neither the training centres nor the factories, nor the recruiting places, and at the time of the national call hardly any vacancies existed. Humble workers, who spent their savings in journeying long distances to London, found themselves unemployed and stranded, and turned to the Guardians for relief; yet even so they were not discouraged. War was war, they felt, and things must be expected to go wrong; and the moment there were any places to be filled they applied in thousands. Grandmothers came forward as eagerly as young girls in their teens; nearly half a million women were ultimately employed, and there was never at any time a shortage of willing volunteers for the work. Nothing daunted them: long hours, night shifts, lack of accommodation, lack of arrangements for meals—all this was in the day's work, and nothing mattered so long as they could get on to the job and feel that they were helping the men at the front; and in shipbuilding, aircraft, ordnance, chemical, rope, rubber, steel, and iron works they cheerfully "did their bit."

[1] Mrs Pankhurst worked after the war for the Canadian Government. She subsequently returned to England and joined the Conservative Party, and was adopted as a candidate for Parliament. She died in June 1928.

The great new munition centres which came into existence in 1915 and 1916 constituted an administrative problem of their own, but they were by no means the only directions in which women's labour was in demand. The Government itself called for thousands of them to staff the new mushroom Ministries in Whitehall. A hundred and sixty-two thousand women found employment in this way, being taken on at first without the least selection or care, and planted wholesale in the new temporary buildings. This army of clerks constituted a serious problem, all the more difficult to deal with because the Civil Service (like the Trade Unions) was very unwilling to trust any women with responsibility, or to allow them to rise to any of the better-paid posts.

Besides these main groups of openings, a whole host of other kinds of substitution gradually came into force. Women were taken into the banks and the business houses; they were used as window cleaners and as plumbers, as signalmen and as porters, as bus conductors, as van drivers, as shepherds and as electricians. Practically nothing came amiss to them, and, though on some of the heavier work, such as cleaning boilers, it took three women to do the work of two men, in many other trades the proportion was reversed.

The success and popularity of substitution grew steadily from the summer of 1915 onwards, and by the middle of 1916 there was a universal chorus of praise for the women. More than one well-known shipbuilder was heard to say publicly that he would be prepared to build the largest ironclads by women's labour alone. The newspapers, a little surprised, but very eloquent, took up all such remarks with enthusiasm and began to say that "the nation is grateful to the women"—not realising even yet that the women WERE the nation just as much as the men were. And the women, a trifle dazzled by their unwonted popularity, their high wages, and their interesting new work, began to know what it was like to be made much of, and to have free scope for their abilities and powers.

While the employment of women was expanding in all directions under the civil authorities and private enterprise, the question of their direct employment with the troops arose. In July 1915 the Women's Legion was organised, and this body, which consisted at first of cooks and motor-drivers, was employed by the War Office in connection with some of the camps at home. The results of using women were so satisfactory—the saving of man-power, of material, and of money was so marked—that at the end of 1916 the War Office made an inquiry as to the numbers of men at the base camps in France who could be replaced by women. The number was considerable, and accordingly early in 1917 the first of the regular women's corps, the Women's Army Auxiliary Corps, came into formal existence. This was followed, shortly after, by the Women's Royal Naval Service and the Women's Royal Air Force Service, and these three were supplemented by special groups of women employed in the Army Pay Office, the Remount Department, the Anti-Gas Department, and the Forage Corps, the Army Records, and the Army Service Corps. In all about 150,000 women were enrolled in these official services, of whom less than a tenth served in France. They were controlled by their own officers and wore uniforms; and although in a legal sense they were not enlisted, they were considered to be, and considered themselves to be, a regular part of the British Armies.

In addition to the work needed to support the fighting forces, there was another great task for the women to carry on, and that was the business of conserving the resources of the country.

The food shortage was a matter which every housekeeper was able to assist, by the economical use of foodstuffs, by the prevention of waste, and by the innumerable devices with which the time abounded. Hay-box cookers, bread substitutes, sugarless fruit-preserving and all such things, which were well within even the traditional sphere of women, were now of national importance; and the growing of potatoes in front gardens, and the keeping of hens in back ones went on all over the country. Moreover, agriculture itself called for more and more labour, and although the farmers were even worse than the trade unionists in their distrust of women workers, a good deal was accomplished in that direction. The Land Army, which was organised in 1917, placed uniformed girls upon the farms and fields, housing them in camps of their own when the farmers did not take them in, and setting them to plough and to milk, to cart and to weed in the neglected fields of the country, and to supervise the thousands of part-time workers who answered the national appeal. Many more found their way into agricultural employment independently (over and above the 80,000 normally so employed), and by the middle of 1918 there were 18,000 whole-time and 300,000 part-time women employed in agriculture in England and Wales alone. These numbers were small compared with the magnitude of the need, but they represented the full extent of what the rural population would allow.

These main divisions of women's war work were of course extended by scores of other miscellaneous activities. There were, for example, a hundred women carpenters working for a private contractor in Calais; there were women organising entertainments for the troops and running continuous canteens at the railway stations; there were others collecting and turning to useful ends the rags and bones and refuse of the big towns, and others still steering barges along the canals and waterways of the country. There were thousands engaged upon the charities and relief works made needful by the war—the pension work, the separation allowances, and all the ramifications of the tasks of the Soldiers' and Sailors' Families Association and the Officers' Relief Fund. There was work for thousands more in the preparation and dispatch of parcels for the prisoners of war, and of comforts, libraries, and lectures for the wounded and the troops. Others were fully busy with the organisation and administration of the welfare schemes devised to meet the needs of the munition areas, and others still were caught up in the War Savings Campaign, and organised great collections and drives for that purpose. There were endless flag days for war objects, and one way and another there was work, intermittent or steady, great or small, for all the women in the country; and they did it eagerly and well.

In addition to all the mass of things which were done by women at home to assist the prosecution of the war, or to help to mitigate its horrors, there was also a great effort made to give help to the Allied Nations. When the British Red Cross rejected the medical women in 1914 they turned elsewhere, and within a very short time hospitals staffed by British women and equipped and maintained by them were at work in France. The first of these, organised by Dr Louisa Garrett Anderson (the daughter of Elizabeth, the pioneer), and Dr Flora Murray, began work in Paris in September 1914, and a month later a second branch hospital was opened at Wimereux which was accepted by the British authorities. These hospitals were so well managed and so successful that the British War Office changed its mind in 1915, and placed these two women doctors in charge of a military hospital of 520 beds in London, which they staffed entirely with women and kept open until the end of the war.

Meantime Dr Elsie Inglis, backed up by the National Union of Women's Suffrage Societies (of whose Scottish Federation she was the honorary secretary), formed the Scottish Women's Hospitals, and under the auspices and at the charge of this organisation (which raised nearly £500,000 for the purpose) fourteen different hospital units were sent out to various parts of the world to work for the Belgian, French, Russian, and Serbian Armies.

One of the units established a magnificent hospital at Royaumont, behind the French lines, and it was continued there from 1914 until February 1919. Most of the other units, however, moved from place to place, working at Calais, Corsica, Troyes, Salonica, and numerous towns in Serbia, Russia, and Roumania. Some of the units shared the retreats and the advances of the Serbian Army, and two units were taken prisoner by the enemy. Another was involved in the great flight of the Russian Army through the Dobrudja, and Dr Inglis, who was herself in charge of this unit, made a successful effort to save the remnants of the Serbian troops from being sacrificed in the turmoil which followed the outbreak of the Russian Revolution. She sent two of her staff to England, with a memorised message of 2500 words for the Foreign Office; and in consequence of the representations made thereafter by the British Government, the Serbian troops were evacuated from Archangel and brought to England. Dr Inglis herself, although she was very ill, stayed by them until all was settled, sailed with them in one of the Admiralty transports, and lived just long enough to bring them safely back, dying, with her task accomplished, the day after she reached home.

The heroism and the courage of women like this came as a surprise to those whose ideas had not been modified by the Women's Movement. When Edith Cavell was shot in 1915, Mr Asquith paid an eloquent tribute to her memory; in ending it, however, he used a self-revealing phrase: "There are thousands of such women," he said, "but a year ago we did not know it." It was quite true; a year ago he, and those who were like him, had been blind to the fact that women shared the virtues and the vices of common humanity; but the war was opening their eyes.

The great success of women's war work, and the great publicity which attended it, startled men of all kinds into forming a new and more favourable judgment of the female sex. It was wildly illogical to be converted to Women's Suffrage because a girl who had been a good milliner could also be a good lift attendant; but so it was. The whole atmosphere and feeling of the country became enthusiastic, and for the time it seemed as if the battle of the Women's Movement were won. More than sixty years before Harriet Martineau had said that the best advocates were yet to come "in the persons of women who are obtaining access to real social business—the female physicians and other professors . . . the women of business . . . the hospital administrators, the nurses, the educators, and substantially successful authors."[1] She had been right. Now, at last, when the war put the opportunity before them, these advocates came into sight, and their effect was immediate and profound.

Another change, even more vital to the Women's Movement than the approval of public opinion, was brought about by the war years, and that was the change in the outlook of women themselves. For the first time hundreds of thousands of them had experienced the joys of achievement; they had been of consequence and had done things they felt to be important; they had been encouraged to show enterprise and ambition, and they had been more or less adequately paid. The false and temporary prosperity of the war period had given women a taste of the power of money; the factory women had been better fed, in spite of the food shortage, than in the days when they did "women's work" in their homes. The married women had had the spending of the separation allowances, and their children were better dressed and in better health than had ever been the case before. They saw what the world was like for men; and neither Act of Parliament nor season of reaction, nor any other thing could thereafter take that knowledge from them.

[1] *Autobiography of Harriet Martineau*, vol. i, 1855.

CHAPTER XIX

THE SUFFRAGE VICTORY. 1916–1918

Policy of the N.U.W.S.S. to use its organisation for national support—Differences of opinion within the union—Mrs Fawcett's policy upheld—Question of new register for men voters raised in Parliament—The N.U. declares that if the basis of franchise is changed Women's Suffrage must be considered—General approval in Press and country for this view—Mr Asquith converted—Unsuccessful efforts of Government to frame a Special Register Bill—Appointment of the Speaker's Conference—Report issued, February 1917, including Women's Suffrage on limited terms—Suffrage Societies endorse this proposal—War workers' demonstration and deputation to Lloyd George—Representation of the People Bill introduced—Debate on Clause IV and favourable majority of 7 to 1—Removal of grille from the ladies' gallery—Improvement of the Local Government Franchise Clause—Debate in the Lords—Lord Curzon's surrender—The Bill passes the Lords by 134 to 71, and receives the Royal Assent, February 1918.

1914 and 1915 and the first half of 1916 passed by in the turmoil and effort of the war, and political questions seemed to be of no importance. The Women's Movement, indeed, was gaining support by the results of the new experiences, and women themselves were learning to look upon their value in the world in a new light, but no one had time or thought to spare to translate these things into legislation. People looked back at the old days of the suffrage commotion with amazement, and said, as if it were a thing of small moment, that of course they now saw that women "deserved the vote"; but it was a matter no one wanted to raise while the crisis was still upon them. The suffrage societies themselves were fully occupied with their war tasks. They did, in fact, keep the machinery of their organisation together, and even in 1915 went through a severe internal crisis; but they made no move towards asking for a Franchise Bill. When the war was over it would be time enough; now their duty was to be as useful and as helpful as they could. This was the opinion of all, but there was not full unanimity as to what the wisest course of usefulness might be. The N.U.W.S.S. was intensely democratic in all its ways; it included in its ranks women, and men too, of all shades of opinion, and its Election Fighting Fund policy had drawn close its connection with the Independent Labour Party and the people of the left wing. As time went on, therefore, and as the relief work at first undertaken began to shade off into activities more directly intended to help in the prosecution of the war, some of the members of the union became uneasy. There were the pacifists, unwilling to take any part or lot in the war; there were others, not so extreme, who thought that the time to discuss peace terms had already come; and others still, who believed that the argument of force was the antithesis of every ideal of the Women's Movement, and disapproved of any corporate action on the part of the suffragists at all. All these factors of discontent, and the hundred other shades of feeling which prevailed at the time, had led in 1915 to the resignation of several of the officers and half the members of the executive committee. Mrs Fawcett was left with a small remnant at headquarters; but in the country at large, and among the rank and file of the members, her course was overwhelmingly approved, and the union, recovering quickly from the trouble, went on its way unchanged.

It was well for the Women's Movement that it was able to do so, for scarcely a year later the object for which it existed came suddenly back into the field of practical politics, and the need for its guidance revived. Bargains, problems, and difficult questions of policy arose once more, and some one was needed who could tell the Government "what the women thought," and who could watch their interests.

The immediate cause of the reappearance of Women's

Suffrage in Parliament was the electoral situation of men. The war, with all its attendant changes of population, had made the existing register of voters a farce, and, moreover, the annual revision of the register had been suspended in 1914. Not one man in five was still to be found at the place where he had been registered when the lists had been made, and, what was more, not one in five was sufficiently stationary to be registered afresh. If an election came, as come it must, the existing registers would be absolutely useless, and if a new one were compiled on the old basis, the fighting men would find no part in it; and there was clearly no advantage in an election on these terms. At the end of 1915, therefore, the possibility of a special register was first mooted, and its character began to be discussed. It was no easy problem to solve, and for some time little that was definite emerged. In May 1916 Sir Edward Carson and a strong group of Members of Parliament began to press for the creation of a new register based on war service, and when this question arose the N.U.W.S.S. felt bound to intervene. They had considered the matter very seriously, and now wrote to the Prime Minister, pointing out to him that women also were doing war work, and that their claims would be pressed if any such plan were adopted. They did not wish to bring forward their controversy during the war, nor to do anything to embarrass the Government; but they could not allow an alteration in the basis of voting for men without the consideration of their question. If, as seemed the only practicable way, the period of qualification was shortened, the effect would be a wide extension of votes to men; and it was their duty, as representatives of the suffragists of the country, not to allow this to be done unless women at the same time had a chance of enfranchisement.

This policy was communicated to the Prime Minister, and to the friendly members of the Cabinet, and it met with sympathy and understanding. Even Mr Asquith, the old enemy, admitted its justice; but for the moment nothing seemed likely to be done. All through the early summer this question simmered in Parliament. One expedient after another was suggested, but none of them met with approval; and the Press said more and more clearly that the subject could not be touched at all without considering, and granting, the women's claim. In July Mr Asquith, who was naturally reluctant to undertake a great Franchise Bill in the midst of the war, put the matter into the hands of Parliament. It was their question, he said; the Cabinet had not solved it, and did not feel called upon to do so, with all the other business which was upon their hands. Parliament must itself find the way out. This was not a very happy suggestion, and the House of Commons did not like it; and when it was rediscussed a week later, and Mr Herbert Samuel pointed out the totally insoluble nature of the problem, and then invited the House to solve it, Members rose in revolt. They threw the measure back at the Cabinet; let them do their own job.

It was now clear that the introduction of some kind of Franchise Bill was inevitable. The existing Parliament had lost its "moral authority," and was largely out of touch with the country. This was all very well during the war, when Parliament was relatively unimportant; but everyone realised that as soon as the fighting was over its power would return, and even in 1916 people were thinking anxiously of the reconstruction period. If democratic government was not to be a farce, there must be an election during or immediately after the war; and in this election the soldiers and sailors must vote. Everyone knew this, and agreed to it, but no one knew how it was to be managed unless by the introduction of a wide change in the basis of the franchise.

The suffragists knew that their opportunity was approaching. Through the summer of 1916, therefore, while the futile negotiations about a Special Register Bill were going on, they resumed their suffrage work. Meetings were not appropriate, nor even necessary; all they had to do was to collect together the expressions of public support which were rising spontaneously on every side, and to mobilise that support so that Parliament should be sure to be aware of it. Busy as they were with their war work, the societies all over the country found time to send deputations to their Members, and the officers interviewed Cabinet Ministers. A Consultative Committee of all the surviving suffrage societies was formed to ensure united action, and this committee endorsed the policy adopted by the N.U.W.S.S. six months before. If the Bill was purely a re-registration Bill they would stand aside; if it introduced a change in the basis of the franchise they would raise their claim. Lord Robert Cecil, Mr Lloyd George, and Mr Arthur Henderson within the Cabinet,[1] and a great volume of public opinion outside approved this decision. Newspapers like the *Observer*, hitherto an extreme opponent, came out with unequivocal support. "In the past we have opposed the claim. . . . We were wrong."[2] From all sides the chorus came.

On 14th August Mr Asquith himself gave up his opposition. "It is true," he said, "(that women) cannot fight in the sense of going out with rifles and so forth, but . . . they have aided in the most effective way in the prosecution of the war. What is more—and this is a point which makes a special appeal to me—when the war comes to an end . . . and when the process of industrial reconstruction has to be set on foot, have not the women a special claim to be heard on the many questions which will arise directly affecting their interests? . . . I say quite frankly that I cannot deny that claim."

The suffragists, when they heard this, held their breath with excitement. It seemed incredible, but it was true;

[1] It is interesting to notice that these three friends belonged each to a different political party.
[2] *Observer*, 13th August 1916.

the old "antis" were converted, the old enemies had become friends. Mr Walter Long, once a strong opponent, committed himself even more deeply. Speaking at a meeting on the subject of the Land Army he used the following extraordinary words: "There are still, unfortunately, villages to be found where the women have become imbued with the idea that their place is the home. That idea must be met and combated!" It seemed altogether too good to be true.

In spite of all this encouragement the situation was a little anxious and exceedingly tangled. Just before the close of the Session in August 1916, however, Mr Walter Long made a proposal which seemed to afford hope, and it was accepted on all sides. His plan was to appoint an all-party conference composed of Members of both Houses, and presided over by the Speaker of the House of Commons, and to charge this conference with the duty of drafting agreed proposals on the franchise and registration difficulty. They were not to suggest any merely temporary expedient. "It is our duty . . . to set ourselves to find a lasting settlement of a very old and difficult problem," said the Colonial Secretary; and the Government and the House of Commons concurred.

In October the Speaker's Conference was appointed, and at once began its work. The Speaker, Mr Lowther, was a noted anti-suffragist, but so far as was known he had selected the members of the conference with strict impartiality in respect to the Women's Suffrage question. Times, however, had changed. No one could with certainty be labelled as an unconverted "anti." Mrs Humphry Ward and Lord Curzon, indeed, still stood firm, but most of their followers had left them. The chief women who had been of their camp openly expressed a change of opinion, and men were deserting wholesale. The suffragists were not afraid of the "impartial" conference, though they were of course exceedingly anxious to know exactly what it would propose.

Its deliberations were conducted in the strictest secrecy. No evidence was taken, and no special pleading heard. Behind closed doors the compromise was worked out, and the debate went on without any contribution from the women; they were, as yet, outside the parliamentary machine, and this was a parliamentary conference. But although they were not allowed to take part in its proceedings, the women knew that they were well represented within. Sir John Simon, who was chief spokesman of their party, was a friend they entirely trusted. He knew their point of view, and shared it; he was, besides, a master in the art of negotiation; they felt sure that he would get for them every ounce of concession it was possible to secure, and so, though they were eager and impatient, they were not alarmed. Success was coming into sight.

Mr Asquith's Cabinet fell, and Mr Lloyd George became Prime Minister before the conference reported; but this change was not allowed to interrupt its labours, and at the end of January 1917 its report was made known. The conference unanimously recommended thirty-three very drastic reforms in the franchise, the most important of which involved the basing of the parliamentary vote for men upon residence, and not "occupation" of premises, and a simplification of the Local Government Register. It also recommended, but by a majority only, that some form of Women's Suffrage should be conferred, and suggested a form which would enfranchise about six million of the possible eleven million adult women. Their method of limiting numbers was twofold: the restriction of the women voters to householders and the wives of householders, and the cutting off of all women who were under the age of thirty or thirty-five.

The appearance of this report was hailed with various feelings by the suffragists, of which, when all allowances were made for disappointment, the predominant one was relief. Here at last was a concrete proposal which had strong official backing. On its merits, of course, it was not a good proposal, and the age limit was absurd; but still it looked like a workable compromise, and if so much were once secured the rest was bound to follow. The fact that there were more women than men in the country had always been a stumbling-block in the way of a really equal Bill; for anti-suffragists had made much of the "risk of handing over the government of the country to women"; and the illogical basis which the report proposed avoided this so-called danger. There was therefore a good compromise case to be made out for the report as it stood.

Conferences of the societies were immediately held, and after much discussion a unanimous agreement to endorse the report was reached. The Labour women, whose assent was very important, were especially reluctant to take this course. They said that the young women who were cut out from the plan were the very ones who needed such protection as the vote could give. The women who would stay in industry after the war, who would be hit most severely by such legislation as the proposed Pre-War Practices Bill and the like—the women, in short, whose claim to enfranchisement even Mr Asquith could no longer deny—were for the most part under thirty; and yet they were to be left out. This was perfectly true, and all the suffragists felt it acutely, but they were unwilling to risk their prospects of partial success by standing out for more; and the Labour men in the House of Commons, who knew what could and what could not be carried, united with them in persuading the Labour women to come in with the rest. Though the negotiations were anxious, and at times difficult, all went well; and the N.U.W.S.S. was soon in a position to tell the Prime Minister that the whole of the feminist forces welcomed and would support a Bill on the lines of the majority report, if the age taken were thirty, and not thirty-five.

So far so good; but it still remained to be seen whether

the Government was prepared to incorporate and stand by the majority recommendation as it would by the unanimous parts of the report. The welcome which the proposal had in the Press and the country, and the general temper of approval of women which prevailed in that year, were good signs; but Mrs Fawcett had a long memory, and knew that nothing is safe until it is done.

In 1870, and again in 1884 and 1911 and 1912, things had looked almost as hopeful; and it would be wise to take every precaution. A renewed effort was therefore made, and a big suffrage demonstration, the first since the outbreak of war, was arranged. It took the form, of course, of a demonstration of women war-workers. Almost all the women of the country were war-workers in one way or another, and there was no other form it could take. Representative women from seventy different trades, ranging from occupations as unlike women's traditional sphere as lamp-lighters, policewomen, engine-cleaners, and post-women, to the more obvious actresses, nurses, head-mistresses, and lace-makers, were on the platform, and the organisations supporting the meeting numbered over two million. A monster deputation of a similar character was gathered together to see the Prime Minister a month later, and in the interval every one of the Cabinet Ministers was individually visited. Although the intentions of the Government were not yet known, these interviews had strengthened the feeling of hope, and when on the 29th of March the war-workers' deputation crowded itself into the Cabinet Room at No. 10 Downing Street, the main point of their demand had already been granted. The night before a motion had been moved in the House of Commons by Mr Asquith himself, calling for the immediate introduction of a Bill on the lines of the Speaker's Conference Report, and he had repeated that in his view women should be included in it. The leaders of every Party had taken the same line, and Mr Lloyd George had eloquently supported it. After a debate in which Women's Suffrage had been the chief topic of discussion, the motion had been carried by 341 votes to 62, and the Prime Minister was thus in a position to tell the deputation that the parliamentary draughtsmen were already at work upon the Bill. Only one point remained to be made clear, and that was whether Women's Suffrage would be in the Bill from the outset, or whether it would have to be put in by amendment; and Mrs Fawcett, remembering the fiasco of 1912, strongly urged that the former course should be adopted. To this Mr Lloyd George agreed and further explained that the whole Bill was to be not a Government but a House of Commons measure, and that although it would be introduced from the Front Bench, and afforded the time that a Government measure secures, it would be open to Members at every stage to vote according to their own convictions, without the Party whips, and this not only on the Women's Suffrage clause, but on the whole Bill.

From many points of view this was a satisfactory plan, and it had the great advantage of doing away with the difference between the unanimous and the majority parts of the report. The suffragists left the Prime Minister happier than they had ever come away from such an occasion before, and devoted their energies for the remaining time until the Bill came on to making sure that all their friends, new and old, should be in their places, and that as many as possible of their remaining enemies should be so much badgered in their constituencies that they would at least abstain from voting.

As the important day drew near it became obvious that success was at hand. When the final lists of supporters were prepared in the National Union Office for the unofficial whips, who had volunteered to see that none of them slipped away from the House before the critical division, these lists were so lengthy that they made quite a bulky volume. Nobody doubted that success was at hand, and the only question was how large the majority would be.

When the second reading of the Representation of the People Bill was taken, most of the discussion centred round the question of Women's Suffrage. The vote, however, was not on that point, but on the question of whether the whole Bill should be proceeded with; and the fact that it was carried by 329 to 40 was thus no real indication of how things would go upon this single issue. It was possible, the pessimists said, that many might have voted for the Bill with the intention of deleting the obnoxious clause; it was too early to feel secure. Nevertheless the fact remained that no such fiasco as that of the previous Reform Bills was now possible. Mr Lloyd George could not throw the women overboard, as Mr Gladstone had done, nor could he withdraw his whole Bill, like Mr Asquith; nor did he want to do these things. The tide had turned, and though they hardly dared to say it, the suffragists knew that victory was sailing in.

For all their certainty, however, the women who thronged the Ladies' Gallery on 19th June, when the House was to take the committee stage of Clause IV (the Women's Suffrage clause), were desperately excited. Often as some of them had sat there before, to hear their cause mocked at, or obstructed, or outvoted in the Chamber below, the scene was still painfully impressive. Through the bars of the absurd little cage in which they were penned they saw chiefly the tops of the heads of the legislators, but the atmosphere of excitement which pervaded the House was noticeable even so. Members trooped in in unwonted numbers, and more than filled the benches. A dense crowd stood below the Bar, and overflowed into the side galleries. All the well-known friends and enemies were in their places, and there was that irrepressible buzz of sound which arises when the attention of the assembly is really aroused.

The debate went its way, noticeable chiefly for the great

number of favourable speakers, and the hopeless tone of the opponents. They spoke, some of them, with all the passion which accrues to the convictions of a lifetime; those who still stood out against the change sincerely believed that it would spell ruin to the State, and disaster to the homes of the country, and spoke, therefore, from their consciences and their hearts. But they were very few. The tide had really turned, and when the time for the division came there were found to be but 55 opponents in the whole House, while 385, seven times their number, went into the other Lobby. This vote was larger than even the most optimistic had expected. It was victory without reserve.

After the critical decision on Clause IV, and before the Report Stage came on in the autumn, a small incident in the domestic history of the House of Commons took place, which added to the happiness of the suffragists, and increased the good humour of the members. The grille or grating behind which the Ladies' Gallery had been shut away had been a joke to the House ever since it had been in existence. In the old House ladies had only been allowed to peep down a ventilating shaft, and when the new House was being built after the fire of 1844 there had been a number of facetious debates about what accommodation, if any, was to be made for ladies. The Ladies' Gallery had seemed a very daring innovation, and the grille had been put up by way of a compromise with those who thought it improper for ladies to come at all. Once or twice in the intervening years attempts had been made to take it down (for it was a terribly uncomfortable arrangement, and shut off sight and sound in an exasperating manner), but none of these attempts had succeeded. Sir Alfred Mond, at this time First Commissioner of Works, was anxious to remove it, and a frivolous little plot was got up between him, Sir Willoughby Dickinson, and the suffragists. A petition was drawn up,[1] and cir-

[1] The text of the petition ran as follows: "To all members of the House of Commons, Sir, We notice with deep interest that your honour-

culated to the wives of the M.P.'s and signed by them with alacrity, and this petition, which was kept quite secret, was found upon their breakfast tables on the day when a motion for the removal of the grille was to come before the House. The debate duly came on, and the Members, mindful of their wives' signatures, made no objection; and accordingly the oriental trappings of the gallery were taken away and placed as a curiosity in another part of the building.

This piece of encouragement was frivolous, but there was another which more clearly demonstrated the value of the coming power of the vote, and which was an improvement in the Bill itself.

The suffragists, feeling almost safe with so magnificent a majority behind them, ventured to criticise the Bill during the summer months. They did not propose to alter the terms of their parliamentary enfranchisement—much though they would have liked to do so. It would have been a breach of faith, and political madness into the bargain, and they did not even consider this course. What they did ask was that the local government franchise for women should be placed upon the same basis as the parliamentary, instead of being left on the old narrow terms. By the existing plan only those women who were themselves householders, unmarried or widowed ladies with property, were entitled to vote; but on the new basis it would be not only these but

able House has had before it a proposal for the removal of the grille from the front of the Ladies' Gallery of the House of Commons.

"We do not wish to attach undue importance to so purely domestic a proposal, nor to attribute to any serious principle a custom which is merely a survival of a more picturesque age; but we beg you to remember in your further deliberations, that it is a very uncomfortable thing to have to sit in a gallery from which little can be heard, and still less seen. We feel this the more acutely because we are assured that the interest of these Debates which we cannot hear, far surpasses that of any other legislative assembly in the civilised world.

"We do most heartily pray you, therefore, to give leave for the removal of this iron grille.

And are,
Your obedient servants."

To this petition the signatures of the wives of 264 Members of Parliament were appended.

also the wives of all male local government electors (provided these wives were over thirty years of age). This seemed to the N.U.W.S.S. to be a perfectly reasonable demand, and one which would not in any way upset the balance of the compromise. The more intelligent of the "antis" had always approved of women taking part in local elections, and it was difficult to see who would object. The Government did so, however, and Sir George Cave refused the amendment not only in the House, but also to a large deputation from the suffragists and the Labour Party. A week-end, however, intervened between this refusal and the final stage of the Bill in the House of Commons; and during that week-end such a phenomenal flood of letters and telegrams poured in upon the Minister from all over the country that he gave way. On 20th November the Government withdrew its opposition, the clause was inserted without a division, and the Bill passed out to the House of Lords, with Women's Suffrage and Women's Local Government Franchise as integral parts of it.

The suffragists had always been afraid of the House of Lords, and in the interval which now elapsed before the discussion in that Chamber their fears awoke once more. The Peers were not susceptible to pressure as were the ordinary M.P.'s. No constituency could be stirred up to send them deputations or telegrams, no threats of withholding support could be held over their heads. Nothing was of any use except the conversion of their minds; and how to convert the minds of the Peerage no one could tell. Such inquiries as it was within their power to make were not very encouraging. The friendly Peers said that although there were many who had come over, there were plenty who had not moved an inch; and it all depended upon who turned up on the day itself. If the "backwoodsmen" came in force, the Bill might easily be lost; and it was doubtful whether attempts to circularise the House might not have exactly the wrong effect.

In this uncertainty the suffragists could do little but wait upon events. They did indeed prepare an elaborate Memorandum setting out the new arguments, the war services, and the claim to be heard on reconstruction problems. They were able to include also the new victories of Women's Suffrage in other parts of the world. Finland and Norway had enfranchised women in 1915, and in this very year, 1917, four additional American States and all the Provinces of Canada except Quebec had followed suit. But what did the Lords care about Finland or Ohio, Norway, or Manitoba? Imposing as the Memorandum was, it was sent out with little confidence, for the most dangerous stage of all was at hand.

The House of Lords had always been the stronghold of the league for opposing Women's Suffrage. Lord Curzon, who was still its president, was the Leader of the House, and there were plenty of others whose opposition was known to be strong and influential—Lord Lansdowne, Lord Halsbury, and Lord Bryce, for example; the last of these all the more damaging because of the great share he had taken in advancing the education of women. It was true there were also strong friends—Lord Lytton, Lord Selborne, Lord Grey, Lord Courtney (the same who had reunited the divided factions of the suffragists in 1878), and many more; but the "antis" seemed to be the more numerous, and they had all that unknown crowd of silent Peers presumably on their side.

As in the House of Commons, the second reading of the whole Bill passed off smoothly, and was carried without a division. There were some speeches on the Women's Suffrage issue, but it was evident that most of these were reserved for the three days' debate on Clause IV, and on 8th January 1918 the last fight began.

New York State had carried Women's Suffrage a few days before, and on 9th January, while the Lords were in full conclave, the American House of Representatives carried the Federal Amendment by the necessary two-thirds majority; these events, though they cheered the suffragists, did not affect the issue. Whatever might be happening in America, their Lordships were still saying that women's place was the home, and that Women's Suffrage would endanger the British Constitution and the safety of the Empire.

As the debate went on, however, the anxious women began to feel more hope. There were speeches of the good old-fashioned type, of course, and there were evidences of unabated prejudice; but there was also the breath of the new understanding. The Peers about whom nothing had been known seemed all to be speaking on the right side, and Mrs Humphry Ward, who sat beside Mrs Fawcett through the debates, looked uneasy and anxious. Her society, it appeared, had lost hope in direct opposition, and was trying at this late hour to secure the submission of the question to a referendum. She went so far as to ask Mrs Fawcett, as they sat there together, whether the suffragists would not support this course; but she must have known it to be a forlorn hope. The proposal was indeed made in the Chamber, and some discussion took place as to whether it should be a referendum to men only, or women only, or to men and women; but it was an unreal point, and presently vanished out of sight, and the last test came near.

Lord Curzon wound up the debate on the afternoon of the 10th of January, and as he rose to speak there was a hush of excitement. One of the policemen at the door, friendly as the police always were to the women, went along the passage to the committee-room, where a number of them were gathered, and put his head round the door. "Lord Curzon is up, ladies," he announced, "but 'e won't do you no 'arm." And so it was. For the President of the Anti-Suffrage League was forced to strike his colours. He said, indeed, that the passage of the Bill would be the ruin of the country; women were politically worthless, and the whole ideal of the Women's Movement was disastrous and wrong; he felt bound to say these things, for he believed them. But when it came to action he could not give so certain a lead. The majority in the House of Commons had been too big, and if the Upper House rejected Women's Suffrage all that would happen would be that the Bill would return to them again with the clause re-inserted. "Are you prepared," he asked, "to embark upon a conflict with a majority of 350 in the House of Commons, of whom nearly 150 belong to the party to which most of your Lordships also belong . . .?" For his part, he said, he could not take upon himself the responsibility of "precipitating a conflict from which your Lordships would not emerge with credit," and he would abstain from voting, one way or the other, upon the clause. With that dramatic and wholly unexpected announcement the discussion ended, and the voting began; and the suffragists, as they waited for the figures, knew that their fight was won. One hundred and thirty-four Peers voted for the clause, 71 against it, and 13 abstained. The Representation of the People Bill was through both Houses; and on 6th February it received the Royal Assent and became the law of the land. The fifty years' struggle was over, and the sex barrier was broken down.

CHAPTER XX

POST WAR. 1918–1928

Immediate effect of Women's Suffrage—Eligibility to Parliament Act, 1918—New development of N.U.W.S.S.—Economic position of women after the war—Demobilisation of women war-workers—Domestic service—Difficulty of finding work—Labour Party's Emancipation Bill superseded by Sex Disqualification Removal Act, which opens legal profession, magistracy, and jury service to women—Election of Lady Astor, 1919—Struggle to secure entry to the Civil Service on equal terms—Unsuccessful attempts to obtain equal pay—Progress of social legislation—Oxford University grants degrees and full membership, Cambridge only "titular degrees"—Equal divorce—Equal guardianship—Widows' pensions—Final extension of the suffrage on equal terms.

THE effect of the passing of "votes for women" was quickly evident. The Representation of the People Act had not been on the Statute Book a fortnight before the House of Commons discovered that every Bill which came before it had a "women's side," and the Party Whips began eagerly to ask "what the women thought?" The precincts of the House of Commons, which had been firmly closed to all women since the early days of the militant agitation, were now opened, and access to Members became wonderfully easy. Letters from women constituents no longer went straight into wastepaper-baskets, but received elaborate answers, and the agents of the women's societies were positively welcomed at Westminster. In 1918 politicians had not realised that women would not vote in a solid block, as women; they feared that perhaps a Women's Party might be formed, and consequently they did not quite know what to be at. They wanted, very naturally, to secure "the women's vote" for themselves, but they did not know how this was to be done; and it was thus the moment for the feminists to put in their word. They had garded the vote not as an end in itself, but as an instrument for securing other reforms; and now they proceeded to use it.

Three Bills of importance to the position of women were passed in 1918, one amending the registration of midwives (which had been unsuccessfully sought for ever since the original Act had scraped through in 1902); one increasing the maximum payment for affiliation orders from 5s. to 10s., and one, initiated by the Government itself, making women eligible (at the age of 21) to be nominated and elected to the House of Commons.

The passing of this Act came as a surprise to the suffragists, who had expected a long struggle on the subject, and who, indeed, in the course of their previous campaign had often repeated that the vote and eligibility to Parliament were different things, and that the grant of the one did not involve that of the other. They were delighted to have been proved wrong, and to see the Bill pass rapidly, and almost without opposition, through both Houses. It reached the Statute Book in November 1918, just three weeks before the General Election, and though this was a terribly short time for candidates to make their preparations, sixteen women came forward in different parts of the country. Only one of these, namely, Christabel Pankhurst,[1] received the approval of the Coalition; the majority of the others stood as Independents, and with one exception they were all defeated. The exception was the late Countess Markovicz, who stood as an Irish Republican; and since, like the others of her Party, she refused to take the Oath, she was not seen at Westminster, and the first Reconstruction Parliament met with no women members. Their absence in person was, however, much less important than it had ever been before, for every Member there knew that he owed

[1] Christabel Pankhurst did not again contest a seat. She turned her attention away from politics, and became a religious preacher, announcing in America and other parts of the world the Second Coming of Christ.

his election to the votes of women as well as of men, so that the whole atmosphere of Parliament was changed.

For nearly a year after the passing of the Suffrage Act the war had been going on. 1918 was indeed, in many ways, the most dreadful year of all, and there had not been much time or energy, before the election of November, to devote to anything but the national crisis. The suffragists, nevertheless, had felt it their duty to take decisions as to the future of their organisation. As was usual in its history, strong differences of opinion existed in the National Union upon this point. Some felt that it must abide strictly by its "feminist" objects, and work only for the removal of the remaining disabilities of women, and the extension of the franchise upon equal terms. Others, and these were slightly in the majority, felt that, now they were enfranchised, there was much more waiting to be done. All the "causes" which had made them care to possess political power rose up in their minds, and they wanted to work within the organisation they knew and loved so well for all sorts of aspects of the betterment of humanity—for the welfare of children, the improvement of health, education, and sanitation, the improvement of international understanding, and the general education of women in the duties of citizenship. The first group urged that there were many other organisations through which to advocate these things; their own duty, as a feminist body, lay along the plain equality line on which they were all agreed. The others answered that this was a dry, academic view; what was the use of having the vote if they were not to use it for all the causes they believed in?

The debate lasted long, and was not by any means ended with the first year's decisions; but the upshot of it, broadly speaking, was a compromise between the two views. The National Union of Women's Suffrage Societies became the National Union of Societies for Equal Citizenship, and its objects remained feminist as before, but with the addition of a phrase authorising it to work "to educate women in the duties of citizenship," under which clause, of course, a great deal could be done. Mrs Fawcett resigned the presidency in 1919, and was succeeded by Miss Eleanor Rathbone; and the executive committee, acting in accordance with the evident desire of the council, deliberately interpreted the objects of the union widely. A "real equality of liberties, status, and opportunities" is an easy phrase to use, but its translation into terms of life, in a world where men are still supposed to support their wives and children, is a harder thing. And time and time again the council meetings of the union, when faced with some concrete proposal, struggled to arrive at its true meaning and did not agree. In the main, however, the course of the Women's Movement was fairly clear. There were still, in 1918, a score of flagrant injustices and inequalities to be cleared away; there were unequal divorce, unequal inheritance and nationality laws, unequal franchise, unequal guardianship of children, unequal standards of morality, unequal chances of employment, and unequal rates of pay.

Important though all these matters seemed to the feminists of 1918, the last of them, namely, the economic inequality of the position of women, was the most pressing of all; and the reason was that the end of the war brought the financial prosperity of women to a sudden stop. No later than the spring of 1919 the demobilisation of women war-workers was in full swing, and the most miserable consequences were following from it. Just as happened a little later with the men who went out of the army, thousands upon thousands of women workers were dismissed, and found no work to do. It was difficult to see how this could have been prevented. All the special war work was at an end, industry was contracting and not expanding, and such jobs as there were had to be kept for the returning soldiers. This was the governing factor, and nothing could change it; and yet it was terribly hard on the women. Everyone assumed, of course, that they would go quietly back to their homes, and that everything could be as it had been before; but, apart altogether from anything the women might wish, this was sheerly impossible. The war had enormously increased the number of surplus women, so that very nearly one woman in every three had to be self-supporting;[1] it had broken up innumerable homes and brought into existence a great class of "new poor." Prices were nearly double what they had been in 1914, and the women who had been able to live upon their small allowances or fixed incomes could do so no more. All these facts, however, were forgotten. Public opinion assumed that all women could still be supported by men, and that if they went on working it was from a sort of deliberate wickedness. The tone of the Press swung, all in a moment, from extravagant praise to the opposite extreme, and the very same people who had been heroines and the saviours of their country a few months before were now parasites, blacklegs, and limpets. Employers were implored to turn them out as passionately as they had been implored to employ them, and their last weeks in their war-time jobs were made miserable by the jeers and taunts of their fellow-workers.

The women themselves acquiesced in the situation. They did not want to stand in the way of the returned soldiers, and, far from being the selfish creatures the Press described, they were only too meek and yielding. They did indeed feel it hard when they were pushed out to make room for a youth who had never fought; but even then they made little protest, and let their gains slip from them, allowing the old rigid exclusions to be reimposed because they thought it was their duty.

Employers were much less willing to let them go altogether. They knew the value of female labour, and had learnt all sorts of lessons from the war years; and if they

[1] The census figures for 1921 show 9,316,753 returned as "unoccupied" (*i.e.* working without wages), and 4,209,408 in the labour market.

had had their way they would have kept women on in dozens of processes from which they were now obliged to turn them out. They wanted, of course, the cheaper labour, and they wanted to break down the troublesome aspects of the Trade Union power—the exclusion of learners, the rejection of piece-work, and the rigid demarcation of jobs. But this was not to be. The Government's promise to restore pre-war practices had to be honoured, and even before it was made positively illegal to employ women in certain trades their exclusion was an accomplished fact.

Women therefore came tumbling out of industry at a great rate and were very difficult to reabsorb. The first solution which occurred to middle-class observers was domestic service, and there was a long-sustained outcry in the Press because, even at the height of the demobilisation troubles, there remained a shortage in this direction. The munition girls were freely accused of being "spoiled by the war," and of having had their heads turned. But the facts were not quite so simple. Women had, indeed, got a new glimpse of what work might be; they had tasted the joys of independent living and of good wages, and in consequence a fourteen-hours' day as a solitary slavey was not very attractive. But they did not hold back from this reason. Keep was keep, and to many of them there was none to be had elsewhere. But the trouble was that they could not do the job. They had none of the necessary clothes, and none of the necessary experience. They were rough, and often wild, and if they had been taken into any ordinary house they would have been turned out again very promptly amid a smash of broken crockery. The over-driven mothers of small children, who longed for help in their domestic burdens, would have found small comfort in these girls who knew nothing of health or cleanliness, and could neither cook nor sew. Even if it could have been managed, nothing could have been gained by forcing industrial women into these positions, and the only possible course was adopted by the

Government when, in 1919, training centres were opened where short courses with maintenance were offered to girls to prepare them for domestic work.

At the best, domestic work could only absorb a fraction of the women who needed work, and though this aspect of the problem loomed very large in the public mind, it was not really so important. From the point of view of the Women's Movement what was important was that industrial women were being driven back into almost the same position they had held before the war, while the non-industrial women were not so treated. In spite of the return of the men, and the wholesale retirement of the women, the occupations in which there were no strong men's unions did not lose women altogether. Here and there, even at the height of demobilisation, a few specially useful women were retained in almost all the new posts, and the tradition of their eligibility remained unbroken. Banks and commercial houses, Government offices and private firms, and a great host of miscellaneous occupations remained theoretically open, and although this did little to ease the pressure of the first years of the peace, it marked a very decided advance in the economic development of women. The old aims of Barbara Bodichon's Employment Society were being realised; the field of choice was widening, and, bad as temporary conditions were, it could never again be so restricted as it had been in the nineteenth century.

Developments such as these, which can be described in general terms, represent in real life a multitude of individual cases; and during the first years after the war the attempt to steer a feminist course among them was almost heartbreaking. The disappointment, the discouragement, and the sheer material needs of the women were painful in the extreme, and their pathetic resignation and patient acceptance of the bottom place only made it harder to endure on their behalf. The London Society for Women's Suffrage, under its new name of Women's Service, had been recruiting women for war service since August 1914, and had placed over 200,000 of them in interesting jobs; and now its office was thronged with these same women, asking where they could turn next.

At first it was possible to urge them to train thoroughly for some special occupation, though many of them, of course, had not the capital required; but the time came when even this suggestion was useless, when all the training centres were full to overflowing, and when competent and proficient women were coming out from them and still finding no work to do. The workers in industrial occupations were to some extent helped by the "dole," but this was not available for the thousands of clerical workers who poured out of the Government offices in 1920 and 1921; and, amid the hardships of the whole unemployment problem, their case was desperate.

The feminist societies realised that in this direction lay a great new field of effort, and early in 1919 they began to attack it in the old pioneering spirit, while at the same time they watched the social legislation of each successive Parliament, and tried to secure the passage of the reforms needed to complete the equality of women before the law.

The actual division of responsibilities among the societies was complicated and variable, and the task of awarding credit for the progress which followed need not be undertaken. With the granting of the vote all the organisations of women became more or less feminist and political, and the doctrines of equal legislation and equal pay became, as it were, common form to them all. The war, too, had left a legacy of co-operation among them, and the co-ordinating and unifying machinery became so complete as almost to stultify its own ends. A member of one of these societies could, if she chose, spend the greater part of her life in attending conferences, congresses, joint meetings and organising committees to secure the united presentation of the feminist point of view; and the internal politics of the movement naturally grew to formidable proportions. Nevertheless, the unifying of so much organised opinion had its effect upon the action of Parliament, and the years which followed the passing of Women's Suffrage brought a big harvest of results.

The first actual Bill to come forward was the Emancipation Bill, introduced by the Labour Party on a Private Members' day in April 1919. This Bill was intended to remove at one sweep all the remaining disabilities of women; it would have equalised the franchise, admitted Peeresses in their own right to the House of Lords, opened the legal profession to women, made them liable for jury service, and eligible for admission to all branches of the Civil Service, and to all societies and corporations controlled by Charter. The Government, influenced no doubt by the permanent officials, resisted this Bill, but the Members of the House of Commons hardly dared to vote against it, not knowing what their female constituents might have to say. After an unusually animated debate for a Friday afternoon, the Bill was carried against the Government, and both the Opposition and the women's societies were greatly delighted. The Coalition Parliament did not regard Government defeats as seriously as normal Parliaments, however, so that no question of resignation arose; and when the Bill reached the Upper House, steps were taken to defeat it. The Peers had no constituents, and therefore were not at all afraid, and they quashed this comprehensive Bill with pleasure. Nevertheless, the Government was not easy in mind, and a short time later it produced a Bill of its own, ostensibly designed to the same end, and called the Sex Disqualification Removal Bill. In its first form this Bill did little more than open the legal profession to women; and although this in itself was a great matter, it was not enough to satisfy the women's organisations. They did not seriously expect the extension of the vote on equal terms so soon, but they did hope, and indeed intend, to secure the opening of the

Civil Service, and they therefore devoted themselves to the effort to improve the Bill. The opposition they encountered was as stubborn as anything in the whole history of the movement. The Civil Service machine seemed absolutely determined not to allow women to come into any but the routine and subordinate grades, and their spokesmen fought with the adroitness of long practice against the threatened interference with their preserves. The women, however, were adroit and experienced too; they knew that their hope lay in Parliament, and that decisions there, though they might be resisted and delayed in administration, would ultimately bear fruit, and they therefore bent all their energies to the task of making the decisions of Parliament on this point explicit and definite. In the Bill itself they were not wholly successful, though some modifications were secured; but when it was passed, and the reforms it achieved were safely harvested, they returned again to the charge.

The passing of the Sex Disqualification Removal Act opened the legal profession in all its branches to women, and led to the immediate appointment of women magistrates. Women also became liable for jury service, a privilege which, disagreeable as it might be, was recognised to be very important; and the subsequent efforts of a few judges and barristers to object to their presence in unpleasant cases were resisted whenever they occurred. The women claimed that these cases were the very ones in which their presence was most required, and this claim was supported by the general sense of public opinion, so that in an amazingly short time this function worked normally and smoothly.

Entry to the legal profession had been one of the objects of the feminist societies for many years, and a special committee, with Mr Samuel Garrett as its chairman, had existed for the purpose of securing this reform. It had always been vehemently opposed by the profession, but Mr Garrett, who had himself been president of the Law Society, Lord Robert Cecil, Major J. W. Hills, and many other friendly solicitors and barristers had prepared the way, so that when the final defeat came the lawyers took it in good part and welcomed the new recruits generously, making it clear that they would be treated, as they wished to be treated, without penalty or privilege. A fair number of women at once began the study of law with a view to practising in the courts, and a smaller number, mostly of those who had some family connection, were articled to solicitors. Everyone predicted that they would have no luck, and that their entry into an already overcrowded profession would be a failure; but in the event it has been found that their prospects are much the same as those of their male contemporaries, and that their appearance in wig and gown has created no revolution in legal circles.

One other effect the Sex Disqualification Removal Act immediately produced, and that was to secure the opening to women of such bodies as the Society of Chartered Accountants. Some of these bodies had voluntarily admitted women before the passing of the Act, notably the Institute of Naval Architects and the Institute of Banking; and after the Act all the others were obliged to follow suit. Even the Royal Society had to give way, and when the question was tested in 1922 Counsel's opinion was that women could no longer be excluded, and Mrs Ayrton, who had been rejected twenty years before, was speedily admitted.

Peeresses in their own right were not dealt with in this Act, and although in 1922 the Viscountess Rhondda secured a judgment from the Committee on Privileges that she was qualified to take her seat in the House of Lords, this decision was subsequently reversed. In the same year that the Act was passed, however, the first woman appeared in the House of Commons, when the Viscountess Astor was returned as a Conservative for the Sutton Division of

Plymouth at a by-election made necessary by her husband's accession to a Peerage. This event was hailed all over the country, and indeed all over the world, as a great achievement; and although there were still a few sulky and old-fashioned M.P.'s who shook their heads, and went out of their way to be politely disagreeable, her reception in the House was better than had been feared. For a time, of course, it was attended with a blaze of publicity. Everything she did or said was reported and exaggerated, and it was fortunate indeed for the movement that she was not only courageous, but also able and witty. Inside the House she speedily won for herself a unique position; and outside she became the symbol of hope to people whom she could never meet. Hundreds of letters poured in upon her daily from every part of the kingdom. "You, Lady Astor, being a woman and a mother yourself, will understand what we feel. . . ." And understand she did. In a very short time she was identified in the public mind with all the social reforms which are dear to ordinary women, as well as being known everywhere as the champion of women's equal rights in every aspect of life.

In the same year that Lady Astor was elected there was a remarkable increase in the number of women returned to Town and Borough Councils. The extension of the local government franchise by the inclusion of married women was in great part the cause; but it is also clear that the willingness of women candidates to come forward for public work, and the willingness of the electors to vote for them, was one of the results of the war. It was not so interesting to serve on a public health committee as to drive an ambulance in France; but it was the same service in a different form.

1919 was the year of the Peace Conference in Paris, and was thus a time of much international activity among all organised "movements." The International Council of Women, and the International Women's Suffrage Alliance were not behindhand, and delegates were sent from England to put forward the views of their respective societies. Through the support of President Wilson and M. Venizelos, and Lord Robert Cecil, that part of their object which related to the equal treatment of women was secured, and in the Covenant of the League of Nations itself[1] the eligibility of women to all posts in the League and the Secretariat was assured.

The following year, 1920, was less prosperous, and was chiefly marked by the continued battle with the Civil Service for the right of equal entry into the profession. The women's societies, inside as well as outside the service, attached more importance to this matter than lay upon the surface; for it was clear that the action of the Government as an employer must have a tremendous effect upon the attitude of all other employers. The fight, therefore, together with the demand which the teachers were at the same time putting forward for equal pay, was taken up with determination, and a contest was begun which is by no means yet at an end. In 1920 Major Hills, who was acting for an important joint committee of women's societies, secured a debate upon the matter, and a straight vote in favour of equal opportunity of employment was obtained. The equal pay aspect of the matter was weakened down by phrases referring to the need for national economy, but a review was promised within three years, and it seemed as if progress had been made. Many were the disappointments which followed. Delays, obstructions, and circumlocutions were piled one upon another, and a great deal of really first-class energy and ability was devoted by the Treasury and other big departments to the task of evading the plain meaning of the decision of Parliament. In August 1921 a second debate was obtained, after a long series of technical manœuvres, and on this occasion an absolutely exact pledge was wrested from the Government that entrance to every grade of the Home Civil Service should be open to women

[1] Article 7.

by the same competitive examinations as admitted men. The first test held under this decision was held in 1925, and three young women from the universities made their way into the sacred preserves and took up their work as "administrative cadets."

After this decision had been reached in 1921 the opposition in the Civil Service took rather a different form. It was henceforward the policy of the Treasury to admit women; but they were in no hurry to implement it, and obstruction took the place of open opposition. The men already employed in all grades had what they considered their "natural expectations," and these were amply and abundantly allowed for. In the long run, it was now agreed, women would have a fair chance; but meanwhile there were all the existing male staff, who objected to having women imposed upon them, who felt outraged at being asked to work under them, and who feared the extra competition for promotion. Thousands of temporary male civil servants had been absorbed, and thousands of ex-soldiers had been taken in; and every one of these, in the official view, had a prior claim over the women. Nevertheless, it was, and is, admitted that this must be a diminishing obstruction, and that the way to equality of opportunity lies clear.

The question of pay proved even more obstinate. The teachers, who were the first to raise their claim, made a valiant fight, but when the whole dispute was sent to Lord Burnham's Committee to be arbitrated, they lost their case. The awards granted them roughly five-sixths of a man's pay, and with that they had, for the time being, to be satisfied. In the Civil Service the scales were more or less similar, and these two standards acted, of course, as a guide to private employers.

In 1921 Mrs Wintringham was elected for Louth. This second woman member was of a different Party from the first, being a Liberal; but opposing principles did not prevent the two women M.P.'s from working very closely together for all "women's causes," which greatly profited by their help. In subsequent years still more women were elected. In 1923 there were eight of them, and their presence at Westminster became fully recognised and accepted. Both the Labour and Conservative Parties included one in their Governments, and the custom of sending a woman among the delegates to the League of Nations Assembly became established. Sixty years after Miss Davies and Miss Beale had been so greatly agitated by being called to give evidence before a Government commission, hardly one such body could be appointed without at least one woman member. The effects of the enfranchisement of women were plain.

In 1920 some small anomalies in the Law of Married Woman's Property in Scotland were put right, and the Law of Property Act of 1922 made husbands and wives, mothers and fathers, sons and daughters equal in cases of intestacy, thus remedying a very old and very grievous injustice. In 1920 it became for the first time legally possible for husbands and wives to steal from each other when they were living apart; and though this privilege was not perhaps very highly valued, the Maintenance Acts of 1922 were a more real advantage, while in 1923 a welcome Act increasing the maximum contributions of fathers for the support of their bastard children was secured. The appointment of women police, which had been tried with admirable results during the war, had been continued, and a small number taken into the metropolitan and other forces. The work of these women, together with that of the increasing numbers of women magistrates, caused the subject of order and morality in the streets to be widely discussed, and a parliamentary commission on the subject of the Criminal Law was appointed in 1922. Lady Astor was a member of this commission, and the publicity which rightly attended its discussions was no longer either sensational or malevolent. What Mrs Butler had had to agonise for, what W. T. Stead had had to go to prison for, the regularly elected woman Member of Parliament obtained as a matter of course; and an Act carrying further Mrs Butler's work was passed with little opposition.

Miss Emily Davies died in 1921. She had lived to record the vote she had so much wanted, and to see some of the results of its power; and she saw the final triumph of the cause of university education at Oxford. In 1920 the women students were admitted to full membership, with degrees, caps, gowns, and an equal share in university government. Miss Davies rejoiced; but at the same time she was saddened by the fact that Cambridge, where her own college had been established, still refused to follow this example. The course of affairs at that perverse university was long and intricate. The position of women became a very sore subject, and was discussed with some of the old animus and much of the old subtlety; and in the end a system was devised which gave the women a thing called a "titular degree," and a share in the teaching affairs of the university, together with the right to use the libraries and laboratories, but denied them the real membership which had been given at Oxford and at every other university in the United Kingdom. It was a decision which disappointed the women graduates of Cambridge, but perhaps rather more with shame for the obscurantist attitude it revealed than for any remaining grievance. They had the substance, and were denied only the shadow; and this was so different from the old state of affairs that it could be accepted with comparative equanimity.

In 1923 a further step towards removing the inequalities of women was taken, when the Matrimonial Causes Act altered the grounds upon which divorce could be obtained, by making them the same for men and women. The immediate increase in undefended suits which followed showed how widespread a difficulty the old arrangement had caused; and although the Bill was unwelcome to those to whom the simplification of divorce seemed an evil, there was no one left to defend the old unequal arrangement.

In 1925 and 1926 seven more Acts of direct importance to the position of women found their way on to the Statute Book. The Guardianship of Infants Act of 1925 at last completed the work which Caroline Norton had begun a hundred years earlier, and put fathers and mothers into an equal position in regard to their rights and powers over their offspring; the Widows' Pensions Act removed the support of widows from the Poor Law, and granted them a pension similar in standing to the Old Age Pension. The Summary Jurisdiction Act removed what had been a serious practical difficulty in the administration of Separation and Maintenance Orders; and the Adoption of Children Act, together with the Act making possible the legitimation of children on the subsequent marriage of their parents, both tended to lessen the undeserved misfortunes of the child born out of wedlock. The Midwives and Maternity Homes Act aimed at improving the conditions and lessening the risks under which children are brought into the world, and carried a step farther the great life-work of Florence Nightingale.

The Criminal Justice Act of 1926, though not primarily concerned with the subject of women, abolished the presumption that a married woman was coerced by her husband when she committed a crime in his presence, and thus restored to her the responsibility for her own actions, and almost completed the legal separation of married people into two individuals, which the Women's Movement had so long desired.

One great disability still, however, remained in the beginning of 1928, and that was the age-limit of thirty, with the other disqualifications as to occupancy, by which the numbers of women voters had been kept down below those of men. In 1924 the Conservative Government, which then came into power, had declared its intention of remedying this anomaly, and in 1926 the feminist societies began to press Mr Baldwin in regard to the fulfilment of this pledge. Some opposition to the project made its appearance, not so much on the old ground that women outnumbered men (for the non-existence of a women's party had destroyed this bogey) but on the ground that young women as a whole were not to be trusted. From time immemorial "the girl of the period" has been considered to be frivolous and flighty; her elders have always said she was a problem; and in 1927 they began to say that she was a danger too. The outcry which arose, however, came from a very restricted class of people, and was not taken up either by the Conservative Party or by the general public. The obvious absurdity of allowing young men of twenty-one to vote, and refusing to allow young women to do so till nine years later was generally admitted; and in the King's Speech of February 1928 the Bill to equalise the franchise occupied a prominent place. It came forward as a Government measure on 29th March 1928, and received the support of both the Opposition Parties. After a debate which revealed the extraordinary change of feeling which ten years' experience of women constituents had produced, the second reading was carried by 387 votes to 10. The further stages quickly followed, and on 23rd of May the Bill passed the House of Lords by a considerable majority. With the passage of this Act the last glaring inequality in the legal position of women was abolished. As the Prime Minister said in the debate, "The subjection of women, if there be such a thing, will not now depend on any creation of the law, nor can it be remedied by any action of the law. It will never again be possible to blame the Sovereign State for any position of inequality. Women will have, with us, the fullest rights. The ground and justification for the old agitation is gone, and gone for ever." [1]

Legal equality is not, of course, the whole aim of the

[1] *Hansard*, 29th March 1928.

movement. There are aspects of it which are not susceptible to victory by law; there are changes of thought and outlook which even yet have not arrived. There are consequences, too, of the victories already won which have not as yet fully emerged; and, above all, economic equality is still a distant dream. The struggle for these things goes on, and must go on, with the development of the British people. But the main fight is over, and the main victory is won. With education, enfranchisement, and legal equality all conceded, the future of women lies in their own hands; and it has been the fundamental belief of the Women's Movement that in those hands it is safe.

CHAPTER XXI

THE DEATH OF MRS GRUNDY

Development of the physical freedom of women—Bicycles—Bloomers—Tight lacing, long skirts, and long hair—Their effect on pre-war athletics—The war clothes—The frivolity of 1919—Changed conventions of to-day—Domestic service—Women's Institutes—Factory conditions—Would anyone go back to Early Victorian behaviour ?

In the ten years between the first instalment of Women's Suffrage and the granting of full political equality the Women's Cause moved fast. The catalogue of reforms contained in the last chapter covers nearly every aspect of the status of men and women which can be equalised by legislation, and, in so far as this goes, the Women's Movement is practically complete. Some of the great aspects of life, however, escape from the government of law. Morals and economics are at the best but indirectly affected by Parliament, and in these two directions the present position of women still falls far short of the ideal which has inspired their movement. The Cause, therefore, will still go on, and though in future its battles will lie in new fields, they will be stiff battles on a wide front. The victories which have been won so far, however, and the changes which those victories have already involved are an earnest of its final vindication.

At this moment, when the Cause stands midway to success, it is possible to look back at the course which has been run, and to try and estimate the losses and gains which have resulted from it. We have already measured them in terms of laws and achievements, where all has been gain; but in manners, customs, and social conditions the results have been equally, if not more, astonishing. A hundred years ago a girl could go nowhere unprotected; to-day there is nowhere she cannot go. The chaperon has vanished with the crinoline, and freedom and companionship between the sexes have taken the place of the old uneasy restraint. In work as much as in play, in study as much as in games, there is now little divergence, and scholarship, athletics, travel, tobacco, and even latch-keys and cheque-books are no longer the sole prerogatives of men.

The widening of the physical world for women which these changed conditions involve did not really begin before 1890. Some years earlier, as we have seen, games were introduced into the more advanced girls' schools, but it was not until the early nineties that the idea that grown-up women could move about freely was at all generally accepted; and the emancipating agent in this reform was the bicycle. The women who first began to ride upon this queer machine were thought to be incredibly venturous, and most people also thought them shocking. In the very early days, indeed, when only men's bicycles were made, the enormity of riding at all was intensified by the fact that it had to be done in Bloomers,[1] and the bold pioneers were freely hooted in the streets. After a time adaptations of the machine were made, so that the voluminous skirts of the period could be heaped up and stowed away, and a perfectly ladylike appearance maintained. The prejudice did not at once diminish, but the achievement was considered worth the persecution, and women persevered. They found in it not only what was then thought to be the exquisite pleasure of rapid motion, but also very great practical convenience. They were no longer prisoners in their own houses; they

[1] Mrs Amelia Bloomer, who was an American suffragist, first invented the costume in 1857. It was worn for a time by a few "advanced" lecturers in America, but did not become a fashion. Mrs Bloomer herself abandoned it in 1865, as she feared her name might go down to posterity in this connection alone; and she wished to be remembered rather for her writings and her serious feminist work. She edited a paper called *The Lily*.

could spin off, if they chose, as far as six or seven miles away; they could go to the nearest town to do their shopping, and they could visit their friends, and be no longer dependent for these joys upon the convenience of the rest of the family, but only upon their own muscles. It was a wonderful change, and one which was rapidly appreciated by all sorts of women who had no conscious sympathy with the Women's Movement at all. No doubt it was this emancipating tendency which caused the opposition to be so acute; certainly it was the reason why a deliberate propaganda in favour of the innovation made its appearance, and a little flock of quaint pamphlets urging women to "conquer the world on wheels" remains to bear witness to this vital social change.

For a long time fashion fought valiantly against any further development of physical freedom for women. Tight lacing claimed many victims, and all through the nineties and the early years of the new century girls, as they reached their teens, were firmly encased in frameworks of whalebone which made anything but the mildest exercise difficult. To add to this they endured as their age increased a gradual lengthening of their skirts, until at about the age of seventeen these symbolical wrappings reached the ground and put a final end to all running and jumping, and made walking, especially in a wind, a sadly fatiguing affair. At the same stage of life a girl's hair was "put up"—that is to say, it was coiled into a heap and attached to the back of her head by pins; and the instability of this arrangement added another to the difficulties of rapid movement. Hats, though they varied in size and style from year to year, were perched somewhat insecurely upon the top of the head, and they had to be kept in place by long skewers, or "hat pins," whose sharp points protruded on one side, and were dangerous at close proximity. Rigged up in this attire, without freedom to breathe or to move their legs or their heads, women were badly handicapped, and it is not greatly to be wondered at that their athletic performances reached but a poor standard. They struggled as best they could against the difficulties which convention imposed, but their golf was rudimentary, and their tennis at the best a mild affair of lobbing from the back of the court. Hockey alone was played in earnest, for since it was seldom played by mixed teams a special costume could be adopted; and the enthusiasm which sprang up in girls' schools for this game led to the formation of innumerable clubs and the organisation of county and even international matches, where a really fast and scientific game was to be seen.

The dress designers, backed no doubt by the conservative tendency of the world, strove hard to keep fashion and hygiene apart. Trains appeared at the end of skirts already long, and women had to hold them up with their hands whenever they moved; high collars, stiffened with whalebone, were fitted close to the neck, and presently the hobble skirt, so narrow at the ankles that only half a step at a time was possible, were superimposed. It seemed that folly could go no farther; and there were some in the feminist ranks who almost questioned whether women who would endure such clothes deserved their enfranchisement!

The war, however, brought deliverance. Under the necessities of the time fashion gave way, and short-skirted uniforms, and even breeches, became familiar sights. Women, when they had once really tasted the joys of this deliverance, refused to be put back into the old costumes. The trade tried, indeed, when the war was over, to reinstate the old ideas; but they did not "take." Skirts grew shorter and shorter, clothes grew more and more simple and convenient, and hair, that "crowning glory of a woman," was cut short. With one bound the young women of 1919 burst out from the hampering conventions, and with their cigarettes, their motor-cars, their latch-keys, and their athletics they astonished and scandalised their elders. All through the course of the movement any widening of outlook had been thought dangerous for women, and now it seemed that these fears were justified. Men had said that the knowledge of good and evil, which was necessary to themselves, would only hurt women, and rub off the peach-bloom of their innocence; and in the changed manners of the first years after the war this prophecy seemed to be coming true. Many young women seemed to be mistaking the meaning of their freedom, and to be using it only for excess of excitement. They spent the morning hours upon the make-up of their faces, idled through the afternoons, and danced all the night. They discarded the semblance of manners and morals, and replaced them by licence and dissipation. These young women figured largely in the minds of the old-fashioned, who enjoyed the belief that the country had now finally gone to the dogs, and that the emancipation of women was the last manifestation of this fact. In reality, however, all this was ephemeral and unimportant, and was more a sign of the reaction after the war strain than of anything to do with the Women's Movement. It passed and died down, and men and women turned away from night clubs to the more wholesome light of day. And yet, in a sense, the pessimists had been right. The new freedom of women *had* destroyed the old ideal on which their fears were based, and it *had* banished the clinging doll-heroine into the shades of the past. Innocence, in the sense of ignorance, existed no more, but in its place there was that of which the pioneers of the Women's Movement had dreamed, namely, the combination of independence with responsibility, of amusement with achievement.

In all ranks of life the pressure of convention is now easier. Domestic service, under the combined influence of the shortage of servants and the new ideas, at last began to turn into a less dreary and dismal trade. Wages rose sharply, and "outings" increased as fast; tobacco, that great comforter of small woes, found its way into every scullery, and labour-saving and back-saving appliances came flooding into the market. In the new post-war houses the basement kitchens and the weary flights of stone stairs are not constructed, and housework, though still far from efficiently organised, begins to assume more reasonable dimensions.

In the villages, where social customs and the minute subdivisions of class feeling had separated neighbour from neighbour, and condemned the home-keeping women to an almost unbelievable loneliness, a complete transformation has taken place. The Women's Institutes, begun during the war as a part of the national effort, developed in the first years of peace, and within a remarkably short time they have become universal. These institutes, democratic in theory and practice, became tremendously popular, and gave to the women of the rural districts exactly the stimulus they required. At the Institute meetings all come together on an equal footing; the distinctions between the tradesman's and the labourer's wife vanish, and friendship (with its exchange of gossip) combines harmoniously with demonstrations of home industries, talks on health and children, and amateur theatricals. It is not too much to say that the lives of country women were transformed by the coming of this organisation, which brought instruction and variety just at the moment when enfranchisement and short skirts were bringing physical and mental development; and it is not surprising that great numbers of those who had worked in the Suffrage Movement turned their energies to this field.

Among the factory population, and in the towns, progress is less apparent. The war indeed wrought changes here. The welfare work and the specialised inquiries of those years convinced employers that the best work comes from the happiest workers, and that sports clubs and canteens and good material conditions are thoroughly paying propositions. But industry was hard hit by the aftermath of the war, and much that would normally have resulted was financially impossible. Moreover, unemployment lies like a spectre across the lives of the working girls; and until that state of affairs can be ended their progress must inevitably be slow.

Surveying the whole female population, however, and comparing it with that over which Queen Victoria began to reign, it is easy to see that there has been progress in every direction. Something, no doubt, has been destroyed, something innocent and restful and pure; but ignorance, ill-health, and the dangerous spirit of dependence have been banished with it, and in their place there is education and self-reliance. No woman of to-day would go back if she could to the conditions which her grandmother endured. No girl would submit to the clothing and the restraints of 1837; no wife would be content to merge her whole legal and financial existence in that of her husband; no matron would agree to put on her cap and retire from life at thirty-five. And even if women would do these things, men would not approve! For as the Women's Movement has gone along its course men, too, have been influenced thereby. They have found better comfort and joy in companions who have shared their own world, and neither sex would now, even if it could, turn back the hands of the clock.

What lies in the future no one can tell. The Women's Movement will go forward, as all the other movements for human progress will go forward, in the hands of the men and women of this generation.

John Stuart Mill, when he introduced the first Women's Suffrage Bill in 1867, ventured upon a prophecy. "When the time comes, as it certainly will come," he said, "when this reform will be granted, I feel the firmest conviction that you will never repent of the concession." Mr Baldwin, when he introduced the last Women's Suffrage Bill in 1928, went even farther. "It may well be," he said, "that men and women, working together for the regeneration of their country, and for the regeneration of the world, each doing that for which they are better fitted, may provide such an environment that each immortal soul as it is born on this earth may have a fairer chance and a fairer home than has ever yet been vouchsafed to the generations that have passed."

It is for the future to fulfil these hopes.

APPENDIX I

THE fragment " Cassandra," here published in full for the first time, forms part of the second volume of Miss Nightingale's unpublished book *Suggestions for Thought to Searchers after Religious Truth*. The second volume is called " Practical Deductions "; and it is with these bitter and impassioned comments upon the position of women, as she herself experienced it, that the volume ends.

The book was written by Miss Nightingale in 1852, when she was thirty-two years old, and it was revised and finally put together in 1859, after her return from the Crimea. In that year she had it privately printed, but on the advice of J. S. Mill, Jowett, and other friends it was not published.

Permission to reproduce this fragment of the book has very kindly been granted by the representatives of her family and executors.

CASSANDRA

By FLORENCE NIGHTINGALE

I

" The voice of one crying in the " crowd, " Prepare ye the way of the Lord."

ONE often comes to be thus wandering alone in the bitterness of life without. It might be that such an one might be tempted to seek an escape in the hope of a more congenial sphere. Yet, perhaps, if prematurely we dismiss ourselves from this world, all may even have to be suffered through again—the premature birth may not contribute to the production of another being, which must be begun again from the beginning.

Such an one longs to replunge into the happy unconscious sleep of the rest of the race! they slumber in one another's arms —they are not yet awake. To them evil and suffering are not, for they are not conscious of evil. While one alone, awake and prematurely alive to it, must wander out in silence and solitude —such an one has awakened too early, has risen up too soon, has rejected the companionship of the race, unlinked to any human being. Such an one sees the evil they do not see, and yet has no power to discover the remedy for it.

Why have women passion, intellect, moral activity—these three —and a place in society where no one of the three can be exercised? Men say that God punishes for complaining. No, but men are angry with misery. They are irritated with women for not being happy. They take it as a personal offence. To God alone may women complain without insulting Him!

And women, who are afraid, while in words they acknowledge that God's work is good, to say, Thy will be *not* done (declaring another order of society from that which He has made), go about maudling to each other and teaching to their daughters that "women have no passions." In the conventional society, which men have made for women, and women have accepted, they *must* have none, they *must* act the farce of hypocrisy, the lie that they are without passion—and therefore what else can they say to their daughters, without giving the lie to themselves?

Suffering, sad "female humanity!" What are these feelings which they are taught to consider as disgraceful, to deny to themselves? What form do the Chinese feet assume when denied their proper development? If the young girls of the "higher classes," who never commit a false step, whose justly earned reputations were never sullied even by the stain which the fruit of mere "knowledge of good and evil" leaves behind, were to speak, and say what are their thoughts employed upon, their *thoughts*, which alone are free, what would they say?

That, with the phantom companion of their fancy, they talk (not love, they are too innocent, too pure, too full of genius and imagination for that, but) they talk, in fancy, of that which interests them most; they seek a companion for their every thought; the companion they find not in reality they seek in fancy, or, if not that, if not absorbed in endless conversations, they see themselves engaged with him in stirring events, circumstances which call out the interest wanting to them. Yes, fathers, mothers, you who see your daughter proudly rejecting all semblance of flirtation, primly engaged in the duties of the breakfast table, you little think how her fancy compensates itself by endless interviews and sympathies (sympathies either for ideas or events) with the fancy's companion of the hour! And you say, "She is not susceptible. Women have no passion." Mothers, who cradle yourselves in visions about the domestic hearth, how many of your sons and daughters are *there*, do you think, while sitting round under your complacent eye? Were you there yourself during your own (now forgotten) girlhood?

What are the thoughts of these young girls while one is singing Schubert, another is reading the *Review*, and a third is busy embroidering? Is not one fancying herself the nurse of some new friend in sickness; another engaging in romantic dangers with him, such as call out the character and afford more food for sympathy than the monotonous events of domestic society; another undergoing unheard-of trials under the observation of someone whom she has chosen as the companion of her dream; another having a loving and loved companion in the life she is living, which many do not want to change?

And is not this all most natural, inevitable? Are they, who are too much ashamed of it to confess it even to themselves, to be blamed for that which cannot be otherwise, the causes of which stare one in the face, *if one's eyes were not closed*? Many struggle against this as a " snare." No Trappist ascetic watches or fasts more in the body than these do in the soul! They understand the discipline of the Thebaid—the life-long agonies to which those strong moral Mohicans subjected themselves. How cordially they could do the same, in order to escape the worse torture of wandering " vain imaginations." But the laws of God for moral well-being are not thus to be obeyed. We fast mentally, scourge ourselves morally, use the intellectual hair-shirt, in order to subdue that perpetual day-dreaming, which is so dangerous! We resolve " this day month I will be free from it "; twice a day with prayer and written record of the times when we have indulged in it, we endeavour to combat it. Never, with the slightest success. By mortifying vanity we do ourselves no good. It is the want of interest in our life which produces it; by filling up that want of interest in our life we can alone remedy it. And, did we even see this, how can we make the difference? How obtain the interest which society declares *she* does not want, and *we* cannot want?

What are novels? What is the secret of the charm of every romance that ever was written? The first thing in a good novel is to place the persons together in circumstances which naturally call out the high feelings and thoughts of the character, which afford food for sympathy between them on these points—romantic events they are called. The second is that the heroine has *generally* no family ties (almost *invariably* no mother), or, if she has, these do not interfere with her entire independence.

These two things constitute the main charm of reading novels.

Now, in as far as these are good and not spurious interests, let us see what we have to correspond with them in real life. Can high sympathies be fed upon the opera, the exhibitions, the gossip of the House of Commons, and the political caricature? If, together, man and woman approach any of the high questions of social, political, or religious life, they are said (and justly—under our present disqualifications) to be going "too far." That such things can be!

"Is it Thou, Lord?" And He said, "It is I." Let our hearts be still.

II

> "Yet I would spare no pang,
> Would wish no torture less,
> The more that anguish racks,
> The earlier it will bless."

Give us back our suffering, we cry to Heaven in our hearts—suffering rather than indifferentism; for out of nothing comes nothing. But out of suffering may come the cure. Better have pain than paralysis! A hundred struggle and drown in the breakers. One discovers the new world. But rather, ten times rather, die in the surf, heralding the way to that new world, than stand idly on the shore!

Passion, intellect, moral activity—these three have never been satisfied in a woman. In this cold and oppressive conventional atmosphere, they cannot be satisfied. To say more on this subject would be to enter into the whole history of society, of the present state of civilisation.

Look at that lizard—"It is not hot," he says, "I like it. The atmosphere which enervates you is life to me." The state of society which some complain of makes others happy. Why should these complain to those? *They* do not suffer. *They* would not understand it, any more than that lizard would comprehend the sufferings of a Shetland sheep.

The progressive world is necessarily divided into two classes—those who take the best of what there is and enjoy it—those who wish for something better and try to create it. Without these two classes the world would be badly off. They are the very conditions of progress, both the one and the other. Were there none who were discontented with what they have, the world would never reach anything better. And, through the other class, which is constantly taking the best of what the first is creating for them, a balance is secured, and that which is conquered is held fast. But with neither class must we quarrel for not possessing the privileges of the other. The laws of the nature of each make it impossible.

Is discontent a privilege?

Yes, it is a privilege for you to suffer for your race—a privilege not reserved to the Redeemer, and the martyrs alone, but one enjoyed by numbers in every age.

The common-place life of thousands; and in that is its only interest—its only merit as a history; viz. that it *is* the type of common sufferings—the story of one who has not the courage to resist nor to submit to the civilisation of her time—is this.

Poetry and imagination begin life. A child will fall on its knees on the gravel walk at the sight of a pink hawthorn in full flower, when it is by itself, to praise God for it.

Then comes intellect. It wishes to satisfy the wants which intellect creates for it. But there is a physical, not moral, impossibility of supplying the wants of the intellect in the state of civilisation at which we have arrived. The stimulus, the training, the time, are all three wanting to us; or, in other words, the means and inducements are not there.

Look at the poor lives we lead. It is a wonder that we are so good as we are, not that we are so bad. In looking round we are struck with the power of the organisations we see, not with their want of power. Now and then, it is true, we are conscious that *there* is an inferior organisation, but, in general, just the contrary. Mrs A. has the imagination, the poetry of a Murillo, and has sufficient power of execution to show that she might have had a great deal more. Why is she not a Murillo? From a material difficulty, not a mental one. If she has a knife and fork in her hands for three hours of the day, she cannot have a pencil or brush. Dinner is the great sacred ceremony of this day, the great sacrament. To be absent from dinner is equivalent to being ill. Nothing else will excuse us from it. Bodily incapacity is the only apology valid. If she has a pen and ink in her hands during other three hours, writing answers for the penny post, again, she cannot have her pencil, and so *ad infinitum* through life. People have no type before them in their lives, neither fathers nor mothers, nor the children themselves. They look at things in detail. They say, " It is very desirable that A., my daughter, should go to such a party, should know such a lady, should sit by such a person." It is true. But what standard have they before them of the nature and destination of man? The very words are rejected as pedantic. But might they not, at least, have a type in their minds that such an one might be a discoverer through her intellect, such another through her art, a third through her moral power?

Women often try one branch of intellect after another in their youth, *e.g.* mathematics. But that, least of all is compatible with the life of "society." It is impossible to follow up anything systematically. Women often long to enter some man's profession where they would find direction, competition (or rather opportunity of measuring the intellect with others) and, above all, time.

In those wise institutions, mixed as they are with many follies, which will last as long as the human race lasts, because they are adapted to the wants of the human race; those institutions which we call monasteries, and which, embracing much that is contrary to the laws of nature, are yet better adapted to the union of the life of action and that of thought than any other mode of life with which we are acquainted; in many such, four and a half hours, at least, are daily set aside for thought, rules are given for thought, training and opportunity afforded. Among us there is *no* time appointed for this purpose, and the difficulty is that, in our social life, we must be always doubtful whether we ought not to be with somebody else or be doing something else.

Are men better off than women in this?

If one calls upon a friend in London and sees her son in the drawing-room, it strikes one as odd to find a young man sitting idle in his mother's drawing-room in the morning. For men, who are seen much in those haunts, there is no end of the epithets we have: "knights of the carpet," "drawing-room heroes," "ladies' men." But suppose we were to see a number of men in the morning sitting round a table in the drawing-room, looking at prints, doing worsted work, and reading little books, how we should laugh! A member of the House of Commons was once known to do worsted work. Of another man was said, "His only fault is that he is too good; he drives out with his mother every day in the carriage, and if he is asked anywhere he answers that he must dine with his mother, but, if she can spare him, he will come in to tea, and he does not come."

Now, why is it more ridiculous for a man than for a woman to do worsted work and drive out every day in the carriage? Why should we laugh if we were to see a parcel of men sitting round a drawing-room table in the morning, and think it all right if they were women?

Is man's time more valuable than woman's? or is the difference between man and woman this, that woman has confessedly nothing to do?

Women are never supposed to have any occupation of sufficient importance *not* to be interrupted, except " suckling their fools "; and women themselves have accepted this, have written books to support it, and have trained themselves so as to consider whatever they do as *not* of such value to the world or to others, but that they can throw it up at the first " claim of social life." They have accustomed themselves to consider intellectual occupation as a merely selfish amusement, which it is their " duty " to give up for every trifler more selfish than themselves.

A young man (who was afterwards useful and known in his day and generation) when busy reading and sent for by his proud mother to shine in some morning visit, came; but, after it was over, he said, " Now, remember, this is not to happen again. I came that you might not think me sulky, but I shall not come again." But for a young woman to send such a message to her mother and sisters, how impertinent it would be! A woman of great administrative powers said that she never undertook anything which she " could not throw by at once, if necessary."

How do we explain then the many cases of women who have distinguished themselves in classics, mathematics, even in politics?

Widowhood, ill-health, or want of bread, these three explanations or excuses are supposed to justify a woman taking up an occupation. In some cases, no doubt, an indomitable force of character will suffice without any of these three, but such are rare.

But see how society fritters away the intellects of those committed to her charge! It is said that society is necessary to sharpen the intellect. But what do we seek society for? It does sharpen the intellect, because it is a kind of *tour-de-force* to say something at a pinch,—unprepared and uninterested with any subject, to improvise something under difficulties. But what " go we out for to seek "? To take the chance of some one having something to say which we want to hear? or of finding something to say which *they* want to hear? You have a little to say, but not much. You often make a stipulation with someone else, " Come in ten minutes, for I shall not be able to find enough to spin out longer than that." You are not to talk of anything very interesting, for the essence of society is to prevent any long conversations and all tête-à-têtes. *Glissez, n'appuyez pas* is its very motto. The praise of a good *maitresse de maison* consists in this, that she allows no one person to be too much absorbed in, or too long about, a conversation. She always recalls them to their " duty." People do not go into the company of their fellow-creatures for what would seem a very sufficient reason, namely, that they have something to say to them, or something that they want to hear from them; but in the vague hope that they may find something to say.

Then as to solitary opportunities. Women never have an half-hour in all their lives (excepting before or after anybody is up in the house) that they can call their own, without fear of offending or of hurting someone. Why do people sit up so late, or, more rarely, get up so early? Not because the day is not long enough, but because they have " no time in the day to themselves."

If we do attempt to do anything in company, what is the system of literary exercise which we pursue? Everybody reads aloud out of their own book or newspaper—or, every five minutes, something is said. And what is it to be " read aloud to "? The most miserable exercise of the human intellect. Or rather, is it any exercise at all? It is like lying on one's back, with one's hands tied and having liquid poured down one's throat. Worse than that, because suffocation would immediately ensue and put a stop to this operation. But no suffocation would stop the other.

So much for the satisfaction of the intellect. Yet for a married woman in society, it is even worse. A married woman was heard to wish that she could break a limb that she might have a little time to herself. Many take advantage of the fear of " infection " to do the same.

It is a thing *so* accepted among women that they have nothing to do, that one woman has not the least scruple in saying to another, " I will come and spend the morning with you." And you would be thought quite surly and absurd, if you were to refuse it on the plea of occupation. Nay, it is thought a mark of amiability and affection, if you are " on such terms " that you can " come in " " any morning you please."

In a country house, if there is a large party of young people, " You will spend the morning with us," they say to the neighbours, " we will drive together in the afternoon," " to-morrow we will make an expedition, and we will spend the evening together." And this is thought friendly and spending time in a pleasant manner. So women play through life. Yet time is the most valuable of all things. If they had come every morning and afternoon and robbed us of half-a-crown we should have had redress from the police. But it is laid down, that our time is of no value. If you offer a morning visit to a professional man, and say, " I will just stay an hour with you, if you will allow me, till so and so comes back to fetch me "; it costs him the earnings of an hour, and therefore he has a right to complain. But women have no right, because it is " *only* their time."

Women have no means given them, whereby they *can* resist the " claims of social life." They are taught from their infancy upwards that it is a wrong, ill-tempered, and a misunderstanding of " woman's mission " (with a great M) if they do not allow themselves *willingly* to be interrupted at all hours. If a woman has once put in a claim to be treated as a man by some work of science or art or literature, which she can *show* as the " fruit of her leisure," then she will be considered justified in *having* leisure (hardly, perhaps, even then). But if not, not. If she has nothing to show, she must resign herself to her fate.

III

" I like riding about this beautiful place, why don't you? I like walking about the garden, why don't you? " is the common expostulation—as if we were children, whose spirits rise during a fortnight's holiday, who think that they will last for ever—and look neither backwards nor forwards.

Society triumphs over many. They wish to regenerate the world with their institutions, with their moral philosophy, with their love. Then they sink to living from breakfast till dinner, from dinner till tea, with a little worsted work, and to looking forward to nothing but bed.

When shall we see a life full of steady enthusiasm, walking straight to its aim, flying home, as that bird is now, against the wind—with the calmness and the confidence of one who knows the laws of God and can apply them?

What *do* we see? We see great and fine organisations deteriorating. We see girls and boys of seventeen, before whose noble ambitions, heroic dreams, and rich endowments we bow our heads, as before *God incarnate in the flesh*. But, ere they are thirty, they are withered, paralysed, extinguished. " We have forgotten our visions," they say themselves.

The " dreams of youth " have become a proverb. That organisations, early rich, fall far short of their promise has been repeated to satiety. But is it extraordinary that it should be so? For do we ever *utilise* this heroism? Look how it lives upon itself and perishes for lack of food. We do not know what to do with it. We had rather that it should not be there. Often we laugh at it. Always we find it troublesome. Look at the poverty of our life! Can we expect anything else but poor creatures to come out of it? Did Michael Angelo's genius fail, did Pascal's die in its bud, did Sir Isaac Newton become a common-place sort of man? In two of these cases the knife wore out the sheath.

But the knife itself did not become rusty, till the body was dead or infirm.

Why cannot we *make use* of the noble rising heroisms of our own day, instead of leaving them to rust?

They have nothing to do.

Are they to be employed in sitting in the drawing-room saying words which may as well not be said, which could be said as well if *they* were not there?

Women often strive to live by intellect. The clear, brilliant, sharp radiance of intellect's moonlight rising upon such an expanse of snow is dreary, it is true, but some love its solemn desolation, its silence, its solitude—if they are but *allowed* to live in it; if they are not perpetually baulked or disappointed. But a woman cannot live in the light of intellect. Society forbids it. Those conventional frivolities, which are called her "duties," forbid it. Her "domestic duties," high-sounding words, which, for the most part, are bad habits (which she has not the courage to enfranchise herself from, the strength to break through) forbid it. What are these duties (or bad habits)?—Answering a multitude of letters which lead to nothing, from her so-called friends, keeping herself up to the level of the world that she may furnish her quota of amusement at the breakfast-table; driving out her company in the carriage. And all these things are exacted from her by her family which, if she is good and affectionate, will have more influence with her than the world.

What wonder, if, wearied out, sick at heart with hope deferred, the springs of will broken, not seeing clearly *where* her duty lies, she abandons intellect as a vocation and takes it only, as we use the moon, by glimpses through her tight-closed window shutters?

The family? It is too narrow a field for the development of an immortal spirit, be that spirit male or female. The chances are a thousand to one that, in that small sphere, the task for which that immortal spirit is destined by the qualities and the gifts which its Creator has placed within it, will not be found.

The family uses people, *not* for what they are, nor for what they are intended to be, but for what it wants them for—its own uses. It thinks of them not as what God has made them, but as the something which it has arranged that they shall be. If it wants someone to sit in the drawing-room, *that* someone is supplied by the family, though that member may be destined for science, or for education, or for active superintendence by God, *i.e.* by the gifts within.

This system dooms some minds to incurable infancy, others to silent misery.

And family boasts that it has performed its mission well, in as far as it has enabled the individual to say, " I have *no* peculiar work, nothing but what the moment brings me, nothing that I cannot throw up at once at anybody's claim "; in as far, that is, as it has *destroyed* the individual life. And the individual thinks that a great victory has been accomplished, when, at last, she is able to say that she has " no personal desires or plans." What is this but throwing the gifts of God aside as worthless, and substituting for them those of the world?

Marriage is the only chance (and it is but a chance) offered to women for escape from this death; and how eagerly and how ignorantly it is embraced!

At present we live to impede each other's satisfactions; competition, domestic life, society, what is it all but this? We go somewhere where we are not wanted and where we don't want to go. What else is conventional life? *Passivity* when we want to be active. So many hours spent every day in passively doing what conventional life tells us, when we would so gladly be at work.

And is it a wonder that all individual life is extinguished?

Women dream of a great sphere of steady, not sketchy benevolence, of moral activity, for which they would fain be trained and fitted, instead of working in the dark, neither knowing nor registering whither their steps lead, whether farther from or nearer to the aim.

For how do people exercise their moral activity now? We visit, we teach, we talk, among " the poor "; we are told, " don't look for the fruits, cast thy bread upon the waters; for thou shalt find it after many days." Certainly " don't look," for you won't see. You will *not* " find it," and then you would " strike work."

How different would be the heart for the work, and how different would be the success, if we learnt our work as a serious study, and followed it out steadily as a profession!

Were the physician to set to work at *his* trade, as the philanthropist does at his, how many bodies would he not spoil before he cured one!

We set the treatment of bodies so high above the treatment of souls, that the physician occupies a higher place in society than the school-master. The governess is to have every one of God's gifts; she is to do that which the mother herself is incapable of doing; but our son must not degrade himself by marrying the governess, nor our daughter the tutor, though she might marry the medical man.

But my medical man does do something for me, it is said, my tutor has done nothing.

This is true, this is the real reason. And what a condemnation of the state of mental science it is! Low as is physical science, that of the mind is still lower.

Women long for an education to teach them *to teach*, to teach them the laws of the human mind and how to apply them—and knowing how imperfect, in the present state of the world, such an education must be, they long for experience, not patch-work experience, but experience followed up and systematised, to enable them to know what they are about and *where* they are "casting their bread," and whether it is "*bread*" or a stone.

How should we learn a language if we were to give it an hour a week? A fortnight's steady application would make more way in it than a year of such patch-work. A "lady" can hardly go to "her school" two days running. She cannot leave the breakfast-table—or she must be fulfilling some little frivolous "duty," which others ought not to exact, or which might just as well be done some other time.

Dreaming always—never accomplishing; thus women live—too much ashamed of their dreams, which they think "romantic," to tell them where they will be laughed at, even if not considered wrong.

With greater strength of purpose they might accomplish something. But if they were strong, all of them, they would not need to have their story told, for all the world would read it in the mission they have fulfilled. It is for common-place, every-day characters that we tell our tale—because it is the sample of hundreds of lives (or rather deaths) of persons who cannot fight with society, or who, unsupported by the sympathies about them, give up their own destiny as not worth the fierce and continued struggle necessary to accomplish it. *One* struggle they *could* make and be free (and, in the Church of Rome, many, many, unallured by any other motive, make this one struggle to enter a convent); but the perpetual series of petty spars, with discouragements between, and doubts as to whether they are right—these wear out the very life necessary to make them.

If a man were to follow up his profession or occupation at odd times, how would he do it? Would he become skilful in that profession? It is acknowledged by women themselves that they are inferior in every occupation to men. Is it wonderful? *They* do *everything* at "odd times."

And if a woman's music and drawing are only used by her as

an amusement (*a pass-time*, as it is called), is it wonderful that she tires of them, that she becomes disgusted with them?

In every dream of the life of intelligence or that of activity, women are accompanied by a phantom—the phantom of sympathy guiding, lighting the way—even if they do not marry. Some few sacrifice marriage, because they sacrifice all other life if they accept that. That man and woman have an equality of duties and rights is accepted by woman even less than by man. Behind *his* destiny woman must annihilate herself, must be only his complement. A woman dedicates herself to the vocation of her husband; she fills up and performs the subordinate parts in it. But if she has any destiny, any vocation of her own, she must renounce it, in nine cases out of ten. Some few, like Mrs Somerville, Mrs Chisholm, Mrs Fry, have not done so; but these are exceptions. The fact is that woman has so seldom any vocation of her own, that it does not much signify; she has none to renounce. A man gains everything by marriage: he gains a "helpmate," but a woman does not.

But if ever women come into contact with sickness, with poverty, and crime in masses, how the practical reality of life revives them! They are exhausted, like those who live on opium or on novels, all their lives—exhausted with feelings which lead to no action. If they see and enter into a continuous line of action, with a full and interesting life, with training constantly kept up to the occupation, occupation constantly testing the training—it is the *beau-ideal* of practical, not theoretical, education—they are re-tempered, their life is filled, they have found their work, and the means to do it.

Women, when they are young, sometimes think that an actress's life is a happy one—not for the sake of the admiration, not for the sake of the fame; but because in the morning she studies, in the evening she embodies those studies: she has the means of testing and correcting them by practice, and of resuming her studies in the morning, to improve the weak parts, remedy the failures, and in the evening try the corrections again. It is, indeed, true that, even after middle age, with such exercise of faculty, there is no end to the progress which may be made.

Some are only deterred from suicide because it is in the most distinct manner to say to God: "I will not, I will not do as Thou wouldst have me," and because it is "no use."

To have no food for our heads, no food for our hearts, no food for our activity, is that nothing? If we have no food for the body, how do we cry out, how all the world hears of it, how all the newspapers talk of it, with a paragraph headed in great capital letters,

DEATH FROM STARVATION! But suppose one were to put a paragraph in the *Times*, Death of Thought from Starvation, or Death of Moral Activity from Starvation, how people would stare, how they would laugh and wonder! One would think we had no heads nor hearts, by the total indifference of the public towards them. Our bodies are the only things of any consequence.

We have nothing to do which raises us, no food which agrees with us. We can never pursue any object for a single two hours, for we can never command any regular leisure or solitude; and in social and domestic life one is bound, under pain of being thought sulky, to make a remark every two minutes.

Men are on the side of society; they blow hot and cold; they say, " Why can't you employ yourself in society? " and then, " Why don't you talk in society? " I can pursue a connected conversation, or I can be silent; but to drop a remark, as it is called every two minutes, how wearisome it is! It is impossible to pursue the current of one's own thoughts, because one must keep oneself ever on the alert, " to say something "; and it is impossible to say what one is thinking, because the essence of a remark is not to be a thought, but an impression. With what labour women have toiled to break down all individual and independent life, in order to fit themselves for this social and domestic existence, thinking it right! And when they have killed themselves to do it, they have awakened (too late) to think it wrong.

For, later in life, women could not make use of leisure and solitude if they had it! Like the Chinese woman, who could not make use of her feet, if she were brought into European life.

Some have an attention like a battering-ram, which, slowly, brought to bear, can work upon a subject for any length of time. They can work ten hours just as well as two upon the same thing. But this age would have men like the musket, which you can load so fast that nothing but its heating in the process puts any limit to the number and frequency of times of firing, and at as many different objects as you please.

So, later in life, people cannot use their battering-ram. Their attention, like society's, goes off in a thousand different directions. They are an hour before they can fix it; and by the time it is fixed, the leisure is gone. They become incapable of consecutive or strenuous work.

What these suffer—even physically—from the want of such work no one can tell. The accumulation of nervous energy, which has had nothing to do during the day, makes them feel every night, when they go to bed, as if they were going mad; and they are obliged to lie long in bed in the morning to let it evaporate and keep it down. At last they suffer at once from disgust of the one and incapacity for the other—from loathing of conventional idleness and powerlessness to do work when they have it. "Now go, you have several hours," say people, "you have all the afternoon to yourself." When they are all frittered away, they are to begin to work. When they are broken up into little bits, they are to hew away.

IV

Moral activity? There is scarcely such a thing possible! Everything is sketchy. The world does nothing but sketch. One Lady Bountiful sketches a school, but it never comes to a finished study; she can hardly work at it two weeks consecutively. Here and there a solitary individual, it is true, makes a really careful study,—as Mrs Chisholm of emigration—as Miss Carpenter of reformatory discipline. But, in general, a "lady" has too many sketches on hand. She has a sketch of society, a sketch of her children's education, sketches of her "charities," sketches of her reading. She is like a painter who should have five pictures in his studio at once, and giving now a stroke to one, and now a stroke to another, till he had made the whole round, should continue this routine to the end.

All life is sketchy—the poet's verse (compare Tennyson, Milnes, and Mrs Browning with Milton or even Byron; it is not the difference of genius which strikes one so much as the unfinished state of these modern sketches compared with the studies of the old masters),—the artist's picture, the author's composition—all are rough, imperfect, incomplete, even as works of art.

And how can it be otherwise? A "leader" out of a newspaper, an article out of a review, five books read aloud in the course of an evening, such is our literature. What mind can stand three leading articles every morning as its food?

When shall we see a woman making a *study* of what she does? Married women cannot; for a man would think, if his wife undertook any great work with the intention of carrying it out,—of making anything but a sham of it—that she would "suckle his fools and chronicle his small beer" less well for it,—that he would not have so good a dinner—that she would destroy, as it is called, his domestic life.

The intercourse of man and woman—how frivolous, how unworthy it is! Can we call *that* the true vocation of woman—

her high career? Look round at the marriages which you know. The true marriage—that noble union, by which a man and woman become together the one perfect being—probably does not exist at present upon earth.

It is not surprising that husbands and wives seem so little part of one another. It is surprising that there is so much love as there is. For there is no food for it. What does it live upon—what nourishes it? Husbands and wives never seem to have anything to say to one another. What do they talk about? Not about any great religious, social, political questions or feelings. They talk about who shall come to dinner, who is to live in this lodge and who in that, about the improvement of the place, or when they shall go to London. If there are children, they form a common subject of some nourishment. But, even then, the case is oftenest thus,—the husband is to think of how they are to get on in life; the wife of bringing them up at home.

But any real communion between husband and wife—any descending into the depths of their being, and drawing out thence what they find and comparing it—do we ever dream of such a thing? Yes, we may dream of it during the season of "passion," but we shall not find it afterwards. We even expect it to go off, and lay our account that it will. If the husband has, by chance, gone into the depths of *his* being, and found there anything unorthodox, he, oftenest, conceals it carefully from his wife,—he is afraid of "unsettling her opinions."

What is the mystery of passion, spiritually speaking? For there *is* a passion of the Spirit. *Blind* passion, as it has most truly been called, seems to come on in man without his exactly knowing why for *this* person rather than for *that*, and (whether it has been satisfied or unsatisfied) to go off again after awhile, as it came, also without his knowing why.

The woman's passion is generally more lasting.

It is possible that this difference may be, because there is really more in man than in woman. There is nothing in her for him to have this intimate communion *with*. He cannot impart to her his religious beliefs, if he have any, because she would be "shocked." Religious men are and must be heretics now—for we must not pray, except in a "form" of words, made beforehand—or think of God but with a pre-arranged idea.

With the man's political ideas, if they extend beyond the merest party politics, she has no sympathy.

His social ideas, if they are "advanced," she will probably denounce without knowing why, as savouring of "socialism" (a convenient word, which covers a multitude of new ideas and offences). For woman is " by birth a Tory,"—has often been said,—by education a " Tory," we mean.

Woman has nothing but her affections,—and this makes her at once more loving and less loved.

But is it surprising that there should be so little real marriage, when we think what the process is which leads to marriage?

Under the eyes of an always present mother and sisters (of whom even the most refined and intellectual cannot abstain from a jest upon the subject, who think it their *duty* to be anxious, to watch every germ and bud of it) the acquaintance begins. It is fed—upon what?—the gossip of art, musical and pictorial, the party politics of the day, the chit-chat of society, and people marry or sometimes they don't marry, discouraged by the impossibility of knowing any more of one another than this will furnish.

They prefer to marry in *thought*, to hold imaginary conversations with one another in idea, rather than, on such a flimsy pretext of communion, to take the chance (certainty it cannot be) of having more to say to one another in marriage.

Men and women meet now *to be idle*. Is it extraordinary that they do not know each other, and that, in their mutual ignorance, they form no surer friendships? Did they meet to *do* something together, then indeed they might form some real tie.

But, as it is, *they* are not there, it is only a mask which is there—a mouth-piece of ready-made sentences about the " topics of the day "; and then people rail against men for choosing a woman " for her face "—why, what else do they see?

It is very well to say " be prudent, be careful, try to know each other." But how are you to know each other?

Unless a woman had lost all pride, how is it possible for her, under the eyes of all her family, to indulge in long exclusive conversations with a man? " Such a thing " must not take place till after her " engagement." And how is she to make an engagement, if " such a thing " has not taken place?

Besides, young women at home have so little to occupy and to interest them—they have so little reason for *not* quitting their home, that a young and independent man cannot look at a girl without giving rise to " expectations " if not on her own part, on that of her family. Happy he, if he is not said to have been " trifling with her feelings," or " disappointing her hopes ! " Under these circumstances, how can a man, who has any pride or principle, become acquainted with a woman in such a manner as to *justify* them in marrying?

There are four ways in which people marry. First, accident or relationship has thrown them together in their childhood, and acquaintance has grown up naturally and unconsciously. Accordingly, in novels, it is generally cousins who marry; and *now* it seems the only natural thing—the only possible way of making any intimacy. And yet, we know that intermarriage between relations is in direct contravention of the laws of nature for the well-being of the race; witness the Quakers, the Spanish grandees, the royal races, the secluded valleys of mountainous countries, where madness, degeneration of race, defective organisation and cretinism flourish and multiply.

The second way, and by far the most general, in which people marry, is this. A woman, thoroughly uninterested at home, and having formed a slight acquaintance with some accidental person, accepts him, if he " falls in love " with her, as it is technically called, and takes the chance. Hence the vulgar expression of marriage being a lottery, which it most truly is, for that the *right* two should come together has as many chances against it as there are blanks in any lottery.

The third way is, that some person is found sufficiently independent, sufficiently careless of the opinions of others, or sufficiently without modesty to speculate thus : " It is worth while that I should become acquainted with so and so. I do not care what his or her opinion of me is, if, *after* having become acquainted, to do which can bear no other construction in people's eyes than a desire of marriage, I retreat." But there is this to be said, that it is doubtful whether, under their unnatural tension, which, to all susceptible characters, such a disregard of the opinions which they care for must be, a healthy or a natural feeling can grow up.

And now they are married—that is to say, two people have received the licence of a man in a white surplice. But they are no more man and wife for that than Louis XIV and the Infanta of Spain, married by proxy, were man and wife. The woman who has sold herself for an establishment, in what is she superior to those we may not name?

Lastly, in a few rare, very rare cases, such as circumstances, always provided in novels, but seldom to be met with in real life, present—whether the accident of parents' neglect, or of parents' unusual skill and wisdom, or of having no parents at all, which is generally the case in novels—or by marrying out of the person's rank of life, by which the usual restraints are removed, and there is room and play left for attraction—or extraordinary events, isolation, misfortunes, which many wish for, even though their imaginations be not tainted by romance-reading; such alternatives as these give food and space for the development of character and mutual sympathies. But a girl, if she has any pride, is so ashamed of having anything she wishes to say out of the hearing of her own family, she thinks it must be something so very wrong, that it is ten to one, if she have the opportunity of saying it, that she will not.

And yet she is spending her life, perhaps, in dreaming of accidental means of unrestrained communion.

And then it is thought pretty to say that "Women have no passion." If passion is excitement in the daily social intercourse with men, women think about marriage much more than men do; it is the only event of their lives. It ought to be a sacred event, but surely not the only event of a woman's life, as it is now. Many women spend their lives in asking men to marry them, in a refined way. Yet it is true that women are seldom in love. How can they be?

How cruel are the revulsions which high-minded women suffer! There was one who loved, in connexion with great deeds, noble thoughts, devoted feelings. They met after an interval. It was at one of those crowded parties of Civilisation which we call Society. His only careless passing remark was, "The buzz to-night is like a manufactory." Yet he loved her.

V

"L'enthousiasme est la faiblesse d'un temps où l'intelligence monte très haut, entrainée par l'imagination, et tombe très bas, écrasée par une réalité, sans poésie et sans grandeur."

Women dream till they have no longer the strength to dream; those dreams against which they so struggle, so honestly, vigorously, and conscientiously, and so in vain, yet which are their life, without which they could not have lived; those dreams go at last. All their plans and visions seem vanished, and they know not where; gone, and they cannot recall them. They do not even remember them. And they are left without the food of reality or of hope.

Later in life, they neither desire nor dream, neither of activity, nor of love, nor of intellect. The last often survives the longest. They wish, if their experiences would benefit anybody, to give them to someone. But they never find an hour free in which to collect their thoughts, and so discouragement becomes ever deeper and deeper, and they less and less capable of undertaking anything.

It seems as if the female spirit of the world were mourning everlastingly over blessings, not *lost*, but which she has never had, and which, in her discouragement she feels that she never will have, they are so far off.

The more complete a woman's organisation, the more she will feel it, till at last there shall arise a woman, who will resume, in her own soul, all the sufferings of her race, and that women will be the Saviour of her race.

Jesus Christ raised women above the condition of mere slaves, mere ministers to the passions of the man, raised them by His sympathy, to be Ministers of God. He gave them moral activity. But the Age, the World, Humanity, must give them the means to exercise this moral activity, must give them intellectual cultivation, spheres of action.

There is perhaps no century where the woman shows so meanly as in this.[1] Because her education seems entirely to have parted company with her vocation; there is no longer unity between the woman as inwardly developed, and as outwardly manifested.

In the last century it was not so. In the succeeding one let us hope that it will no longer be so.

But now she is like the Archangel Michael as he stands upon Saint Angelo at Rome. She has an immense provision of wings, which seem as if they would bear her over earth and heaven; but when she tries to use them, she is petrified into stone, her feet are grown into the earth, chained to the bronze pedestal.

Nothing can well be imagined more painful than the present position of woman, unless, on the one hand, she renounces all outward activity and keeps herself within the magic sphere, the bubble of her dreams; or, on the other, surrendering all aspiration, she gives herself to her real life, soul and body. For those to whom it is possible, the latter is best; for out of activity may come thought, out of mere aspiration can come nothing.

But now—when the young imagination is so high and so developed, and reality is so narrow and conventional—there is no more parallelism between life in the thought and life in the actual than between the corpse, which lies motionless in its narrow bed, and the spirit, which, in our imagination, is at large among the stars.

The ideal life is passed in noble schemes of good consecutively

[1] At almost every period of social life, we find, as it were, two undercurrents running different ways. There is the noble woman who dreams the following out her useful vocation ; but there is also the selfish dreamer now, who is ever turning to something new, regardless of the expectations she has voluntarily excited, who is ever talking about "making a life for herself," heedless that she is spoiling another life, undertaken, perhaps, at her own bidding. This is the ugly reverse of the medal.

followed up, of devotion to a great object, of sympathy given and received for high ideas and generous feelings. The actual life is passed in sympathy given and received for a dinner, a party, a piece of furniture, a house built or a garden laid out well, in devotion to your guests—(a too real devotion, for it implies that of all your time)—in schemes of schooling for the poor, which you follow up perhaps in an odd quarter of an hour, between luncheon and driving out in the carriage—broth and dripping are included in the plan—and the rest of your time goes in ordering the dinner, hunting for a governess for your children, and sending pheasants and apples to your poorer relations. Is there anything in *this* life which can be called an Incarnation of the ideal life within? Is it a wonder that the unhappy woman should prefer to keep them entirely separate? not to take the bloom off her Ideal by mixing it up with her Actual; not to make her Actual still more unpalatable by trying to *inform* it with her Ideal? And then she is blamed, and her own sex unites against her, for not being content with the " day of small things." She is told that " trifles make the sum of human things "; they do indeed. She is contemptuously asked, " Would she abolish domestic life ? " Men are afraid that their houses will not be so comfortable, that their wives will make themselves " remarkable " women, that they will make themselves distasteful to men; they write books (and very wisely) to teach themselves to dramatise " little things," to persuade themselves that " domestic life is their sphere " and to idealise the " sacred hearth." Sacred it is indeed. Sacred from the touch of their sons almost as soon as they are out of childhood—from its dulness and its tyrannous trifling *these* recoil. Sacred from the grasp of their daughters' affections upon which it has so light a hold that they seize the first opportunity of marriage, *their* only chance of emancipation. The " sacred hearth "; sacred to their husband's sleep, their sons' absence in the body and their daughters' in mind.

Oh! mothers, who talk about this hearth, how much do you know of your son's real life, how much of your daughter's imaginary one? Awake, ye women, all ye that sleep, awake! If this domestic life were so very good, would your young men wander away from it, your maidens think of something else?

The time is come when women must do something more than the " domestic hearth," which means nursing the infants, keeping a pretty house, having a good dinner and an entertaining party.

You say, " It is true, our young men see visions, and our maidens dream dreams," but what of? Does not the woman intend to marry, and have over again what she has at home? and the man ultimately too? Yes, but not the same; she *will* have the same, that is, if circumstances are not altered to prevent it; but her *ideal* is very different, though that ideal and the reality will never come together to mould each other. And it is not only the unmarried woman who dreams. The married woman also holds long imaginary conversations but too often.

VI

We live in the world, it is said, and must walk in its ways.

Was Christ called a complainer against the world? Yet all these great teachers and preachers must have had a most deep and ingrained sense, a continual feeling of the miseries and wrongs of the world. Otherwise they would not have been impelled to devote life and death to redress them. Christ, Socrates, Howard, they must have had no ear for the joys, compared to that which they had for the sorrows of the world.

They acted, however, and we complain. The great reformers of the world turn into the great misanthropists, if circumstances or organisation do not permit them to act. Christ, if He had been a woman, might have been nothing but a great complainer. Peace be with the misanthropists! They have made a step in progress; the next will make them great philanthropists; they are divided but by a line.

The next Christ will perhaps be a female Christ. But do we see one woman who looks like a female Christ? or even like " the messenger before " her " face," to go before her and prepare the hearts and minds for her?

To this will be answered that half the inmates of Bedlam begin in this way, by fancying that they are " the Christ." [1]

People talk about imitating Christ, and imitate Him in the little trifling formal things, such as washing the feet, saying His prayer, and so on; but if anyone attempts the real imitation of

[1] It is quite true that insanity, sensuality, and monstrous fraud have constantly assumed to be " the Christ," *vide* the *Agapemone* and the Mormons. " Believing " a man of the name of Prince " to be the tabernacle of God on earth," poor deluded women transfer to him all their stock in the Three per Cents. We hear of the Mormons, etc., being the " recipients and mouth-pieces of God's Spirit." They profess to be " incarnations of the Deity," " witnesses of the Almighty," " solely knowing God's will, and being the medium of communicating it to man," and so forth. It does not appear to us that this blasphemy is very dangerous to the cause of true religion in general, any more than forgery is very dangerous to commerce in general. It is the universal dishonesty in religion, as in trade, which is really dangerous.

Him, there are no bounds to the outcry with which the presumption of that person is condemned.

For instance, Christ was saying something to the people one day, which interested Him very much, and interested them very much; and Mary and His brothers came in the middle of it, and wanted to interrupt Him, and take Him home to dinner, very likely—(how natural that story is! does it not speak more home than any historic evidences of the Gospel's reality?), and He, instead of being angry with their interruption of Him in such an important work for some trifling thing, answers, "Who is my mother? and who are my brethren? Whosoever shall do the will of my Father which is in heaven, the same is my brother and sister and mother." But if *we* were to say that, we should be accused of "destroying the family tie, of diminishing the obligation of the home duties."

He might well say, "Heaven and earth shall pass away, but my words shall not pass away." His words will never pass away. If He had said, "Tell them that I am engaged at this moment in something very important; that the instruction of the multitude ought to go before any personal ties; that I will remember to come when I have done," no one would have been impressed by His words; but how striking is that, "Behold my mother and my brethren!"

VII

The dying woman to her mourners:—"Oh! if you knew how gladly I leave this life, how much more courage I feel to take the chance of another, than of anything I see before me in this, you would put on your wedding-clothes instead of mourning for me!"

"But," they say, "so much talent! so many gifts! such good which you might have done!"

"The world will be put back some little time by my death," she says; "you see I estimate my powers at least as highly as you can; but it is by the death which has taken place some years ago in me, not by the death which is about to take place now." And so is the world put back by the death of every one who has to sacrifice the development of his or her peculiar gifts (which were meant, not for selfish gratification, but for the improvement of that world) to conventionality.

"My people were like children playing on the shore of the eighteenth century. I was their hobby-horse, their plaything; and they drove me to and fro, dear souls! never weary of the play themselves, till I, who had grown to woman's estate and to the ideas of the nineteenth century, lay down exhausted, my mind closed to hope, my heart to strength.

"Free—free—oh! divine freedom, art thou come at last? Welcome, beautiful death!"

Let neither name nor date be placed on her grave, still less the expression of regret or of admiration; but simply the words, "I believe in God."

APPENDIX II

BIBLIOGRAPHICAL NOTE

A FULL list of the books and documents consulted in the preparation of this history would occupy many pages, and be of little interest or value to the general reader. Nearly everything which has been written about the nineteenth century contains some reference to the position of women, though generally not much more than a footnote. Where no mention is made, the omission is itself relevant to the Women's Movement!

The short list which follows includes those books which give reliable information concerning the main points touched on in this history, and the student who wishes to read more fully can easily pursue the subject from the indications contained in them. The Library of the London and National Society for Women's Service includes all these books, and through the Central Library for Students it can be easily consulted.

There is a great deal of very interesting material relating to the period between the publication of Mary Wollstonecraft's book, *A Vindication of the Rights of Women* (1792), and the accession of Queen Victoria (1837), none of which is here referred to. The best way to find it is to begin with a study of the biographies and letters of the women of the period, for example, Jane Austen, Charlotte Brontë, Caroline Chisholm, Mary Berry, Elizabeth Fry, Hannah More, Maria Edgeworth, and Harriet Martineau. No mention is made in this list of the fiction of the period between 1837 and 1928. It is of course exceedingly important to an understanding of the changing position of women, but it has been so abundantly studied, and is so easily accessible that no detailed tabulation seems necessary. One author, however, deserves special mention, namely, Charlotte M. Yonge. Her delightful tales were written between 1847 and 1890, and they give pictures of the lives of educated families between those years which are irresistibly convincing. The author was herself a convinced anti-feminist, but her characters lived and developed with the times, and a detailed study of their fortunes is a most agreeable and instructive pastime. Some of the greater writers of the last century were deliberate feminists, as, for example, Elizabeth Barrett Browning, George Eliot, and George Meredith. Others, like Dickens and Trollope, faithfully preserved the old ideal of feminine foolishness. But it is not by the works of either of these classes that the progress of the Women's Movement is to be measured. The change in the type of heroine required for " best sellers " is the real test, and it is not until the " strong silent hero " ceases to " dominate " the gentle heroine that the end of the Women's Movement will have arrived.

BIBLIOGRAPHY

I. Biographical:

Dorothea Beale of Cheltenham, by Elizabeth Raikes, 1908.
Life of Sophia Jex-Blake, by M. Todd, 1918.
Life of Catherine Booth, by W. T. Stead.
Josephine Butler, An Autobiographical Memoir, by G. W. and A. L. Johnson, 1909.
Life and Work of Mary Carpenter, by J. Estlin Carpenter, 1879.
Memoir of Ann Jemima Clough, by B. A. Clough, 1897.
Life of Frances Power Cobbe as told by Herself, 1904.
Emily Davies and Girton College, by Barbara Stephen, 1927.
What I Remember, by Millicent Garrett Fawcett, 1925.
Memorial of the Life and Work of Anna Jameson, by G. Macpherson, 1878.
Autobiography of Harriet Martineau, 1877.
Life of Frederick Denison Maurice, by his Son.
Autobiography of J. S. Mill (new edition), 1908.
Life of Florence Nightingale, by Sir E. Cook, 1913.
Life of Mrs Norton, by J. G. Perkins, 1910.
My Own Story, by Emmiline Pankhurst, 1914.
Pioneer Work in Opening the Medical Profession to Women, by Elizabeth Blackwell, 1895.
Personal Reminiscences of a Great Crusade, by Josephine Butler, 1896.
Life of W. T. Stead, by F. Whyte, 1925.
Recollection of Life and Work, by Louisa Twining, 1893.

II. General:

A Vindication of the Rights of Women, by Mary Wollstonecraft, 1792.
The Subjection of Women, by J. S. Mill, 1869.

Women's Suffrage, by Millicent Garrett Fawcett, 1911.
The Woman's Victory and After, by M. G. Fawcett, 1920.
Record of Women's Suffrage, by Helen Blackburn, 1902.
The Evolution of Women from Subjection to Citizenship, by G. W. Johnson, 1926.
Women under English Law, by Arthur Rackham Cleveland, 1896.
The Emancipation of Englishwomen, by Lyon Bleaze, 1910.
British Freewomen, by C. C. Stopes, 1894.
Prisons and Prisoners, by Lady Constance Lytton, 1914.
History of Factory Legislation, by Hutchins and Harrison, 1911.
Women in Trade Unions, by Barbara Drake, 1920.
Women in the Printing Trade, by J. Ramsay MacDonald, 1904.
La Femme Anglaise et son Évolution, d'après le Roman Anglais Contemporain, by Leonie Villard.
See also *Hansard*; Government Reports on the Employment of Women, and the Reports and Publications of the Suffrage Societies.

III. Periodicals:

The Englishwoman's Journal, 1858–1864.
The Englishwoman's Review, 1866–1894.
The Women's Suffrage Journal, 1870–1890.
The Englishwoman, 1909–1921.
The Common Cause, 1909–1920.
The Woman's Leader, 1920–1928.
Votes for Women, 1908–1915.
The Anti-Suffrage Review, 1908–1918.

INDEX